Pragmatics of Internet Humour

Francisco Yus

Pragmatics of Internet Humour

palgrave
macmillan

Francisco Yus
Filología Inglesa
University of Alicante
Alicante, Spain

ISBN 978-3-031-31901-3 ISBN 978-3-031-31902-0 (eBook)
https://doi.org/10.1007/978-3-031-31902-0

This Palgrave Macmillan imprint is published by the registered company Springer Nature Switzerland AG.
The registered company address is: Gewerbestrasse 11, 6330 Cham, Switzerland

This book is dedicated to all the internet users who have made me laugh or smile.

CONTENTS

List of Figures

List of Tables

CHAPTER 1

Introduction

Pragmatics of Internet Humour brings together more than 20 years of research on internet-mediated communication from the perspective of *cyberpragmatics* (e.g. Yus 2011) and parallel research on humorous communication (e.g. Yus 2016), both of them anchored in cognitive pragmatics and more specifically *relevance theory* (Sperber and Wilson 1995). Unlike other publications on internet humour (which do not abound), this book assumes an explicitly cognitive pragmatics standpoint to explain what is at stake in the (un)successful generation of humorous effects online.[1]

Relevance theory and cognitive pragmatics (as a higher-order research trend) focus on how more gets communicated than has been said, as the famous definition of pragmatics by Yule (1996) summarises. The so-called *underdeterminacy thesis*, i.e. the claim that all utterances communicate more information than the one literally coded in them, also holds true for humorous discourses, which must be developed into contextualised interpretations by addressees. And relevance theory offers an ideal framework to understand how humorous interpretations are inferred and which

[1] This book has been funded by the research project "PROMETEO/2021/079: Etiquetaje pragmático para un observatorio de la identidad de mujeres y hombres a través del humor. La plataforma Observahumor.com" (*Pragmatic labelling for the analysis of men's and women's identities. The plaform Observahumor.com*).

F. Yus, *Pragmatics of Internet Humour*,
https://doi.org/10.1007/978-3-031-31902-0_1

specific inferential strategies are performed for that purpose. In a nutshell, during the analysis of humorous discourses by cognitive pragmatics, the analyst takes the discourse and uses it to track down the discourse creator's predictions about the addressee's inferential strategies, which generally have as their aim (a) to build up an explicit interpretation of the discourse produced (*explicatures* in relevance-theoretic terminology); (b) to derive implicatures should these be required to grasp the communicator's full intended interpretation; and (c) to retrieve from context the amount of information necessary to obtain (b) and (c).

How fine-grained can an analyst's predictions about the addressee's performance of strategies (a-c) be? Of course, it is impossible for us to enter people's minds; however, relevance theory proposes an unavoidable cost-benefit mental heuristic invariably used for the inferential selection of interpretations and context accessibility which can be more or less monitored, exploited and manipulated to a greater or lesser extent to achieve humorous effects. More precisely, according to relevance theory, during every act of communication, the communicator has the ability to predict which stimulus in the interlocutor's environment is likely to attract their attention; which background information from their memory will most probably be retrieved and used in processing this stimulus (e.g. the contextual information most relevant to process it optimally); and which inferences the interlocutor is likely to draw in order to reach a relevant explicit and/or implicated interpretation (Sperber and Wilson 2002).

Therefore, when devising a humorous text, the creator is quite sure, for instance, that a certain referent will be selected for a pronoun (reference assignment of indexicals), that one sense of a potentially ambiguous word is bound to be selected as the most likely and relevant one (inferential disambiguation) and so on, these choices then usually becoming invalidated and re-interpreted with the aim of generating humorous effects. Needless to say, these are not humour-specific inferential strategies, but rather ones applied to every instance of communication, which aids in them being predictable to a certain extent. As argued in Yus (2016), inferential mechanisms have a universal and biologically rooted status in human psychology and consequently come into play too when humorous discourses are interpreted and their effects generated. In other words, we own a single unitary cognitive criterion, and all the claims made by this theory regarding how discourses are interpreted are also at work in the interpretation of humorous discourses.

In sum, several claims underpin a relevance-theoretic analysis of humour:

1. A more or less substantial informational gap exists between what the speaker codes in a discourse (or to put it in another way, says, writes, types…) and the interpretation intended with that discourse (and inferred from it). This becomes crucial in humorous communication, since this inferential gap-filling may be guided in a certain interpretive direction for the sake of humour.
2. Humour does not lie in the discourse itself, but in how that discourse is inferred and contextualised. It stems from the discourse creator's strategy, which leads the audience to engage in a specific process of interpretation and contextualisation of the humorous discourse, possibly yielding the desired humorous effects.
3. Human cognition characteristically exhibits a rooted tendency (i.e. an evolved psychological capacity) to search for relevant interpretations and subsequently select them, together with undertaking contextualisation in the most effort-relieving way. When an utterance is interpreted, several possible interpretations arise in the specific context where its utterance takes place, and we hold the ability to assess the strength and likelihood of these interpretations, eventually choosing only one of them. Crucially for an analysis of humour, human cognition performs this assessment of interpretations mostly at a sub-conscious level (we cannot possibly stop to compute all the possible interpretations and then select the most relevant one every time we interpret other people's utterances). Therefore, the speaker can play with the likelihood of interpretations, predict that one of them stands a better chance of being selected, and then invalidate it to finally show that (a) previously undetected interpretation(s) was/were feasible as well.
4. Relevance-oriented inferential strategies operate on a systematic (and unavoidable) basis when pairing the inference of discourse content and the one centred upon contextualisation. Again, these strategies may be predicted and manipulated for the sake of humour.

These general relevance-theoretic ideas will be developed in greater detail throughout the chapters of this book. However, one of its essential qualities is that it focuses specifically on internet humour, an environment for communication that entails a set of parameters different from those associated with the prototypical dyadic face-to-face interaction that relevance theory usually assumes when explaining its theoretical assumptions. Indeed, as noted in Yus (2021, 120–121), on the internet we: (a) find *new sender users* (not only the typical single communicator but also users engaged in collective creation, with hybridisation of communicators-audiences, etc.); (b) who produce *new types of discourse* (audio-visual, multimodal, with link-mediated choices for the flow of communication, etc.); (c) through *new interfaces* (new verbal-visual designs, multimodality, interfaces aiming at usability); (d) directed at a *new kind of user* (an active and dynamic one often contributing to the authorship of the online discourse); and (e) who comes up with a *variety of interpretations* (the initial user's intended interpretation -if any- becomes diluted and the responsibility for the choice of interpretations often falls upon the audience).

All of these qualities (a–e) just mentioned imply an adjustment both of the application of the theoretical assumptions of relevance theory and of the way in which humorous discourses are devised, conveyed to other users, interpreted in the context of a certain interface and inferred by the audience, which is frequently multiple and heterogeneous (as in Facebook users' lists of Friends) and likely to react to a specific humorous discourse in radically different manners. And the same applies to humorous communication, which takes up a variety of formats, with different expectations of context accessibility and often directed at multiple audiences online.

1 Overview of the Chapters

The second chapter (*Relevance theory, humour and internet communication*) provides the main theoretical scaffolding of this volume, exemplified with several instances of humorous internet discourses, which corroborates the suitability of this theory to address humour online. The chapter starts with several important notions in relevance theory such as intention, inference and the innate search for relevance, as well as a differentiation between the cognitive and communicative principle of relevance. The former revolves around the general human tendency to focus on potentially relevant inputs (including inputs not tied to an act of communication), whereas the latter is specific of communication and refers to the quality of intentionally communicated utterances to generate a presumption of its eventual relevance. This quality arguably sets in motion the addressee's inferential activity to enrich the schematic words of a discourse into contextualised explicit interpretations (*explicatures*) and derived *implicatures* (if necessary), as well as to retrieve contextual information.

In this chapter, a relevance-theoretic distinction between *communicative intention* and *informative intention* is also drawn, followed by a Section on context and mutuality of information (deemed essential for the planning and the expectation of generating humorous effects). The next Sections specify interpretive strategies within discourse comprehension that lead to explicatures and implicatures and describe how these are predicted and exploited in humorous communication. Chapter 2's final Section addresses the famous *incongruity-resolution* humorous strategy, which is said to be fully compatible with the relevance-theoretic analysis of humour, and likewise applied to several instances of internet humour.

Chapter 3 *Internet humour* introduces the main topic of this publication and specifies the scope of this label. It is argued that not all of the humorous discourses that abound online are genuinely qualified as fitting the "internet humour" label. In an attempt to explain the coverage of this term, three types of humour online are proposed: (a) *replicated humour*, which comprises humorous discourses created outside the Net for an offline audience and subsequently uploaded online. These would lie outside the narrow definition of internet humour proposed in this book. Examples include online joke repositories and stand-up comedy performances recorded in theatres and then uploaded on YouTube. (b) *Spontaneous internet humour*. These humorous discourses are either created on the Net or designed offline exclusively to be uploaded and interpreted online, and constitute the object of analysis in this book. This sort of humour becomes visible in all the range of typical internet discourses such as memes, stickers, GIFs, emojis, humorous comments on a social networking site entry, humorous online reviews and humour-centred blogs, among others. And (c) *hybrid internet humour*. The examples fitting this label combine replicated and spontaneous discourses within one single instance of internet communication. Examples appear in humorous comments to a replicated discourse or humorous discussions stemming from a replicated film or TV show on YouTube.

The chapter also includes reviews in the debate revolving around whether face-to-face humour outperforms its online counterpart or vice versa. Besides, some space is devoted to general issues regarding what constitutes a humorous discourse on the Net in its verbal, visual or multimodal qualities.

Contextual constraints on internet humour constitute the focus of attention in Chap. 4. Previous research has laid an emphasis on the fact that all internet communication is framed by a number of user- and interface-related constraints that influence the quality and quantity of content produced, causing a similar impact on what will eventually be interpreted from these discourses. As the introduction to the chapter specifies, although contextual constraints exist prior to the internet-mediated interaction (hence not appearing to be an inherent object of pragmatic research), their role in the quality of internet communication outcomes makes their analysis relevant when it comes to determining why online communication (and more specifically humour-centred internet communication, as addressed in this book) ends up being fruitful or fruitless.

This fourth chapter lists a number of interface-related contextual constraints on interactions taking place through interfaces for messaging as well as on social networking site interactions, each of which imposes certain communicative practices and prevents others due to their interface affordances. As for user-related constraints, the chapter studies users' personality in some depth. Furthermore, among these user-related constraints stand out inherited macro-features such as sex, ethnic origin and nationality, alongside other more context-dependent features, among them the task at hand or the user's mood upon engaging in interactions online. This chapter centres upon one of them: sex roles and how they impact everyday humorous interaction online.

Chapter 5, entitled *Humour in messaging interactions*, focuses on interactions occurring via the interface of the popular application WhatsApp, although it additionally assigns some space to comparing these interactions with the ones performed on WeChat. The chapter starts with some comments on humorous interactions and about the extent to which relevance theory is suited to study them, given the fact that this theory has traditionally used dyadic dialogues in its analysis. The specification of several benefits associated with interactive humour follows, together with a list of five key elements in the analysis of humorous interactions. A Section is then devoted to laughter and to how users convey it through messaging interactions.

The central part of the chapter deals with humorous interactions on WhatsApp, starting with an analysis of the role played by laugh particles (e.g. haha) and emojis in these interactions, and finishing with a long Section that studies turn-taking patterns during humorous interactions on WhatsApp. This chapter comes to an end with the aforementioned comparison between the way in which humorous interactions respectively develop on WhatsApp and WeChat.

Chapter 6, which addresses *Humour on social networking sites*, begins with a number of comments on the specificity of social networking sites and their interfaces when it comes to collecting and sharing humorous discourses. Then some space is devoted to the multiple formats (i.e. discursive modes) in which humour may be shaped on these sites.

Most importantly, this chapter divides humour on social networking sites into a number of humour parameters: by a single user, compiled on certain sites, on sites where social groups of users converge and their specificity usually becomes emphasised by the ability to understand and create certain kinds of humour, humour from commented posts and in-comment interactions, and finally corporate humour.

One of the most pervasive discourses online nowadays, the meme, is the object of analysis in Chap. 7, which goes under the title of *Meme-mediated humorous communication*. The chapter starts with an introduction to meme discourse and some references to the history of the term "meme." Attention is subsequently paid to the relationship between text and image in humorous memes, after which another Section shows how humorous effects may stem from the exploitation of different inferential strategies intended to turn the literal verbal-visual discourse coded in the meme into meaningful (and eventually humorous) contextualised interpretations.

The next Section deals with the incongruity-resolution humorous strategy applied to memes, followed by a short Section on the adjustment of visual referents in memes for the sake of humour. This chapter is brought to an end with an account of Covid-19 memes and their humorous strategies, the analysis of which evidences that these memes exhibit alternative purposes in the context of the pandemic and lockdown to the ones devised for non-Covid memes.

The title of the last chapter in this book is *Beyond humour: Relevant affective effects*. This chapter has as its main aim to show that several relevant non-propositional effects (feelings, emotions) are part of the humorous act of internet communication (or triggered by it) too. These effects, generated in parallel to humorous ones, may match what the sender user intends upon engaging in a humorous interaction, but they sometimes also *leak* from the act of communication beyond the sender user's intentions and nevertheless end up being relevant to the audience.

After an account of relevance theory's approach to the analysis of non-propositional effects and the degree to which the internet is specific in how these effects are generated, four groups of relevant non-propositional effects are listed: at a personal level; at an interactive level; at a medium-sized group level; and at a large-sized group level. Effects stemming from such humorous interactions include those which are identity-centred, based on the exploitation of shared discursive conventions arising from the ability that humour has to mark group boundaries and emphasise the mutuality of information, focusing on bonding and solidarity, and so on.

In sum, *Pragmatics of internet humour* offers a unique pragmatic overview of how humour is devised, coded, manipulated and ultimately inferred online. The reader will obtain a thorough explanation of the way in which these communicative humorous strategies unfold in the medium, which differs from the typical dyadic face-to-face environment which has so often been analysed in the literature on offline humour.

References

Sperber, Dan, and Deirdre Wilson. 1995. *Relevance. Communication and Cognition*. 2nd ed. Oxford: Blackwell.

———. 2002. Pragmatics, Modularity and Mind-Reading. *Mind and Language* 17 (1–2): 3–23. https://doi.org/10.1111/1468-0017.00186.

Yule, George. 1996. *Pragmatics*. Oxford: Oxford University Press. https://doi.org/10.1017/S0272263198224053.

Yus, Francisco. 2011. *Cyberpragmatics. Internet-Mediated Communication in Context*. Amsterdam and Philadelphia: John Benjamins. https://doi.org/10.1075/pbns.213.

———. 2016. *Humour and Relevance*. Amsterdam: John Benjamins. https://doi.org/10.1075/thr.4.

———. 2021. *Smartphone Communication. Interactions in the App Ecosystem*. Abingdon: Routledge. https://doi.org/10.4324/9781003200574.

CHAPTER 2

Relevance Theory, Humour and Internet Communication

1 Introduction

Pragmatics can be described as a branch of semiotics that analyses how *more* gets communicated than is literally *said* (Yule 1996). As such, it lays emphasis on the role played by context when interlocutors fill the gap between what has been literally said and what is meant and eventually interpreted. Relevance theory (henceforth RT), a cognitive pragmatics theory, seems particularly suited to accounting for utterance interpretation and to explaining the selection of context as well as its combination with inferred content to yield satisfactory (i.e. relevant) interpretations (Sperber and Wilson 1995).[1] As will be described in the following Sections, RT is not only a theory of human communication but also a proposal of how human cognition works as a whole, and it proves useful to explain both face-to-face interaction and internet-mediated communication (Yus 2001, 2010a, 2011,[2] 2021a), alongside humorous communication (Yus

[1] For general comments on RT, see Allott (2013), Assimakopoulos (2017a), Blakemore (1992, 2011), Carston (2011), Carston and Powell (2005), Clark (2013), Wilson (2014, 2017), Wilson and Sperber (1987, 2002, 2004, 2012) and Yus (1998a, 2003a, 2006, 2010b, 2016b). For bibliographical references, see Yus (1998b) and the online resource *Relevance Theory Online Bibliographic Service* (http://personal.ua.es/francisco.yus/rt.html).

[2] The book *Cyberpragmatics* (2011) is available (open access) here: https://benjamins.com/catalog/pbns.213.

F. Yus, *Pragmatics of Internet Humour*,
https://doi.org/10.1007/978-3-031-31902-0_2

2016a, 2017) and a combination of both, *internet humour*, as proposed and analysed in this book.

The chapter is organised as follows. In Sect. 2, a review of RT's main tenets will be provided, together with general applications to humorous communication. Section 3 will in turn focus on the well-known incongruity-resolution humorous strategy addressed from an RT perspective.

2 Relevance Theory and Humour

2.1 Intention, Inference and Search for Relevance

Humans possess an evolved cognitive mechanism that allows them to focus their attention on what they are likely to find rewarding, or *relevant*, in the technical sense adopted within RT. Once a potentially relevant stimulus has been identified (especially if intentionally produced), our cognitive system automatically engages in its processing and tries to achieve relevant effects. Although this cognitive task works with all inputs to our cognitive system, RT has focused on inputs of an intentional nature and recognised as such (i.e. with an *ostensive* quality) when coming from communicators (nonverbal behaviour, utterances). As Wilson (2014, 4) remarks, "the aim is to define relevance not only for utterances or other communicative acts, but (also) for any external stimulus or internal mental representation which can provide an input to cognitive processes, so that not only utterances but (also) sights, sounds, smells, thoughts, memories or conclusions of inferences may all provide potentially relevant inputs (for an individual, at a time)."

In sum, inputs subjected to human processing for relevance include verbal utterances, nonverbal behaviour, elements in the physical surrounding, as well as the individual's thoughts and background knowledge retrieved at a particular communicative situation. When do these inputs acquire relevance? In general, other things being equal, when a positive trade-off exists between the reward obtained from their processing (*positive cognitive effects* in RT terminology) and the mental effort that their processing demands.

Different inputs compete for our attention at every stage of our lives, and it has been crucial for human cognition to develop an ability to filter out potentially irrelevant stimuli and consequently to focus exclusively on what is thought to be interesting and rewarding: "as a result of constant selection pressures towards increasing cognitive efficiency, the human cognitive system has developed a variety of mental mechanisms or biases (some innate, others acquired) which tend to allocate attention to inputs with the greatest expected relevance, and process them in the most relevance-enhancing way" (Wilson 2017, 83). This cognitive strategy is covered by the so-called *cognitive principle of relevance*: "Human cognition is geared to the maximisation of relevance." Broadly speaking, an input becomes relevant to an individual when it fruitfully interacts with contextual information that the individual has access to and yields new, worthwhile effects:

> The main idea underlying the cognitive principle of relevance is that our perceptual systems are constantly trying to pick up the stimuli which are bound to be relevant; similarly, our background information is accessed in a relevance-driven way, retrieving relevant information in specific contexts, and our inferential systems are geared to the maximisation of cognitive effects. Processing in this way is seen as something that happens automatically, in ways that are generally outside our control. These 'subpersonal' processes are carried out by heuristics that arise from the way the mind is organised. (Yus 2016a, 9)

This relevance derived from a trade-off of effects and effort also holds true for the interpretation of utterances: "For communication to succeed, the speaker needs the addressee's attention. Since attention tends to go automatically to what is most relevant at the time, a prerequisite to successful communication is that the addressee must take the utterance to be relevant enough to be worth attending to. Then a speaker, by the very act of addressing someone, communicates that the utterance meets this precondition" (Wilson 2017, 85), as specifically reflected in the parallel *communicative principle of relevance* (Sperber and Wilson 1995, 266–278): "Every utterance communicates a presumption of its own optimal relevance." Of course, this effects/effort trade-off also takes place in humorous discourses, whose interpretation often entails increased mental effort to cause the desired effects. As stated in Yus (2016a, 50),

> unlike other forms of ostensive communication, a person telling a joke pushes the interlocutor into assuming an eventual relevance despite the fact that the joke itself is probably not going to be very informative or interact with the current context of the interaction in fruitful ways. Indeed, hearers sometimes have to interpret absurd scenarios with strange characters inside

the joke for the sake of humour, but will still assume that the presumption of relevance applies and that it will eventually lead to a positive interpretive outcome, that is, that the eventual amusement and even laughter will make up for the effort involved in processing the joke.

Both principles are at work in most daily instances of interpretation. Crucially, when an utterance is intentionally directed at us (*ostensively* communicated), it not only activates our search for relevance but also the relevance-related search for explicit and implicated interpretations, technically referred to as *explicature* and *implicature*, respectively (more on this in Sect. 2.4 below). An adaptation was suggested in Yus (2021a) for the dialogue in (1), from Sperber and Wilson (2015: 121), including additional relevant information that might be communicated and/or inferred. In this example, the explicit interpretation (*explicature*) from the official's utterance would roughly match the version provided in (2). Furthermore, the passenger would be expected to infer the official's *propositional attitude*[3] upon answering the question, in this case a warning (3). An extension was also suggested in Yus (ibid.) to include not only propositional information intended but also the official's *affective attitude* (feelings and emotions felt as well as intended) that he might also wish to communicate, as in (4). Concerning *implicatures*, (5) would count as a *strong implicature* (clearly intended by the official), whereas the possibilities listed in (6) would be *weak implicatures* (perhaps inferred by the passenger beyond the official's intentions), likewise triggered by the utterance (more on explicatures/implicatures in Sect. 2.4 below):

(1)	Passenger:	[*Reaching the station at 12:45 and talking to an official*]. What time is the next train to Oxford?
	Railway official:	[*With an alarmed look on his face and marked intonation*]. At 12.48!!!

[3] As remarked in Yus (2016a, 137), propositional attitudes matter for successful interactions, since they introduce an additional metarepresentational level of information beyond the explicit utterance content. These attitudes relate to a variety of mental experiences, such as emotional reactions, feelings and judgements, which may be consciously or unconsciously held by the speaker towards the utterance. Natural languages offer speakers a whole range of linguistic means which can be used to code propositional attitudes. These include *that*-clauses introduced by an attitudinal verb ("I *regret* that you failed your exam"), parenthetical clauses ("It's time to go, I *guess*"), verbal moods ("*Come* here right now!"), illocutionary adverbials ("*Frankly*, I am not surprised"), and evidentials ("*No doubt* he is the best candidate for the job").

(2) The next train to Oxford departs at 12.48 on this day.
(3) The official is warning the passenger that the next train to Oxford departs at 12.48.
(4) The official feels concerned about whether the passenger will board the train in time.
(5) You'd better hurry or you'll miss the train.
(6) The train is not going to wait for passengers who arrive late at the platform.
The seats on the train are filling up fast.
The platform is further away than the passenger might have thought.

All the interpretive outcomes listed in (2–6) result from the official's utterance, and the passenger will be engaged in obtaining the most relevant interpretive outcome from this utterance. This whole process would be covered by the *communicative principle of relevance*. However, consider the possibilities listed in (8–9) regarding situation (7) right after the dialogue in (1):

(7) The passenger runs to the platform but, right when he arrives, he sees the train departing.
(8) It takes an hour for the train to arrive in Oxford.
No further trains are departing any time soon.
My job interview is at 13:45.
(9) I will miss the job interview.
My family will criticise me for stupidly missing the interview.

When the passenger reaches the platform, many visual inputs compete to catch his attention, among them several other passengers at the platform, the new benches of the station or a new bar that has just opened beside the platform. However, following the *cognitive principle of relevance*, only the train departing will be deemed worth processing. The passenger is thus likely to combine the visual input in (7) with background information such as (8) to reach relevant conclusions like those in (9), which may be categorised as *hearer-centred implications*. He might equally entertain other *leaked* effects, for instance, regarding the reliability of trains, feelings about passengers' or colleagues' reaction upon him not turning up at the interview, or overall satisfaction with the punctuality of British trains, to quote but a few.

In short, hearers normally focus their cognitive resources on obtaining the highest possible reward in return for the least mental effort involved. They will automatically select the most likely interpretation unless further evidence leads them to opt for alternative interpretive paths. This turns out to be crucial to understand humorous communication, and specifically internet humour, as this book aims to show. All the above becomes evident in the general comprehension heuristic proposed by RT:

a. Follow a path of least effort in constructing an interpretation of the utterance (and in particular in resolving ambiguities and referential indeterminacies, adjusting lexical meaning, supplying contextual assumptions, deriving implicatures, etc.).
b. Stop when your expectations of relevance are satisfied.

The fact that, once the hearer has found a satisfactory interpretation deemed to be the most relevant, the hearer will stop and infer no further, is key for humour. By way of example, jokes based on polysemy (as in numerous puns) typically entail the hearer's initial choice of one interpretation for a word or stretch of discourse that is found sufficiently relevant for them to stop inferring. In this case, the hearer will not consider the existence of other senses. The speaker then invalidates that relevant choice and replaces it with a different one, which the hearer could not have taken into account, thus triggering humorous effects. An explanation for this, provided in Yus (2003b, 1309–1310), relies on distinguishing the initial part of *multiple-graded interpretations* framed within the humorous discourse from its subsequent *single covert interpretation* part.

In a nutshell, even though the initial part of many jokes has multiple interpretations, they are graded according to their accessibility (or expressed differently, according to their relevance). The hearer is led to automatically select a first interpretation for the initial part of the text (often in a garden-path way). Suddenly, the hearer realises that the subsequent text has a *single covert interpretation*, other than that initially selected, which eventually becomes the correct one and the one providing an overall coherent interpretation for the whole text. That second interpretation surprises the hearer (it seems incongruous with the on-going interpretation, see Sect. 3 below) and its resolution by finding an overall coherent interpretation of the whole text, together with the addressees' awareness that they have been fooled into selecting a specific interpretation, will most probably trigger a humorous effect. Examples include (10):

(10) "Things don't look good. The only chance is a brain transplant. This is an experimental procedure. It might work, but the bad news is that brains are very expensive, and you will have to pay the costs yourselves." "Well, how much does a brain cost?" asked the relatives. "For a male brain, \$500,000. For a female brain, \$200,000." The patient's daughter was unsatisfied and asked, "Why the difference in price between male brains and female brains?" "A standard pricing practice," said the head of the team. "Women's brains have to be marked down because they have actually been used."

Overt accessible interpretation in the initial part:
"Women are less intelligent than men."
Covert (and unlikely) interpretation of second part and fitting the whole joke:
"Women are more intelligent than men."

The interpretive steps listed in (a-b) above are automatic inferential procedures triggered by ostensive (i.e. intentional) communicative behaviour and in charge of a specialised comprehension module,[4] often referred to as *ostension processor*, which forms part of a broader *mindreading module* devoted to attributing mental states in others.[5] RT has placed the emphasis on intentional (*ostensive*) communication in this regard, leaving unintentionally transferred information outside the scope of pragmatic

[4] The term *module* comes from Fodor's (1983) *modularity thesis.* His conceptualisation of the mind included a powerful (and still highly mysterious) central processor fed with information from a number of highly specialised, encapsulated and domain-specific modules that are in charge of identifying a specific type of information. For instance, the *perception module* only activates itself when visual information becomes available to be sent to the central processor. Similarly (and despite this claim not being devoid of controversy, see Clark 2013, 94f), the activation of the *language module* would not take place until words which the hearer can possibly understand reach this module. The *ostension processor module* appeared as a development and refinement of this initial proposal by Fodor.

[5] As summarised by Carston (2002, 44), the main argument to claim that this is a distinct mental module hinges on the assumption that the comprehension process requires a particular pattern of inference which distinguishes it from the inferential processes involved in interpreting non-ostensive behaviour such as watching people pass by us: "In interpreting an instance of ostensive behaviour, the desirable effect (which is that the addressee grasp the communicator's meaning) cannot be achieved without the addressee's prior recognition of the communicator's intention to achieve that effect."

analysis. Indeed, accidental transmissions of information (where the speaker simply gives off or exudes information without an intention to communicate it) would lie outside RT's scope of analysis. In the words of Sperber and Wilson (1997, 150): "The issue is not, of course, whether non-ostensive forms of information-transmission exist, but whether they should be treated as communication. In Relevance, we argue that, in general, unintentionally transmitted information is subject merely to general cognitive rather than specifically communicative constraints." For example, concerning the similar situations (11) and (12), only the latter would deserve pragmatic analysis, even though inference is devoted to making sense of the other person's behaviour in both of them (Yus 2021a):

(11) Tom is walking along a street that leads to the railway station and sees his friend Peter, who is carrying a suitcase. While walking fast, he looks at his watch, worried. Tom correctly infers that Peter is hurrying to catch a train and that he is worried because he is late.

(12) Tom is walking along a street that leads to the railway station and sees his friend Peter, who is carrying a suitcase. Tom waves at him. Peter waves back and, while looking at him, Peter points at his watch, with a worried expression. Tom correctly infers that Peter is trying to communicate that he is hurrying to catch a train, that he is late and has no time to talk to him.

Within this view of intentional communication, Sperber and Wilson predict the existence of two intentions: the *communicative intention*, which alerts the hearer to the speaker's willingness to communicate some information (to *make* it *manifest* in RT's technical sense) to the hearer; and the *informative intention*, which concerns the actual information (*a set of assumptions* in relevance-theoretic terminology) that the speaker means to communicate (and which is revealed by parallelly identifying the communicative intention). In RT terms,

Informative intention
An intention to make a set of assumptions manifest or more manifest to the audience.
Communicative intention
An intention to make it mutually manifest both to the audience and to communicator that the latter has this informative intention.
Ostensive-inferential communication

> The communicator produces a stimulus which makes it mutually manifest both to the communicator and to the audience that the former wants to use this stimulus with the aim of making a set of assumptions manifest or more manifest to the audience.

Authors such as Assimakopoulos (2021) have recently put forward the idea that, despite its non-intentional nature, non-ostensive behaviour -including utterances not directed at us- may also trigger relevance-seeking inferential strategies (rather than general cognitive operations). Imagine, for instance, that I am sitting at a table in a bar and cannot help but overhear a conversation between two women at a nearby table. At some point, one of them says (13) to the other:

(13) Yes, Mary did arrive at the party, but really, really late. And instead of thanking me for inviting her, she started complaining that the party was a disaster, that there was nobody there and no drink.

Obviously, (13) is not addressed to me, but that does not stop me engaging in some inferential strategies to turn what the woman literally said into a (somewhat) meaningful interpretation. Despite my obvious inability to find a referent for "Mary," I can still infer that "her" and "she" allude to Mary, that the meaning of *nobody* has to be relaxed, rather than inferred literally (some people were still at the party), and that *drink* specifically means "alcoholic drinks" (more on these inferential strategies in Sect. 2.4 below).

Humorous communication likewise includes a communicative intention that reveals an informative intention. The addressee may be either overtly alerted to the humorous intention underlying the discourse about to be uttered (e.g. "have you heard the one about…?") or humorously taken by surprise, so to speak. In any case, what matters most in humour is that the inferential strategies to interpret a humorous discourse do not differ from those used in non-humorous ones, insofar as

> we are biologically endowed with one single ability to turn schematic stimuli into contextualised interpretations, and we do not possess different cognitive capabilities to process different kinds of stimuli (…) In short, a relevance-theoretic analysis of humour predicts that the hearer decodes the schematic text (a joke, for instance) and uses it as evidence of the speaker's (or writer's) humorous intention. As researchers, we can mind-read the speaker's intentions when devising the humorous text (or when using an already available one, if it is part of the collective archive of humorous representations stored in the culture) with specific predictions of how this joke is expected to be

> processed and what quality and quantity of context is bound to be accessed in the search for a relevant interpretation of the humorous text. (Yus 2016a, 38).

RT also acknowledges this ability to foresee the mental states and inferential patterns of others as part of the general human tendency to maximise relevance (Sperber and Wilson 2002). More precisely, speakers can predict: (a) which stimulus[6] belonging to an individual B's environment is likely to attract B's attention (i.e. the most relevant stimulus in that environment); (b) which background information from B's memory is likely to be retrieved and used while processing such stimulus (that is, the background information most relevant to its processing); and (c) which inferences B is likely to draw (in other words, those which yield enough cognitive benefits for B's attentional resources to remain on the stimulus instead of being diverted to alternative potential inputs competing for the same resources).

Similarly, the communicator of a humorous discourse expects it to be the most attractive stimulus in the interlocutor's environment (a), which additionally allows the former to make fine-grained predictions regarding (b) the addressee's accessibility to the necessary contextual information required to reach a relevant interpretation of this humorous discourse and to derive parallel humorous effects (more on context in Sect. 2.2 below); and (c) the addressee's inferential steps towards a relevant interpretation of that humorous discourse. Needless to say, the same holds true for humorous internet discourses. Let us discuss the multimodal meme in (14) and the Facebook entry in (15):

(14) Image: A man at a hotel reception counter talking to the receptionist, a woman.
He: Oiga, la chica que pasó conmigo la noche en mi habitación, ¿ha dejado alguna nota aquí en recepción?
[*Excuse me, the woman who spent the night with me in my room, has she left a note here at reception?*].
She: Sí. Un 4.
[*Yes, a 4*].

(15) Apparently, Elton John has put on so much weight he has to have his trousers specially made. Goodbye Normal Jeans

[6] "Stimulus" is an umbrella term covering a whole range of intentionally conveyed inputs, mainly utterances but also nonverbal behaviour.

Meme (14) illustrates prediction (c) above. The meme plays with the polysemy of *nota* in Spanish, which means either *note* or *mark*. The sender user knows that, given the setup of the joke (hotel reception, customer inquiring, etc.), the reader is bound to select "has she left a note?" as the intended interpretation of *¿ha dejado alguna nota?* Crucially, as explained above, upon finding that interpretation, the internet user will discard the existence of any other possible interpretation for *nota*. However, the woman's reply, *Sí. Un 4* ("Yes, a 4"), makes the user suddenly realise that *mark* is also a possible meaning of *nota*, albeit much less likely or relevant at first. On the other hand, (15) illustrates prediction (b) above. The Facebook user expects his audience to have access to the necessary background contextual information regarding Elton John's song "Candle in the Wind (Goodbye Norma Jean)," and accordingly to identify the phonetic similarity with "normal jeans," which will enable them to draw the intended humorous effects.

It goes without saying that predictions (b) and (c) are not mutually exclusive and, in fact, interlocutors very often need both (predicted context accessibility and predicted content inference) to optimally derive humorous effects. For example, a recent post on Facebook (Fig. 2.1) pictured a woman in bed beside a huge pipe and a man standing beside the bed while she says "Darling, it's not what it looks like!" Given the frequency of such an utterance in that specific scenario (and in the media, for that matter), the audience are bound to select the text between square brackets in (16) below as the referent for *it*. However, the pipe depicted closely resembles the famous pipe drawn in Rene Magritte's painting belonging to the series *The treachery of images* (1929), which portrays a pipe and, below it, the text "Ceci n'est pas une pipe" ("This is not a pipe"), thus criticising our overreliance on the figurativeness of images.[7] Therefore, the creator of the joke *also* expects the audience to be aware of this contextual information and, consequently, to be capable of replacing the initial accessible referent in (16) with the one between square brackets in (17), the clash of predictable/unlikely referents possibly triggering the desired humorous effects.

(16) [My being in bed with someone] is not what it looks like.
(17) [The pipe in bed beside me] is not what it looks like.

[7] See the painting here: https://www.renemagritte.org/the-treachery-of-images.jsp

Fig. 2.1 A meme demanding reference assignment and context accessibility

2.2 *Context and Mutuality of Information* (Manifestness)

It is widely agreed within pragmatics that context plays a major role when turning the schematic meaning literally uttered (or written, recorded, typed…) into communicatively meaningful and relevant interpretations. However, there are differences as for how context has been conceptualised and its accessibility pictured throughout the history of pragmatics. As a matter of fact, within the so-called *static view of context* in pragmatics that prevailed during the 1980s and 1990s, analysts acknowledged the importance of context in human communication; nonetheless, they were concerned to a greater extent with isolating types of contexts than with explaining the way in which context is selected and used to obtain an appropriate interpretation. Added to that, context was somehow taken for granted or given beforehand, and *inserting* -so to speak- the utterance in the context sufficed to obtain the right interpretation. By contrast, RT belongs to the *dynamic view of context*, according to which context is not given but actively sought as part of the utterance interpretation process. Isolating types of contexts looks fruitless, since context is always "information" (*a set of assumptions* in RT terminology) that we retrieve during utterance interpretation.

Of course, contextual information may stem from multiple sources, including the person's store of background information or information from the immediate physical surroundings.[8] RT defines context as

> a psychological construct, a subset of the hearer's assumptions about the world. It is these assumptions, of course, rather than the actual state of the world, that affect the interpretation of an utterance. A context in this sense is not limited to information about the immediate physical environment or the immediately preceding utterances: expectations about the future, scientific hypotheses or religious beliefs, anecdotal memories, general cultural assumptions, beliefs about the mental state of the speaker, may all play a role in interpretation. (Sperber and Wilson 1995, 15–16).

In any case, and most importantly, it is the utterance that pushes the hearer into a specific "contextualising direction" (i.e. into selecting some specific information from context) when searching for a relevant interpretation of the utterance, rather than context being simply "there" or given beforehand (Assimakopoulos 2017b, 223).

The assumptions making up the context upon which an utterance is interpreted exhibit an important quality: they have to be mentally represented by the hearer, so that they can feed the "ostension processor" and combine optimally with the information literally provided by the utterance in order to yield a relevant interpretation: "A context comprises mentally represented information of any type -beliefs, doubts, hopes, wishes, plans, goals, intentions, questions…- and is constructed or selected in the course of the comprehension process from a range of potential contexts available to the individual. One reason for treating these more general notions as basic is that considerations of relevance play a fundamental role not only in communication but also in cognition" (Wilson 2017, 82).

In RT terms, in every situation where interpretations are obtained the hearer has access to a huge amount of contextual information (i.e.

[8] "This set of assumptions, which comprises not only immediately observable information but also general beliefs about the world, as well as dispositions towards the communicator in that particular instance, constitutes the context against which the content of the communicative stimulus will be processed with a view to recovering the communicator's intended meaning or, as relevance theorists call it, her informative intention" (Assimakopoulos 2017a, 311).

assumptions) that makes up the hearer's *cognitive environment*. Such assumptions are the ones that the hearer is capable of mentally representing and accepting as true in the situation in question. The speaker's utterance provides the hearer with information (*manifest information*, according to RT) which is in turn inferred against the store of assumptions underpinning the hearer's cognitive environment. Therefore, when communication succeeds, the speaker makes information manifest to the hearer, this information eventually becoming *mutually manifest* to both interlocutors. Communication basically consists in making information mutually manifest to both interlocutors.

Regarding humorous communication, speakers (and "sender internet users" too, in the context of this book) also predict the existence of this mutuality of information when devising their humorous discourses and sending/forwarding them to other users via social media and messaging apps. It is frequently the case that the key to the humour in such discourses lies precisely in the vivid mutual awareness of the audience's capacity to access the context needed to obtain relevant interpretations and parallel humorous effects. Consider the memes in Fig. 2.2, the top-left one translated in (18), bottom-left in (19), and the one on the right in (20):

(18) -Shit, Paco, what an amazing car you bought.
-It's because I iron the clothes at night.

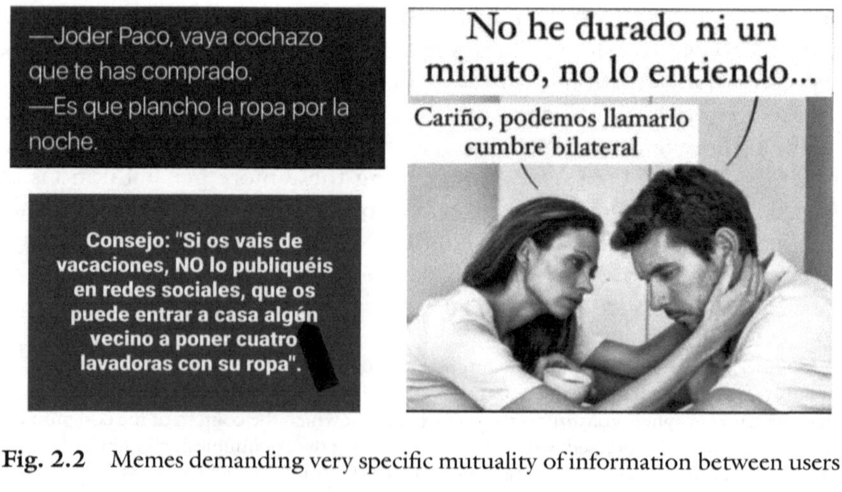

Fig. 2.2 Memes demanding very specific mutuality of information between users

(19) Advice: "If you go on holiday, do NOT post that information on social media, because a neighbour might break into your house and use your washing machine 4 times with their clothes."

(20) He: I didn't even last one minute, I don't understand...
She: Darling, we can call it bilateral summit.

To ensure effectiveness in the humorous interpretation of the textual memes[9] (18–19), the audience must be able to access very specific contextual (i.e. background) information, and the awareness about the mutuality of this information between sender user and their audience should suffice to trigger the desired humorous effects. Similarly, the absence of this mutuality would lead to unresolved incongruity, rather than to humour. Specifically, these two textual memes deal with the change in the electricity tariff that was implemented in 2021 in Spain, which made the price of electricity increase considerably during the day and decrease at night. Spanish people started using household appliances at night to save money, and both social media and messaging apps were flooded with memes humorously criticising this new scenario. As for (20), this meme demands accessibility to even more fine-grained background assumptions. Given the look of the man portrayed in the meme, the audience will have no problem elaborating "I didn't even last one minute" into "I didn't even last one minute [in bed making love to you]" (on enriching inferential strategies, see Sect. 2.4 below). The audience is then expected to access background information about the recent bilateral summit between U.S president Joe Biden and Spanish president Pedro Sánchez, which was overtly criticised by opposition leaders precisely for lasting only one minute. Again, the mutual awareness of this information between the sender user and their audience should succeed in triggering the desired humorous effects. Since we cannot enter other people's minds, the successful

[9] Despite both memes on the left of Fig. 2.2 being textual, they are actually forwarded and shared as images, and retrieved as such from the images in the photo library of the smartphone (when not directly forwarded through social media or messaging apps). As argued in Yus (2021a), this use of text-turned-image entails a reinterpretation of what "an image" is in the context of smartphone-mediated communication.

derivation of humorous effects is an effective way to signal and foreground this mutuality of information.[10]

2.3 *Inferring from What Is Coded*

One basic idea in RT is the so-called *underdeterminacy thesis*, i.e. the fact that what the speaker (or internet user) codes (or expressed differently: says, writes, records, types…) always turns out to be less informative than both the interpretation that the speaker/user has in mind and the interpretation finally obtained by the addressee. RT pictures two main stages during comprehension, a minimal *decoding* one and a major one that revolves around *inferring*. The former basically seeks to identify the words uttered and arrange them in a basic grammatical string or schema. The language module in the brain (à la Fodor 1983) is in charge of this basic and context-free identification (no context-bound inference takes place at this stage). The latter has far more importance, when the central processor (or *ostensive processor*, as now labelled in recent RT research) receives this schematic string of words, called *logical form* in RT terminology, as input and enriches it inferentially to yield a relevant interpretation (see next Section). More precisely, the processor "performs the tasks of (a) developing [the logical form] into a full proposition that corresponds to the one that the speaker intended to communicate in the first place; (b) selecting an appropriate set of contextual assumptions against which it will calculate the speaker-intended cognitive effects; and (c) calculating these cognitive effects" (Assimakopoulos 2017a, 313).

On most occasions, the aforementioned language module comes up with a single logical form for the words uttered by the speaker/user. However, two (or more) logical forms are sometimes equally valid (or both are possible even if one prevails over the other).This multiplicity of

[10] As described in Yus (2016a, 48–49), the mutuality of knowledge (*mutual manifestness*) between interlocutors becomes so important for humour (as much as for communication in general) that one theory exists which has as its main theoretical premise to stress the role of shared knowledge: the *encryption theory of humour* (Flamson and Clark Barrett 2008; Flamson and Bryant 2013). As stated above, according to this theory, humorous effects depend on accessibility to implicit information shared by speaker and audience. The same as in any type of encryption, it faces us with a public product, the joke, which needs to be deciphered and its intended meaning can only be deduced if the audience hold the key to decrypt the message, and audiences can be more or less certain that the speaker has access to this key too.

Fig. 2.3 Memes humorously exploiting the existence of two possible logical forms for the utterance

logical forms is sometimes exploited by the creators of humorous discourses -including those found on the Internet- either because the two logical forms are perfect candidates for the utterance at hand or because the speaker/user forces a second logical form upon the one initially obtained by the language module, this option being quite frequent as a humorous strategy. Let us discuss the memes from Fig. 2.3 (copied and translated in (21–24)):

(21) -Lo voy a ayudar con su problema de próstata.
[*I am going to help you with your prostate problem*].
-Gracias doctor. Mearia muy feliz.[11]
[*Thanks doc. I would piss happily / You'd make me very happy*].

(22) -Anoche me robaron la televisión mientras estaba con mi mujer en la cama.
[*Last night someone stole my TV while I was in bed with my wife*].
-¿Consumando?
[*Having sex? / With its remote?*].
-Si, si. Con los cables y todo.

[11] Some of the words in the examples in Spanish exhibit orthographic mistakes (e.g. *Mearia* should be *Mearía*). In this book, these mistakes are maintained when copied and/or translated.

[*Yes, yes. And the cables and all*].

(23) ¿Para usted cuál es su ministro favorito?
[*For you, who is your favourite minister?*].
El suministro de cerveza, sin duda alguna.
[*The beer supply, without a doubt*].

(24) He: Can I ask you about the menu please?
She: The men I please is none of your business.

In (21), one of the logical forms, *Mearía muy feliz* ("I would piss happily"), is more accessible to the hearer, mainly due to the visual input of the words in that phrase. However, the humourist plays with another logical form that is pronounced exactly the same: *me haría muy feliz* ("You would make me very happy"), which can be an equally valid candidate for a logical form of the utterance, and even more so if the meme is listened to and not read. In (22), only one possible logical form with a single word makes sense: *Consumando?* ("Having sex?"). However, the continuation of the meme is incongruous (see Sect. 3) and reminds the user of a second, more unlikely albeit still possible logical form, this time made up of three words: *Con su mando?* ("With its remote?"), which turns out to be the one compatible with the end of the meme: *Sí, sí. Con los cables y todo* ("Yes, yes. And the cables and all"). Similarly, when reading (23), the internet user is expected to construct a logical form that includes *su ministro* ("your minister," in two words, again very prominent due to the visual input of the words), only to realise that a parallel possible logical form includes *suministro* ("supply," in a single word); and its pairing with "beer" humorously surprises the addressee. Finally, the reader of (24) is expected to come up with a predictable logical form containing *the menu please* (3 words), helped by the situation in which the utterance takes place (a restaurant, tables, customer, waitress). What then comes as a surprise to the reader is that another possible -but much more unlikely- logical form exists for this utterance (and with a similar pronunciation too): *the men you please* (4 words).

In any case, it would sound naïve to state that hearers (or addressee internet users) wait until the speaker (or sender user) has finished speaking (or writing or typing) to start inferring the most relevant interpretation from the discourse produced. Instead, RT predicts a mental interpretive procedure that comprises three parallel tasks (i.e. tasks in a *mutual parallel adjustment*): (a) to identify the speaker's intended explicit interpretation (*explicature*); (b) to derive, if necessary, implicated conclusions (*implicatures*) from the utterance; and (c) to access as much contextual information as is required to fulfil tasks (a) and (b). For instance, in the dialogue quoted in (25), upon inferring Mary's utterance, John will construct Mary's intended explicit interpretation or *explicature* (26) (notice how this explicature entails narrowing the default meaning of *drink* into a more adequate and relevant *drink alcohol*, a case of *conceptual narrowing*, see below). He will likewise need to access contextual assumptions such as the ones in (27) (also known as *implicated premises* in RT terminology) so that he can derive the intended implicature (*implicated conclusion* in RT terminology) in (28), which is the actual answer to John's question.

(25) John: Are you still going out with Peter?
Mary: I drink too much.
(26) Mary drinks too much alcohol.
(27) Peter is an ex-alcoholic.
Ex alcoholics do not like having people around them drinking alcohol.
(28) Mary is no longer going out with Peter.

These three tasks are performed and adjusted in parallel as the utterance is interpreted, i.e. for every chunk or stretch that shapes the utterance (Wilson 2017, 89). Crucially, the previously inferred content also becomes context on which the interpretation of the next chunk/stretch relies. Figure 2.4 pictures how hearers and addressee users identify the words in

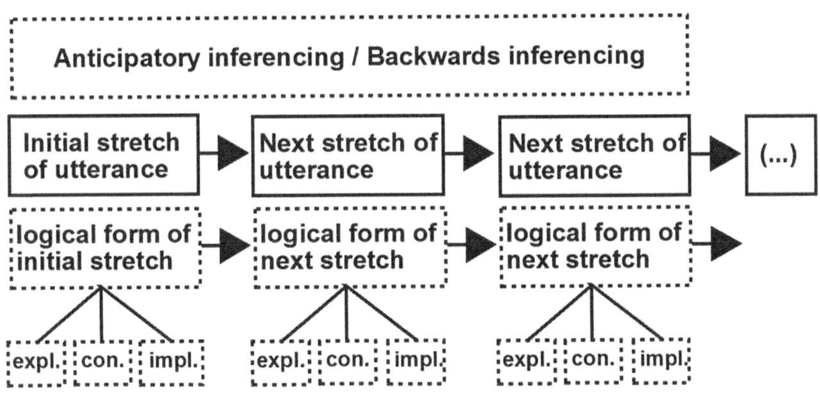

Fig. 2.4 Comprehension as mutual parallel adjustment (Yus 2016a, 20)

the initial stretch of the utterance (its logical form) and access contextual information (abbreviated to "con." in Fig. 2.4), extract an explicit interpretation (expl.) and perhaps already derive implicatures (impl.) from this stretch of the utterance (see Carston and Hall 2011).

Figure 2.4 includes the terms *anticipatory inferencing* and *backwards inferencing* as well. In the former, the hearer can anticipate certain structures or even lexical items in the light of the chunk of text that has just been processed (see Dikker et al. 2014):

> Consider someone about to process some new information. He still has in mind some of the assumptions he has just been processing. People do not come to the processing of new information with a 'blank mind'; they have some kind of short-term memory store (or several such stores, or devices functionally equivalent to short-term memory stores) whose contents are simply never erased, at least when the individual is awake. (Sperber and Wilson 1995, 138).

Backwards inferencing in turn occurs when the information provided by a subsequent stretch of discourse invalidates what the hearer has already taken on board inferentially based on previous stretches of discourse, forcing them to backtrack and re-interpret that previous discourse. This typically happens in humorous communication (e.g. puns), where the speaker often causes the hearer to interpret an initial part of the joke in a certain way only to invalidate that interpretation in a subsequent stretch of discourse (Yus 2020). This is the humorous strategy at work in the following meme:

(29) -¿Qué hay de menú?
[*What's on the menu?*].
-Tenemos tres primeros y tres segundos para elegir…
[*We've got three first [courses] and three second [courses] to choose (from)*].
-MIERDA, en tres segundos no me da tiempo a decidirme…
[*Shit, I've got not time to make up my mind in three seconds*].

The creator of (29) knows that, having processed the initial part of the meme, including *menu*, the hearer will construct an appropriate mental situation for the meme (what in Sect. 3 will be called *make-sense frame*), within which *tres primeros* is bound to be interpreted as "three first courses" and this previously processed information will act as the preliminary context from which a fast interpretation of *tres segundos* as "three second courses" will be obtained, this being considered the only possible understanding of that phrase. The hearer is then forced to invalidate that accessible and frame-congruent interpretation and replace it with the alternative and far less likely interpretation of *tres segundos* as "three seconds," as shown in the subsequent content of the meme.

2.4 Explicatures and Implicatures

As explained above, what the addressee initially grasps from an utterance is its schematic, context-free logical form (also called *semantic representation*). This grammatical string of words has to be enriched into a meaningful and relevant proposition possibly matching the one that the communicator had in mind when uttering these words (or to put it in another way, into the utterance's *explicature*). According to Wilson (2017, 90), an explicature has "two defining features: (a) it is a communicated proposition (i.e. part of the speaker's meaning); and (b) it is identifiable by a combination of decoding and inference (i.e. by inferentially developing an encoded logical form into a full proposition)."

This explicature plus contextual information act as premises to derive (where necessary for a relevant interpretive outcome) *implicated conclusions* or *implicatures.* Several inferential strategies may be applied to the logical form depending on relevance-based inferential constraints and discursive demands. These explicature-oriented strategies will be outlined below, additionally exemplifying their widespread application to humorous communication. In general, though, two major groups of inferential operations can be distinguished. The examples in (30a-f) (inspired in a similar analysis by Hall 2017, 343–344) will prove illustrative:

(30) a. Said by a mother to her son: "You're not going to die."
You're not going to die [*from this wound*].

b. Mary is the best candidate.
Mary is the best candidate [*for the job of editing assistant*].

c. Mary left John and he started going to therapy.
Mary left John and [*as a consequence of the breakup*] he started going to therapy.

d. Yes, she was there with him.
Yes, [*Ruth Thomas*] was [*at last Saturday's party*] with [*Paul Smith*].

e. I've got nothing to wear for the party.
I've got [*nothing elegant, classy, appropriate*] to wear for the party.

f. You can buy a house if you've got money.
You can buy a house if you've got [*a substantial amount of money*].

The sentences in (30a-c) entail the retrieval of some *unarticulated constituent* not coded in the utterance but nevertheless essential to arrive at a relevant explicature of these utterances (the one provided in the added content between square brackets).[12] Although such unarticulated constituents tend to be easily retrieved, sometimes misunderstandings arise if there is a wrong prediction of the hearer's accessibility to contextual information. This occurs in sub-sentential utterances whose omitted content has to be retrieved by the hearer, and mismatches may arise between the intended proposition and the one constructed by the hearer. Yus (2016a, 30) provides an illustrative example of the sub-sentential utterance "Shameless" in (31), from a dialogue in the TV series *Frasier*, which leads to a misunderstanding:

(31) Frasier: I've tried dealing with this problem on my own but he insists on interrupting my show with his foolish pranks.
Kate: I heard.
Frasier: Yes, well I did not spend eight years at Harvard to be mocked by that jackass!
Kate: Shameless!
Frasier: Oh, he's beyond shameless!
Kate: I'm talking about the way you manage to get Harvard into every conversation.

Of course, the addressee's retrieval of unarticulated constituents can also be exploited for humorous purposes. Let us look at the tweet in (32):

(32) -Qué llevarías a una isla desierta?
[*What would you take to a desert island?*].

[12] As explained in Escandell-Vidal and Leonetti (2020, 95), the general RT position is that inference and being guided by an inherent search for relevance suffice to explain the existence and retrieval of these unarticulated constituents, however other possibilities exist, including the idea that these constituents are indeed represented in the syntax by means of silent categories and projections, or the idea that they are better explained in terms of pre-semantic implicatures (as advocated in some neo-Gricean approaches).

-A mi suegra.
[*My mother-in-law*].
-Te irías con tu suegra???
[*You'd go there with your mother-in-law???*].
-Ah. Que yo también tengo que ir?
[*Ah. Am I supposed to go, too?*].

The author of this tweet knows that the audience will automatically elaborate on the first utterance through the addition of the missing unarticulated constituent ("what would you take to a desert island [with you]?") and then invalidates such enrichment in the subsequent utterances, thus generating humour.

By contrast, the utterances in (30d-f) above exemplify the "*pragmatic modification* of a simple concept in the encoded logical form so that the concept that forms a constituent of the speaker's meaning replaces the encoded one" (Hall 2017, 344, italics added). This is performed via strategies required to reach a relevant interpretation of these utterances. In these cases, the encoded meaning of some word or phrase needs to be adjusted in context so as to yield a relevant interpretation. (30d) is filled with indexicals whose default "empty" meaning has to be completed with a referent. (30e) and (30f) entails adjusting the meaning of the encoded concepts *nothing* and *money* into more contextually appropriate interpretations (categorised as *ad hoc concepts* in RT research), once more provided between square brackets.

When applied to humour, these enriching inferential strategies are predicted and manipulated for the sake of generating the desired effects. Some examples are provided below involving text-based memes massively shared and forwarded on social networking sites and messaging apps.

1. *Reference assignment*. As shown in (30d) above, some words -among which stand out pronouns, some adverbs and proper names- only have a schematic default meaning and need to be completed with a referent with the aid of context. This strategy is harnessed in plenty of humorous internet discourses. Several examples of memes appear in Fig. 2.5. The creators of these memes hold precise expectations about which referent the audience will inevitably select for the pronouns inside these discourses in their search for an optimal interpretation, these expectations allowing them to manipulate and invalidate this fairly automatic referent assignment for the sake of humour. In

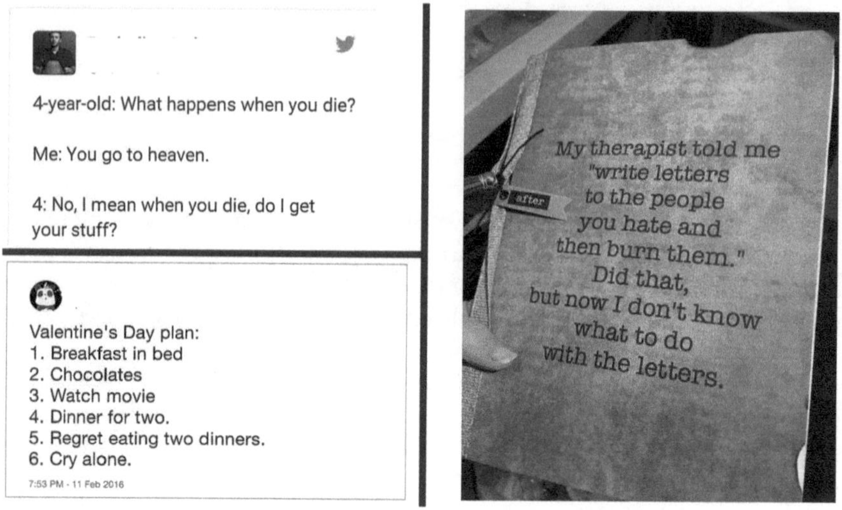

Fig. 2.5 Memes exploiting the inferential strategy of reference assignment

the top-left meme, the audience are bound to select a generic "people" for "you" in "What happens when you die?" but the continuation of the meme forces a substitution of that referent, this time a specific person: the father. Something similar holds true for the bottom-left meme. Its beginning makes the audience frame it as a romantic plan typically involving two people (lovers, a couple…). In this scenario, the referent of "two" in "Dinner for two" is unavoidably interpreted as "two people [celebrating their love]." That accessible referent becomes invalidated when we continue reading the "Valentine's Day plan" in the meme (being substituted for "enough dinner for two people"). Finally, the reader of the meme on the right will have no trouble assigning a referent to "them" in "burn them" (i.e. "the letters"). This being a very accessible and relevant referent, the reader will stop processing at this point, unaware of other possible referents. As the meme progresses, though, the reader is reminded of another far more unlikely referent (i.e. "the people you hate").

2. *Disambiguation*. Sometimes the hearer must choose between two senses of the same word which are equally likely to match the one intended by the speaker, as in (33):

(33) I saw John by the *bank* [river bank / financial institution].

Yus (2016a, 23; 2020) argues that, since comprehension is a cumulative inferential activity where the interpretation of a previous chunk of discourse becomes the preliminary context upon which subsequent stretches are processed, hearers most often disambiguate meanings without even realising that alternative senses of the same word or phrase exist, only because the already-processed information biases the choice of one sense of the word or another. Therefore, in reality, hearers frequently do nothing but *select* a single meaning rather than ***disambiguate*** between several candidate meanings. The meme in (34) is an example thereof:

(34) -Para tener sexo deberías probar algún gel.
[*To have sex, you should try some gel*].
-¿De efecto frío o calor?
[*One with a cold or hot effect?*].
-De ducha a ser posible.
[*Shower gel if possible*].

In this meme, the creator knows that once its initial part has been processed for relevance, it will become a preliminary context from which "gel" is inferred. Despite the word being potentially polysemous, the creator has no doubt whatsoever that "lubricant gel" will be the first and only interpretation of that word, not even realising that other interpretations such as "shower gel" are possible. Of course, the meme also bases it humorous effects on possible implicatures arising from the end of the meme (most importantly about the person's bad health habits).

This gradation of senses -one very relevant and likely, and the other(s) not even considered- provides a perfect environment for humourists when devising their discourses, as it happens in the memes pictured at the bottom row of Fig. 2.6. An additional disambiguation-based humorous strategy consists in presenting a setup of the discourse in such a way that the audience cannot possibly choose a referent from a range of possible and relevant options. This becomes evident in the memes of the top row in Fig. 2.6, translated as (35–36) below.

(35) -Paco, qué haces?
[*Paco, what are you doing?*].
-Aquí, pescando
[*Here, fishing*].
-Y qué usas de cebo?
[*And what are you using as bait?*].

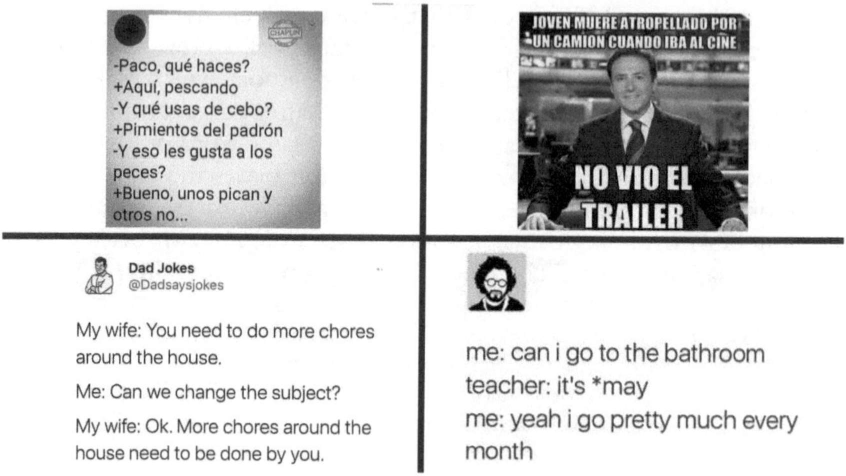

Fig. 2.6 Memes exploiting the inferential strategy of disambiguation for humorous purposes

-Pimientos del padrón
[*Padrón peppers*].
-Y eso le gusta a los peces?
[*And do fish like that?*].
-Bueno, unos pican y otros no…
[*Well, some bite/some are hot and others don't/aren't…*].

(36) Joven muere atropellado por un camión cuando iba al cine
[*Young man is run over by a truck while going to the cinema*].
No vio el trailer
[*He didn't see the trailer*].

As mentioned above in passing, the memes at the bottom row of Fig. 2.6 are examples of the humorous strategy based on taking advantage of the fact that, once a relevant meaning of a word or phrase has been selected, no other meanings are considered. Upon reaching the question "Can we change the subject?" any reader of the bottom-left meme will think that the only meaning of "subject" is "topic," the interpretation of the whole utterance consequently being "Can we change the topic [of the conversation]?" At the same time, they will be totally unaware that "subject" may also mean "grammatical subject," the utterance then coming to be understood as "Can we change the grammatical subject of the utterance?" This alternative meaning surprises the reader. Similarly, although the context in the bottom right meme makes an interpretation of "may" as "a modal to ask for permission" very likely, the reader is immediately reminded of another possible, albeit much less likely interpretation ("May" as one of the months in a year).

As opposed to the above, the memes at the top row of Fig. 2.6 -and translated in (35–36)- show discourse setups designed to provide two equally valid interpretations of a subsequent word or phrase. This goes against the relevance-seeking inferential procedure that normally selects a single interpretation as the intended one and discards any other candidates, which are not consciously entertained. Meme (35) cunningly combines reference assignment and disambiguation to create an environment of inferential puzzlement among the audience. The setup design gives the same validity to two referents for *unos* (*some*, meaning "some fish" or "some peppers") and to two senses for *pican* (i.e. "bite" vs. "are hot"). In the same fashion, the setup of (36) leads to two equally valid senses of *trailer* ("lorry" vs. "a series of extracts from a film or broadcast, used for advance publicity").

3. *Concept adjustment*. On many occasions (if not all), the concept literally coded by a word is not sufficiently relevant and has to be adjusted pragmatically, as a result of which the communicated concept in a context (called *ad hoc concept*) differs, to a greater or lesser extent, from the original literally coded concept. This communicated concept may be *narrower* than the coded one (in other words, the coded concept is too general and needs to be narrowed in meaning), as in (37); or *broader* (that is, the coded concept seems so specific that an inferential broadening becomes necessary), as in (38); or a combination of narrowing and broadening that characterises many metaphors such as the one shown in (39) (see Mateo and Yus 2021). In all these cases, the *ad hoc concept* eventually communicated (DRINK*, EMPTY* and PRINCESS*[13]) only resembles the concept coded in the utterance:

(37) I am worried about Jim... He drinks too much.
[narrowing: *specifically, Jim drinks too much alcohol*].

(38) We entered the pub but we left since it was empty.

[13] Adjusted (i.e. *ad hoc*) concepts conventionally appear with an asterisk after them in RT-based research. The encoded concept "empty" is represented as EMPTY* when adjusted in context. If a need arises to distinguish two ad hoc concepts corresponding to the same encoded word, then two, three or more asterisks are added.

[broadening: *not literally empty; rather, with few people, including the waiter*].

(39) I am thrilled with my daughter. She is a princess.
[*The ad hoc concept communicated is broader than the coded one because it also includes women like the daughter, who are not princesses. On the other hand, the ad hoc concept communicated also has a narrower scope than the coded one, since it only includes a sub-group of princesses, those who are beautiful, charming, lovely, etc.*].

The picture is one of a "unified account on which lexical narrowing and broadening (or a combination of the two) result from a single interpretive process that fine-tunes the interpretation of almost every word" (Wilson and Carston 2007, 231). Sperber and Wilson (2005, 376) stress that

> from the general claim that an utterance is a piece of evidence about the speaker's meaning, it follows, at the lexical level, that the function of words in an utterance is not to encode but merely to indicate the concepts that are constituents of the speaker's meaning. We are not denying that words do encode concepts (or at least semantic features), and that they are (at least partly) decoded during the comprehension process; however, we are claiming that the output of decoding is merely a point of departure for identifying the concepts intended by the speaker.

Concept adjustment is also at work in some humorous discourses, including those on the internet (see Yus 2021b). For example, the meme in (40) exemplifies *broadening*. The reader encounters *perdí la vida* (I lost my life) -which in Spanish means "I died"- and is expected to broaden the underlying concept so as to meet the expectations of relevance and accommodate other, more metaphoric ways of losing one's life such as "I lost the way I used to live happily before I got married."

(40) -En esa curva yo perdí la vida.
[*In that curve I lost my life*].
-¿Vas a decir la misma tontería cada vez que pasemos por la iglesia donde nos casamos?
[*Are you going to say the same nonsense every time we pass by the church where we got married?*].

The inferential strategies commented on above give as a result the so-called *proposition expressed* by the utterance which, if communicated, is labelled as *explicature*.[14] This communicated proposition, together with further contextual information (known as *implicated premise(s)* in RT research) will yield -if necessary for the relevance of the utterance- an *implicature*, or *implicated conclusion*, as RT research names it. These implicatures may be *strong*, when clearly intended and backed up by the speaker, or *weak*, if they continue to be triggered by the act of communication but their derivation partly (or totally) depends on the hearer. An example would be (41). After obtaining the explicature of Sue's utterance, Ann will also access (42) as the contextual information (implicated premise) that she needs to derive the strong implicature in (43). Moreover, Ann may likewise derive some weak implicatures such as those listed in (44), probably by her sole responsibility, instead of being overtly intended by Sue upon producing her utterance:

(41) -Ann: [*Pointing to a nearby clothes shop*] Shall we enter and buy some nice stuff for the trip?
-Sue: I don't enter shops that sell cheap clothes.
(42) That shop I am pointing to sells cheap clothes.
(43) Sue does not want to enter that shop I am pointing to.
(44) Sue is elitist.
Sue earns a lot of money.
Sue misses the chance to wear some nice clothes just because they are cheap.

As highlighted in Yus (2016a, 46–47), some jokes only rely on implicated premises and conclusions to achieve humorous effects. Examples thereof are the implicatures listed in (46) for the joke (45), which become essential to obtain the intended humorous effects:

(45) A woman in bed with a man. The phone rings and she answers it. "Yes darling… No problem… OK… See you later." The man: "Who was it?" The woman: "It was my husband. He said he's going to come home very late today because he is in an important meeting with you."
(46) a. The man and the woman are lovers.
b. The woman's husband has a lover.

[14] On most occasions, the proposition expressed is communicated and hence becomes an explicature of the utterance. Sometimes, though, this proposition is not meant to be communicated, as typically occurs with ironies, for example.

c. She knows that her husband has a lover.
d. Her lover and her husband know each other.
e. Her husband does not know that this man is his wife's lover.

In a nutshell, the joke quoted in (45) deserves special attention because its humorous effects depend on implicated premises and conclusions retrieved by the hearer, some of them clearly intended by the speaker (as strong implicatures), while others are weakly communicated, and for these the hearer takes certain (and sometimes full) responsibility for their derivation.

3 Incongruity-Resolution. A Relevance Theory Account

One of the most influential theories ever proposed to explain the way in which humour generation takes place is *incongruity-resolution*. Many jokes exhibit this pattern, including humorous discourses on the internet (see, for example, the proposal of incongruity-resolution patterns in memes provided in Chap. 7). This theory has also importantly proved compatible with RT's predictions about how discourses are inferred for relevance.

Basically, incongruity-resolution theory claims that, for humorous effects to be derived, the addressee first has to encounter some kind of *incongruity* while interpreting the humorous discourse, the *resolution* of which triggers such humorous effects. Several authors have embraced this theory to a greater or lesser extent, and proposed classifications of jokes according to this general inferential pattern, including Ritchie (2004, 2006, 2009) and Dynel (2012a, 2012b). Suls (1972, 1977, 1983) stands out as the main proponent of incongruity-resolution. The theory, summarised in Yus (2016a, 68), predicts an initial stage in which an incongruity is detected by the hearer during the joke interpretation process. Then, while the hearer tries to solve the incongruity (and make sense of the joke as a whole), they will search for a cognitive rule able to reconcile the incongruous parts through which a resolution to the incongruity becomes possible, thus allowing the hearer to feel relieved and perhaps humorously entertained too.

For an RT reinterpretation of this theory, readers can refer back to Yus (2016a), according to whom it becomes essential to distinguish two major types of incongruity: one based on the inference of the humorous discourse itself and another supported on the hearer's construction of a situation suited to understand the joke (called *make-sense frame*), although combinations of both types abound. The former is the one generated out of the addressee's inferential gap-filling already mentioned in Sect. 2 above; or expressed differently, the inference to turn the schematic logical form into a communicatively relevant proposition. This involves inferential joke interpretation strategies such as reference assignment (47), disambiguation (48) and concept adjustment (49).

(47) Lucy, aged 11, was walking down the street leading a cow by a rope. She met the vicar who said, "Little girl, what are you doing with that cow?" Lucy said: "it is my father's cow and I am taking her to the bull." "Disgusting," said the parson, "can't your father do that?" "No," said Lucy, "it has to be the bull."

(48) After successfully delivering the first child of a Canadian couple visiting Scotland, the doctor popped into the waiting room to tell the anxious husband the good news. "It's a boy -eight pounds exactly!". "Oh", replied the flustered father. "Will you take a check?"

(49) -How is your daughter doing with her piano lessons?
-Good! Her fingers are like streaks of lightning.
-Because they are so fast?
-No, because you don't know where they are going to fall.

In (47), the humourist creates an incongruity by altering the accessible assignment of a referent for "that" in "can't your father do that?" (i.e. "do the job of taking the cow to the bull"), which clashes with the continuation of the joke ("No… it has to be the bull") and the resolution comes through the replacement of this accessible referent with a more unlikely but still possible referent: "do the job of making the cow pregnant." (48) in turn plays with the disambiguation of "pounds" and the gradation of senses in terms of inferential accessibility (pounds of weight vs. pounds of money). Finally, (49) resorts to the adjustment of the concept *streaks of lightning*, which has several possible metaphoric interpretations that yield different *ad hoc concepts*, as provided in the setup and punchline of the joke. In all of these jokes (47–49), the incongruity-resolution pattern revolves around the addressee's inference of the humorous discourse.

The second kind of incongruity arises when the addressee builds up a suitable situation within which the text of the humorous discourse needs to be inferred, the so-called *make-sense frame* (Yus 2013a, 2013b, 2016a). Yus (2016a, 80) defined it as follows:

> it is clear that inferring the intended interpretation of a joke (and of any utterance in general) also involves the extraction of general information

> about the world and everyday situations that is stored as accessible chunks of encyclopaedic information (specifically stored as "I conceptualize X as *p*" or as a more factual "I believe that *p*"). This information is often retrieved almost unconsciously in order to make sense of the intended scenario for the comprehension of jokes and other utterances (…). This storage of information allows us to frame situations and save mental effort when facing a new input such as a joke.

Thielemann (2020, 33–36) further comments on this notion. Frames are said to influence categorisation of what we are engaged with conversationally and what we say and interpret. In general terms, fitting my definition, "frames refer to structured sets of expectations and formats, within which experience is organized and available as knowledge. Frames provide the background against which we interpret and understand an activity or a text" (ibid., 35). She also proposes two major concepts of *frame*: ***interactive frames*** and ***knowledge frames*** (the latter also referred to as *schemas* or *scripts* in the bibliography). Knowledge frames describe the way humans organise knowledge and use this knowledge while understanding. They represent chunks of general knowledge about the world we live in and are hence stored in the long-term memory. By contrast, interactive frames refer to a delimitation of what activity the interlocutors are being engaged in, and how they mean what they say. Interactive frames are typically at work in conversations, where interlocutors understand and interpret what is going on as a social encounter of a particular type.

In this kind of frame-based incongruity, it is the construction of that suitable situation that becomes invalidated and puzzles the addressee, as in the change of situation between the initial and accessible "loving wife scenario" and the final "murdering wife scenario" portrayed in (50):

(50) Bill sat alone in the hospital room at his dying wife's beside. It was difficult to hear her above the many life-sustaining devices, as her voice was little more than a hoarse whisper. "Bill darling," she breathed. "I've got a confession to make before I go… I… I'm the one who took the $10,000 from your safe in the house… I spent it on a fling with your best friend Jimmy. For years I've been going to bed with Jimmy, as well as with several of the neighbours." "That's all right, dearest; I knew that already," said Bill, "that's why I poisoned you."

Make-sense frame is an umbrella term covering others proposed in the bibliography for this kind of inferential build-up of a suitable situation so as to comprehend discourses, including humorous ones:

Frame This term similarly refers to stereotypical chunks of information that are retrieved from encyclopaedic knowledge in order to rapidly process a new situation, including those depicted in jokes.

Schema This similar term suggested in the bibliography describes a basic chunk of information that allows us to engage in daily experiences and classify them as prototypical, that is, "a dynamic mental representation that enables us to build mental models of/for the world" (Martin 2006, 85; see also Brubaker et al. 2004, 41).[15]

Script It refers more to sequences of actions such as ordering a meal in a bar or posting a letter at the post office. When the script is activated, we expect certain activities to take place in a certain order. Scollon and Scollon (2001, 66–67) illustrated scripts with this example: In American coffee shops, customers expect a regular pattern of activities which follow a sequence with minor variations: (1) You find a seat. (2) You decide your order. (3) You place your order with the waiter or waitress. (4) You receive your food. (5) When you finish eating, you pay your bill at the cash desk.

Many humorous discourses on the internet involve this kind of frame-based incongruity, which has become particularly popular among meme creators. The examples provided in Fig. 2.7 -and translated in (51–56)- are quite illustrative.

(51) -Al menos, cariño, este confinamiento ha hecho que tengamos una relación más fluida y nos escuchemos el uno al otro.
[*At least, honey, this lockdown has made us have a more fluid relationship and listen to each other*].
-No sé, espaguetis.
[*I don't know, spaghetti*].

[15] As pointed out in Yus (2016a, 83–84), a quality that schemas share with frames is the rather unconscious process of situation labelling that occurs when the schema is activated. In general, upon interpreting a new utterance (e.g. a joke), the hearer automatically activates a corresponding schema that saves mental effort when picturing what is happening in the utterance, and all that beyond conscious awareness. This is why hearers are often utterly surprised when a schema is altered by a subsequent stretch of discourse in the joke punchline, and very often this is the very moment when they realise that they had activated an initial schema in the first place.

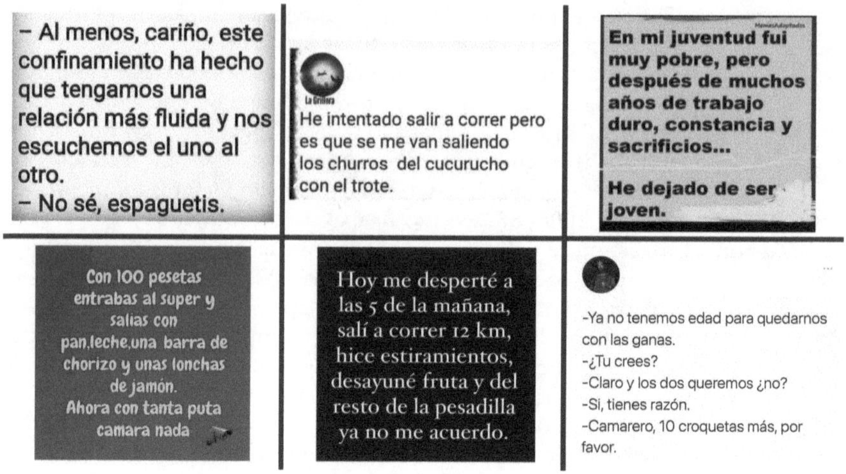

Fig. 2.7 Memes exploiting frame-based incongruities for humorous purposes

(52) He intentado salir a correr pero es que se me van saliendo los churros[16] del cucurucho con el trote.
[*I have tried going running but the churros keep coming out from the cone with the trot*].

(53) En mi juventud fui muy pobre, pero después de muchos años de trabajo duro, constancia y sacrificios… He dejado de ser joven.
[*In my youth I was very poor, but after many years of hard work, perseverance and sacrifices... I am no longer young*].

(54) Con 100 pesetas entrabas al super y salias con pan, leche, una barra de chorizo y unas lonchas de jamón… Ahora con tanta puta camara nada.
[*With 100 pesetas you entered the supermarket and left with bread, milk, a chorizo bar and some slices of ham… Now with so many fucking cameras, nothing*].

(55) Hoy me desperté a las 5 de la mañana, salí a correr 12 km, hice estiramientos, desayuné fruta y del resto de la pesadilla ya no me acuerdo.
[*Today I woke up at 5 a.m., went out for a 12 K run, did some stretching, had fruit for breakfast and I no longer remember the rest of the nightmare*].

(56) -Ya no tenemos edad para quedarnos con las ganas.
[*We are old enough not to restrain ourselves*].

[16] *Churros* are snacks or breakfast food popular in Spain and Latin America, consisting of a long tube of dough (= a flour and water mixture) fried in hot oil, covered in sugar and often eaten with a hot chocolate sauce (Cambridge Dictionary).

-¿Tu crees?
[*Do you think so?*].
-Claro y los dos queremos ¿no?
[*Of course, and both of us want this, don't we?*].
-Si, tienes razón.
[*Yes, you're right*].
-Camarero, 10 croquetas más por favor.
[*Waiter, 10 more croquettes, please*].

All the memes in (51–56) base their humorous effects on frame-based incongruities, that is, they are designed to clash at some stage with the inferential construction of a situation suited to interpret these memes properly. (51) activates a familiar situation of a couple making up for deteriorated in-marriage communication that becomes radically invalidated by the husband's reply ("I don't know, spaghetti"), which clearly indicates that he has not been paying any attention to his partner's words. (52) innovates by creating a clash of activities within a situation, rather than a clash of situations. Specifically, although going jogging and eating *churros* at the same time appear to be mutually exclusive, they are brought together for humorous purposes. (53) is an example of a make-sense frame helping us to make anticipatory inferences regarding the discourse that is coming up next; these expectations are invalidated in this case, though. The text comments on how hard life has been for that individual and we expect to read about a final reward for all the hard work, which is not provided eventually. (54) depicts a situation often found in nostalgic Spaniards who think that everything was cheaper when "the peseta" was the national currency. This easily built situation stops being valid at the end of the meme, the reader being forced to change the scenario of "buying a lot of stuff with little money" into "stealing goods from a supermarket." As for (55), it provides another sharp contrast of frames, switching from the general picture of a healthy person to the criticism of this very lifestyle by qualifying it as nightmare. Finally, in (56) the situation looks like the typical talk used to encourage sex; however, the end of the meme invalidates this accessible make-sense frame and replaces it with a different one.

Furthermore, analysing incongruity-resolution from an RT perspective raises an important question. If incongruity-based humorous discourses demand more mental effort, invalidate initially relevant interpretive choices and often provide the interlocutor with no substantive relevant content, why (or how) do they end up being humorous (and relevant)? A number of possible reasons are suggested in Yus (2003b, 2016a):

1. *The expectation of humorous effects as part of the mutually manifest information between the interlocutors.* If the addressee is aware of the humorous intention underlying the production of the humorous discourse along with the expectation of associated cognitive reward, they may be willing to invest additional cognitive resources to work out the incongruity and seek a resolution to ensure the achievement of these humorous effects.
2. *Pleasure in solving incongruities.* Encountering incongruities may not be pleasurable for human cognition, but the satisfaction at solving them will most probably offset any increased effort demanded in exchange (Yus 2003b, 1314; see also Hurley et al. 2011). Finding the resolution to incongruity gives us a feeling of discovery that resembles the sense of triumph experienced when we solve a problem (Curcó 1998, 311–312). Morreall (2009, 15) remarks that the pleasure of humour "is not the enjoyment of incongruity, but the enjoyment of a kind of puzzle solving similar to what scientists do" (also colloquially referred to as the *aha-moment*).
3. *Realisation of having been fooled by the speaker.* It has already been stressed that RT pictures interpretation as a general two-phase procedure: (a) consider interpretations in order of accessibility; and (b) stop when your expectations of relevance have been satisfied. In the course of this two-phase inferential activity, human cognition can compare potential interpretations and contextual information in parallel and select the interpretation that is bound to be more relevant -possibly matching the speaker's intended interpretation too- while other potential interpretations are discarded and not even entertained at a conscious level. Therefore, it comes as a great surprise for humans to discover that the interpretation which was supposedly the most relevant one (i.e. the one providing the best balance between interpretive reward or gains -cognitive effects- and mental effort) eventually turns out to be incorrect. Yus (2016a, 89) offers an interesting example in (57) that revolves around the need to find a correct referent for the indexical "it" in "tried it":

(57) An elderly couple walk into a doctor's office. The man tells the doctor, "Doctor, we want to have a baby." The doctor replies, "At your age I don't think it's possible, but I'll give you a jar, come back in a few days with a sperm sample." So the couple comes back a few days later. They give the doctor an empty jar. The doctor says, "Just as I feared." The old man says, "No, it's not what you think. I tried it

with my left hand. I tried it with my right hand. She tried it with her left hand. She tried it with her right hand. She tried it with her teeth in. She tried it with her teeth out. But we couldn't get the lid off the jar."

Concerning this joke, the most accessible referent for the indexical in *tried it* is "to produce a sperm sample," and after selecting it as the most relevant candidate, the hearer will stop looking for any other possible candidate referents. However, the hearer is then reminded that another possible referent exists for the indexical, namely "to open the jar." Therefore, the hearer is both surprised at this previously unnoticed sense and also fully aware of having been fooled by the speaker, a realisation that the hearer should accept with amusement.

4. *A positive interaction of the joke with the addressee's cognitive environment.* As claimed in Yus (2003b, 1315), humorous discourses and underlying intentions are not simply identified and interpreted from scratch; they have to be accepted by the hearer before they can produce any humorous effect. Since many humorous discourses lack interest from an informational point of view, and some jokes are even patently false (Attardo, pers. comm.), the effectiveness of such discourses -often related to social (i.e., phatic) uses of language (cf. Žegarac and Clark 1999) must rely on an intended pleasurable effect on the hearer, whose personal beliefs, background assumptions and feelings can only be predicted to a certain extent. These personal beliefs, background assumptions and feelings, together with further information accessible to the hearer during the conversation, influence the joker's achievement of the humorous intention. Furthermore, we ought to bear in mind that cognitive environments are strongly impacted on by constraints associated with the social sphere, from which many encyclopaedic assumptions are constantly retrieved. This holds true especially for sexist or racist jokes, which, despite being objectively humorous, may simultaneously offend some interlocutors rather than pleasurably amuse them.

3.1 A Classification of Incongruity-Resolution Patterns

Yus (2016a) made a proposal to classify possible incongruity-resolution patterns. These will subsequently be applied to memes in Chap. 7, with the necessary adjustments and adaptations to their multimodal nature. In a nutshell, these patterns arise from combining three parameters that play a key part both in the design of the joke and in its interpretation:

1. A differentiation between *discourse-based incongruities* and *frame-based incongruities.* As already commented upon, the former relate to the inferential strategies that the hearer applies to the coded input (the joke) so that it can become a fully contextualised proposition (reference assignment, disambiguation, concept adjustment…), whereas the latter focus on the situation that the hearer constructs to make sense of what is happening in the joke (*make-sense frame*).
2. A threefold classification of resolutions depending on what the hearer is expected to do in order to solve the incongruity:
   2.a. *Discourse-based resolution*, when the hearer must perform a supplementary inferential task in order to make sense of the incongruity detected while inferring some portion of the joke text, for instance, to select a different sense for a word, to locate a referent for an indexical other than the one initially chosen, to opt for a different *ad hoc concept* for a word in a context, and so on and so forth. This kind of resolution has a very narrow scope, since it applies only to inferential strategies carried out by the hearer in order to turn the schematic logical form of the joke into a fully contextualised proposition (*proposition expressed*) matching the explicature of the utterance.
   2.b. *Frame-based resolution*, when the hearer has to alter the current make-sense frame constructed for the situation and replace it with a different frame that solves the incongruity.
   2.c. *Implication-based resolution*, which refers to (a) cases where the hearer must look for the resolution outside the joke text through the inference of implicated conclusions (implicatures); and (b) cases in which the hearer looks for implications that allow for the derivation of (further) humorous effects after having fully understood the joke.
3. A distinction between incongruities whose source is located at the initial part[17] of the joke (the *setup*) and those whose source becomes

[17] *Initial part* does not necessarily mean the very beginning of the joke. Its setup may take up most of the space in the joke, to such an extent that the potential position of the incongruity-triggering element near the end of the joke does not prevent it from belonging to the initial part of the joke (setup).

visible at its final part (the *punchline*). The former often demand some kind of inferential backtracking from the hearer, that is, to return to an already processed part of the joke and re-interpret it in the light of the new evidence arising from processing a subsequent joke stretch. Instead, the latter (incongruity-triggering elements placed at the end of the joke) often requires the hearer's participation with the derivation of implicatures that are necessary to make sense of the joke and obtain the desired humorous effects. Notice, as argued in Yus (2016a, 102), that the source of incongruity as well as its actual identification could be located in different parts of the joke. Example (58), also from Yus (ibid.), was suggested to clarify this with the explanation in (59):

(58) Tom and Jim talking to each other, Tom says: "You know, Jim, my wife and I were very happy for 25 years." His friend asks, "And then... what happened?" "We met," replies Tom.

(59) In this joke, the hearer activates a typical scenario of the married couple's loving marriage. The last part of the joke (punchline) invalidates this frame and forces a resolution involving a replacement with a different frame, this time suggesting unsatisfactory marriage. However, the source of incongruity does not appear in the punchline, but in the setup, more precisely in the phrase "very happy for 25 years," which in the initially activated make-sense frame is inevitably understood as "very happy [together] for 25 years" and later as "very happy for 25 years [before meeting]." Therefore, the joke would exhibit a frame-based incongruity, with its source in the setup and a frame-based resolution.

The combination of the three parameters described above yields the cases listed in Table 2.1. They will be defined in (60a-71a) below, exemplified (60b-71b) and explained in (60c-71c). Note that these 12 cases are not clear-cut and mutually exclusive ones exhibiting very clearly delimited ways in which both discourse- and frame-based incongruities are at work in the successful humorous outcome. Quite the opposite, a great deal of cross-breeding exists between these strategies, which actually very often "collaborate" to ensure the generation of humorous effects.

(60) [1] [frame-based incongruity] [setup] [discourse-based resolution]

a. This incongruity-resolution pattern (henceforth IRP) entails the hearer's construction of a make-sense frame in the setup that even-

Table 2.1 Incongruity-resolution cases (Yus 2016a)

	Type of incongruity	*Location*	*Type of resolution*
1	Frame-based	Setup	Discourse-based
2	Frame-based	Punchline	Discourse-based
3	Frame-based	Setup	Frame-based
4	Frame-based	Punchline	Frame-based
5	Frame-based	Setup	Discourse-based
6	Frame-based	Punchline	Discourse-based
7	Discourse-based	Setup	Frame-based
8	Discourse-based	Punchline	Frame-based
9	Discourse-based	Setup	Discourse-based
10	Discourse-based	Punchline	Discourse-based
11	Discourse-based	Setup	Frame-based
12	Discourse-based	Punchline	Frame-based

tually becomes incongruous with the frame built up for the subsequent part of the joke. The hearer then reconciles the incongruous parts by resorting to some discourse-based inferential strategy

b. No samples found in the corpus built by Yus (2016a).

c. This IRP is hard (or impossible) to find since, normally, when the hearer notices a frame-based incongruity, they normally build up another frame that replaces the initial one and provides coherence for the whole joke, rather than engage in a discourse-based resolution.

(61) [2] [frame-based incongruity] [punchline] [discourse-based resolution]

a. In this IRP, the hearer constructs a make-sense frame unobstructed until the frame no longer applies at the final part of the joke (punchline). Therefore, incongruity arises with the assumptions that they have hitherto taken on board while interpreting the joke. The resolution of the incongruity requires the hearer to re-interpret some part of the joke.

b. A man calls his family doctor. Man: "Doctor, for the last week my wife has thought that she was a rabbit." Doctor: "OK, bring her in and I'll try to help." Man: "Fine, but whatever you do, don't cure her."

c. The hearer activates the frame typically associated with being at the doctor's. When any hearer encounters the word "rabbit," they devote little mental effort to finding the exact quality of the wife's resemblance to a rabbit. At the end of the joke, the phrase "Don't cure her" contradicts the usual frame for being at the doctor's, which typically includes a desire for the patient to recover. The hearer is thus forced to backtrack and perform a more fine-grained conceptual adjustment of the word "rabbit" and to reflect on why some quality typically associated with rabbits can possibly apply to a human being in such a way that a lack of cure becomes desirable. The hearer ultimately discovers the intended quality of rabbits, applied to the wife: "Rabbits engage in frequent sexual intercourse."

(62) [3] [frame-based incongruity] [setup] [frame-based resolution]

a. This IRP shows the hearer finding an incongruity during her construction of an appropriate make-sense frame for the joke. The source of this incongruity appears in the setup, the resolution demanding some frame alteration or substitution so as to obtain a congruent interpretation for the whole joke.

b. A young man moves into a new neighbourhood, alone and without any friends. He's only been there a couple of days when there's a knock on the door. "Hi," says the visitor. "I'm Colin, I live just down the hall from you and I thought I could come and introduce myself." "Thanks," says the young man. "I'm Mike." "Well, Mike, would you like to come over to a party at my place on Saturday night? There'll be plenty of booze, great music and lots of sex." "Wow, that sounds good, what do you reckon I should wear?" says Mike. "Oh, come as you are, there'll only be the two of us."

c. The initially activated frame for "a party" includes the stereotypical meeting of several people and, in this particular case, there is a prospect of sex (understood as heterosexual sex). The punchline reminds the hearer that another (initially unlikely but also possible) interpretation existed, namely "a party with sex", this time involving only two people and homosexual sex, as a result of which the hearer must re-interpret the frame that they had already constructed.

(63) [4] [frame-based incongruity] [punchline] [frame-based resolution]

a. The structure of this IRP includes an incongruity supported on choosing a make-sense frame that will become eventually invalidated. The source of incongruity is located at the punchline of the joke and its resolution requires an alteration or re-interpretation of the initially selected frame.

b. I have this friend who faces a real dilemma. His wife won't give him a divorce until she figures out a way of doing it without making him a happy man.

c. The hearer activates the frame "divorce as a painful experience," which seems easy to construct, accessible and relevant for most of the joke text, until the punchline eventually forces the hearer to replace this frame with a different and unexpected one. The source of incongruity stems from the drastic change in the frame constructed until that moment and its substitution for a new surprising one.

(64) [5] [frame-based incongruity] [setup] [implication-based resolution]

a. Not very frequent. Its structure predicts an incongruity resulting from the construction of an adequate make-sense frame for the joke. The hearer finds an incongruity located in the setup and her attempts to solve it include the inference of implicated premises and/or conclusions.

b. A plane crashed in deepest, darkest Africa and there were only five survivors, four men and one woman. It soon became obvious that they would never be rescued, so they decided to start a small community and make the most of what they had. Everything went well for a while except that they all got sexually frustrated and eventually came to an agreement that the woman would spend one week with each man in turn. As it happened, this worked very well until three years later the woman fell sick and died. It turned out to be disastrous for the men. The first week proved difficult, the second awful, the third horrifying and the fourth so impossible that at the beginning of the fifth week, they buried her.

c. he hearer cannot help thinking that the appropriate make-sense frame includes the hard time that the men are having, week after week, because they no longer have a woman with whom to engage in sexual intercourse. The source of incongruity stems from two possible situations depicted in the text. In order to arrive at this eventually correct interpretation (and parallel resolution of the incongruity triggered by the punchline), the hearer has to draw appropriate implications about what had happened in these four weeks before the men were forced to bury the woman.

(65) [6] [frame-based incongruity] [punchline] [implication-based resolution]

a. The hearer encounters an incongruity related to the construction of a suitable make-sense frame for the joke. This time, the source of incongruity appears in the punchline, and its resolution requires the derivation of implications (implicatures).

b. A woman in bed with a man. The phone rings and she takes the call. "Yes darling… No problem… OK… I'll see you later." The man asks: "Who was that?" "It was my husband. He's going to come home very late tonight because he is in an important meeting with you."

c. The joke, already cited in this chapter, leads the hearer to alter the initially constructed frame for the situation depicted in the joke, and the eventual humorous effects result from a number of stronger or weaker implications that the hearer has to take full responsibility over constructing after the punchline alters the accessible frame construction.

(66) [7] [discourse-based incongruity] [setup] [discourse-based resolution]

a. The hearer engages in a pragmatic enrichment of the joke text in order to reach a contextualised proposition. The speaker predicts that one interpretation of an element located in the setup is bound to be selected because it offers a better balance between effects and effort, not even noticing other competing interpretations. Then the punchline makes the hearer realise that another interpretation of that initial chunk of text was possible, albeit far less likely (and hence undetected until the speaker foregrounds it). The hearer is thus forced to engage in some inferential backtracking and to re-interpret that part of the text differently, so that the joke as a whole can finally achieve congruence.

b. A guy came into a bar one day and said to the barman "Give me six double vodkas." The barman says "Wow! you must have had one hell of a day." "Yes, I've just found out my older brother is gay." The next day the same guy came into the bar and asked for the same drinks. When the bartender asked what the problem was today, the answer came back, "I've just found out that my younger brother is gay too!" On the third day the guy came into the bar and ordered another six double vodkas. The bartender said "Jesus! Doesn't anybody in your family like women?" "Yeah, my wife..."

c. The joke makes it very easy to select "any man" as the candidate referent for "anybody." The speaker then obliges the hearer to backtrack and link the word to a female referent instead.

(67) [8] [discourse-based incongruity] [punchline] [discourse-based resolution]

a. The source of the discourse-based incongruity is located in the punchline of the joke. This probably illustrates the most typical case in which the two senses of an ambiguous part of the joke are entertained (and enjoyed) simultaneously, rather than one simply replacing the other, since the joke ends with an ambiguity or different candidate interpretations, and the resolution of incongruity comes after the meaning of the whole joke has been interpreted.

b. A young husband with an inferiority complex insisted he was just a little pebble on a vast beach. The marriage counsellor, trying to be creative, told him, "If you wish to save your marriage, you'd better be a little bolder."

c. The joke plays with the homophony of *bolder* and *boulder*. In the context of counselling, the first interpretation should be selected as the intended one. However, the character in the joke talks metaphorically about feeling like a *pebble*, thus making the boulder interpretation as likely as *bolder*, and both are entertained simultaneously.

(68) [9] [discourse-based incongruity] [setup] [frame-based resolution]

a. This IRP is more unusual, as it involves discourse-based incongruity whose source is located in the setup, and its resolution demands a variation of the make-sense frame constructed so far while interpreting the joke.

b. Mary Clancey came up to Father O'Grady in tears." What's bothering you so, dear?" inquired Father O'Grady." Oh, father, I've got terrible news," replied Mary." Well, what is it, Mary?" "Well, my husband, passed away last night, Father." "Oh, Mary" said the father, "that's terrible. Tell me Mary, did he have any last requests?" "Well, yes he did father," replied Mary." What did he ask, Mary?" Mary replied, "He said, 'Please, Mary, put down the gun."

c. This joke is based on the potential ambiguity in the phrase "last requests," which the Father intends in one sense ("the husband's last will"), and for which the joke eventually shows a different sense ("the husband's begging for his life"). This re-interpretation of the phrase entails a drastic change of make-sense frame from the initially accessible "grieving woman upon her husband's death" to the more unlikely but eventually correct "grieving woman after killing her husband."

(69) [10] [discourse-based incongruity] [punchline] [frame-based resolution]

a. This IRP is not very common either, the difference with Pattern 9 being the location of the incongruity source, now placed in the punchline.

b. No samples found in the Yus (2016a) corpus.

(70) [11] [discourse-based incongruity] [setup] [implication-based resolution]

a. The source of the incongruity appears in the setup of the joke and focuses upon an inferential strategy to turn the coded input into a contextualised proposition (discourse-based incongruity). The resolution of the incongruity —and the eventual enjoyment of the joke— becomes possible if the hearer derives implications from the text of the joke.

b. A man and his alligator walk into a bar and the man asks, "Does this bar serve lawyers?" "Of course we do," replied the bartender. "Great," said the man, "I'd like a beer... and give me a lawyer for my alligator."

c. The joke plays with the dual possible objects that come after serve: "serve a person" and "serve a drink," which allows for the ambiguity in "do you serve lawyers?," meaning "to serve a drink to lawyers" or "to serve lawyers as drink," the former being the only likely interpretation. The disambiguation of "serve" and the consequent humour requires the extraction of implications regarding the speaker's negative opinion about lawyers.

(71) [12] [discourse-based incongruity] [punchline] [implication-based resolution]

a. This IRP exhibits a structure resembling that of the previous pattern, since implicated premises or implicated conclusions derived from the joke become essential to the eventual humorous effects. The source of the incongruity is located in the punchline of the joke this time, though.

b. "You are up before this court for the hideous crime of making love to your wife after she had died. Do you have anything to say in your defence?" "Yes, your honour. I didn't know she was dead; she'd been like that for years."

c. The joke demands a conceptual adjustment so that the wife's literal death can be applied to her behaviour (specifically in bed). This conceptual adjustment permits to derive a number of implications concerning the husband's opinion about her wife and his dissatisfaction with their sex life, among others.

4 Concluding Remarks

Pragmatics takes an interest in how we turn what people say into meaningful interpretations with the aid of context. RT has proved effective to explain the inferential strategies that people use during their everyday interpretation of other people's utterances and other intentional behaviours.

Regarding humorous communication, the initial assumption is that people engage in similar inferential strategies when interpreting these discourses. The difference lies in how these strategies are predicted and manipulated for the purpose of generating the desired humorous effects.

Finally, concerning internet humour, again no differences initially exist in terms of the way in which these discourses are inferred for humour.

What distinguishes internet humour, as this book aims to explain, is, on the one hand, the impact caused by the various platforms and interfaces on how these discourses are created, communicated and inferred; and on the other hand, the quality of the audiences of these discourses, often scattered worldwide, which makes predictions about mutuality of information riskier. Actually, being able to emphasise in-group mutuality of information very often suffices to amuse these scattered audiences. Some such internet-specific issues will be analysed in the next chapters of this book.

References

Allott, Nicholas. 2013. Relevance Theory. In *Perspectives on Linguistic Pragmatics*, ed. Alessandro Capone, Franco Lo Piparo, and Marco Carapezza, 57–98. Berlin: Springer. https://doi.org/10.1007/978-3-319-01014-4_3.

Assimakopoulos, Stavros. 2017a. Relevance. In *The Routledge Handbook of Pragmatics*, ed. Anne Barron, Gerard Steen, and Gu Yueguo, 310–322. Abingdon: Routledge.

———. 2017b. Context in Relevance Theory. In *Formal Models in the Study of Language. Applications in Interdisciplinary Contexts*, ed. Joanna Blochowiak, Cristina Grisot, Stephanie Durrleman, and Christopher Laenzlinger, 221–242. Cham: Springer. https://doi.org/10.1007/978-3-319-48832-5_12.

———. 2021. Beyond Meaning$_{NN}$ and Ostension: Pragmatic Inference in the Wild. In *Beyond Meaning*, ed. Elly Ifantidou, Louis de Saussure, and Tim Wharton, 11–28. Amsterdam: John Benjamins. https://doi.org/10.1075/pbns.324.c1.

Blakemore, Diane. 1992. *Understanding Utterances*. Oxford: Blackwell.

———. 2011. Relevance Theory. In *The Pragmatics Reader*, ed. Dawn Archer and Peter Grundy. Abingdon: Taylor & Francis.

Brubaker, Rogers, Mara Loveman, and Peter Stamatov. 2004. Ethnicity as Cognition. *Theory and Society* 33: 31–64. https://doi.org/10.1023/B:RYSO.0000021405.18890.63.

Carston, Robyn. 2002. *Thoughts and Utterances*. Oxford: Blackwell. https://doi.org/10.1002/9780470754603.

———. 2011. Relevance Theory. In *Routledge Companion to the Philosophy of Language*, ed. Gillian Russell and Delia Graff Fara, 163–176. London: Routledge.

Carston, Robyn, and Allison Hall. 2011. Implicature and Explicature. In *Cognitive Pragmatics*, ed. H.-J. Schmid and D. Geeraerts, 47–84. Berlin: Mouton de Gruyter. https://doi.org/10.1515/9783110214215.47.

Carston, Robyn, and George Powell. 2005. Relevance Theory – New Directions and Developments. *UCL Working Papers in Linguistics* 17: 279–299.

Clark, Billy. 2013. *Relevance Theory*. Cambridge: Cambridge University Press. https://doi.org/10.1017/CBO9781139034104.

Curcó, Carmen. 1998. Indirect Echoes and Verbal Humour. In *Current Issues in Relevance Theory*, ed. Villy Rouchota and Andreas Jucker, 305–326. Amsterdam and Philadelphia: John Benjamins. https://doi.org/10.1075/pbns.58.13cur.

Dikker, Suzanne, Lauren J. Silbert, Uri Hasson, and Jason D. Zevin. 2014. On the Same Wavelength: Predictable Language Enhances Speaker-listener Brain-to-Brain Synchrony in Posterior Superior Temporal Gyrus. *Journal of Neuroscience* 34 (18): 6267–6272. https://doi.org/10.1523/JNEUROSCI.3796-13.2014.

Dynel, Marta. 2012a. What RT Cannot Do, IR Can: On the Incremental Interpretation of Jokes in (Non)relevance-Theoretic Terms. In *Relevance Theory: More than Understanding*, ed. Ewa Wałaszewska and Agnieszka Piskorska, 147–166. Newcastle upon Tyne: Cambridge Scholars Publishing.

———. 2012b. Garden Paths, Red Lights and Crossroads: On Finding Our Way to Understanding the Cognitive Mechanisms Underlying Jokes. *Israeli Journal of Humor Research* 1 (1): 6–28.

Escandell-Vidal, Victoria, and Manuel Leonetti. 2020. Relevance Theory in Spanish Pragmatics. In *The Routledge Handbook of Spanish Pragmatics*, ed. Dale A. Koike and J. César Félix-Brasdefer, 91–108. Abingdon: Routledge.

Flamson, Thomas, and Gregory A. Bryant. 2013. Signals of Humor. Encryption and Laughter in Social Interaction. In *Developments in Linguistic Humour Theory*, ed. Marta Dynel, 49–73. Amsterdam: John Benjamins. https://doi.org/10.1075/thr.1.04fla.

Flamson, Thomas, and H. Clark Barrett. 2008. The Encryption Theory of Humor: A Knowledge-Based Mechanism of Honest Signaling. *Journal of Evolutionary Psychology* 6 (4): 261–281. https://doi.org/10.1556/JEP.6.2008.4.2.

Fodor, Jerry. 1983. *The Modularity of Mind*. Cambridge, Mass: The MIT Press.

Hall, Allison. 2017. Enrichment. In *The Routledge Handbook of Pragmatics*, ed. Anne Barron, Gerard Steen, and Gu Yueguo, 341–353. Abingdon: Routledge.

Hurley, Matthew M., Daniel C. Dennett, and Reginald B. Adams. 2011. *Inside Jokes. Using Humor to Reverse-Engineer the Mind*. Cambridge, Mass: The MIT Press.

Martin, Rod A. 2006. *The Psychology of Humor: An Integrative Approach*. London: Academic Press.

Mateo, José, and Francisco Yus. 2021. Ad Hoc Concepts in Humorous Financial Metaphors. A Pragmatic Approach. In *Metaphor in Economics and Specialised Discourse*, ed. José Mateo and Francisco Yus, 17–39. Bern: Peter Lang.

Morreall, John. 2009. *Comic Relief. A Comprehensive Philosophy of Humor*. Chichester: Wiley-Blackwell. https://doi.org/10.1002/9781444307795.

Ritchie, Graeme. 2004. *The Linguistic Analysis of Jokes*. London: Routledge. https://doi.org/10.4324/9780203406953.

———. 2006. Reinterpretation and Viewpoints. *Humor* 9 (3): 251–270. https://doi.org/10.1515/HUMOR.2006.014.
———. 2009. Variants of Incongruity Resolution. *Journal of Literary Theory* 3 (2): 1–20. https://doi.org/10.1515/JLT.2009.017.
Scollon, Ron, and Suzanne Wong Scollon. 2001. *Intercultural Communication. A Discourse Approach*. Oxford: Blackwell.
Sperber, Dan, and Deirdre Wilson. 1995. *Relevance. Communication and Cognition*. 2nd ed. Oxford: Blackwell.
———. 1997. Remarks on Relevance Theory and the Social Sciences. *Multilingua* 16: 145–151. https://doi.org/10.1515/mult.1997.16.2-3.145.
———. 2002. Pragmatics, Modularity and Mind-Reading. *Mind and Language* 17 (1-2): 3–23. https://doi.org/10.1111/1468-0017.00186.
———. 2005. Pragmatics. *UCL Working Papers in Linguistics* 17: 353–388.
Sperber, Dan, and Deidre Wilson. 2015. Beyond Speaker's Meaning. *Croatian Journal of Philosophy* XV (2): 117–149.
Suls, Jerry M. 1972. A Two-Stage Model for the Appreciation of Jokes and Cartoons: An Information-processing Analysis. In *The Psychology of Humor: Theoretical Perspectives and Empirical Issues*, ed. J.H. Goldstein and P.E. McGhee, 81–100. New York: Academic Press. https://doi.org/10.1016/B978-0-12-288950-9.50010-9.
———. 1977. Cognitive and Disparagement Theories of Humour: A Theoretical and Empirical Synthesis. In *It's a Funny Thing, Humour*, ed. A.J. Chapman and H.C. Foot, 41–45. Oxford: Pergamon Press. https://doi.org/10.1016/B978-0-08-021376-7.50012-7.
———. 1983. Cognitive Processes in Humor Appreciation. In *Handbook of Humor Research, Vol. 1: Basic Issues*, ed. P.E. McGhee and J.H. Goldstein, 39–57. New York: Springer-Verlag. https://doi.org/10.1007/978-1-4612-5572-7_3.
Thielemann, Nadine. 2020. *Understanding Conversational Joking. A Cognitive-Pragmatic Study Based on Russian Interactions*. Amsterdam: John Benjamins. https://doi.org/10.1075/pbns.310.
Wilson, Deirdre. 2014. Relevance Theory. *UCL Working Papers in Linguistics* 26: 1–20.
———. 2017. Relevance Theory. In *Oxford Handbook of Pragmatics*, ed. Yan Huang, 79–100. Oxford: Oxford University Press. https://doi.org/10.1093/oxfordhb/9780199697960.013.25.
Wilson, Deirdre, and Robyn Carston. 2007. A Unitary Approach to Lexical Pragmatics: Relevance, Inference and Ad Hoc Concepts. In *Pragmatics*, ed. N. Burton-Roberts, 230–259. Basingstoke: Palgrave. https://doi.org/10.1093/oxfordhb/9780199234769.003.0018.
Wilson, Deirdre, and Dan Sperber. 1987. An Outline of Relevance Theory. *Notes on Linguistics* 39: 5–24.

———. 2002. Relevance Theory. *UCL Working Papers in Linguistics* 14: 249–290.
———. 2004. Relevance Theory. In *Handbook of Pragmatics*, ed. Gregory Ward and Larry Horn, 607–632. Oxford: Blackwell. https://doi.org/10.1002/9780470756959.ch27.
———. 2012. *Relevance and Meaning*. Cambridge: Cambridge University Press. https://doi.org/10.1017/CBO9781139028370.
Yule, George. 1996. *Pragmatics*. Oxford: Oxford University Press. https://doi.org/10.1017/S0272263198224053.
Yus, Francisco. 1998a. A Decade of Relevance Theory. *Journal of Pragmatics* 30: 305–345. https://doi.org/10.1016/S0378-2166(98)00015-0.
———. 1998b. Relevance: A Thematic Bibliographical List. *Revista Alicantina de Estudios Ingleses* 11: 261–285. (special issue devoted to relevance theory).
———. 2001. *Ciberpragmática. El uso del lenguaje en Internet [Cyberpragmatics. The use of language on the Internet]*. Barcelona: Ariel.
———. 2003a. *Cooperación y Relevancia. Dos Aproximaciones Pragmáticas a la Interpretación (2nd revised edition) [Cooperation and relevance. Two pragmatic approaches to interpretation]*. Alicante: University of Alicante, Servicio de Publicaciones.
———. 2003b. Humor and the Search for Relevance. *Journal of Pragmatics* 35 (9): 1295–1331. https://doi.org/10.1016/S0378-2166(02)00179-0.
———. 2006. Relevance Theory. In The Encyclopedia of Language and Linguistics (2) 10, by Keith Brown, 512–519. Amsterdam: Elsevier. https://doi.org/10.1016/B0-08-044854-2/00313-8
———. 2010a. *Ciberpragmática 2.0. Nuevos Usos del Lenguaje en Internet [Cyberpragmatics 2.0. New uses of language on the internet]*. Barcelona: Ariel.
———. 2010b. Relevance Theory. In *The Oxford Handbook of Linguistic Analysis*, ed. Bernd Heine and Heiko Narrog, 679–701. Oxford: Oxford University Press. https://doi.org/10.1093/oxfordhb/9780199677078.013.0027.
———. 2011. *Cyberpragmatics. Internet-Mediated Communication in Context*. Amsterdam and Philadelphia: John Benjamins. https://doi.org/10.1075/pbns.213.
———. 2013a. An Inference-Centered Analysis of Jokes: The Intersecting Circles Model of Humorous Communication. In *Irony and Humor: From Pragmatics to Discourse*, ed. Leonor Ruiz Gurillo and Belén Alvarado, 59–82. Amsterdam: John Benjamins. https://doi.org/10.1075/pbns.231.05yus.
———. 2013b. Analyzing Jokes with the Intersecting Circles Model of Humorous Communication. *Lodz Papers in Pragmatics* 9 (1): 3–24. https://doi.org/10.1515/lpp-2013-0002.
———. 2016a. *Humour and Relevance*. Amsterdam: John Benjamins. https://doi.org/10.1075/thr.4.

———. 2016b. La Teoría de la Relevancia [Relevance theory]. In *Enciclopedia de lingüística hispánica*, ed. Javier Gutiérrez Rexach, vol. 2, 297–304. London: Routledge.

———. 2017. Relevance-Theoretic Treatments of Humor. In *The Routledge Handbook of Language and Humor*, ed. Salvatore Attardo, 189–203. Abingdon: Routledge.

———. 2020. Disambiguation Should Not Exist (But it Does in Humour). Paper delivered at the *9th International Symposium on Intercultural, Cognitive and Social Pragmatics* ("Communication in the 21st Century: Intercultural, Cognitive and Social Pragmatics"). Seville, Spain.

———. 2021a. *Smartphone Communication. Interactions in the App Ecosystem.* Abingdon: Routledge. https://doi.org/10.4324/9781003200574.

———. 2021b. Pragmatics of Humour in Memes in Spanish. *Spanish in Context* 18 (1): 113–135, special issue on humour. https://doi.org/10.1075/sic.00070.yus.

Žegarac, Vladimir, and Billy Clark. 1999. Phatic Interpretations and Phatic Communication. *Journal of Linguistics* 35: 321–346. https://doi.org/10.1017/S0022226799007628.

CHAPTER 3

Internet Humour

1 Introduction

As remarked in Yus (2016, 37), humour is an inherently human trait that defies a unitary analysis or a single perspective, since the term covers a whole range of communicative, social and psychological aspects of human behaviour. Humour appears pervasively in today's interactions and takes different shapes depending on the culture (Martin 2006, 4). Humour also stands out as one of the most valued qualities that men and women seek in a potential partner as well as a key element in personal attraction (Cann et al. 1997, 2011). Despite stressing group solidarity and a sense of belonging by emphasising a certain mutuality of assumptions, it proves equally useful to exclude individuals from a group. It lubricates conversations, relieves tension in business negotiations and facilitates interactions at work, among other qualities.

Being so important in present-day interactions, it comes as no surprise that humour is also pervasive on the internet. And yet, not all humorous discourses on the Net can properly be labelled as internet humour. In fact, as proposed in this book, the term has a rather narrow scope (see below), with a more specific range of humorous discourses under study than those addressed in other books on this topic, including Taiwo et al. (2016) or Chiaro (2018). By contrast, Vásquez (2019) did restrict her analysis to

F. Yus, *Pragmatics of Internet Humour*,
https://doi.org/10.1007/978-3-031-31902-0_3

specific instances of humour which are solely found on the internet, thus fitting the label *internet humour* used in this book, since it covers inherently digital humorous discourses such as Twitter accounts, Tumblr chats or Amazon reviews, among others.

2 What Constitutes Internet Humour?

The internet hosts millions of humorous discourses, but not all of them can genuinely be referred to as *internet humour*. For the purposes of this book, internet humour will be defined as "any discourse (verbal, visual, multimodal) with an underlying humorous intention that is either autonomously produced on the internet or created offline for the sole purpose of being uploaded and interpreted online." As such, this definition leaves outside its scope all the humorous effects stemming from discourses produced without a humorous aim. And most importantly, the definition also excludes every discourse which, despite being uploaded on the Net, was initially created offline and intended for an offline audience. For example, Shifman's (2014, 389) definition of internet humour as "any type of humorous interaction or performance that is manifest on the Internet" would clearly include discursive instances not covered by the definition of this label adopted in this book.

In order to understand the suggested narrow scope of the label *internet humour*, it seems convenient to resort to Shepherd and Watters' (1998) proposal for types of internet genres (Fig. 3.1) and check the extent to which these adapt to the humorous discourses available online. As summarised in Yus (2021a, 122), according to these authors cyber-genres are initially divided into *extant* and *novel*. The former rely on genres that already exist outside the Net, while the latter depend entirely on the digital qualities of the interface. Extant genres in turn divide into *replicated* and *variant*. The former proliferated in the early stages of the internet, when it was thought that it was only necessary to scan and upload documents online. The variant genres, instead, take advantage (to a certain extent) of interface specificity, such as the inclusion of links or the cutting of texts to adapt them to the new reading area of the screen. The text often matches the one in the printed version, but format fidelity ceases to be maintained, and neither is it expected by users.

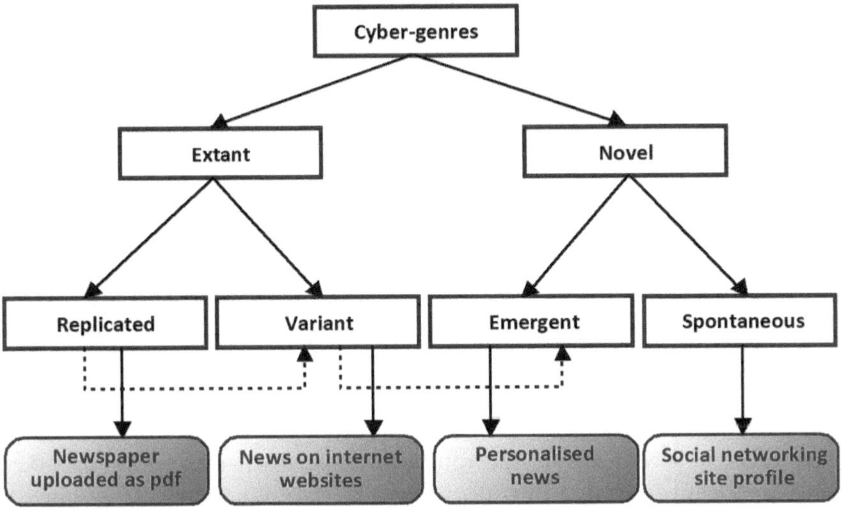

Fig. 3.1 Evolution of cyber-genres (Shepherd and Watters 1998)

Continuing with Fig. 3.1, *novel* genres fall into two types: *emergent* and *spontaneous*. The former are evolutions of offline genres adapted to the Net, to such an extent that they hardly resemble their printed counterparts. There are substantial changes in form and content and, therefore, substantial changes resulting from the processing of the information contained in both versions become evident as well. Finally, the spontaneous genres have no printed counterpart. They have been born within the internet and take advantage of the technology and the design of interfaces to generate various readings and modes of interaction, as exemplified by the profiles of social networking sites such as Facebook.

From this proposal, three main types of humour appear on the internet: *replicated humour* (which would lie beyond the scope of this book), *spontaneous humour* (the main object of analysis in this book and the one neatly fitting the label *internet humour*) and *hybrid humour* (which combines aspects or elements of the other two categories). These are briefly described below.[1]

1. *Replicated internet humour*. These humorous discourses, created outside the Net for an offline audience, would lie outside the narrow definition of internet humour proposed in this book. Examples include online joke repositories, stand-up comedy performances recorded in theatres and then uploaded on YouTube or humour-related printed publications that are subsequently digitalised (e.g. turned into a pdf file) and uploaded on the Net (see Hirsch 2017). The forwarded jokes through emails that Oring (2012, 79) places within the so-called *online folklore* also belong here.

   Weitz (2017, 506) stressed how with the rise of the digital age and new media capabilities, the internet affords an unprecedented personalised access to humour-related performances in the broadest application of the term, an archive open to the connected public for comic performance past and present. It is then possible to visit some of the great comic performers from as far back as recording technology has allowed. These would be examples of replicated internet humour.

   Similarly, Tsakona (2020, 170) wrote about *joke circles*. These "constitute folk taxonomies of jokes that were initially circulated orally and became written when their producers, collectors, and eventually researchers attempted to maintain them, thus further contributing to their dissemination." Again, these jokes were first

[1] Stefani (2020, 329) makes a (rather reductive) twofold distinction between old and new types of internet humour. Among the former, she lists discourses such as (1) *joke* (a short story with a punch line), (2) *home video* (a slapstick-based video that captures people in embarrassing /surprising situations), (3) *the commercial* (advertisements created in order to be circulated via e-mail from person to person), and (4) *cartoon*. According to her, the new types of internet humour include (1) *interactive humour* (a humorous text which forces its receiver to perform an activity that is additional to reading, watching or hearing), (2) *funny photo* (a photograph that conveys a humorous message, often accompanied by a funny written text, (3) *maniphoto* (an explicitly manipulated photograph that usually combines with other visual forms), (4) *phanimation* (a crude animation of static photos -phanimation is a blend resulting from photo + animation), (5) *celebrity soundboards* (collections of digitized celebrity sound bites taken from movies, radio and TV which are presented on the internet to facilitate prank calls, and (6) *PowerPoint humour* (a humorous text that takes the form of a Powerpoint presentation.

told offline and then uploaded online, thus fitting the label of replicated internet humour.

Chiaro (2018, 35) also commented on the role played by repositories and cable channels when it comes to making humorous discourses available to users. Nevertheless, she also underlines another important feature of replicated internet humour: the fact that these replicated humorous discourses are re-located elsewhere, in a new communicative context other than the one in which they were initially produced and also interpreted by a different audience, which in turn has obvious pragmatic implications too: Clips are by their very nature divorced from the whole where they originally occurred, let alone their historical context. In other words, a user who uploads a favourite comic clip provides something that is partly original; it might be his or her favourite part of a film, for instance. However, that same clip can be later seen and revisited repeatedly by others, and yet at the same time, it will remain devoid of its original context.

For example, when a joke is told in a face-to-face scenario during a dyadic conversation, the speaker may hold fairly clear expectations of which information from context can easily be accessed by the addressee (or is *mutually manifest* in relevance-theoretic terminology) and how the joke will interact with that person's background store of beliefs, ideas, etc. (crucial in sex- or race-connoted jokes, see next chapter), depending on whether this addressee is a friend or an acquaintance. By contrast, an offline -and then replicated online- joke shared on a social networking site profile, for instance, may be read by a multiplicity of users whose context accessibility and background assumptions can only be predicted to a certain extent, with the obvious risk of failed humour. The same holds true for offline jokes shared on messaging app groups. Bronner (2012) pointed in a similar direction. After initially studying online Jewish joke repositories, clearly filled with replicated humorous discourses, he also stressed that "internet transforms folkloric genres by providing a different communicative medium and a novel play frame. From this perspective, digital media are not simulating or stirring a face-to-face interactive context; instead, they serve to redefine the social setting and reorganize the cultural frame, thus allowing users to create a fresh expressive form" (pp. 121–122).

2. *Spontaneous internet humour.* These humorous discourses were either created on the Net or designed offline exclusively to be

uploaded and interpreted online. Examples include memes, stickers, GIFs, emojis, humorous comments on a social networking site entry, humorous online reviews (see Vásquez 2017, 2019) and humour-centred blogs, among others. These discourses, some of which constitute the object of analysis in this book, cannot usually be reproduced offline or they lose their specificity and communicative purpose. For example, Fiadotava (2020, 100) remarked that sharing humour digitally is popular because "some genres of humour are too specific to digital communication and cannot be transmitted orally even if the family members are together and have an opportunity to engage in humour at the same time." Furthermore, such spontaneous humorous discourses often become embedded within other internet media, e.g. memes shared on messaging apps or humorous comments on a social networking site entry. Among these, memes stand out as the quintessential example of internet humour. Tsakona (2020, 170) correctly contended that memes have become the most typical and popular online humorous genre through the combination of text, image and even moving images (see Chap. 7). They are also regarded as prototypical instances of today's internet culture fostering user creativity and involvement, and also serve to represent and disseminate of complex ideas and values, often in an unconventional manner. As such, they are not always meant to be humorous, because they may also convey harsh political criticism.

Some of the new humour types listed in Shifman (2007) fit this spontaneous internet humour label:

a. *Interactive humour*. Since this type requires its receiver to perform an activity in addition to reading, watching or hearing the discourse, the eventual humour is produced and conveyed solely online. She mentions the example of the *squirrel name generator*, where people are invited to type their names, press the 'submit' button, and wait until their true 'inner squirrel' name appears on the screen. The same mechanism is at work in game-like sites such as *Give Bush a brain*, in which the player has to drop a brain into the President's head.
b. *Funny photo*. In this case, a photograph has been designed to convey a humorous message, frequently accompanied by a funny written text (hence similar to memes). Although these funny photos already existed before the advent of the internet (e.g. in

Fig. 3.2 Staged funny photo (Shifman 2007)

family albums, calendars or postcards), they are nowadays not imported from offline photos but created from scratch for the only purpose of being shared online (thus fitting the label of spontaneous internet humour). She distinguished two main kinds of funny photos in her study: (a) photos showing strange or unexpected phenomena; and (b) 'staged' photos in which someone has created a special situation for the camera (an example thereof is reproduced in Fig. 3.2).

c. *Maniphoto*. This explicitly manipulated photograph usually combines with other visual forms. What mainly distinguishes a maniphoto from a funny photo is that no doubts whatsoever exist about the picture having been manipulated in the former. The origins of maniphotos can be traced back to the practice of photomontage, prior to the internet era mainly as a form of art that was not widespread in mass media. Again, these maniphotos are solely meant to be shared and consumed online, which makes the label spontaneous internet humour applicable to them.
d. *Phanimation*. A crude animation of static photos (Phanimation = photo + animation) most commonly produced by professionals due to the technical command demanded. Needless to say, they are also created on the Net for users to watch and comment on them.

3. *Hybrid internet humour*. The discourses fitting this label combine replicated and spontaneous discourses within one single instance of internet communication. Examples include humorous comments to a replicated discourse, or humorous discussions stemming from a replicated film or TV show on YouTube.

In a similar vein, Shifman (2007, 188) proposes the term *humour hub*, a large, dynamic repository of visual and verbal humour about various topics. These hubs tend to embody the strong linkage between Web and email circulation of humour: They are often based on contributions of material that has circulated by email and they also encourage visitors to distribute their content to friends via email. As such, humour hubs may contain not only humorous discourses replicated from their production and interpretation in an offline environment but also others created specifically on the internet, thus acquiring a hybrid quality.

Table 3.1 brings together examples of internet humour fitting the label of replicated, spontaneous and hybrid.

3 Humour across Online/Offline Environments

General consensus exists that offline communication and interaction are contextually richer than internet-mediated communication, even regarding internet interactions carried out through video (e.g. Zoom, Meet). As argued in Yus (forthcoming), although video-mediated interactions online exhibit, on paper, the richest medium in terms of options for contextualisation, the medium itself remains limited compared to face-to-face communication. Authentic expressions of emotion (mostly in face-to-face scenarios) are essential to our understanding. But those nonverbal clues disappear on pixelated video or even become frozen, smoothed over, or delayed. Indeed, to recognise emotion, we have to embody it, which makes mirroring essential to empathy and connection, and "when we can't do it seamlessly, as happens during a video chat, we feel unsettled because it's hard to read people's reactions and, thus, predict what they will do" (Murphy 2020: NA). Does the same hold true for the distinction between internet humour and offline humour? Several positions, briefly summarised below, may be isolated in this debate; however, all of them start off from the premise that humour is as pervasive (or even more so) online as it is offline, against some general intuition otherwise (see Hancock 2004a; Adams 2012, 16).

Table 3.1 Examples of replicated, spontaneous and hybrid humorous internet discourses

Internet Discourse	*Label*
A humorous TV programme, aired offline and recorded, then uploaded on YouTube	REPLICATED
A meme consisting of text only, text-image combinations or other discursive modes	SPONTANEOUS
A sequence of humorous comments to a replicated offline humorous discourse[a]	HYBRID
A repository of jokes told offline and then collected on a website	REPLICATED
A funny tweet on any newsworthy event	SPONTANEOUS
A web repository compiling jokes from both offline and online sources	HYBRID
A stand-up comedy performance recorded in a theatre and subsequently made available online	REPLICATED
A humorous sequence of comments to a user's entry on Facebook	SPONTANEOUS
A meme containing a playful combination of offline image and text[b]	HYBRID
A cartoon published in a printed newspaper and reproduced on the artist's website	REPLICATED
A humorous online review of a product (see Vásquez 2019)	SPONTANEOUS
A typed comment (*danmu*) on the screen while watching a programme recorded offline[c]	HYBRID

[a]See, for instance, Page's (2018) analysis of humorous comments on YouTube videos. If these videos are replicated, these would constitute an instance of hybrid internet humour. If the videos are also spontaneous, the videos + comments would make up a single piece of spontaneous humorous internet discourse

[b]This kind of hybrid meme comprising a still from an offline TV program or film and new (spontaneous) text matches the label of ***second-order incongruity*** proposed in Yus (2021b) for certain memes. The incongruity lies in the clash between the meme text and the image as it was initially produced offline, rather than in the clash between the image and the top-bottom texts inside the meme (in fact, texts and image are very often fully compatible). Expressed differently, instead of arising from the interpretation of text and image within the meme, the clash actually takes place between the text and that image as it had initially been produced offline and interpreted in the offline context of the film or the TV programme

[c]As described in Yus (2021a, 180), ***danmu*** is a sort of collaborative textual annotation on videos, films or TV programmes. Users watching these may write comments on the video/film/TV discourse, each comment becoming synchronised with the image. Furthermore, several users typically engage in interactions about the video by typing ***danmu*** on it, to the extent that it is often difficult to see the image itself, with the text blocking out most of it, causing a visual effect that resembles ***danmaku*** ("bullet curtain" in Japanese)

1. *Face-to face humour is richer than internet humour.* The most frequent position, as already mentioned for online/offline communication in general (see Proekt 2019). Hancock (2004b, 57) suggested a number of reasons why online humour could be a risky business compared to offline (i.e. face-to-face) humour. First, and true at

least at the time of publication, because online communication was massively text-based, users have fewer cues available to signal their humorous intent when they are online. Second, face-to-face humour importantly tends to reveal a high degree of coordination and/or complicity between the interlocutors involved. The online humourist, however, cannot always receive appropriate -instant- feedback on whether the intended humour was successful or failed. This especially happens in asynchronous forms of communication, such as email and newsgroups, but also applies to supposedly synchronous interactions (e.g. through messaging apps) in which it is equally acknowledged that the addressee user might take some time to reply to a message.

Certainly, conveying humour by means of typed messages entails more difficulties, especially considering that laughter often occurs in simultaneity with verbal utterances. As McKay (2020, 99) correctly contended, text-based communication clearly places restrictions on typed laughter due to which it must be used somewhat differently from physical laughter. Most transparently, physical laughter may be uttered "paraverbally" so that it overlaps with the production of words, both the laugher's own words and those of other participants. However, it deserves to be stressed that users do not normally complain about the limitations of the medium used for humorous communication; instead, they make the most of the options that the interface affordances provide them with, rather than be critical about the lack of options offered. As argued in Yus (forthcoming), internet users exploit to the fullest extent these possibilities (interface affordances) and often obtain as much contextual information and are as capable of conveying their humorous intentions as they are in a richer scenario such as a face-to-face conversation. Users even act upon those interface affordances with a view to achieve greater richness and better options to manage their interactions. Actually, users adapt and reshape technologies to their own communicative needs. This is what happened when the dissatisfaction with its interface options led Twitter users to start labelling tweets by using hashtags, as well as creating the *retweet* nomenclature. These end-user innovations were eventually incorporated into the Twitter interface.

2. *Face-to face humour is less rich than internet humour.* A position held by few scholars. It is true that internet humour abounds on the Net,

sometimes even more so than offline humour, but does this correlate with the richness of the medium? Chiaro (2018, 3–4) mentions the so-called *disaster jokes*, like those produced immediately after the 11S terrorist attack in New York, as evidence that the web facilitated a massive voicing and ease of pain via humour that face-to-face humorous interactions failed to attain. Even though internet humour actually seems to be richer than its face-to-face counterpart in these specific instances, there is general agreement that, pragmatically speaking, offline humour offers more options for contextualisation or expectations of mutuality of information, among other things.

3. *Face-to face humour is similar to internet humour*. According to the pragmatic perspective adopted in this book, only one inferential system is in charge of turning the schematic words uttered (or images uploaded) by the speaker into meaningful and contextualised interpretations, and the same holds true for the interpretation of humorous discourses in general and, more precisely, of humorous internet discourses. In this sense, internet humour and offline humour would be similar, the main difference lying, according to cyberpragmatics (Yus 2010, 2011) in the options and/or limitations favoured or imposed by the specific interfaces (their *affordances*) upon this inferential pattern. Analysts such as Vandergriff and Fuchs (2012) point in a similar direction.
4. *Face-to face humour is different from internet humour*. Although this is a counter-intuitive position, given the aforementioned unicity of humour processing for both online and offline discourses, differences indeed exist in how they are performed and through which medium, together with constraints imposed upon a successful humorous production, interpretation and desired outcome. For example, Weitz (2017, 507) seems to emphasise the differences between these discourses without meaning that one outperforms the other: "joking in an online context necessitates interceding steps that stretch the time between a thought and its public utterance and eliminate the possibility of overlapping responses. Participants are able to take at least a bit of time to think about how best to 'perform' their jokes, how to phrase or otherwise construct them, and they even have the capacity to edit posts after the fact."

Fiadotava (2020, 99–100) proposed certain differences between online and offline humour. The first one has to do with *performative devices*. The production of humour requires certain skills, and its appreciation also depends on its performance. Again, the repertoire of performative devices is said to be much more limited in digital settings than oral face-to-face communication, the latter offering voice modulations, facial expressions and gestures, as well as other contextualisation cues. Digital messages are nearly devoid of the performative aspect, which is less apparent than in face-to-face interaction. The second difference regards the *spatiotemporal level*: digital communication is not always as immediate as oral interactions. Besides, users are faced with a large amount of information, but it is often very ephemeral and if one does not engage with it immediately, they might not be able to trace it back anymore. Hence, users are pushed into non-stop attention in today's world of attention scarcity, and this ultimately determines the popularity of some humorous internet discourses over others. Finally, another differentiating aspect is the temporal patterns of communication. Unlike oral communication, digital sharing of humour often works asynchronously, and participants may not engage in the conversation at the same time. Such asynchronous nature of online communication reduces the pressure to respond instantly, but humorous communication may trigger another type of pressure associated with a need to come up with a humorous reply or a funny example of our own. It also entails differences regarding co-constructed humour in face-to-face conversations compared to online (a)synchronous ones (Mullan 2020, 137; Weitz 2017, 509; Farnia and Karimi 2019, 25).

4 The Discourse of Internet Humour. General Issues

Today's internet humour takes advantage of all the possibilities that the medium provides users with, both in terms of interaction and regarding interface affordances, which have opened up throughout the development of internet from its initial stages, when limited options were offered to generate and derive humorous effects. Shifman (2014, 389) proposed a wide array of areas in which internet humour is pervasive, and suggested a wide scope, including both interactional vs. situational vs. spontaneous humour, with users reacting to one another humorously in settings such as forums and bulletin boards, and "pass along" humour, which comprises artifacts such as jokes, funny photos and videos that are disseminated and shared across different contexts. This proposal needs to be updated, of course, to incorporate social networking sites and messaging applications, the sites where most of today's internet humour appears.

Overall, three types of humorous internet discourses may be isolated:

1. *Textual*. Before the advent of Web 2.0, with its emphasis on social media and the proliferation of all kinds of discourses uploaded and exchanged online, the largest part of internet communication and interaction was text-based. Albeit apparently a clear limitation compared to the richness of today's multiplicity of genres, authors such as Vandergriff (2010, 26) find advantages in text-based discourse compared, for example, to the wealth of face-to-face interactions. Text-only internet communication provides researchers with a way to look at language as an interactive unimodal system without the "noise" of conveyed information such as physical appearance, proxemics, pitch, and other cues that are part and parcel of speech despite being absent in the online universe.

   In this phase, most of the humour arose from the playful use of nicknames (*nicks*), text alteration[2] (repetition of letters, capitalisation, acronyms, creative use of punctuation) and the incorporation of emoticons created out of typed text (see Yus 2014). These are the main topics in the seminal research on text-based internet humour undertaken by Danet and others (Danet 1995, 2001; Danet et al. 1996). They drew a metaphoric comparison between creative typed text and a piano keyboard: "On the piano, in addition to playing individual notes to create a melody, one can also produce chords by playing several notes together, much expanding the expressive possibilities of the instrument. On the computer keyboard, creative individuals sometimes produce amazing effects merely with the mundane options of upper and lower case, numbers, and typographic symbols" (Danet et al. 1996). This basically applies to emoticon use. Nicks are likewise foregrounded as a humour-generating strategy. Danet (2001) is probably the best study on internet humour during this initial, mainly text-based Web 1.0 period, characterised by the playful use of text alteration compensating for vocal qualities of the human voice and emoticons together with so-called

[2] *Text alteration* (Yus 2021a) was called *textual deformation* in Yus (2005) and *oralised written text* in Yus (2011).

iconic stage directions (e.g. *John laughs his socks off*, see Yus 2011) for visual nonverbal communication.

Nowadays, some of these text-based strategies continue to be popular (except the aforementioned stage directions), including the transcription of laugh (also called laugh particles or e-laughter, as in "hahaha") and humour-related acronyms. However, with the evolution of interfaces and of the internet itself towards web 2.0, the range of options available for users to accomplish their humorous intentions has increased to an enormous extent and with obvious pragmatic implications. The latter will be the main focus of analysis in this book, spanning emoji, stickers and GIFs on messaging apps (Chap. 5); textual, visual and multimodal discourses on social networking sites (Chap. 6) and memes (Chap. 7).

2. *Visual.* Owing to increased broadband and the integration of mobile and smartphone cameras with other apps making up an *app ecosystem* (Yus 2021a), humour is now frequently shared online in a visual format, including funny photos and selfies (Baran 2009, 172; Ge 2019, 11). As explained in Yus (2021a, 149), thousands of photos are taken daily with no intention to preserve them (or not primarily) in today's smartphone-dominated era. Instead, they serve to perform actions and provoke effects, which clearly resonates with one of the main purposes of humour. Despite the current photo-taking capabilities, smartphone-mediated images often lack aesthetic quality because this is by no means the main point of taking and sharing them; generating humorous effects often is, though. As Peters and Allan (2018, 365) noted, smartphone technology creates the possibility of an 'always-on' connection, i.e. different places are experienced by participants not only in terms of their immediate surroundings but also regarding the potential social and informational connections that they enable, which humour-laden interactions facilitates as well. Berry (2016, 54) added that "visual images in these social media ecologies, enabled by the assemblages of smartphones and networked technology, take on phatic and phenomenological aspects in order to evoke a sense of what it is like to be here and now in the physical world in a visceral multisensory way."
3. *Multimodal.* A high tendency equally arises today towards conveying humour through multimodal discourses that mainly combine text and image but without discarding other possible mode combinations

(Marone 2016, 51), very typical nowadays in the shape of videos (e.g. on TikTok, see for example Barry and Graça 2018; Wang 2020; Haines 2021) and verbal-visual memes (see Chap. 7). Another example is visual collages, in which

> various phrases and images from popular media are assembled in incongruous combinations, thus producing a humorous effect. These visual collages are often based on genre play -they juxtapose news footage, children's programs, advertisements, and other genres in amusing and unexpected ways. Whereas creators of media messages try to introduce them in a smooth and easy-to-digest format, concealing the assemblage of bits and pieces that underlie them, the creators of Internet jokes do the opposite. Internet humor highlights the "cut and paste" process underpinning it: It plays with genres and conventions of visual culture in an explicit and self-conscious manner. (Shifman 2014, 390).

Memes archetypically illustrate multimodal internet humorous discourse. Users of social networking sites such as Facebook, Instagram or Twitter have also increasingly conveyed their humorous intentions via multimodal discourses. In this case, an interesting research issue could be which mode in the multimodal discourse, for example the image or the text, draws the user's attention to a greater extent at an initial stage of interpreting it, alongside the consequences derived from combining this initial processing with the subsequent inference of the other modes that make up the discourse. Along these same lines, Simarro Vázquez et al. (2021) analysed multimodal tweets and came to the conclusion that "generally speaking the processing is not linear; images tend to attract the attention of the participants; written text is a close second and requires more effort/time to process. The relatively smaller size of the text, compared with the size of the images, may also be responsible for the prevalence of the image-first processing strategy" (p. 169).

5 Concluding Remarks

Millions of humorous discourses are uploaded, commented upon, shared and forwarded on the internet. Not all of them fit the narrow label of *internet humour* proposed in this book, namely, humorous discourses created online or created offline with the sole purpose of being posted and interpreted online. A three-fold distinction of humorous discourses on the internet has been proposed in this chapter: replicated, spontaneous and hybrid, only the second one truly deserving the label of internet humour.

This chapter has also addressed a comparison between offline and online humour, with different positions regarding the (dis)advantages of one environment over the other.

References

Adams, Audrey. 2012. Humor Markers in Computer-Mediated Communication. MA Thesis. Texas A&M University-Commerce.

Baran, Anneli. 2009. Visual Humour on the Internet. In *Estonia and Poland: Creativity and Change in Cultural Communication: Vol. 1 Jokes and Humour*, ed. Liisi Laineste, Dorota Brzozowska, and Wladislaw Chlopicky, 144–158. Tartu: EKM Teaduskirjastus. https://doi.org/10.7592/EP.1.baran.

Barry, James M., and Sandra S. Graça. 2018. Humor Effectiveness in Social Video Engagement. *Journal of Marketing Theory and Practice* 26 (1-2): 158–180. https://doi.org/10.1080/10696679.2017.1389247.

Berry, Marsha. 2016. Out in the Open: Locating New Vernacular Practices with Smartphone Cameras. *Studies in Australasian Cinema* 10 (1): 53–64. https://doi.org/10.1080/17503175.2015.1084173.

Bronner, Simon J. 2012. The Jewish Joke Online: Framing and Symbolizing Humor in Analog and Digital Culture. In *Folk Culture in the Digital Age. The Emergent Dynamics of Human Interaction*, ed. Trevor J. Blank, 119–149. Boulder: Utah State University Press.

Cann, Arnie, Lawrence G. Calhoun, and Janet S. Banks. 1997. On the Role of Humor Appreciation in Interpersonal Attraction: It's No Joking Matter. *Humor* 10: 77–89. https://doi.org/10.1515/humr.1997.10.1.77.

Cann, Arnie, Christine L. Zapata, and Heather B. Davis. 2011. Humor Style and Relationship Satisfaction in Dating Couples: Perceived Versus Self-Reported Humor Styles as Predictors of Satisfaction. *Humor* 24 (1): 1–20. https://doi.org/10.1515/humr.2011.001.

Chiaro, Delia. 2018. *The Language of Jokes in the Digital Age*. Abingdon: Routledge.

Danet, Brenda. 1995. Language, Play and Performance in Computer-Mediated Communication. *Journal of Computer-Mediated Communication* 1 (2).

———. 2001. *Cyberplay. Communicating Online*. Oxford: Berg.

Danet, Brenda, Lucia Ruedenberg-Wright, and Yehudit Rosenbaum-Tamari. 1996. "Hmmm...Where's That Smoke Coming From?" Writing, Play and Performance on Internet Relay Chat. *Journal of Computer-Mediated Communication* 2 (4). https://doi.org/10.1111/j.1083-6101.1997.tb00195.x.

Farnia, Maryam, and Keihaneh Karimi. 2019. Humor Markers in Computer Mediated Communication: Emotion Perception and Response. *Teaching English with Technology* 19 (1): 21–35.

Fiadotava, Anastasiya. 2020. Sharing Humour Digitally in Family Communication. *European Journal of Humour Research* 8 (1): 95–111. https://doi.org/10.7592/EJHR2020.8.1.fiadotava.

Ge, Jing. 2019. Social Media-Based Visual Humour Use in Tourism Marketing: A Semiotic Perspective. *European Journal of Humour Research* 7 (3): 6–25. https://doi.org/10.7592/EJHR2019.7.3.ge.

Haines, Zachary. 2021. Humorous Judgment of Incongruity in Short Internet Videos. MA Thesis. Kent State University College.

Hancock, Jeffrey T. 2004a. Verbal Irony Use in Face-to-Face and Computer-Mediated Conversations. *Journal of Language and Social Psychology* 23 (4): 447–463. https://doi.org/10.1177/0261927X04269587.

———. 2004b. LOL: Humor Online. *Interactions* 11 (5): 57–58.

Hirsch, Galia. 2017. Humor Appreciation in the Digital Era. *Lingua* 197: 123–140. https://doi.org/10.1016/j.lingua.2017.06.016.

Marone, Vittorio. 2016. Looping Out Loud: A Multimodal Analysis of Humour on Vine. *European Journal of Humour Research* 4 (4): 50–66. https://doi.org/10.7592/EJHR2016.4.4.marone.

Martin, Rod A. 2006. *The Psychology of Humor: An Integrative Approach*. London: Academic.

McKay, Isabel. 2020. Some Distributional Patterns in the Use of Typed Laughter-Derived Expressions on Twitter. *Journal of Pragmatics* 166: 97–113. https://doi.org/10.1016/j.pragma.2020.05.009.

Mullan, Kerry. 2020. Pile of Dead Leaves Free to a Good Home: Humour and Belonging in a Facebook Community. In *Studies in Ethnopragmatics, Cultural Semantics, and Intercultural Communication. Ethnopragmatics and Semantic Analysis*, ed. Kerry Mullan, Bert Peeters, and Lauren Sadow, 135–159. Cham: Springer. https://doi.org/10.1007/978-981-32-9983-2_8.

Murphy, Kate. 2020. Why Zoom is Terrible. *The New York Times*, 29-4-2020.

Oring, Elliott. 2012. Jokes on the Internet: Listing toward Lists. In *Folk Culture in the Digital Age. The Emergent Dynamics of Human Interaction*, ed. Trevor J. Blank, 98–118. Boulder: Utah State University Press.

Page, Ruth. 2018. *Narratives Online. Shared Stories in Social Media*. Cambridge: Cambridge University Press. https://doi.org/10.1017/9781316492390.

Peters, Chris, and Stuart Allan. 2018. Everyday Imagery: Users' Reflections on Smartphone Cameras and Communication. *Convergence* 24 (4): 357–373. https://doi.org/10.1177/1354856516678395.

Proekt, Yulilla L. 2019. Humor as a Communication Strategy in Social Networking Services. Paper delivered at 2019 IEEE Communication Strategies in Digital Society Workshop. St. Petersburg, 61–64.

Shepherd, M., and Carolyn Watters. 1998. The Evolution of Cybergenres. In *Proceedings of the 31st Annual Hawaii International Conference on System Sciences*, Hawaii. https://doi.org/10.1109/HICSS.1998.651688

Shifman, Limor. 2007. Humor in the Age of Digital Reproduction: Continuity and Change in Internet-Based Comic Texts. *International Journal of Communication* 1: 187–209.

———. 2014. Internet Humor. In *Encyclopedia of Humor Studies*, ed. Salvatore Attardo, 389–393. London: Sage.

Stefani, Claudiu. 2020. Humor During Pandemic in Romania on Facebook. *Culture e Studi del Sociale* 5 (1): 323–334.

Taiwo, Rotimi, Akinola Odebunmi, and Akin Adetunji, eds. 2016. *Analyzing Language and Humor in Online Communication*. Hershey: Information Science Reference.

Tsakona, Villy. 2020. Tracing the Trajectories of Contemporary Online Joking. *Media Linguistics* 7 (2): 169–183. https://doi.org/10.21638/spbu22.2020.202.

Vandergriff, Ilona. 2010. Humor and Play in CMC. In *Handbook of Research on Discourse Behavior and Digital Communication: Language Structures and Social Interaction*, ed. Rotimi Taiwo, 235–251. Hershey: Information Science Reference. https://doi.org/10.4018/978-1-61520-773-2.ch016.

Vandergriff, Ilona, and Carolin Fuchs. 2012. Humor Support in Synchronous Computer-Mediated Classroom Discussions. *Humor* 25 (4): 437–458. https://doi.org/10.1515/humor-2012-0022.

Vásquez, Camilla. 2017. "My Life Has Changed Forever!" Narrative Identities in Parodies of Amazon Reviews. *Narrative Inquiry* 27 (2): 217–234. https://doi.org/10.1075/ni.27.2.02vas.

———. 2019. *Language, Creativity and Humour Online*. Abingdon: Routledge.

Vázquez, Simarro, Nabiha El María, Phillip Hamrick Khatib, and Salvatore Attardo. 2021. On the Order of Processing of Humorous Tweets with Visual and Verbal Elements. *Internet Pragmatics* 4 (1): 150–175. https://doi.org/10.1075/ip.00060.sim.

Wang, Yunwen. 2020. Humor and Camera View on Mobile Short-Form Video Apps Influence User Experience and Technology-Adoption Intent, an Example of *TikTok* (*DouYin*). *Computers in Human Behavior* 110. https://doi.org/10.1016/j.chb.2020.106373.

Weitz, Eric. 2017. Online and Internet Humor. In *The Routledge Handbook of Language and Humor*, ed. Salvatore Attardo, 504–518. Abingdon: Routledge.

Yus, Francisco. 2005. Attitudes and Emotions Through Written Text: The Case of Textual Deformation in Internet Chat Rooms. *Pragmalingüística* 13: 147–174.

———. 2010. *Ciberpragmática 2.0. Nuevos Usos del Lenguaje en Internet [Cyberpragmatics 2.0. New uses of language on the internet]*. Barcelona: Ariel.

———. 2011. *Cyberpragmatics. Internet-Mediated Communication in Context*. Amsterdam and Philadelphia: John Benjamins. https://doi.org/10.1075/pbns.213.
———. 2014. Not All Emoticons Are Created Equal. *Linguagem em (Dis)curso* 14 (3): 511–529. https://doi.org/10.1590/1982-4017-140304-0414.
———. 2016. *Humour and Relevance*. Amsterdam: John Benjamins. https://doi.org/10.1075/thr.4.
———. 2021a. *Smartphone Communication. Interactions in the App Ecosystem*. Abingdon: Routledge. https://doi.org/10.4324/9781003200574.
———. 2021b. Incongruity-Resolution Humorous Strategies in Image Macro Memes. *Internet Pragmatics* 4 (1): 131–149. https://doi.org/10.1075/ip.00058.yus.
———. forthcoming. Social Media and Computer-Mediated Communication. In *The Cambridge Handbook of Language in Context*, ed. Jesús Romero-Trillo. Cambridge: Cambridge University Press.

CHAPTER 4

Contextual Constraints on Internet Humour

1 Introduction

The prototypical act of humorous internet communication, as pictured within cyberpragmatics (Yus 2010, 2011a, 2021), starts with a "sender user" who holds a humorous intention towards an audience (single or multiple) accessible through an interface (e.g. a messaging app, a social networking site profile). To achieve such humorous intention, this user produces a discourse (textual, visual, multimodal) for that audience to interpret in certain predictable ways. The schematic discourse -a context-free string of words or multimodal combinations with images- has to be enriched inferentially by the audience with the aid of contextual information so as to be communicatively valid (i.e. relevant). Inferential strategies in this direction include, as commented upon in Chap. 2, reference assignment, disambiguation and concept adjustment. The aforesaid inferential enrichment yields a fully contextualised and communicatively valid proposition called *explicature*, which may also combine with further contextual information to produce an *implicature*.[1] The sender user may exploit all of

[1] Explicature and implicature are propositional interpretations obtained from linguistic decoding. However, a proposal was made in previous research (e.g. Yus 2008, 2021) to speak about *visual explicatures* and *visual implicatures* when they derive from the comprehension of visual inputs (images, photos, pictures and so on). As summarised in Yus (2021, 144), "images may also convey explicit and implicated interpretations as long as the rigid conceptualisation of that linguistic anchorage is 'relaxed' so as to incorporate inferential interpretations of images."

F. Yus, *Pragmatics of Internet Humour*,
https://doi.org/10.1007/978-3-031-31902-0_4

these inferential strategies involved in discourse comprehension to achieve their humorous intentions.

However, previous research (Yus 2011b, 2015a, 2016b, 2017, 2018, 2019, 2021) has claimed that this cyberpragmatic (relevance-theoretic) picture of comprehension does not suffice to analyse and explain all forms of internet-mediated communication and should therefore be complemented with a key term: *contextual constraint*, which *frames*, as it were, the act of internet-mediated communication, specifically *constraining* the choice of which information is communicated and to whom, as well as the effort involved in choosing and accessing the intended interpretation, together with the options for communication offered by the interface (*interface affordances*). Although contextual constraints exist prior to the internet-mediated interaction and hence do not appear to be an inherent object of pragmatic research, their role in the quality of the outcome of internet communication makes their analysis relevant when it comes to determining why online communication (and more specifically humour-centred internet communication, as addressed in this book) ends up being satisfactory or fruitless.

In this sense, a distinction can be drawn between contextual constraints related to the use of an interface (*user-to-system communication*) and those which have to do with the exchange of information among users or the qualities of individual users that eventually affect both the quantity and quality of information coded/inferred and the relevance achieved, such as the user's personality (*user-to-user communication*). Finally, contextual constraints may relate either to the sender user or to the addressee user (or addressee audience), thus introducing further elements which might play a part in how (un)successful internet communication turns out to be, and will be signalled as essential to understand why certain forms of internet-mediated humour fail to succeed in generating the desired effects.

2 Interface-Related Contextual Constraints on Internet Humour

As briefly mentioned above, interface-related contextual constraints are features of the interface which favour or limit humour-centred online interaction or communication. Since humour normally relies on performing of a number of parallel communicative actions, notably nonverbal ones (vocal, visual), the interface's capacity to facilitate the transfer of such parallel sources of information will largely influence the (un)successful accomplishment of the humorous intention and whether the act of internet communication manages to generate the desired effects in the audience. Similarly, an increased effort to obtain the desired humorous effects due to defective interface design impacts on the mental effort side of the relevance formula. Dynel and Chovanec (2021, 152) point in the same direction when they state that "it is not just the fact that much interpersonal communication has now shifted into the online space; each (new) communicative platform or format tends to offer new technical affordances, prompting users to adjust their communicative practices to such innovations. Numerous technology-mediated forms of interpersonal communication not only are normative on various social media (e.g. Facebook, YouTube, Twitter or TikTok) but also affect the way traditional media content is received." The next Sections will deal with some of these interface-related constraints, particularly as far as messaging apps and social networking sites are concerned.

2.1 *Interface-Related Contextual Constraints on Messaging Apps*

These constraints basically have to do with the *usability* of the app/site interface during messaging interactions. Usability, as conceptualised in this book, is mainly linked to interface ease of use, "the extent to which a product can be used by specified users to achieve specified goals with effectiveness, efficiency and satisfaction in a specified context of use" (Oghuma et al. 2016, 36), which could be rephrased in our context as the extent to which the interface allows its users to achieve their humorous communicative goals.

As highlighted in Yus (2017), because usability affects users' mental effort when using an interface, managing an app or surfing the Net, it clearly influences the eventual relevance of the information accessed through that interface, alongside the ultimate appreciation of the sender user's humorous intention. For example, despite messaging interactions taking place through an interface initially designed for cues-filtered text-based communication, today's messaging interactions are aided by emojis, GIFs, stickers and multimedia attachments (images, videos...), all of which can help to accomplish humorous intentions.

On paper, such cues-filtered type of communication (albeit aided by the aforementioned "props" -emojis, stickers, GIFs- and strategies for text alteration[2]) should be negatively constrained, thus eventually leading to cognitive dissatisfaction, both at coding (trying to make up for the expressive limitations of typed text) and inferring (trying to work out the intended interpretation of typed text plus these "props"). As Vandergriff (2010, 239) remarked, widespread agreement exists that joking seems to be more difficult in a faceless environment because spontaneous language play is hardly ever flagged overtly by linguistic markers such as an explicit "just kidding." During face-to-face interactions, subtle cues, including stylistic deviations, laughter and prosodic or mimetic cues, signal humorous intent. Instead, situational, gestural, mimetic, paralinguistic or other nonverbal cues are lacking in text-based internet communication, which makes it harder for internet users not only to signal a joke but also to understand it correctly derive the desired humorous effects (see Kotthoff 2006, 7). Likewise, Adams (2012, 19) claimed that the participants in an internet-mediated act of communication are at a great disadvantage when it comes to producing humorous or ironic utterances compared to those involved in face-to-face interactions, since users taking part in the former do not share the same physical space and are granted limited access to the contextual cues that facilitate humour comprehension.

Nonetheless, users of messaging apps obtain rewarding humorous effects in the use of typed messages which are not possible with more contextualised app-enabled phone or video calls. Indeed, those messaging app users perceive the interface as manageable enough, because it serves their communicative needs (including humorous ones) without the negative effects associated with using the phone/video call (intrusive quality, exuding too much nonverbal information about the user, too little time to plan messages or lack of colourful communicative creativeness, to quote but a few).

[2] Text alteration covers a wide range of enriching strategies for typed text, among them creative use of punctuation marks, repetition of letters and use of emoji. Pirzadeh and Pfaff (2012, 493) proposed five strategies when compensating for lack of orality in typed texts: (a) *vocal spelling* (altering spelling to mimic a specific vocal inflection, e.g. weeee, soooo), (b) *lexical surrogates* (textual representations of vocal sounds that are not words, e.g. uh huh, haha), (c) *spatial arrays* (pictographs constructed from punctuation and letters, e.g.: (for a sad face, or :-D to indicate laughing), (d) *manipulation of grammatical markers* (alterations of the presentation of words, e.g. capital letters, strings of periods or commas), and (e) *minus features* (deliberate or inadvertent neglect of conventional formatting elements, e.g. lack of capitalization or paragraphing).

Wang et al. (2012, 90) correctly argued that individuals experience the advantages of adopting a phatic technology, typed text through a messaging app in this case, and gradually place more reliance on this interface and depend on it to accomplish their social (phatic) goals, including the humorous ones, which also own a phatic quality. After a prolonged period of phatic technology utilisation, these individuals simply become accustomed to using it to fulfil these goals and obtain rewarding non-propositional effects, despite being aware of the availability of other technologies (such as in-app phone/video calls) which may potentially offer higher efficiency.[3] This is so because they trust the technology to such an extent that their sense of security and relaxation while carrying out the activity is deeply rooted in this particular phatic technology. Similarly, Ogara et al. (2014, 454) emphasised how user experience and familiarity when choosing an interface make users be willing to sustain interactions through this medium, especially if their peers also use that interface, as a result of which this medium becomes a natural form of interaction. This definitely holds true for interactions of a humorous kind.

All the same, messaging apps do exhibit certain contextual constraints, for example, those shared with chat rooms and texting, since both interfaces entail typing and sending messages that a server rigidly allocates in a fixed order (Yus 2003, 2005a, 2017). This acquires especial prominence in the case of co-constructed humour in messaging groups, since users may find turns disordered, with the comment on a picture sent by a user sometimes arriving at the addressee's mobile before the picture itself, all of which inevitably results in confusion. Delay of response has likewise been highlighted as a limitation for humorous online communication. According to Adams (2012, 19), in face-to-face interactions successful humour often depends on coordination between speaker and listener, as feedback facilitates mutual awareness of whether the humorous interactions are being properly recognised, understood and appreciated or not. By contrast, in internet interactions, this feedback is greatly delayed (particularly in

[3] It was suggested in Yus (2014) that users show greater interest in the cognitive satisfaction that engaging in and through these apps or sites provides, regardless of the existing options for contextualisation. In other words, this cognitive satisfaction does not depend upon the purely informational relevance (*maximal relevance*) favoured by the qualities of the interface, but focuses instead on cognitively rewarding non-propositional qualities such as emotions, feelings, sensations, and even aesthetic effects that are triggered by propositional content (*optimal relevance*).

asynchronous communications) and sometimes never provided at all, with obvious negative consequences for the successful outcome of the humorous intention.

Furthermore, one of the major negative constraints reported in Yus (2017) concerns the management of long lists of contacts who demand equal attention from the user. Although messaging apps treat all contacts on an equal basis, to the user some interactions and interlocutors are more important than others, in the same way as a user may have greater expectations of accomplishing their humorous intentions with some contacts (with whom they share more information, for example) than with others. The interface should consequently make it possible for the user to prioritise certain contacts and the associated variable intensity of interactions.

Once again, the above-mentioned interface limitations do not discourage users of messaging apps from utilising them or from typing plain text instead of engaging in more clearly contextualised phone/video calls. In short, users have found in these apps a convenient solution to meet their interactive needs and to accomplish their humorous intentions (Dolev-Cohen and Barak 2013, 59). It also offers options for the exchange of humorous multimedia discourses and in-group humour-centred interaction, by trading images and videos as an additional phatic strategy, their role being that of foundations which can foster and underpin humorous effects (Lo and Leun 2009, 163; Ogara et al. 2014; Cui 2016, 21).

Moreover, it should be noted that a specific interface-related constraint may eventually prove positive to some users while discouraging and ending up negative to others, depending on a specific user's command, familiarity with the interface and personal issues that software companies can only partly predict (these would constitute *user-related contextual constraints*, see below). An example cited in Yus (2021) is interface personalisation, which in theory should generate an offset of positive non-propositional effects on how a user feels that they are treated as a unique individual whose specific preferences and usage patterns are catered for by the app. Users may like to feel part of the group, network or community, but they also enjoy "standing out from the crowd" and feeling unique when experiencing the app. Needless to say, some users will be overwhelmed by the wide range of options for personalisation, ultimately deriving negative effects through lack of control over these interface options.

2.2 *Interface-Related Contextual Constraints on Social Networking Sites*

A social networking site profile provides users with different affordances that restrict or enhance the kinds of discourses that may be used therein, ranging from text to images, videos, etc., which becomes crucial for the humorous strategies implemented on such sites. These profiles have evolved to a large extent, with companies incorporating features from rival sites for the purpose of offering the richest possible environment to upload information, engage in dialogues and exchange feedback (see Yus 2021, ch. 12). In the context of this book, the aim sought by profile designers consists in making those profiles as user-friendly as possible, so that humorous strategies can be devised and successfully conveyed, designers expecting to provide an effortless experience while handling their desktop versions and parallel smartphone apps. As stressed by Reid (2018, 185) in relation to apps, engaging with our smartphone, regardless of why we do so, leads us to allocate a fraction of our information processing ability towards the device and away from our immediate surroundings. The level of attention expended by our cognitive resources depends on how we use our smartphone; a social utilisation (e.g. scrolling through Instagram photos) is less taxing than other tasks (e.g. reading or composing text), which demand more from our cognitive reserves.

What matters most from the (cyber)pragmatics point of view is whether users' interactions are favoured or limited depending on social networking site design. Similarly, van Dijck (2013) highlighted the implications of platform design when she remarked that platforms act as mediators rather than intermediaries. These design constraints become crucial in smartphone apps, where users show less willingness to expend effort in managing their social networks on small screens. Desktop profiles and their smartphone counterparts are generally similar; however, some features inevitably need to be discarded or rearranged from the main desktop interface to the smartphone app in order to reduce the number of items displayed on the screen and make app management more user-friendly. What kind of humorous strategy is chosen, through which kind of discourse and embedded in which kind of social networking environment will depend on these interface affordances.

3 User-Related Contextual Constraints on Internet Humour

Several user-related constraints exist in humorous internet-mediated communication that have to do with the actual use of the interface. Other constraints such as the sex, race and age of interlocutors constrain humorous communication both online and offline. Some of these constraints will be addressed in the next Sections.

3.1 User-Related Contextual Constraints on Interface Use and Management

Yus (2017) stated that users may positively or negatively influence both the production of content and the outcome of an internet-mediated act of communication, a claim that holds true for humorous interactions on messaging apps and social networking sites too. Somewhere between the interface and the user we can find constraints regarding the management of the interface by particular individuals. For example, the task at hand while using an app may constrain the quality and quantity of the interactions carried out therein, as well as the amount of information, and the use of other complementing discourses such as emojis, for instance. Equally in-between the interface and the user lies the user's familiarity with an interface and their command for internet-mediated interactions, as already mentioned above. Although an objective interface usability may be established for the app or site at hand, the user's familiarity or command (or lack thereof) will most probably enhance or decrease the feeling of interface usability, thus variations in this interface-related constraint are produced due to each user's specificity (Ogara et al. 2014, 458). Yus (2011a, 65–66) pointed out in this respect that "the user's familiarity with the interface, even if it is not user-friendly, and also the user's intuitive ability to interact with the interface also affect the balance of cognitive effects and mental effort involved in processing information from this interface, generating multiple outcomes of (in)efficient interpretations. And frequency of use is a parallel variable affecting relevance."

Furthermore, an aspect that covers both interface and user constraints when holding a humorous intention online is the devised environment for interactions (*interface constraint*) that correlates with content uploaded there (*user constraint*). For example, Vandergriff (2010, 242) exemplified this with chat rooms:

> one needs to distinguish between publicly available chat rooms (i.e., non-institutionalized), in which participants communicate primarily for recreational purposes, and institutionalized (moderated or unmoderated) chats, since the contextual variables may play an important role in how adjacency pairs get disrupted and what types of humor and play are perceived as appropriate. Examples of differences between public chat rooms and institutionalized chat rooms include the organization of the chat by the teacher or moderator, joint tasks or goals, previously determined themes, fluctuation and number of participants, and familiarity of participants.

Personality (and related terms such as *self-esteem*, *self-concept* and *self-identity*) stands out as one of the user-centred constraints, together with associated feelings (e.g. joy, loneliness, depression), which impact on the quantity of messages sent through messaging apps and social networking sites, the frequency of these messages and their content (Michikyan et al. 2014, 180), including humorous messages. Indeed, several aspects of the user's identity are likely to impact the text typed and the non-propositional effects generated. For example, although shyness inhibits users from social activity in physical scenarios, these users may find in virtual interactions such as messaging apps the channel to express themselves without the burden of physical co-presence (Lo and Leun 2009, 164; Shen et al. 2015, 32; Marriott and Buchanan 2014, 171). Messaging apps and social networking sites can provide protection from some of the negative effects of self-preoccupation through the elimination of physical cues. It would therefore make sense for shy individuals to use such interfaces for their interactional needs, among them humour-centred ones (Bardi and Brady 2010, 1722).

What kind of humour is shared online and what outcome the humorous intention produces likewise depends on the relationship between interlocutors and the associated amount of mutuality of information that both interlocutors can rely on for these humorous purposes. This prediction of mutuality tends to be absent in humorous discourses shared with large audiences, characterised by heterogeneity and unpredictability as to how they will react to the humorous discourse. In today's scenario of *context collapse* (boyd 2011; Marwick and boyd 2011), users face a very heterogeneous audience on their social networking sites (close friends, acquaintances, former students, relatives and so on), who may react to the humorous discourse in radically different ways. This is particularly the case of numerous contemporary internet jokes (including memes) whose humorous effects rely on a very specific newsworthy event that needs to be shared by all the users involved so that a successful humorous outcome can be obtained (Tsakona 2020, 170). Even though positive effects are likely to derive from this awareness of mutuality, negative effects may also be triggered in those unable to find the point of the humorous discourse and acknowledge this lack of mutuality. Such in-group (i.e. *bonding*) vs. out-group identification (i.e. *bounding*) through humour often becomes strategic when it comes to determining group membership (Phillips and Milner 2017, 92).

Fiadotava (2020, 106) points in a similar direction when she remarks that

> creators and sharers of digital humour have to account for multiple factors and employ a certain form of self-censorship while seeking to provoke a desired reaction. When sharing humour digitally with one's family members, however, people have a much better understanding of their audience and the forms and topics of humour that can be relevant to them. This implicit knowledge can to some extent compensate for the lack of both immediate conversational context and the nonverbal features found in an oral performance.

She also comments on how digital sharing of humour acquires more prominence between partners or spouses than with acquaintances (once more, due to these predictions about mutuality of information). Similarly, sharing humour within a generation is more popular than sharing it across generations. Regarding online-offline correlations, this scholar concludes that "digital sharing is not a means to fill in the gaps that exist in the offline interaction, but rather an alternative and complementary way to reinforce relationships that are also regularly maintained in an offline form (cf. with text messaging during the previous decades)."

Finally, one additional constraint on interface use stems from the culture to which users belong and where they carry out their interactions, with parallel effects on what kind of humour is shared on these interfaces, with whom and how often (Tsakona 2020, 171; Adeloti and Filani 2016, 276). Although global trends of interface use exist, for instance in the way emoji clarifies messages and adds propositional attitudes or emotional load, some cultures constrain the quality and quantity of information exchanged on a site or an app. In fact, many of these exchanges exhibit a phatic quality, and several studies have evidenced the mediation of cultural background in the use of such small talk. Thus, Jaworski (2000) provides many examples to support the claim that different communities apply different degrees of phatic interaction in the same kind of event; and Rygg (2016) exemplifies culture-mediated phatic communication with specific cases. It would seem reasonable to conclude that phatic interactions through interfaces are similarly constrained by cultural factors.

3.2 "Inherited" User Attributes as Constraints on Humorous Internet Communication

In Yus (2015b), a triangle-shaped picture of the discursive management of offline vs. online identity was proposed. After schematising offline sources of identity as an inverted triangle where the broad section at the top represented "inherited" sources such as nationality, sex, and race/ethnicity, a section in the middle of the triangle portrayed "optional" identity sources, mainly associated with social groups to which the individual chooses to belong (often with group-specific jargons). Finally, a very narrow section at the bottom of the inverted triangle represented the human self, linked to unique discursive features (idiolect), which develop and take shape by means of everyday face-to-face interactions.

As far as internet-centred sources of identity are concerned, Yus (ibid.) claimed that the above-mentioned triangle becomes *re-inverted* in online environments. First, the formerly broad section of inherited attributes at the top appears to narrow because of virtual communication and the depersonalisation of networked interactions. Hence, inherited attributes, so obvious in face-to-face encounters, may become blurred and their identity-shaping effect be weakened or invalidated. Such inherited features as race and sex are additionally suppressed or at least minimised in text-based interactions. Second, the middle section of optional discursive sources of identity, normally channelled by self-socialisation through interactions within groups shaped by specific linguistic patterns, remains more or less in the same medium-sized section of the triangle. On the Internet, these specific discourse groups with their limited-access jargons reproduce in parallel forms of organisation: the so-called discussion forums, messaging groups and social media groups, alongside distribution lists via e-mail, which also exploit the same sense of group-membership language specificity that we can find in real-life social instances. Third, the previously narrow vertex of personal self in the inverted triangle now broadens to a great extent due to the multiplicity of selves (often anonymous, too) that can be used in conversational exchanges thanks to various forms of internet communication such as chats or avatars in 3D virtual worlds.

As opposed to the physical world, where the body provides explicit (and stable) clues of inherited and personal qualities shaping the person's identity, on the internet these attributes are not explicitly conveyed, and users portray as many electronic identities and selves as they are willing and/or able to create, all of which frequently presented with no corporeality. As Mitchell (1995) rightly states regarding the initial stage of internet interactions, the process of mutual construction of identities on the internet usually gives very little away. Because communication often takes place without bodily presence or the sound of users' voices, others who "know" a user quite well may not realise how he or she looks, and thus may be unable to make their usual inferences. And even more importantly, on the internet people can also very easily conceal or mask ambiguous information, or falsely signal gender, race, age, body shape, and economic status.

More recent research (Yus 2007, 2010, 2011a) acknowledges that this idea of discursive sources of identity as triangles (inverted for physical identity; re-inverted for virtual identity) clashes not only with today's tendency to hybridise personal networks in physical and virtual settings, but also with today's picture of users shaped up as a node of intersecting online-offline networks, as well as with an increasing presumption of online/offline identity congruence (especially on social networking sites). Therefore, rather than a picture of 'either' physical 'or' virtual sources of identity, as can be deduced from those two triangles that do not touch, we should now view a picture of several sources of identity which undergo a process of mixture, hybridisation and imbrication at a time when the dividing line between physical and virtual realms has become increasingly blurred.

These "inherited" sources of identity -such as sex and race- permeate humour mainly through lingering stereotypes, often conveying a negative, unfair or derogatory picture of the individuals who fit these inherited qualities. It is at this point that they become user-centred contextual constraints on (in)effective humorous online communication. On the sender user's side, the medium provides a safe ground to disseminate such unfair stereotypes due, among other reasons, to the lack of physical co-presence in humour production. On the addressee user's side, because of the aforementioned "context collapse," the audience may comprise multiple kinds of users, some of whom will find these stereotype-connoted jokes funny, while others will be utterly disgusted by the portrayal of these unfair stereotypes, thus provoking a failure in the sender user's humorous goals.

The pervasiveness and spread of stereotypes through humorous communication has been conceptualised in previous research through the interface between *private representations* and *metarepresented cultural representations* (see Yus 2001, 2002, 2004, 2005b, 2016a). In a nutshell, individuals store prototypical information about their culture and community. Added to the personal storage of representations of the kind "I conceptualize X as *p*" or "I believe that *p*" (private representations), in this case the individual acknowledges that certain information is typically cultural, stored as "in this culture, X is conceptualised as *p*" or "in this culture, it is believed that *p*." Personal and cultural representations may overlap to a greater or lesser extent, which entails that some cultural stereotypes will probably become part of the individual's private representations too, while other stereotypes will be rejected by that same individual. In any case, though, the existence of metarepresented cultural representations is acknowledged; or expressed differently, people can very often identify underlying social stereotypes in everyday interactions despite not personally supporting those stereotypes on a personal basis. Pilkington (2000, 112f) offered the following example:

(1) Richard is a gorilla.
(2) a. Gorillas are fierce, nasty, prone to violence.
b. Gorillas are shy, sensitive creatures, given to bouts of sentimentality.

This metaphor relies on cultural stereotypes regarding the gorilla's behaviour in (2a) which are subsequently metaphorically mapped onto Richard's own attributes. However, an ethologist might as well have reached a different conclusion intuitively, after a direct observation of gorillas, for instance (2b). Even so, the ethologist will still understand (2a) when being told (1). The explanation for this dual-access, parallel view about the behaviour of gorillas lies in the aforementioned double mental storage, direct and factual in (2b), that is, directly grasped from observation and becoming incorporated to the person's private representations; and metarepresentationally stored following a schema such as "in this culture/society it is believed that *p*" in (2a). Cultural stereotypes like the qualities in (2a) are normally salient to a whole community, becoming what we usually call *collective representations* attributed to an entire social group and need not be erased when an individual privately constructs parallel but differing beliefs about the same referent.

This duality of private vs. metarepresented cultural mental representations was initially proposed for the specific context of stand-up comedy monologues, where the audience arrives at the venue with their own set of private mental representations plus parallel metarepresentationally acquired cultural representations. The private/cultural interface plays an important role when explaining why certain monologues arouse laughter in the audience and others fail to do so. Arguably, one of the main sources of humour in stand-up comedy monologues is, precisely, the audience's realisation that many thought-to-be privately stored representations (about the world, society, lifestyle, etc.), are actually collective cultural representations shared by a high number of audience members. Laughter constitutes the most evident signal of mutual cultural awareness in stand-up comedy, providing a direct insight into the cultural quality of their representations. This re-shaping of the audience's attitude towards representations spreads in a virus-like way across the venue, bringing out the collective imaginary in each individual.

Similarly, if a user posts or shares any of the sexist memes collected in Fig. 4.1, they will trigger an array of (non-)humorous reactions depending

Fig. 4.1 Sexist memes

on the audience's specific private and metarepresented cultural beliefs, a clear constraint on the eventual success of the user's humorous intention. An excessive overlap between these types of beliefs will cause humorous effects to stem from user's sex role-centred beliefs being strengthened by these memes, thus making it possible to enjoy such humour. Woodzicka et al. (2020, 220) correctly remarked in this sense that both men and women who have sexist attitudes are particularly likely to be amused rather than offended by sexist humour. By contrast, other users with little or no overlap between these private/collective beliefs on sex roles will feel utterly disgusted by these memes, no humorous effects deriving from them. Furthermore, some people may not exhibit this overlap but still find some of these memes amusing because of the cunning way in which they are constructed. In any case, the stereotype will spread and linger on even if the user does not hold similar sexist beliefs on sex roles, since the audience can simultaneously hold private and metarepresented cultural beliefs about sex roles, as already remarked.

One of these social stereotypes in humour, namely *sex roles*, will be briefly addressed in the next Section, additionally paying some attention to how this stereotype, frequently used in humour, is transferred and enacted in internet environments, and ascertaining whether it is also successfully contested online. As suggested above, we treat such stereotypes as a user-centred constraint in this book, since they determine the kind and amount of information (and how much) is provided online (on the sender user's side) along with the positive-negative reactions that it provokes in the single or multiple audiences that interpret such sex role stereotype-connoted humorous discourses (on the addressee user's side).

3.2.1 *User-Related Constraints on Internet Humour: The Case of Sex Roles*

As highlighted in Yus (2002), a huge amount of bibliography has dealt with sex-role stereotypes and their possible qualities and sources. These mainly refer to general men-women roles in society, and also to linguistic stereotypes associated with the way men and women typically speak.

Sex roles are acquired via different validating contexts, including the authority underlying parents' language, which is later complemented with the values acquired at school and through different mass media discourses such as literature, film, television, magazines or advertising. Most importantly for this book, validation equally stems from certain users on internet sites and social media, more precisely celebrities and influencers with whom a wide audience may form parasocial relationships that strongly influence their beliefs on sex roles.

These media have usually emphasised the traditional male and female roles in society, and overrate the importance of physical appearance over personality in women's lives. Furthermore, there are linguistic stereotypes concerning both sexes, such: (a) women use linguistic markers of politeness more often, (b) women use less unacceptable language (swearwords, taboo words...); (c) women have a cooperative attitude in their conversations; (d) women speak a lot (e.g. the stereotype of women's tendency to gossiping); and (e) there are female-specific conversational topics.

Reasons of space prevent us from thoroughly discussing all the aspects related to the enduring quality of sex-role cultural beliefs. What interests us here is, basically, the existence of several sources of mental representations about these sex roles: private representations and, fitting or contradicting these representations, parallel metarepresented cultural representations. As illustrated in (3), from an English alternative comic (Yus 2002), private beliefs acquired through an authoritative source (parents in this case) provides no guarantee that metarepresented cultural beliefs will disappear from the person's mental background knowledge:

(3) [A father -C- and a mother -A- talk to their son -B-]
A: Tarquin, go and help Malcolm tidy the house up... and the tea needs cooking and the washing doing... I'm going to my study to meditate...
B: Aren't you going to help us?
A: Oh Tarquin! You know we don't enforce sexual stereotypes in this house... It would be sexist for me to do any housework.
C: She's right, Tarquin! Men have been oppressing women for centuries and are responsible for all the world's evil, so it's only fair that we should make up for it now.
B: Housework's for girls... I want to go and play war. ("The Modern Parents", *Viz* 60 [June 1993], p. 20).

Humorous discourses that focus on sex roles generally tend to portray and consider men and women according to their deep-rooted, archetypical roles in society, thus fostering the spread of these stereotypes, despite them being overtly contested.[4] Whether they are humorously appreciated or not thus depends on the extent to which each person's private beliefs regarding sex roles overlap with their metarepresented cultural beliefs on these roles, as already stated. Stereotypes listed in the bibliography available include aggressive men vs. passive women (Niketic 2019), competitive, patient and critical men vs. cooperative, impatient and supportive women (Alam 2021), and emotionally inexpressive, independent, agentic and goal-oriented men vs. women as sexual objects, judged on physical look, dependent on others, talkative, emotionally expressive and gold diggers (Cendra et al. 2019). Some sex role stereotypes refer to humour appreciation too, once again focusing on the depth and extent of the constraints that affect the eventual quality of the humorous intention (see Ryan and Kanjorski 1998, 745; Hay 1995, 30; Lemish and Reznik 2008, 117).

Concerning sex roles as person-centred contextual constraints, they influence any communicative instance that involves an exchange of humorous discourses, including internet-mediated ones. Indeed, in such humorous communicative situations, the speaker has to predict and bear in mind the addressee's reaction to these sex role-connoted jokes, for example the addressee's sex, the kind of relationship between the interactants, or the interlocutors' personal beliefs (see Lampert 2014, 260; Gray and Ford 2013, 278). As Parrott and Hopp (2020, 117) remark specifically in relation to sexist humour, its communication involves a number of cues beyond the joke's actual content, such as whether a man or a woman is telling the joke and how audience members respond to the intended humorous effects (e.g. laughter, condemnation)" (see Crawford 2003, 1422–1423).

Moreover, constraints stem from both the sender and the recipient of a humorous discourse. For example, Martin (2014, 124–125) listed a

[4] Billig (2005) proposed an interesting distinction between types of humour related to this idea: *disciplinary* and *rebellious*. In a nutshell, disciplinary humour is intended to mock those placed outside well-established social norms. By contrast, rebellious humour targets and contests established rules and conventions. However, and crucially, Billig (ibid.) also suggests caution in this apparently clear-cut distinction, since even humour that at first appears rebellious may actually serve to reinforce dominant social norms. This has to do with the notion put forward above that even if the addressee rejects the sex-role stereotype depicted in the joke and, for instance, critically tells others about that unfortunate joke, they may still be aware of their existence and unconsciously engage in the spread and reinforcement of these stereotypes.

number of these sender-receiver constraints which affect the humorous outcome. Firstly, individuals may exhibit not only differences in their ability to perceive the intended incongruity during the development of the joke but also difficulties in properly producing humorous jokes and stories. Secondly, sense of humour influences the extent to which one enjoys particular types of humour and certain themes such as sexuality or aggression. Thirdly, Martin (ibid.) mentions differences in temperament ("the degree to which one is generally cheerful and playful, taking a non-serious perspective on situations") concerning habitual humorous communication patterns. Finally, individuals are likewise said to differ in their style of humour: "whether they use it in an affiliative manner to enhance relationships, as a means of coping with stress, in an aggressive manner to diminish others, or in an ingratiating manner to amuse others at their own expense."

An illustrative example of how the sex of the speaker/addressee(s) acts as a contextual constraint is provided by sexist humour, defined as "a form of disparagement humor, communication in which one person or group (the disparager) insults another person or group (the target) on the basis of characteristics that are often key to our social identity, including race, age, intelligence, weight, and sex" (Parrott and Hopp 2020, 116). Since underlying such humour there are sexist beliefs about the inferiority of women, portraying them as stupid, illogical, ignorant, or irresponsible, and with a tendency to build on their sexual objectification as women (Bergman 1986). It is in this kind of sex role-connoted humour that we can find the most striking differences in (un)successful humorous effects according to the sex of the speaker and that of their audience. Men are thus commonly believed to enjoy this kind of humour more than women, as is also the case regarding sexual humour (Mundorf et al. 1988, 231; Martin 2014, 124; Woodzicka et al. 2020, 220).

It additionally deserves underlining that the impact of sex role-centred humorous discourses on the audience's pre-existing beliefs concerning these roles is influenced by what may generically be labelled as *minimising effect* of humorous communication in general and of special contexts of humorous production/reception in particular, such as online environments. Summing up, when sexist attitudes and beliefs are embedded in a humorous frame, its impact tends to be diluted or minimised, and the speakers of these jokes have the chance "to distance themselves from potentially offensive content, and to evade complaints of uncivility from its targets" (Greenwood and Gautam 2020, 266). The same applies to sex role-connoted discourses online. Nasreen (2021, 152) argued that "the laughability and unserious nature of jokes make them more 'likeable' than to be rejected: when many people 'like' masculine jokes, reiterating patriarchal ideology instead of gender equality in the household, it further embeds existing societal perceptions of gender relations and makes confronting that ideology even harder." Another example is the so-called *RoastMe humour*[5] on Reddit, which is potentially harmful to female users but instead received with amusement and regarded as innocuous across male-female audiences (see Chap. 6): "RoastMe centres on trading creative jocular insults hurled at individuals who have willingly submitted their pictures for (good-willed) roasting, a type of humorous activity performed for its own sake. When targeted at women, RoastMe insults (…) may rely on several forms of sexualisation, which humorously and playfully echo (but do not necessarily endorse) prevalent sexist ideologies" (Poppi and Dynel 2021, 432; see also Dynel 2019).

Focusing now on internet humour linked to sex role stereotypes, the internet supposedly provides an interesting venue to contest entrenched beliefs about sex roles as portrayed in many existing offline jokes. This is so thanks to the possibly to reach millions of users via social media and messaging apps, which would allow for the achievement of relevance by contradicting and erasing existing stereotypical (and unfair) beliefs. In any case, it should be noted that user-centred contextual constraints multiply due to the very nature of virtual interactions. On the one hand, anonymity may prevent certain users from limiting the amount of sexist humour that they circulate online; and on the other hand, the above-mentioned *context collapse* makes users harbour doubts about who is going to read their sex role-connoted jokes or what their reaction could be.

According to the research available on internet-mediated humour concerning sex-role stereotypes, there is ample agreement that these unfair stereotypes are also pervasive and spread by means of internet humour (see Drakett et al. 2018, 119–120; Alam 2021, 16; Shifman and Lemish

[5] "RoastMe is conceptualised as an online humorous activity which, similar to the traditional roast (including the celebrity roast genre), is centred on ritual insults addressed to the target who has agreed to be roasted for the sake of humour. RoastMe is enclosed within a humorous frame (regardless of whether or not insults are truthful, i.e. communicate roasters' true beliefs) and thrives on its community members' unbounded creativity. Roasting comments can also be seen as mock impoliteness, constituting utterances that display overtly pretended face-threat, while being oriented towards amusement and solidarity-building among anonymous users" (Dynel 2019, 1).

2010, 2011), despite being sometimes wrapped up in different or innovative digital formats (Shifman and Lemish 2012, 91). This holds true for every type of internet humour proposed in Chap. 3: *replicated*,[6] *spontaneous* and *hybrid*.

As contended by Al-Rawi et al. (2021, 139), "social media spaces are public and an anonymous paradigm, and this hyper-masculine presence often results in gender stereotyping which is consistent with biased gender representation seen in other media like advertisements or television." For instance, Gbadegesin (2019) identified several female stereotypes rooted in the memes under analysis. One of them is "woman as dependent." Under the widespread, hegemonic masculinity, dependency is linked to females and meme creators reproduce the sex-biased ideology by associating this attribute with females, thereby building the "dependent other" identity for them. Examples include (4), a meme accompanied by an image of a black man with glasses and a cap:

(4) **FACTS** Help a woman when she is in trouble and she will remember you when she is in trouble again.

This meme includes strategic uses of language to stereotypically portray women as dependent. There is a salient use of capitalisation in the word "facts" that reinforces the information provided by the meme. Furthermore, the use of "a" in "a woman" entails strategic generalisation (i.e. it applies to any woman). The repetition of "she" provides supplementary emphasis, and the opposition between "help" and "trouble" parallels the we-versus-them ideology, the latter being in constant need of help. Besides, the incongruity generated in "remember when she is in trouble again" allows the meme creator to present the woman as ungrateful and opportunistic.

Nasreen (2021, 150) refers to the prevalence of sex role stereotypes on the internet as well. Although technological developments have transformed the way in which people share jokes, and new forms have emerged, such as internet memes (see Chap. 7), the Net has always been a favourable setting for sexist and racist jokes, fostered by anonymity. Today, the

[6] An example of sex-role stereotypes found in replicated internet humour is the *pastiche*: "the re-use of elements borrowed from popular culture in new contexts… while potentially the vernacular can combine elements from popular culture in order to challenge mainstream discourse, in the case of internet humor about gender, the pastiche is employed commonly to reiterate entrenched beliefs and mass mediated stereotypes" (Shifman and Lemish 2011, 268).

rise of social media has created an environment of online-offline congruence (Yus 2021), and yet users continue to be openly willing to make sexist jokes as part of a process of normalisation and acceptance of sexism online much more widely than offline. Indeed, "while challenging sexism where it occurs is usually an effective way of fighting it, it is not so effective online, as the feelings of fear, anger, shame, shock or panic that the 'real-life' experience of sexism generates may differ greatly online, largely due to the fact that in digital space, anonymity of the perpetrator and the victim is almost impossible" (Nasreen 2021, 152).

However, despite this tendency to standardise the reproduction of these discourses, there is room on the internet to contest unfair sex role stereotypes (Brantner et al. 2020, 688): "Social media sites provide a platform for the production and distribution of humor and offer an opportunity to question power dynamics by disrupting traditional, well-established stereotypes, thereby exposing gendered power structures" (Lawrence and Ringrose 2018, 214). And along these lines of counter-stereotype online action, the trend of (post-)feminist humour deserves a special mention, since it has attempted to achieve relevant effects via contradicting and possibly erasing offline stereotypes, with greater or lesser success. Gallivan (1992, 373) characterised feminist humour as that which reveals and ridicules the absurdity of gender stereotypes and inequalities.

In turn, Sundén and Paasonen (2021, 224) remarked that under what looks like a surface of ubiquitous online sexism, a growing number of social media initiatives exist which produce spaces for what Rentschler and Thrift (2015) label as *networked laughter*, connoted with feminist critique and political agency. These networked feminisms emerge as reactions against sexism and harness strategies such as irony, parody, mockery and ridicule to counter typically sexist humorous strategies (e.g. unsolicited dick pics and slut-shaming), combined with strong associated feelings, especially anger, but also frustration and outrage.

Sometimes, feminism uses the very same discourses that patriarchal trends have adopted in sexist humour online. Take, for instance, the cliché of women's obsession with body shape and looks, replicated in online discourses (selfies, social media, parasocial relationships with influencers, etc.) from similar offline discourses (press, TV, films). An example is the campaign #distractinlysexy mentioned in Brantner et al. (2020) as part of the so-called *hashtag feminism*, with photographic self-representations and selfies that tend to be stigmatised as narcissistic expressions of naive girls, but which actually serve to empower women and to debunk gender stereotypes.

4 Concluding Remarks

All humorous interactions on the internet are influenced by contextual constraints. Interface-related constraints favour or limit the quantity and quality of the interactions carried out through certain interfaces (messaging app, social networking site, etc.). When attempting humorous effects, the interface may make it harder for the audience to contextualise the discourse in the expected way so as to derive these humorous effects.

Similarly, humorous communication online also depends on a number of user-centred constraints, some more stable (nationality, sex, ethnic origin…) and some more temporary (user's mood, task at hand, command of the interface, relationship held between the interlocutors…). In this chapter some emphasis has been laid upon one of these constraints and its impact on humorous outcomes: sex role stereotypes and their maintenance or resistance online.

References

Adams, Audrey. 2012. Humor Markers in Computer-Mediated Communication. MA Thesis. Texas A&M University-Commerce.

Adeloti, Oluwatomi, and Ibukun Filani. 2016. Contextual Beliefs and Pragmatic Strategies in Online Humour: An Example of Akpos Jokes. In *Analyzing Language and Humor in Online Communication*, ed. Rotimi Taiwo, Akinola Odebunmi, and Akin Adetunji, 274–291. Hershey: Information Science Reference. https://doi.org/10.4018/978-1-5225-0338-5.ch015.

Alam, Mahbubul. 2021. 'Know Girl, Know Pain; No Girl, No Pain': Portraying Woman as Stereotyped Entity in the Humorous Posts of Facebook. *Journal of Research in Humanities and Social Science* 9 (4): 11–17.

Al-Rawi, Ahmed, Maliha Siddiqi, Xiaosu Li, Nimisha Vandan, and Karen Grepin. 2021. A Thematic Analysis of Instagram's Gendered Memes on COVID-19. *Journal of Visual Communication in Medicine* 44 (4): 137–150. https://doi.org/10.1080/17453054.2021.1941808.

Bardi, C. Albert, and Michael F. Brady. 2010. Why Shy People Use Instant Messaging: Loneliness and Other Motives. *Computers in Human Behavior* 26: 1722–1726. https://doi.org/10.1016/j.chb.2010.06.021.

Bergman, Memo. 1986. How Many Feminists Does It Take to Make a Joke? Sexist Humor and What's Wrong with it. *Hypatia* 1 (1): 63–82. https://doi.org/10.1111/j.1527-2001.1986.tb00522.x.

Billig, Michael. 2005. *Laughter and Ridicule. Towards a Social Critique of Humour*. Thousand Oaks: Sage.

boyd, danah. 2011. Social Network Sites as Networked Publics: Affordances, Dynamics and Implications. In *A Networked Self: Identity, Community, and Culture on Social Network Sites*, ed. Zizi Papacharissi, 39–58. Abingdon: Routledge.

Brantner, Cornelia, Katharina Lobinger, and Miriam Stehling. 2020. Memes against Sexism? A Multi-Method Analysis of the Feminist Protest Hashtag #Distractinglysexy and its Resonance in the Mainstream News Media. *Convergence*26(3):674–696.https://doi.org/10.1177/1354856519827804.

Cendra, Anastasia Nelladia, Teresia Dian Triutami, and Barli Bram. 2019. Gender Stereotypes Depicted in Online Sexist Jokes. *European Journal of Humour Research* 7 (2): 44–66. https://doi.org/10.7592/EJHR2019.7.2.cendra.

Crawford, Mary. 2003. Gender and Humor in Social Context. *Journal of Pragmatics* 35: 1413–1430. https://doi.org/10.1016/S0378-2166(02)00183-2.

Cui, Di. 2016. Beyond "Connected Presence": Multimedia Mobile Instant Messaging in Close Relationship Management. *Mobile Media & Communication* 4 (1): 19–36. https://doi.org/10.1177/2050157915583925.

Dolev-Cohen, Michal, and Azy Barak. 2013. Adolescents' Use of Instant Messaging as a Means of Emotional Relief. *Computers in Human Behavior* 29: 58–63. https://doi.org/10.1016/j.chb.2012.07.016.

Drakett, Jessica, Bridgette Rickett, Katy Day, and Kate Milnes. 2018. Old jokes, New Media –Online Sexism and Constructions of Gender in Internet Memes. *Feminism & Psychology* 28 (1): 109–127. https://doi.org/10.1177/0959353517727560.

Dynel, Marta. 2019. Risum Teneatis, Amici?: The Socio-Pragmatics of RoastMe Humour. *Journal of Pragmatics* 139: 1–21. https://doi.org/10.1016/j.pragma.2018.10.010.

Dynel, Marta, and Jan Chovanec. 2021. Creating and Sharing Public Humour across Traditional and New Media. *Journal of Pragmatics* 177: 151–156. https://doi.org/10.1016/j.pragma.2021.02.020.

Fiadotava, Anastasiya. 2020. Sharing Humour Digitally in Family Communication. *European Journal of Humour Research* 8 (1): 95–111. https://doi.org/10.7592/EJHR2020.8.1.fiadotava.

Gallivan, Joanne. 1992. Group Differences in Appreciation of Feminist Humor. *Humor* 5: 369–374. https://doi.org/10.1515/humr.1992.5.4.369.

Gbadegesin, Victoria O. 2019. Gender Ideology and Identity in Humorous Social Media Memes. *Digital Scholarship in the Humanities* 35 (3): 529–546. https://doi.org/10.1093/llc/fqz039.

Gray, Jared Alan, and Thomas E. Ford. 2013. The Role of Social Context in the Interpretation of Sexist Humor. *Humor* 26 (2): 277–293. https://doi.org/10.1515/humor-2013-0017.

Greenwood, Dara, and Richa Gautam. 2020. What's in a Tweet? Gender and Sexism Moderate Reactions to Antifat Sexist Humor on Twitter. *Humor* 33 (2): 265–290. https://doi.org/10.1515/humor-2019-0026.

Hay, Jennifer. 1995. Gender and Humour Beyond a Joke. MA Thesis. Victoria University of Wellington.

Jaworski, Adam. 2000. Silence and Small Talk. In *Small Talk*, ed. Justine Coupland, 110–132. Harlow: Longman.

Kotthoff, Helga. 2006. Gender and Humor: The State of the Art. *Journal of Pragmatics* 38: 4–25. https://doi.org/10.1016/j.pragma.2005.06.003.

Lampert, Martin Daniel. 2014. Psychological Aspects of Gender and Humor. In *Encyclopedia of Humor Studies*, ed. Salvatore Attardo, 259–261. Thousand Oaks: Sage.

Lawrence, Emilie, and Jessica Ringrose. 2018. @NoToFeminism, #FeministsAreUgly, and Misandry Memes: How Social Media Feminist Humor is Calling out Antifeminism. In *Emergent Feminisms: Complicating a Postfeminist Media Culture*, ed. Jessalynn Keller and Maureen E. Ryan, 211–232. Abingdon: Routledge.

Lemish, Dafna, and Shiri Reznik. 2008. To Laugh or Not to Laugh? Performing Girlhood through Humor. *Girlhood Studies* 1 (1): 114–137. https://doi.org/10.3167/ghs.2008.010107.

Lo, Olivine Wai-Yu, and Louis Leun. 2009. Effects of Gratification-Opportunities and Gratifications-Obtained on Preferences of Instant Messaging and E-mail among College Students. *Telematics and Informatics* 26: 156–166. https://doi.org/10.1016/j.tele.2008.06.001.

Marriott, Tamsin, and Tom Buchanan. 2014. The True Self Online: Personality Correlates of Preference for Self-Expression Online, and Observer Ratings of Personality Online and Offline. *Computers in Human Behavior* 32: 171–177. https://doi.org/10.1016/j.chb.2013.11.014.

Martin, Rod A. 2014. Humor and Gender: An Overview of Psychological Research. In *Gender and Humor. Interdisciplinary and International Perspectives*, ed. Delia Chiaro and Raffaella Baccolini, 123–146. Abingdon: Routledge.

Marwick, Alice, and danah boyd. 2011. I Tweet Honestly, I Tweet Passionately: Twitter Users, Context Collapse, and the Imagined Audience. *New Media & Society* 13 (1): 114–133. https://doi.org/10.1177/1461444810365313.

Michikyan, Minas, Kaveri Subrahmanyam, and Jessica Dennis. 2014. Can You Tell Who I Am? Neuroticism, Extraversion, and Online Self-Presentation among Young Adults. *Computers in Human Behavior* 33: 179–183. https://doi.org/10.1016/j.chb.2014.01.010.

Mitchell, William J. 1995. *City of Bits*. Cambridge, MA: The MIT Press.

Mundorf, Norbert, Azra Bhatia, Dolf Zillmann, Paul Lester, and Susan Robertson. 1988. Gender Differences in Humor Appreciation. *Humor* 1 (3): 231–243. https://doi.org/10.1515/humr.1988.1.3.231.

Nasreen, Zobaida. 2021. 'Have You Not Got a Sense of Humour?': Unpacking Masculinity Through Online Sexist Jokes During the COVID-19 Pandemic. *Society and Culture in South Asia* 7 (1): 148–154. https://doi.org/10.1177/2393861720977632.

Niketic, Predrag. 2019. Social Harm(lessness) of Gender Humour: Critical Analysis of Gender-Disparaging Verbal Humour. *TEME* XLIII: 827–838. https://doi.org/10.22190/TEME160126050N.

Ogara, Solomon, Chang E. Koh, and Victor R. Prybutok. 2014. Investigating Factors Affecting Social Presence and User Satisfaction with Mobile Instant Messaging. *Computers in Human Behavior* 36: 453–459. https://doi.org/10.1016/j.chb.2014.03.064.

Oghuma, Apollos Patricks, Christian Fernando Libaque-Saenz, Siew Fan Wong, and Younghoon Chang. 2016. An Expectation-Confirmation Model of Continuance Intention to Use Mobile Instant Messaging. *Telematics and Informatics* 33: 34–47. https://doi.org/10.1016/j.tele.2015.05.006.

Parrott, Scott, and Toby Hopp. 2020. Reasons People Enjoy Sexist Humor and Accept it as Inoffensive. *Atlantic Journal of Communication* 28 (2): 115–124. https://doi.org/10.1080/15456870.2019.1616737.

Phillips, Whitney, and Ryan M. Milner. 2017. *The Ambivalent Internet. Mischief, Oddity, and Antagonism Online*. Cambridge: Polity.

Pilkington, Adrian. 2000. *Poetic Effects. A Relevance Theory Perspective*. Amsterdam: John Benjamins. https://doi.org/10.1075/pbns.75.

Pirzadeh, Afarin, and Mark S. Pfaff. 2012. Emotion Expression under Stress in Instant Messaging. *Proceedings of the Human Factors and Ergonomics Society Annual Meeting* 56 (1): 493–497. https://doi.org/10.1177/1071181312561051.

Poppi, Fabio I.M., and Marta Dynel. 2021. Ad Libidinem: Forms of Female Sexualisation in Roastme Humour. *Sexualities* 24 (3): 431–455. https://doi.org/10.1177/1363460720931338.

Reid, Alan J. 2018. *The Smartphone Paradox. Our Ruinous Dependency in the Device Age*. Cham: Palgrave Macmillan. https://doi.org/10.1007/978-3-319-94319-0.

Rentschler, Carrie A., and S.C. Thrift. 2015. Doing Feminism in the Network: Networked Laughter and the 'Binders Full of Women' Meme. *Feminist Theory* 16 (3): 329–359. https://doi.org/10.1177/1464700115604136.

Ryan, Kathryn M., and Jeanne Kanjorski. 1998. The Enjoyment of Sexist Humor, Rape Attitudes, and Relationship Aggression in College Students. *Sex Roles* 38 (9–10): 743–756. https://doi.org/10.1023/A:1018868913615.

Rygg, Kristin. 2016. Was Malinowski Norwegian? Norwegian Interpretations of Phatic Talk. *Journal of Intercultural Communication* 40 (1).

Shen, Jianqiang, Oliver Brdiczka, and Juan Liu. 2015. A Study of Facebook Behavior: What does it Tell about your Neuroticism and Extraversion? *Computers in Human Behavior* 45: 32–38. https://doi.org/10.1016/j.chb.2014.11.067.

Shifman, Limor, and Dafna Lemish. 2010. Between Feminism and Fun(ny)mism. Analysing Gender in Popular Internet Humour. *Information, Communication & Society* 13 (6): 870–891. https://doi.org/10.1080/13691180903490560.

———. 2011. "Mars and Venus" in Virtual Space: Post-Feminist Humor and the Internet. *Critical Studies in Media Communication* 28 (3): 253–273. https://doi.org/10.1080/15295036.2010.522589.

———. 2012. Virtually Blonde. Blonde Jokes in the Global Age and Postfeminist Discourse. In *The Handbook of Gender, Sex, and Media*, ed. Karen Ross, 88–104. Oxford: Wiley-Blackwell. https://doi.org/10.1002/9781118114254.ch6.

Sundén, Jenny, and Susanna Paasonen. 2021. "We Have Tiny Purses in Our Vaginas!!! #Thanksforthat": Absurdity as a Feminist Method of Intervention. *Qualitative Research Journal* 21 (3): 233–243. https://doi.org/10.1108/QRJ-09-2020-0108.

Tsakona, Villy. 2020. Tracing the Trajectories of Contemporary Online Joking. *Media Linguistics* 7 (2): 169–183. https://doi.org/10.21638/spbu22.2020.202.

van Dijck, José. 2013. The Culture of Connectivity. In *A Critical History of Social Media*. Oxford: Oxford University Press. https://doi.org/10.1093/acprof:oso/9780199970773.001.0001.

Vandergriff, Ilona. 2010. Humor and Play in CMC. In *Handbook of Research on Discourse Behavior and Digital Communication: Language Structures and Social Interaction*, ed. Rotimi Taiwo, 235–251. Hershey: Information Science Reference. https://doi.org/10.4018/978-1-61520-773-2.ch016.

Wang, Victoria, John V. Tucker, and Kevin Haines. 2012. Phatic Technologies in Modern Society. *Technology in Society* 34: 84–93. https://doi.org/10.1016/j.techsoc.2012.01.001.

Woodzicka, Julie A., Robyn K. Mallett, and Kala J. Melchiori. 2020. Gender Differences in Using Humor to Respond to Sexist Jokes. *Humor* 33 (2): 219–238. https://doi.org/10.1515/humor-2019-0018.

Yus, Francisco. 2001. *El Discurso Femenino en el Cómic Alternativo Inglés [Women's discourse in alternative English comics]*. Alicante: Universidad de Alicante, Servicio de Publicaciones.

———. 2002. Stand-up Comedy and Cultural Spread: The Case of Sex Roles. Babel A.F.I.A.L., special issue on humour studies, 245–292.

———. 2003. El Chat como Doble Filtro Comunicativo [Chat as a double communicative filter]. *Revista de Investigación Lingüística* 2 (5): 141–169.

———. 2004. Pragmatics of Humorous Strategies in *El Club de la Comedia*. In *Current Trends in the Pragmatics of Spanish*, ed. Rosina Márquez-Reiter and María Elena Placencia, 320–344. Amsterdam: John Benjamins. https://doi.org/10.1075/pbns.123.25yus.

———. 2005a. Attitudes and Emotions Through Written Text: The Case of Textual Deformation in Internet Chat Rooms. *Pragmalingüística* 13: 147–174.

———. 2005b. Dave Allen's Stand-Up Monologues: An Epidemiological Approach. In *Thistles. A Homage to Brian Hughes. Volume 2: Essays in Memoriam*, ed. José Mateo and Francisco Yus, 317–344. Alicante: University of Alicante, Department of English Studies.

———. 2007. *Virtualidades Reales. Nuevas Formas de Comunidad en la Era de Internet [Real Virtualities. New Forms of Community at the Internet Age]*. Alicante: University of Alicante, Servicio de Publicaciones.

———. 2008. Inferring from Comics: A Multi-Stage Account. In *El Discurs del Còmic (Quaderns de Filologia, Estudis de Comunicació, vol. III)*, ed. Pelegrí Sancho Cremades, Carmen Gregori Signes, and Santiago Renard, 223–249. Valencia: University of Valencia.

———. 2010. *Ciberpragmática 2.0. Nuevos Usos del Lenguaje en Internet [Cyberpragmatics 2.0. New uses of language on the internet]*. Barcelona: Ariel.

———. 2011a. *Cyberpragmatics. Internet-Mediated Communication in Context*. Amsterdam and Philadelphia: John Benjamins. https://doi.org/10.1075/pbns.213.

———. 2011b. Relevance Equations of Effective Internet Communication. In *Interdisciplinarity and Languages. Current Issues in Research, Teaching, Professional Applications and ICT*, ed. Barry Pennock and Francisca Suau, 65–86. Berlin: Peter Lang.

———. 2014. Turismo Móvil: Discurso, Interactividad y Usabilidad en las 'Apps' de Turismo. Paper delivered at *Discurso y Géneros del Turismo 2.0*. University of Valencia and IULMA, Valencia.

———. 2015a. The Role of Cognition and Relevance in New Digital Narratives. In *Prospettive Multilingue e Interdisciplinari nel Discorso Specialistico*, ed. Elena Carpi, 81–107. Pisa (Italy): Pisa University Press.

———. 2015b. Discourse and Identity. In International Encyclopedia of the Social and Behavioral Sciences (2nd edition), volume 6, ed. by James D. Wright, 498–502. Oxford: Elsevier. https://doi.org/10.1016/B978-0-08-097086-8.54004-5

———. 2016a. *Humour and Relevance*. Amsterdam: John Benjamins. https://doi.org/10.1075/thr.4.

———. 2016b. Towards a cyberpragmatics of mobile instant messaging. In *Yearbook of Corpus Linguistics and Pragmatics 2016: Global Implications for Culture and Society in the Networked Age*, ed. Jesús Romero-Trillo, 7–26. Berlin: Springer. https://doi.org/10.1007/978-3-319-41733-2_2.

———. 2017. Contextual Constraints and Non-Propositional Effects in WhatsApp Communication. *Journal of Pragmatics* 114: 66–86. https://doi.org/10.1016/j.pragma.2017.04.003.
———. 2018. The Interface between Pragmatics and Internet-Mediated Communication: Applications, Extensions and Adjustments. In *Pragmatics and its Interfaces*, ed. Cornelia Ilie and Neil Norrick, 267–290. Amsterdam: John Benjamins. https://doi.org/10.1075/pbns.294.12yus.
———. 2019. An Outline of Some Future Research Issues for Internet Pragmatics. *Internet Pragmatics* 2 (1): 1–33. https://doi.org/10.1075/ip.00018.yus.
———. 2021. *Smartphone Communication. Interactions in the App Ecosystem.* Abingdon: Routledge. https://doi.org/10.4324/9781003200574.

CHAPTER 5

Humour in Messaging Interactions

1 Introduction

Nowadays, messaging has become an essential means to engage in interactions with single or collective audiences online, mainly through dedicated smartphone apps such as WhatsApp, WeChat, Line, Telegram, Messenger or Snapchat, among others, each of them with specific affordances and limitations to sustain interactions therein. Many of the interactions held on the aforesaid apps exhibit a humorous quality, these being precisely the object of analysis in this chapter, mainly devoted to WhatsApp, one of the most popular apps in the Western world.[1]

The generic label used here will be "humour in messaging interactions," and *interactive humour* is also preferred to *conversational humour*, even though the latter label has its supporters (e.g. Dynel 2009, 1286). Chovanec (2011, 245) further specified conversational humour as one aiming to construct humorous effects in dialogic interactions, and thus differing from joke-telling. Chovanec and Tsakona (2018, 8) added that this label usually refers to a spoken interaction mode. Likewise, its conceptualisation would exceed the scope of other related labels such as *conversational joking*, which constitutes only one of the possible realisations of

[1] This chapter is an extension and update of the research carried out in Yus (2003, 2005, 2010, 2011a, 2014a, 2016a, 2016b, 2017, 2021a, 2021c, 2022a, 2022b, 2022c) and Yus and Hu (submitted).

F. Yus, *Pragmatics of Internet Humour*,
https://doi.org/10.1007/978-3-031-31902-0_5

conversational humour (see also Attardo 2011, 144; Dynel 2011). Chovanec and Tsakona (ibid.) also mentioned the label *humour in interaction*, which tends to be associated with oral conversations too. They contend that most recent research on humour, including the one done in this book, has shifted its attention towards "non-linguistic features of humor production and reception in contexts that involve various forms of interactions, including new and emerging forms of multimodal interactions, particularly as far as computer-mediated and technology-mediated communication is concerned" (p. 9). For this reason, they consider a broader concept like *interactional humour* -similar to *interactive humour*- more feasible. As proposed in this book, both of them do justice to the co-operative construction of humour in diverse interactional contexts:

> There are several features that characterize our conception of *interactional humor*. First, it takes a variety of physical forms in spoken, written, and technology-mediated communication. Second, it is based on the principle of sequentiality, that is, the minimal structural composition consisting of an act and some reaction (follow-up), whether linguistic or non-linguistic. Finally, and most importantly, it involves the co-participation of multiple parties, giving rise to more complex humorous macro-acts. These are made up of semiotic interaction that can, in the broadest sense of the word, be described as dialogical or polylogical. What matters, then, is that interactional humor becomes characterized by the joint negotiation of the humorous potential of forms, situations, and utterances. (Chovanec and Tsakona 2018, 9).

A special emphasis will be laid in this chapter upon the notion of *turn* in messaging interactions, simultaneously paying attention to the ways in which turn structure and turn sequences are managed between the users involved in humorous messaging interactions. The structure of such turns will reveal interesting information about how users intend, handle and generate humorous effects on messaging apps. These turns make up *humorous sequences* exhibiting "sustained" humour. This quality can only be achieved through the presence of several ingredients listed in Ruiz-Gurillo (2021, 164): (a) different individuals co-construct humour; (b) the adoption of a humorous mode is maintained via reciprocation (e.g. irony responds to irony); (c) humour support exists, since the interlocutor validates the intended humorous effect attempted by the addresser; and (d) long turns are dominated by the addresser. The interlocutor reacts to these using backchannels, which guide the conversation towards the desired sustained humour.

Furthermore, exactly like in any other kind of interaction (and as underlined several times in this book) effective humorous interaction ultimately relies on assumed mutuality of information among the interactants (*mutual manifestness*) and may also prove useful to *reveal* this mutuality (Holmes 2006, 27; Norrick 1993, 107). As Padilla Cruz (2020, 170) contends, humorists must make attributions of what the audience may know, together with their attitudes or feelings toward certain events, issues, or people. This enables them "to prompt the audience to access certain information, and anticipate the logical, effortless, and highly salient interpretations that the audience may consider."

2 Humorous Face-to-Face Interactions and Relevance

According to Yus (2016a), relevance theory (RT) has mainly exemplified its theoretical assumptions on communication by resorting to fictional dyadic dialogues where a single addressee selects a relevant interpretation from the addresser's (schematic) coded utterance. Therefore, relevance-theoretic analyses about the multifarious quality of multi-party conversations are scarce. For example, Moeschler (1993) admitted that RT has not focused on conversational issues (or on the structure of conversations, on their progression, on which rules participants should obey when interacting, etc.). However, conversations should not behave differently in terms of search for relevance and the manner in which interpretations are inferred from what multiple users co-construct in the course of a humorous interaction: "One of the important predictions that relevance theory makes about conversation is that no specific sequencing or interpretive principles should be necessary to explain conversational data. We can go a little further and say that, if human cognition is relevance oriented, the conversational behaviour of participants should not escape the general relevance orientation of cognition: utterances in conversation should be relevance oriented" (p. 151).

Certainly, there is no reason why RT should not be able to tackle the analysis of humorous interactions, even multi-party ones. Nevertheless, to do so, it should address methodological issues such as the ones specified in Viana (2013, 220–221) linked to humorous *moves* (a participant's action within the conversation to generate certain effects on other participants) in the interaction: (a) how humorous moves match the ongoing interactional structure within which they take place; (b) how the participants deal with the metalinguistic possibilities that humour opens up, including the management of puns and verbal humour; and (c) how humorous moves, regarded as part of the current interaction, influence both the management of that interaction and its purposes.[2]

Interactive humour in dyadic or multi-parti conversations equally performs a number of functions that have been outlined in the bibliography (see Attardo 2002, 51–56; Hay 2000; Dynel 2007). An interesting attempt to cross-cut these proposals of functions can be found in Yus (2016a):

1. *Strengthening ties and solidarity between the interlocutors.* Typical in many conversational settings and gatherings of friends, or in more formal contexts such as the workplace. It normally results from the joint construction of a *play frame.* The term was proposed by Bateson (1953), for whom we categorise our communicative actions as *serious* or as *play* when interacting with others. The participants in the conversation can frame their talk as humorous by signalling *This is play* through either verbal or nonverbal means. The notion of a *play frame* captures an essential feature of humour, namely that it should not be considered serious, and at the same time avoids being too specific about the kinds of talk that may occur within a play frame, or expressed differently, anything has the potential to be funny. For a play frame to be established in talk, conversational participants need to collaborate with each other, because in such a context the interlocutors display the extent to which they are collaborative and tuned-in to each other (Coates 2007, 31; see also Lampert and Ervin-Tripp 2006, 54), which in turn explains why this function is also compared to a *social cement* that keeps people together by emphasising solidarity and similarity among group members. Holmes (2006, 33) described how jointly constructed humour frequently unfolds between those who are familiar with one another, co-constructed humour contributing to the solidarity of the group as well. This is achieved, as Hay (2000, 716) contends, by expressing not only solidarity with other interlocutors but also a respectful attitude and emphasised status inside the group, all of

[2] He added that certain agreement exists on two facts about humorous moves in conversation: (a) they open the current cognitive frame to a different interpretation; and (b) they reorient the interactional sequence and perhaps the whole communicative event according to the new information that is given. Therefore, the meaning and implications of humorous turns in interactions entail the interlocutors' ability to reorient current conversational purposes and to diversify goals as well as results.

which seemingly go hand in hand. Furthermore, successful humour generates an increased awareness of the portion of each interlocutor's cognitive environment that is mutually manifest, a truly relevant piece of information in its own right.

2. *Mitigating aggressive acts.* Humour can serve to mitigate inherently aggressive acts of communication (*face-threatening acts* in Brown and Levinson's 1987 terminology), ranging from criticism or reprimanding to the performance of directives, to quote but a few (Dynel 2007). Ritchie (2011, 483) also stresses that humour frequently softens implied criticisms and the imposition of directives, helps to negotiate differences regarding power and authority, and introduces potentially offensive or controversial information without taking direct responsibility for it.
3. *Broad social bonding.* Conversational humour has a cohesive social effect on the interactants. Successful humorous outcomes reveal mutually manifest assumptions related to general issues of their lives and shared social context, thus fostering in-group cohesiveness and membership. Long and Graesser (1988, 57) also argued that humour often works as a catalyst to strengthen social bonds and foster group cohesiveness. Inevitably, though, the very same humour that binds some people together ends up excluding other individuals or groups who do not share the information that is highly manifest (and mutually manifest) to these interactants (Lynch 2002, 434). In short, humour has a *bonding* and *bounding* effect on users.
4. *Exerting or resisting power.* This final function becomes interesting, since humour can serve both to exert and to resist the power deployed during a conversation. Authors such as Schnurr (2010, 313) went so far as to assert that "the inherently ambiguous nature of humour implies that it may be used to perform these two functions simultaneously, and that solidarity and power are inextricably intertwined with each other in humour."

2.1 Humorous Conversations and Relevance Theory

Yus (2016a) raises the question of whether RT is suitable to analyse conversational humour, the answer being *yes* (or it should be). No reason prevents us from extending the notions of relevance and search for relevance to the information transmitted and exchanged in conversational interactions. A different issue is whether the effects generated by conversational humour and the functions that this humour can have for the interlocutors while interacting easily fit within the theoretical assumptions of this theory. In general, at least two possibilities for RT-based analysis of conversational humour were isolated in Yus (ibid.):

1. During the conversation, one speaker holds the conversational floor and tells a joke to a number of interlocutors in the group. In this situation, the general proposal of the relevance-theoretic comprehension procedure -essential throughout this book- would also suit this kind of communication, since the structure is the same as that of the prototypical one-to-one scenario typically studied within RT, though developed in parallel one-to-one instances this time (the same joke is told by one addresser to several interlocutors, and each one of them makes sense of the joke individually).
2. A more challenging option for RT arises when humour stems from multi-party conversations where the effects cannot be located in one single utterance told by one single speaker to one or more interlocutors but demand the cooperation and collaboration of every interactant, all of whom co-construct the humorous turns and their effects by humorously replying, adding comments and continuing the initial humorous utterance, or even completing an initiated turn that requires the help of others to achieve the desired humorous effects. Although the default expectation of relevance still applies, this expectation does not revolve around one single utterance by a single addresser, and a single addressee (or a parallel multiple audience) is not responsible for the derivation of the intended effects either.

In this sense, Coupland and Jaworski (1997, 236) remind us that RT does not deny the fact that meaning often results from co-construction: "While it is evidently true that two participants will usually both be active in progressively building the propositional content of a conversation, [...] the process of co-construction is nevertheless analysable as a tightly linked but sequentially set of individual ostensions and inferences" (see Chiera 2014, 12; Liedtke 2001, 244). The same holds true for the instances of conversational humour where several interlocutors cooperate and work towards building up the effects pursued.[3] The interest now lies in a more specific collective co-construction of discourse by several interactants for the sake of generating eventual humorous effects. In these cases, humour turns out to be suitable to study collaborative conversational activity, to which must be added that it typically develops between people who know each other well.[4]

Even though this chapter will focus on dyadic interactions in Spanish humorous messaging interactions taking place on WhatsApp, multi-party co-constructed humour (also characteristic of messaging groups) is a feature of humorous interactions that RT needs to tackle. It was claimed in Yus (2016a) that such an endeavour might require the use of new terminology, albeit not necessarily departing from the central relevance-theoretic claims on inference. A proposal of relevance subtypes apt for use in this kind of future analysis was made:

a. *Partial relevance.* The relevance obtained from processing a single turn within an interaction, but with the hearer's awareness and certainty that this recently obtained relevance is only a part of the overall interactional relevance, and hence it will be taken over or adjusted by the relevance added after processing subsequent turns. These will surely alter the initial relevance and simultaneously add further sources of relevance to the whole exchange. Exactly the same applies to humorous communication, where several humorous effects achieved from a single conversational turn may be considered part of a larger humorous interaction.
b. *Sustained relevance.* In this situation, every turn adds new information, thus managing to generate an offset of sustained effects and the mutually manifest impression that a whole humorous conversation has been co-constructed by all interactants. This typically happens when friends joke and build upon each other's turns while successfully sustaining an appropriate level of humour throughout the interaction.

[3] See Cheng (2003, 288), Holmes (2006, 33), Priego-Valverde (2006, 84), Coates (2007, 31), Feyaerts (2013, 244), Dynel (2008, 244; 2011, 225), and Chovanec (2011, 245), among others.

[4] Holmes (2006, 31) proposes two types of co-constructed humor: *supportive contributions*, which "agree with, add to, elaborate, or strengthen the propositions or arguments of previous contribution(s)"; and *contestive contributions*, which "challenge, disagree with, or undermine the propositions or arguments put forward in earlier contributions."

c. *Transitional relevance.* The relevance of a turn can sometimes be obtained only if the information provided by a prior or subsequent turn is processed for relevance (and humorous effects) too. On this occasion, the humorous effects build upon the succession of turns which create a storyline that eventually becomes an overall co-constructed humorous interaction. To a certain extent, sustained relevance would be achieved by adding up instances of transitional relevance throughout the interaction.
d. *Deferred relevance.* Here, the interlocutors assess all the assumptions brought to bear in the production of the different turns that make up the interaction and come up with an overall, broad relevant humorous outcome for the interaction taken as a whole interactional unit. This is more or less the general humorous outcome derived from the succession of partial conversational relevance.

2.2 Five Elements in the Analysis of Humorous Interactions

Chovanec and Tsakona (2018) propose five elements that play a central role in humorous interactions, which in turn are also at work in humorous messaging counterparts. These elements are summarised below and complemented with further research on them.

1. *Framing devices* refer to elements which somehow signal the presence of humour, including laughter, smile, prosodic and intonational features, gestures, and so on and so forth. They work as *contextualising cues* (Gumperz 1982), i.e. hints that the discourse which has just been produced should be inferred as humorous. This is usually referred to as *mode adoption* (Attardo 2001; Attardo et al. 2013, 410; Bell 2009, 1826; Dynel 2011, 225): The listener reacts to attempted humour with humour, thus giving rise to several humorous interventions in this new *mode*. Therefore, this framing role involves the addressee as well. In fact, "interactional roles such as 'humor producer' or 'humorist' and 'humor recipient/addressee' are not so easy to distinguish from one another and it may be difficult to assign those roles to specific interactants in real settings" (Chovanec and Tsakona ibid., 3).
2. *Reactions* signal whether the addressee has understood the humorous intention in the right way, or the addresser has failed to convey their humorous intention. Reactions are frequently shaped as humorous too, often encouraging further continuation to the

already-initiated play frame, which is likewise usual during humorous messaging interactions (see below). This alignment takes place when the interlocutor engages in what Holmes (2006) called *supportive contribution*, subsequently fleshed out by Hay (2001) in three stages: (a) the addressee's recognition of the humorous intention; (b) an understanding of the intended humour; and (c) a supportive appreciation of that humorous intention (see also Attardo et al. 2011, 226).

3. *Sociocultural parameters* relate to the specific cultural and social variables qualifying both addresser and addressee, additionally including the specificities of the community within which humorous discourses are produced and circulate. Some of them are labelled as *inherited features* in this book, e.g. the interlocutors' sex, ethnic origin or age. Other features fitting these parameters include social class, religion, political affiliation and profession. They all play a fundamental role in the eventual (un)successful outcome of a humorous intention: "different sociocultural communities have different preferences and norms concerning which contexts humor is expected (or not expected) to be used in, which humorous topics and targets are considered appropriate or inappropriate given specific audiences and settings, whether there are institutionalized restrictions on the use of humor, and how they are imposed on the members of the/a community" (Chovanec and Tsakona ibid., 5).
4. *The reasons.* Several possible goals are meant to be achieved through the use of humour in an interaction. One of them consists in emphasising the mutuality of information about the views, socially connoted assumptions and cultural values of the interlocutors involved in a specific humorous interaction. This emphasis, alongside failed/successful inferential outcomes, also brings to the surface the differences with people who do not belong to that culture or social group. As part of their humorous strategy, users often take for granted the mutuality of certain information and may fail in this expectation, the lack of mutuality inevitably leading to misunderstandings, or even to a complete lack of understanding. The following messaging interaction illustrates it:

(1) Luis: [Sends a photomontage of a famous football player holding a volume of *The Descriptive Grammar of the Spanish Language*].
Luis: Oximoron visual 🤣
[*Visual oxymoron* 🤣].

Juan: No lo pillo.
[I don't get it].
Luis: [Sends a close-up photo of the book the player is holding].
Luis: Gramática + [nombre del jugador].
[Grammar + player's name].
Juan: Sabía que tenía que ver con alguien que no soliera tener en sus manos una gramática, pero es que no sabía qué cara tiene [ese jugador]; el fútbol no es lo mío.
[I knew it had to do with someone that doesn't usually carry a grammar, but the thing is, I didn't know [this player's] face; I am not fond of football].
Juan: Jajaja.
[Hahaha].
Luis: 🤦‍♂️

5. *Genres* tend to be relatively stable. However, humorous genres constantly undergo re-shaping on the Internet and often mash up into new genres, some of which become long-lasting while others have a more ephemeral nature (Yus 2011b, 2015, 2021a). The genre under analysis in this chapter (i.e. humorous messaging interaction) remains relatively stable in app-mediated communication. Nevertheless, the gradual improvement of apps with new affordances, some of them crucial for a proper contextualisation of typed utterances (see next Section), results in this genre exhibiting certain variations and developments which eventually influence how humorous discourses are created, typed and inferred on these apps.

2.3 Laughter in Humorous Interactions

One of the key signals revealing the humorous quality of an interaction is the presence of laughter, likewise important during messaging interactions in the shape of *laugh particles* (e.g. typing "hahaha" in English or "jajaja" in Spanish, see Sect. 4.1.1 below). Laughter may occur in one (typically the addressee) or in both interlocutors holding the conversation. Furthermore, it may overlap with words or be produced separately, that is, in the role of what Poyatos (1975, 2002) calls *alternants*, or expressed differently, words and laughter "alternating" in the utterance production flow.[5]

[5] And defined as "nonverbal, marginal and nonspeech sounds or clusters of sounds, articulated or not [...] which do not affect the verbal utterance [...] Alternants occur either isolated or alternating with the verbal utterance and with the kinesic behaviour" (Poyatos 1975, 294).

Normally, laughter serves to acknowledge that the humorous intention has been successful (Hay 2001, 57), for instance, as a backchannel indicating humour appreciation (Attardo et al. 2013, 410; Archakis and Tsakona 2005); it can play other relevant roles, though, even beyond a link to humour (Holt 2010, 1514). Indeed, several functions have been suggested for the role of laughter in conversation. Some of them, either proposed or collected by these authors, are listed in Table 5.1. One of the key

Table 5.1 Proposals for functions of laughter in conversation

Author(s)	*Functions of laughter*
McKeown (2016)	(a) To signal social bonding; (b) to regulate and repair conversational interactions; (c) to ensure that social norms of conversational interactions are adhered to; and (d) to signal the degree of intimacy between the interlocutors
Attardo (2015)	(a) To show appreciation of humour; (b) to terminate talk; (c) to "cover" delicate passages in conversation; and (d) to demonstrate understanding
Adams (2012)	(a) To terminate a turn; (b) to laugh at the interlocutor or third person; (c) to mitigate embarrassing situations; and (d) to react to the speaker's turn
Holt (2010)	(a) To help lead the interaction towards a conclusion or closure; (b) to react positively to a previous turn with a feedback function (*backward looking*); and (c) to serve as a "hinge" for the introduction of a new conversational topic
Lynch (2002)	(a) To manage turn-taking; (b) to display hearership; and (c) to show affiliation
Glenn (2003)	(a) To show a certain state of mind to others and infer the addresser's state of mind; (b) to show affiliation towards others, which entails not only exhibiting mutual understanding but also a mutual connection between the interlocutors; (c) to mark a text as humorous; and (d) to generate group bonding and mutual awareness
Norrick (1993)	(a) To manipulate talk and participants in various ways; (b) to realign ourselves with respect to others; (c) to relieve tension and foster a friendly interaction; and (d) to manage conversational turn-taking
König (2019)	(a) To index power relationships; (b) to manage potentially face-threatening acts; and (c) to convey an affective, evaluative or epistemic stance toward one's own or other interlocutors' utterances
Petitjean and Morel (2017)	(a) To show a humorous intention; (b) to take the conversational floor; (c) to manage conversational topics; and (d) to bypass problematic or delicate moments
Sampietro (2021a)	(a) To indicate the existence of a humorous effect; (b) to highlight the solidarity between the interlocutors (i.e. to show involvement in the conversation); and (c) to structure the humorous conversation
Sampietro (2021b)	(a) To structure the conversation, strategically placing it at certain points in the speaking turns; (b) to mark a text in a humorous way; and (c) to deictically mark a referent (one laughs at a specific referent)

(*continued*)

Table 5.1 (continued)

Author(s)	*Functions of laughter*
Thielemann (2020)	(a) To soften the emotional or social impact of potentially threatening actions, delicate topics or surprising and paradoxical situations; (b) to hedge, allowing the speaker to dissociate themselves from what is said; (c) to modify the potential of face threatening acts for recipients, that is, in facework (e.g., mitigating as well as aggravating critique, ridicule) or protect the speaker's face needs during presentations of lapses or failures; and (d) to index and express a specific emotional attitude towards a stretch of talk

implications of these functions is that no tight or unique relationship exists between laughter and humour. As highlighted by Priego-Valverde et al. (2018, 565), neither humour automatically triggers laughter nor laughter is always provoked by humour. Moreover, lack of laughter in the interlocutor does not necessarily mean that the humorous intention has failed, insofar as it can also perform a strategy of conversational support. Finally, these authors stress the importance of considering the emotional dimension of laughter in addition to the typical connection with humour.

3 The Genre of Messaging Interactions: Interface- and User-Related Constraints

Although humour in messaging apps shares certain qualities with face-to-face humorous interactions, some differences exist between them because the former takes place through the imposed design of an interface and with mainly a text-based quality. Undoubtedly, as already explained in Chap. 4, the *affordances* of messaging apps entail certain constraints on what kind of humorous interaction may be held on these apps, on how users code their utterances for humorous purposes, on the inferential strategies applied by the interlocutors and on the eventual quality of their interpretations. These interactions were initially text-based (and strictly so in the case of SMS, the precursor of messaging; see Yus 2011a, 2021a) and hence cues-filtered (i.e. not good at conveying all the subtleties of oral speech, among which stand out vocal and visual nonverbal behaviour).

However, these apps have incorporated the use of discourses such as emojis, stickers, GIFs, alongside the utilisation of photos, videos, and other multimedia content that allow users to convey their intended interpretations in a more accurate, contextualised way, as well as to generate the desired humorous effects.[6] In sum, the evolutions of messaging interfaces provide users with a highly suitable environment for synchronous interactions, including those for humorous purposes. Not surprisingly, these sorts of apps fit what Wang et al. (2012) call ***strong phatic technologies***, that is, technologies designed for their users to establish frequent interactions within an environment of permanent connectivity. More specifically, users see such apps as a context where they can often engage in conversations with the explicit intention of generating humorous effects on their interlocutors and groups of contacts.

In any case, limitations still exist in messaging apps if compared to the contextual richness of face-to-face interactions which apply to humorous messaging interactions too. According to Moalla and Ben Amor (2020, 82), interface constraints can make the recognition of a play frame a challenging process. For example, the contextualisation and identification of nonverbal cues, so crucial for the derivation of humour, are not readily available for participants. Similarly, turn-taking and adjacent sequences do not function in such an organised and controlled manner as they do in face-to-face conversations. Moreover, a simple directed gaze or the use of exaggerated intonation, as well as low and high tones, may signal a humorous intention, but these resources are not so easy to implement in messaging conversations due to the aforementioned cues-filtered quality.

A major drawback of app interfaces lies in the strict sequential order of posts managed by the system and in the fact that turn arrangement may not coincide with the actual messaging interaction flow, as already mentioned above. For example, the following real WhatsApp conversation between a female (A) and a male (B) user reproduced in Yus (2016b) deals with A's cat's naughty behaviour.

[6] Tagg and Lyons (2022) propose the terms ***polymedia repertoire*** (which encompasses the full configuration of semiotic and technological resources accessed by networked individuals in the contemporary age) and ***polymedia nest*** (a resource into which other resources are embedded, including various communicative modes or channels). During an act of humorous messaging interaction, interlocutors have at their disposal a wide polymedia repertoire of options to enrich their texts that can be grouped into three categories (p. 81): (a) linguistic and multimodal signs brought along by users from their offline contexts and collaboratively reconstructed in mobile interactions (e.g. photos and videos taken in physical contexts); (b) linguistic and multimodal signs made available through particular apps or platforms (app affordances: typeface, layout, colour, emoji/sticker galleries…); and (c) linguistic and multimodal signs accessible through the wider network (e.g. by sharing links or copying and pasting from other sites, including tools or resources collectively imbued by cultural meaning from elsewhere on the internet).

(2) A: La voy a facturar en el aeropuerto.
[*I'm going to check her in at the airport*].
B: Eso.
[*That's right*].
A: Egipto, que allí los idolatran.
[*To Egypt, since they idolise them there*].
A: O a Marruecos pa q aprenda lo que vale un peine.
[*Or to Morocco, so that she learns the tough way*].
Q está muy mimadita.
[*because she's so spoilt*].
B: Yeah.
A: Yastan aqui mis padres.
[*My parents are here already*].
B: Que vea que la vida no es solo hacer trastadas.
[*She has to realise that life is not all about playing tricks around*].
A: 😩
B: Ohhhh. Planazo.
[*Ohhhh. Great plan*].
A: Total.
[*Totally*].
B: Yo iré al gym luego.
[*I'll go to the gym later*].

The initial topic in this interaction shows how angry A is with her naughty cat. Half-way through the dialogue, A informs B that her parents have just arrived (*Yastan aqui mis padres*), but B's next message still relates to the naughty cat, since the WhatsApp system has reproduced messages in strict order of arrival. Similarly, A's next message, an emoji of anguish which conveys a whole proposition (roughly "my parents' visit depresses me"), does not refer to the cat either, although it follows B's cat-related message. These mixed-up threads on WhatsApp conversations may be a potential source of misunderstandings or increased processing effort. Furthermore, and unlike what happens in face-to-face interactions, users can only interpret other users' messages when they arrive at their apps in their entirety, or to put in another way, users cannot interpret messages as they are being typed and engage in anticipatory inferences about what the other user might intend with their text. In König's (2019, 157) words,

> Hearers of spoken interaction 'witness' in real time how an utterance is produced incrementally, but users engaged in written dialogues only see the final product of a foregoing production process. This is essentially reflected in the concept of a posting as the minimal unit a user can contribute to a

> dialogue. Whatever happens during the production phase (typing, deleting, editing, inserting, etc.) cannot be perceived by the addressee. The posting only becomes a topic of the dialogue after it has been posted to the screen protocol as a whole; only then does it constitute a contribution to the ongoing discourse.

Needless to say, as remarked in Yus (2017), messaging apps are also welcome by users because of what they offer despite their interface-related constraints. For instance, they are key to users' phatic purposes: to show readiness for interaction, to enact and sustain connections, or to feel acknowledged by their peers. By way of example, Nardi et al. (2000) claimed that these apps offer an ideal environment to create a sense of social awareness and to perceive the readiness of friends and acquaintances for interaction, hence forming social bonds through the exchange of trivial information (a relevant non-propositional effect, see Chap. 8). Unless the option is disabled by the user, the system on most apps likewise alerts of incoming messages, a useful option that might nevertheless overwhelm certain users. This happens because they feel unable to cope not only with so many incoming messages (an example of a negative non-propositional effect) but also with the additional pressure to reply shortly, a kind of user-to-user contextual constraint related to the default expectations which characterise these messaging interactions. In any case, the aforesaid alerts foster a near synchronous quality of messaging interactions, since these reminders largely help to reduce the time gap between messages sent and replied to (Knop et al. 2016, 1078; Park and Sundar 2015, 122).

To these interface-related constraints must be added other user-centred ones which cross-cut similar interlocutor-centred constraints found in humorous face-to-face interactions. Some of them were also addressed in Chap. 4, more precisely the user's gender constraint. Among these, the following user-related contextual constraints stand out in messaging interactions: (a) the *kind of relationship* existing between the interlocutors. Humour is frequent between friends but may be awkward in certain working environments. Social distance and the degree of intimacy have also been suggested as relationship-based constraints (Schnurr 2010, 316); (b) the *interlocutors' sex*, both regarding sex/gender stereotypes and when it comes to different senses of humour and topics of humorous discourses used (Glenn 2003, 153); and (c) *culture and ethnicity*. Humour may be used in particular ways across cultures and that actually provides us with a source of knowledge about the norms, beliefs and values which prevail in those cultures. It also goes without saying that interlocutors from different cultures may not interpret humour in the same way, which paves the way to misunderstandings (Cheng 2003, 288).

4 Humorous Discourse on Messaging Interactions

Plenty of everyday interactions on messaging apps exhibit a humorous quality. These may be native in-app interactions or based on discourses imported from other apps or the internet (e.g. via links) and trigger humorous responses along with further interactions, frequently through a viralisation process (Cruz-Moya and Sánchez-Moya 2021, 62). With the aid of emojis, stickers, GIFs, text alteration and a playful use of punctuation, users face no major problems to convey that they intend to generate humorous effects or that they want the messaging conversation to shift into a *play frame*.

Humour in messaging interactions has a number of positive effects. Hsieh and Tseng (2017) stress that such playful interactions arouse good feelings such as happiness and joy in users, reducing their stress levels and offering them an escape from everyday routines. They can strengthen exiting friendships too: "friendship-building interactions, such as leaving and sending messages that playfully poke fun at friends within a group, are evident in messaging practice. The playfulness may take various forms, such as storytelling, teasing and joking in the instant messaging conversational threads (…) engaging in play is likely to create a positive affective experience that contributes to the emotional capital of a relationship" (p. 407–408). Some aspects of these messaging interactions will be covered in the following sub-sections.

4.1 *Conveying Humorous Nonverbal Cues during Messaging Interactions*

4.1.1 *Laughter*

Laughter, an important nonverbal element in humorous conversations, can perform several roles beyond showing appreciation of the humorous intent, as shown in Table 5.1 above.

Laughter commonly appears in (near-)simultaneity with verbal content in the course of daily face-to-face conversations. By contrast, in messaging conversations, laughter necessarily has to be typed separately from its

Table 5.2 Laugh particles in Spanish, Chinese and English (Yus and Hu submitted)

Spanish	*Chinese*	*English*	*Frequency of use (Chinese)* *1 = most frequent* *5 = least frequent*
jajajaja	哈哈哈哈	hahahaha	1
jejejeje	呵呵呵呵	hohohoho	4
jajajaja	啊哈哈哈哈	ahhahahaha	2
jejejeje	嘿嘿嘿嘿	heyheyheyhey	3
pufjajajaja	噗哈哈哈哈	puffhahahaha	2
jojojojo	吼吼吼吼	hohohoho	4 (mainly among the Chinese youths)
jajajaja	hahahaha	hahahahaha	4
jajajaja	hhhh	hhhh	3

accompanying text in the shape of ***laugh particles*** which pervade humorous messaging interactions (Chiaro 2018, 123). These are typed transcriptions of vocal laughter that exhibit cross-cultural variations (*hahaha* in English; *jajaja* in Spanish, for instance). Yus and Hu (submitted) draw a comparison between these particles in English, Chinese and Spanish (see Table 5.2).

Of course, laugh particles become crucial to manage humorous messaging interactions. As König (2019, 159) underlines, laughter allows the interlocutors to take stances of an affective, evaluative or epistemic kind towards their own utterances or those of their interlocutors. Laugh particles can be a helpful means for WhatsApp users to decide whether to treat or contextualise an utterance as non-serious, humorous or potentially face-threatening or intrusive. This stance-taking, König (ibid.) contends, is always framed within a particular interactional context, the means with which speakers take stances being also adapted to this particular context.

In short, these particles show how users understand a prior message or how they want their message to be understood (König 2019, 157) and, in that function, they resemble emojis as well (see below). Furthermore, users place these particles in different message positions or formats seeking to either close or continue the topic at hand. König (ibid., 159) proposes two main roles based upon their location in the message: *projective*, when they act as announcements of a forthcoming laughable message (either the one attached to the laugh particle or a subsequent one); or *responsive*, when they comment on a laughable message produced before the laugh particle (be it in the same message or in a previous one). A typical schema in the implementation of laugh particles can be seen in dialogue (3), where the first laugh particle used by Juan[7] serves to show humorous appreciation of Luis's previous message, whereas the second one marks the accompanying text with a humorous connotation:

(3) Juan: Me imagino que estarás en Ibiza, así que disfruta, desconecta y descansa
[*I guess you'll be in Ibiza, so enjoy yourself, disconnect and rest*].
Juan: Abrazo.
[*Hug*].
Luis: Abrazo.
[*Hug*].
Luis: Enjoy [your village] capital 😂
Juan: Jajajajajajaja.
[*hahahahaha*].
Juan: Llegué ayer y ya see me cae la casa encima.
[*I arrived yesterday and I feel like the walls are coming in on me*].
Juan: Jajajajajajaja.
[*hahahahaha*].

Similarly, messaging conversation (4) contains several instances of laugh particles. The first one, in a separate message, instructs Juan that his message should be understood within a joking frame. In the second one, Juan laughs at his own message about his age and Luis replies with "jeje" to show appreciation. The same holds true for the next laugh particle use, this time acknowledged by Luis with emojis, and for the last example, which also modifies Luis's message and is used by Juan to show appreciation.

(4) Luis: Textual meme: "When people talk about 30 years ago, I think they mean the 1970s, but they actually mean 1991 and now I need a lie down."
Juan: 😂😂😂
Luis: Dinosaur Luis?
Luis: Jaja.
[*haha*].
Juan: Ya ves, y tanto!
[*Indeed! Very much so!*].
Juan: Creo que mi mente dejó de computar mi verdadera edad hace años ya.
[*I think my mind stopped computing my true age years ago*].

[7]The names of the interlocutors in messaging interactions have been changed to preserve their anonymity throughout this chapter.

Juan: Jajajajajajaja.
[*hahahahaha*].
Luis: Jeje same here.
Juan: A veces me da que sigo en los veintimuchos o los taipocos.
[*Sometimes I feel like I am still in my twenty-many or my thirty-few*].
Juan: Jajajajajajaja.
[*hahahahaha*].
Luis: 😂😂
Luis: Eso es lo malo… que tenemos alma de veinteañeros en un "body serrano" del cretácico Jajaja.
[*That's the bad thing… that we have the soul of a twenty-something in a body from the Cretaceous*].
Juan: Pozí, jajajajajaja.
[*Indeed, hahahaha*].

A note of clarification regarding turns during messaging interactions becomes necessary at this point: as far as we are concerned, a turn includes all the messages that a user sends before another user intervenes (or replies) with another message, which would immediately constitute a different turn. In the messaging interaction (4) above, Juan sends two texts in separate messages, after which he sends laugh particles in another message. These different messages by Juan appear in a row, which for the purposes of analysis in this chapter will be considered a single conversational turn.

An interesting preliminary account of laugh particles relates to whether or not their variations (*hahaha* vs. *hehehe*) and length (*haha* vs. *hahahahaha*) convey added meanings with pragmatic implications.[8] Yus (2005) carried out an empirical analysis about how users infer letter repetition (hellooooo) in typed text while interacting in chatrooms and smile repetition [:-)))))))] in typed emoticons, which has parallels with the analysis of laugh particle length too. According to the preliminary hypothesis, higher letter repetition and an increased number of smiles in emoticons

[8] Inferences of the role of letter repetition in laugher date back to the times of the telegraph. For example, McKay (2015) cites a New York Times article dated in 1890 in which the author instructs on the possible meanings of repeated "ha's": "Operators laugh over a wire, or rather, they convey the fact that they are amused. They do this by telegraphing "ha, ha." Great amusement is indicated by sending "ha" slowly and repeating it several times, and a smile is expressed by sending "ha" once or perhaps twice. Transmitting it slowly and repeating it tells the perpetrator of the joke at the end of the wire that the listener is leaning back in his chair and laughing long and heartily."

would convey greater intensity in the feelings intended by the user. For example, it was hypothesised that, beyond the default version of the greeting by User 1 in (5) and smiling in (6), User 3 would be happier than User 2 in (5) when greeting the other user through increased letter repetition, and also that User 3 would convey a higher degree of happiness in (6) by adding more smiles in the typed emoticons.

(5) User 1: hello.
User 2: helloooooo.
User 3: hellooooooooooooooo.
(6) User 1: :-)
User 2: :-)))))
User 3: :-))))))))))))

A survey was administered to a number of informants but, contrary to the initial expectations, the results showed that chatroom users hold a basic *default vs. connoted* attitude towards repetition. In a nutshell, the informants found a difference in intensity between the default version (User 1) and the ones including variation with repetition (Users 2–3); however, they found no difference regarding the amount of repetition (no inferred differences between the intensity of happiness conveyed by User 2 and 3 related to the amount of letter or smile repetition). In other words, repetition seems to be a "black-or-white" phenomenon: if the user types repeated letters or emoticon smiles, they infer higher intensity, but no degrees of intensity are inferred out of the greater or lesser level of repetition, probably because, after all, typing repeated items is easy with the keyboard. We can now extrapolate this finding to *laugh particle repetition*. Do different quantities of typed laugh particles generate additional conveyed meanings? To assess this, I posted the following question on Twitter and Facebook (both in English and Spanish) for my contacts to give their opinion:

> One question: if you post a joke on Facebook and a user (A) replies with "hahaha", while a user (B) replies with "hahahahahahahahahahaha", do you think that (B) was more amused by the joke than (A) because (B) has typed "ha" more times? Or the quantity of "ha" does not matter?

The question yielded mixed results. Most users replied that quantity does make a difference. Today's users are lazy and typing more "ha's" necessarily suggests added emphasis. Another user, by contrast, answered that typing is easy, as already stated, and therefore we do not find it difficult to type a lot of "ha's" if it seems necessary to us. Other users also emphasised the importance of capitalisation (*hahaha* vs. *HAHAHA*) which, as it happens with *flaming* online, tends to add a supplementary layer of emphasis to the typed text, including laugh particles. Comments by users also remarked the relevance of certain constraints, both user-centred (mood, task at hand while replying) and interface-related ones (predictive text easily turns a single "ha" into multiple "ha's" with no additional effort involved), as well as those linked to cultural issues (a user commented on the Asian culture, which considers less than three ha's impolite or reflecting an unsuccessful humorous intention).

Furthermore, no consensus apparently exists on what interpretations are conveyed through variations in laugh particles (e.g. *hahaha* vs. *hehehe*). An interesting Twitter thread recently tackled this issue regarding the Spanish version of laugh particles (i.e. *jajaja* vs. *jejeje*). The initial post and the replies are reproduced in Figs. 5.1, translated in (7a-d), and 5.2, translated in (7e-h). These show the extent to which interpretations of laugh particles may vary, even if major misunderstandings derived from their use are unlikely among messaging users.

(7) [A] User 1: Do you distinguish semantically between? jajaja / jejeje / jijiji /jojojo / jujuju?
Will it be jajajá with accentuation or will there be variations?

[B] User 2: "jajaja" as standard laughter / "jejeje" as a pseudo-laughter of complicity or as pseudo-laughter when the conversation reaches a dead point / "jijiji" as a

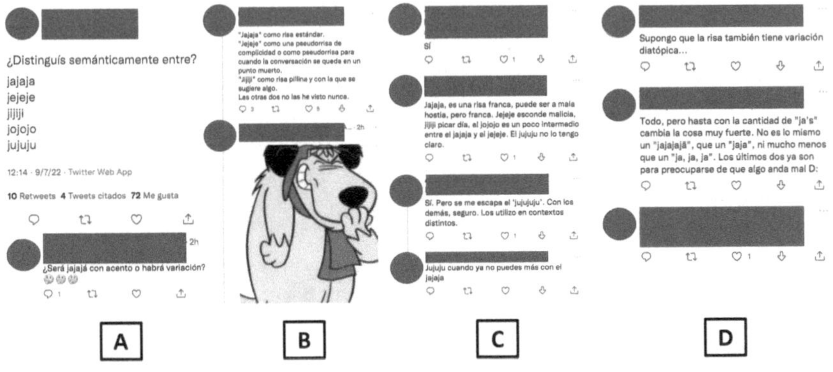

Fig. 5.1 Different interpretations of laugh particles in Spanish

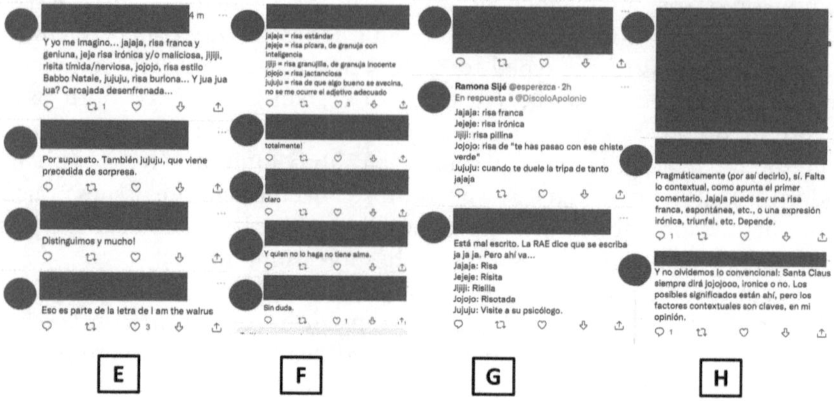

Fig. 5.2 (Continued) Different interpretations of laugh particles in Spanish

		naughty laughter with which you are suggesting something / the other two I've never come across.
	User 1:	Just like he is laughing? [image of dog laughing].
[C]	User 3:	Yes.
	User 4:	Jajaja is an honest laughter, could be out of anger, but honest. Some malicious attitude underlies jejeje, jijiji a swearword, jojojo is half-way between jajaja and jejeje. I have no clear idea what jujuju means
	User 5:	Yes, but jujuju escapes my knowledge. The others for sure. I use them in different contexts.
	User 6:	Jujuju when you had enough of jajaja
[D]	User 7:	I guess laughter also has diatopic variation…
	User 8:	Everything, but even that quantity of "jas" changes things strongly. "jajaja" is not the same as "jaja", and it also differs from "ja, ja, ja". The last two indicate that something is not going well D:
[E]	User 7:	And I imagine… jajaja, honest and genuine laughter, jeje malicious or ironic laughter, jijiji shy/nervous laughter, jojojo laughter Babbo Natale style, jujuju fun-making laughter… and jua jua jua? Insatiable laughter…
	User 9:	Of course. Also jujuju, preceded by surprise.
	User 10:	We distinguish them; a lot, actually!
	User 11:	That's part of the lyrics of "I am the walrus."

[F] User 12: jajaja = standard laughter / jejeje = mischievous laughter, of a rascal with intelligence / jijiji = rascal laughter, of innocent rascal / jojojo = boasting laughter / jujuju = laughter indicating that something good is coming up, I can't find the right adjective.

User 13: [Reply to User 12] Totally.

User 14: [Reply to User 12] Of course.

User 15: [Reply to User 12] And those who don't do it have no soul.

User 16: [Reply to User 12] No doubt.

[G] User 17: jajaja: honest laughter / jejeje: ironic laughter / jijiji: naughty laughter / jojojo: laughter meaning "you went too far with that sexual joke" / jujuju: when your tummy hurts of so much jajaja.

User 18: It's misspelled. RAE [Royal Academy of the Spanish Language] says it should be written ja ja ja. But here we go… jajaja: laughter / jejeje: little laughter / jijiji: giggle / jojojo: guffaw / jujuju: you should see a psychologist.

[H] User 19: Pragmatically (so to say), yes. We lack context, as the first comment hints. Jajaja can be an honest, spontaneous laughter, or an ironic, triumphant expression, etc. It depends.

And don't forget conventions: Santa will always say jojojo, regardless of whether an ironic intention exists or not. The possible meanings are there, but contextual factors play an essential role, in my opinion.

Clearly, laugh particles perform several functions beyond acknowledging a successful humorous intention. In Manokaran and Nian (2020), informants provided functions such as topic management, apology, embarrassment, empathy, and support, among others. Petitjean and Morel (2017, 2) emphasised the significant utilisation of laugh particles to manage delicate interactional moments, especially in the joint negotiation of key points during asynchronous conversations such as topic termination (especially to close the current play frame, see Sampietro 2021a, 99), and how users adapt their interactional skills to the rules of the "messaging game." Laughter, these authors add, likewise proves useful to show a user's competence in managing the app's technological affordances and to display an identity as a competent texter.

4.1.2 Emojis

Emojis are iconic displays of facial expressions that play a fundamental role in the management of messaging humorous interactions. Alongside laugh particles, Sampietro (2021a, 103) points out that most of the functions proposed for laughter in face-to-face scenarios are equally performed by emojis in messaging interactions, namely: to evidence amusement and appreciation of a humorous text; to show involvement in the ongoing interaction, to mark solidarity (e.g. in a humorous interaction co-constructed by several interlocutors); and to structure playful talk (both in signalling speakers' recognition of the establishment of a play frame and in identifying its end). For instance, laugh particles and emojis become crucial to maintain the play frame throughout the WhatsApp interaction because, without them, it might well be interpreted as a sequence of non-humorous texts. Instead, they either tag the interaction humorously or signal staged or faked seriousness, both of these discourses (laugh particles, emojis) ensuring that these messaging turns will be properly understood. Thus, (8) clearly starts with a humorous text, and the subsequent turns maintain this just-initiated humorous frame with the aid of emojis and laugh particles that tinge the accompanying texts with a humorous quality:

(8) Saúl: Solo para que lo sepáis, he sido voluntario para probar una vacuna rusa del Covid-19. He recibido la primera dosis y quería comentaros que es totalmente segura y sin efectos secundarios. Me sientoshкı χoρoshó я чувствую себя немного странно и я думаю, что вытащил ослиные уши.
[Just for you to know, I have volunteered to test the Russian Covid-19 vaccine. I got the first jab and I wanted to tell you that it is completely safe and with no side effects. I am feelingshкı χoρoshó я чувствую себя немного странно и я думаю, что вытащил ослиные уши].
Luca: El pobre...
[*Poor guy*].
Luca : Al menos, ha aprendido una lengua sin esfuerzo ni clases.
[*At least, he has learned a language with no effort or classes*].
Luca : 😂😂😂😂
Saúl: Jajaja.
[*hahaha*].
Luca: A mí el finlandés me atrae.
[*I am interested in Finnish*].
Saúl: Pero esa lengua es complicada... necesitas 5 dosis.
[*But that language is complicated... you need 5 doses*].
Saúl : 😂😂

In more specific terms, emojis have proved useful to set the *play frame* underlying an interaction. They also perform shared laughter, which helps to build up solidarity among interlocutors who generate feelings of in-group bonding via humour recognition and appreciation. Emojis also serve to terminate this *play frame*, in which case they typically make up the sole content of the message and are often repeated. Sequences of equal laughing emojis, such as the famous "face with tears of joy" emoji, often close short informal interactions. For Sampietro (2016, 103), this reveals a clear difference between texting and face-to-face or even phone-mediated communication, where farewells are an essential part of the structure of a successful interaction.

Table 5.3 lists some of the numerous pragmatic functions of emojis proposed in the bibliography. Yus (2019, 2021a) also made a proposal, grouping emoji functions into three main categories:

A. *Emoji within (the text).*

Table 5.3 Proposals for functions of emoji

Author(s)	*Functions of emojis*
Durante (2016)	(a) To repeat what is sent verbally; (b) to substitute for parts of the text message or the entire text message); (c) to complement or clarify the text message; (d) to contradict the text message; (e) to emphasise or elaborate the text message; and (f) to moderate text messages (establish conversational rhythm, moderate, regulate text messaging conversations)
Herring (2018)	(a) To express emotion and playfulness; (b) to modify the tone of textual messages; (c) to soften illocutionary force; (d) to illustrate portions of text; (e) to express virtual actions; (f) to convey private meanings; and (g) to open and/or close conversations
Al Rashdi (2018)	(a) To express emotions; (b) to keep a conversational connection; (c) to add tone; (d) to engage recipients; (e) to maintain or manage relationships; (f) to engage in phaticness; and (g) to add humorous tinges to the text
Ge and Herring (2018)	(a) To express emotion; (b) to modify tone; (c) to substitute for nonverbal behaviour; (d) to open and close conversations; (e) to enhance interpersonal relationships; (f) to share secret meanings; (g) to foster social connectedness between users; (h) to express one's identity; and (i) to increase perceived intimacy
Herring and Dainas (2018)	(a) To add personal identity expression; (b) to add playfulness to a message; (c) to maintain relationships; and (d) to modify the tone of the message
Sampietro (2019)	(a) To signal the illocutionary force of the message; (b) to add politeness and rapport building devices; (c) to clarify the message; (d) to express emotion; (e) to create conversational connection; and (f) to soften or strengthen the message

(*continued*)

Table 5.3 (continued)

Author(s)	*Functions of emojis*
Siever (2020)	(a) Modal function, divided into (a.1) extension of the proposition (sub-divided into provide additional information, provide propositional attitude, decoration), (a.2) repetition of parts of the proposition; and (b) referential function, divided into (b.1) replacement of a letter, (b.2) replacement of parts of words, (b.3) replacement of a complete words, and (b.4) replacement of a complete word with multiple emojis
Völkel et al. (2019)	(a) To add emotional or situational meaning; (b) to convey a more intense expression; (c) to adjust the tone of a message; (d) to make a message more engaging or playful by providing additional stimuli; (e) to manage the conversation; and (f) inside jokes or references within a relationship
Siever and Siever (2020)	(a) Allographs for individual letters; (b) semantic specifier (of intended meaning); (c) cohesive device; (d) deictic element; (e) structuring device; and (f) hashtag
Panckhurst and Frontini (2020)	(a) Redundant addition (an emoji is used as well as written text, but it is not required in order to understand the text); (b) necessary addition (an emoji is used as well as written text, and its inclusion is necessary in order to avoid misinterpretation); and (c) lexical replacement (an emoji is used instead of a word)

The typical scenario in which the emoji influences how the accompanying text should be interpreted. In this first category, we usually find a sender user thinking that their text would be more accurately interpreted with the addition of an emoji, or expecting that the latter will facilitate the derivation of additional (or different) propositional effects, together with possible affective effects. As such, within the perspective of this book, the inclusion of an emoji is seldom regarded as gratuitous or redundant, even when it only seems to "add colour" to a message without any further communicative role). It is our contention that emoji inclusion nearly always aims at relevance and leads the addressee in certain interpretive directions, including the direction towards the derivation of humorous effects.

In the functions listed below it is generally assumed that the emoji adds certain information to the content of the accompanying text (see Maíz-Arévalo 2014, 182). On other occasions, the emoji has a more ***procedural role***, that is, it does not convey much information by itself but mainly instructs the addressee user about how the text next to it ought to be processed. Functions in this category include the following:

A.1. To signal the propositional attitude underlying the message which would be difficult to identify in the absence of the emoji. Propositional attitudes are important to interpret utterances correctly. For example, if someone asks "Can you help me to find work?" and the interlocutor sadly answers that she cannot help him, we could establish an explicature of her answer ("She cannot help him to find work") and also an explicature plus attitude (called *higher-level explicature* in relevance-theoretic terminology) expressed through the same response, such as "she *regrets* not being able to help him to find work."

Similarly, internet users are expected to embed their messages in a particular attitude under which the message is typed. For that purpose, they may resort to text alteration and emojis in order to fulfil this communicative task, thus facilitating the identification of an appropriate attitudinal schema, as in (9–11), where the emojis help to frame the text within an *I regret that…* attitudinal schema:

(9) A: What was the exam like?
B: My mind went blank! 😖😖

(10) I am sooo old!!! 😭

(11) I have no time to get bored, nor to read 😖

A.2. To communicate higher intensity in relation to a propositional attitude which is already coded verbally (i.e. already typed). The user does resort to a linguistic means to communicate their propositional attitude and the emoji adds an additional level of intensity to the way this attitude is held, as in (12), where the attitude "I hope that…" has been typed:

(12) *I hope that* you'll always remember my Spanish lessons ☺

A.3. To contradict the explicit content of a message (a): joking. This is the function that interests us most in the context of this book: to signal that the accompanying text should not be understood literally, and that the underlying intention consists in joking about some state of affairs. The relevance of the emoji lies in its ability to direct the reader away from a literal interpretation of the message. (13–14) below are examples thereof.

(13) A: How are the exams going? 😌😌
B: Ufff... Really well!!! 😂

(14) A: Feel like starting [the new academic year]?
B: Yes, a little, to be honest.
A: Me too, but only for the gossip 😂

A.4. To contradict the explicit content of a message (b): irony. A similar case is contradicting propositional content when seeking to convey irony. Yus (2014a, 522) provided the examples in (15) for the role of (typed) emoticons as markers of an ironic intention:

(15) a. A: I would click on "don't like" if I could... hehe.
B: Hahaha User 1, I know that, deep down inside you, you like them: -)
b. What a hard life you lead xD.
c. A: These scenes ring a bell, don't know why...: -).
B: Really? Well, I don't know why they do, either;-).

In (15a), B knows that A dislikes the content of the entry but pretends to like it; by using the emoticon, she makes it clear (ironically) that both agree on the quality of the content. As for (15b), it is a typical example of irony where the user communicates the opposite while, at the same time, foregrounding the real quality of the addressee's life. Finally, in (15c), both users know which scenes are being talked about but behave as if they did not; the outcome is an increased awareness about the mutuality of this information.

A.5. To add a feeling or emotion towards the propositional content of a message (*affective attitude* towards the latter). Here, emoji use adds emotional valence and affect and can be used, at times strategically, to imbue the messaging interaction with affective information in ways that satisfy this fundamental human need for affection, interpersonal closeness and intimacy in communication.

In general, the range of textual options to convey emotions is arguably limited compared to the vast number of subtleties and shades of meanings that emotions can acquire, which is why users often resort to emojis. In this function, then, the user takes advantage of an emoji to show a certain feeling or emotion towards the content of the accompanying message. Consider the examples below:

(16) A: Will they let you do it [the exam] again?
B: I don't know... As things stand I doubt it 😭
(17) A: What are you doing on New Year's Eve?
B: Mmm 🤤🤤
B: Why are you asking? Do you have any idea? 😮
(18) A: He finished his marriage really fast xD
B: Indeed! 😂

In (16), B uses a specific emoji to express a feeling of sadness or dismay at the fact that her teachers will probably not allow her to retake the exam. In (17), B incorporates a sense of uncertainty into her verbal message. Finally, B adds a laughter-inducing feeling referred to a sub-sentential utterance (*Indeed*) that confirms what the initial user had typed in (18).

A.6. To communicate the intensity of a feeling or emotion that has already been coded verbally. The examples in (19) show textually coded feelings (in italics), the emoji contributing a supplementary layer of intensity:

(19) a. This is on my sister and the dances of the 80 s, we *love* them 😊
b. I don't like it, I *love* it! You've really *moved* me, my friend 😊
c. Oleeee olee olee!! *look forward to* meeting the little baby 😊
d. Sounds great!! So *excited* to see you!! 😍
e. I was *pleased* to see that after waking up... 😊

A.7. To replace verbal elements inside a message, a function exemplified in (20), where several emojis replace their corresponding verbal elements (added in square brackets):

(20) A: Congratulations Lau!!! 🎂🎈🎈
32 already!!!
👀 you tmw? [see you tomorrow?]
B: 😱😱😱😱😱😱😱
I'm so old!
It's 👍👍 👍👍👍 for me. [It's ok for me]
We'll have to have some 🍺🍺🍺🍺🍺🍺 [some beers]
A: Friday 🍝 + 🍺 + 💃 ??? [Shall we have dinner, beers and go dancing on Friday?]
B: 👏👏👏👏👏👏
Friday 👍👍👍👍 [Friday ok]
I suggest tomorrow ["cup of coffee" emoji] + 🎂 in my 🏠 and Friday 🍝 + 🍺 + 💃 [coffee and cake in my place]
A: 👌

B. *Emoji without (the text).*

This category portrays the emoji as the only source of information in the messaging act of communication, also found in humorous messaging interactions. This happens especially when the emoji has no accompanying text (the so-called *naked emoji*). Several functions fit the category.

B.1. To communicate a single referent. In this first function, the emoji's prototypical meaning, without a great informational gap, to what the user intends to communicate with it. This is a clearly ***denotative*** function illustrated in (21):

(21) [User A uploads a picture of a thermometer showing a very low temperature].
A: ⛄
B: 😱

B.2. To communicate an *ad hoc* visual referent. Here, the addressee user will need to adjust the prototypical referent of the emoji by using contextual information such as previous information communicated in the messaging conversation, or the mutuality of information expected between the interlocutors, among other contextualisation sources. A single emoji may have slightly different meanings based on previous/subsequent texts in the interaction.

B.3. To communicate a whole proposition. In this case, the emoji has to be inferentially developed into a full proposition with the aid of contextual information, as in (22), where the emoji is to be inferred as the whole interpretation provided between square brackets:

(22) A: How is the exam going?
B: 😔
[The exam is going really bad].

B.4. To construct a story (***emojis in a row***). Finally, ***naked emojis*** may be utilised in sequences to construct stories. A famous example is the novel *Emoji Dick* by Fred Benenson, a transcription into emojis of Herman Melville's famous novel *Moby Dick*.

C. *Emoji beyond (the text)*.

In this third category, the emoji does not qualify the content of the typed message; instead, it connotes the act of communication as a whole, providing an affective attitude or a propositional attitude towards the broader act of communication rather than focusing directly on the specific content of the message typed. Functions include the following:

C.1. To add visual imagery without qualifying the accompanying text substantially. Here, the user's decision to resort to emojis does not seek to connote or qualify the content of the message that they are typing. These emojis are often added simply to convey visual imagery, also called

colourful addition, that is, emojis whose function is just to provide colourful look to the accompanying text without influencing the meaning of that text (Siever and Siever 2020). Illustrations can be found in (23–25):

(23) A: What was the trip like? ☺☺
B: It was great fun 😜
A: I can imagine 🛫🛫
(24) You've got Thursday's units of [the subject] Culture in your email 📩😘
(25) Happy birthday! 🎂🎈🎈

C.2. To facilitate conversational management. Emojis may likewise play a part in messaging interaction management. They more or less work like facial gestures that can help to handle conversations in physical scenarios (e.g. nodding as feedback to paying attention). Roles include turn-taking management and backchannel reactions, among others. Sampietro (2018) proposes the example (25) below, in which the "blow a kiss" emoji 😘 serves to announce the end of the conversation, while the "smile" emoji 😊 in (26) conveys a backchannel reaction showing that the user is being attended to, even if the user does not contribute verbally to the interaction:

(25) A: If you want, we could meet next weekend and have dinner together.
B: Okay, we'll talk about it on Friday if you want.
A: Ok
A: Talk to u soon 😘
B: 👍😘
(26) A: When does Clara come?
B: On our way.
B: She arrives in 10 minutes.
A: 😊
B: Do I say something to her?

C.3. To add a feeling, emotion or attitude towards the whole communicative act. In physical scenarios, people's nonverbal behaviour sometimes has a more social connotation (the typical quality of phatic exchanges) in which the speakers show what the interaction is making them feel, and hence nonverbal behaviour arises in parallel to verbal content, thereby endowing the whole communicative act with an affective attitude, rather than directly qualifying the propositional content encoded in the utterances. In Yus (2021a), the example (27) can be found.

(27) Ann: how pretty!!! Great parties you go to, you never stop!!!! 🙂
Betty: Next time I'll let you know, in case you feel like it!!! 🙂

Here, Ann will enrich Betty's message inferentially so as to yield a relevant explicit (and/or implicated) interpretation. In this specific case (27), the inferred proposition will roughly be (28), its *explicature*, where the additional inferred content appears between square brackets:

(28) CONTEXTUALISED EXPLICIT INTERPRETATION
Next time [I go to a party] I'll let you know [about that party] in case you feel like [coming with me to that party].

Ann will equally infer Betty's attitude when she says her utterance yielding the so-called *higher-level explicature*. Specifically concerning (27), a possible higher-level explicature might be the one provided in italics in (20):

(29) PROPOSITIONAL ATTITUDE (towards the content of message)
[*I inform you that*] next time [I go to a party] I'll let you know [about that party] in case you feel like [coming with me to that party].

Now, another question arises at this point: is (29) all that Betty intends to communicate? Of course not. She also wants Ann to know that she would love it if Ann joined her at the party -or expressed differently, Betty wishes to communicate her *affective attitude*, for which purpose the "slightly smiling face" emoji (🙂) proves very helpful. Crucially, Betty's use of the emoji has nothing to do with her being *happy that she will let A know* about a future party or *happy to ask whether A will be willing to go*. Instead, she shows the kind of nonverbal behaviour triggered by the fact that she is conversing with Ann, by the prospect of getting together at the party and, in general, by her emotions *while* typing that message for Ann (including a feeling of bonding or enhanced friendship). In other words, the emoji ends up qualifying the higher-level explicature (*I inform you that...*) and not the explicature itself (*Next time...*), which means that it qualifies the act of communication as a whole.

Furthermore, Betty wants to evidence that this is not simply an open-ended question; she intends to convey that some insistence and urge underlie this invitation, which she ultimately does by repeating the exclamation mark so as to achieve her communicative purposes. The resulting proposition would roughly look like the one quoted in (30) below:

(30) AFFECTIVE ATTITUDE (towards the whole communicative act)
[I am happy while] [I inform you that] next time [I go to a party] I'll let you know [about that party] in case you feel like [coming with me to that party] [and I insist that you accept to come].

C.4. To strengthen/mitigate the illocutionary force of a speech act. In this function, the emoji qualifies a speech act performed during a messaging interaction, either by strengthening or mitigating it. As such, this is an emoji *beyond* function, since it impacts on the interpretation of the overall speech act, rather than that of the content of the message encoded in the speech act.

The literature often refers to this function as *tone modification* -commonly regarded as one of the main functions of emojis (Danesi 2016, 14). Authors more recently favour the term *illocutionary force indicator*, thereby facilitating the ascription of the user's intentionality to the act of communication (Dresner and Herring 2010, 2012; dos Reis et al. 2018, 148; Sampietro 2016, 104). On this occasion, the emoji upgrades or downgrades the force of the speech act. By way of example, the emoji in (31) softens a speech act that sounds too imposing and minimises the possible rejection to the arrangement:

(31) A: Hi!
A: Shall we meet tomorrow to organise the paper?
A: At 8.
A: If you want and can.
B: I can't tomorrow at 8. I could at 9 😰

C.5. To communicate the politeness involved in the act of messaging interaction. Following Brown and Levinson's (1987) politeness theory, many instances of messaging communication are *face-threatening* and the user draws on emojis to convey an underlying polite attitude (Vandergriff 2014; Sampietro 2017). Politeness under this theory can be divided into *positive politeness* (the desire that the speaker's intentions are accepted by others, for example, that one's ideas are agreed with or that one's opinions are endorsed) and *negative politeness* (the desire that the speaker's intentions are not thwarted by interlocutors, for instance, that an order is fulfilled or that a request has the desired effect. Emojis may likewise serve to express these types of politeness, including polite openings and closings, expressions of gratitude, markers of solidarity or compliments, to quote but a few.

For the purposes of this chapter, emojis most importantly carry out the function of signalling the humorous quality of the accompanying text (performing an *emoji within* function) or showing appreciation for a previous humorous message from another user (using either an *emoji within* or an *emoji without* function) and even qualify the whole act of communication (*emoji beyond* function). A wide range of emojis can fulfil these humorous objectives. Most apps, among them WhatsApp, rely on the emoji galleries provided by the smartphone. However, WeChat offers its users a specific set of emoji galleries as part of the app's interface affordances. Figure 5.3 shows samples of emojis typically used for humorous purposes on WhatsApp and WeChat.

In this regard, we should not forget that certain WeChat-specific emojis such as "facepalming with tears of joy" emoji (fourth from the left in Fig. 5.3) do not exist on WhatsApp and are thus likely to cause miscommunication, because while Spanish users tend to infer the laughing connotation, WeChat users emphasise the facepalming part (I cannot accept what you just typed.../I can't believe you typed this..., etc.).[9]

Fig. 5.3 Emojis typically used for humorous purposes on WeChat and WhatsApp

[9] The "face with tears of joy emoji" is probably one of the most frequently used with a humorous intention on both apps (Zhang et al. 2021, Sampietro 2021a). However, it has been pointed out in the literature that the WeChat "facepalming with tears of joy" emoji relatively often leads to misunderstandings. Chui (2020, 109) stresses that this emoji has both tears (negative sentiments) and an open smile (positive sentiments), which faces users with a choice of interpreting it as sheer bliss or as wailing. Sun et al. (in press) extend (unjustifiably in my opinion) this convergence of positive and negative emotions to the "face with tears of joy" emoji. Although they acknowledge that this emoji generally appears when someone says or does something so funny as to make the addressee laugh to tears, it may be interpreted differently by some users for including negative (tears) as well as positive (laugh) feelings.

In any case, emojis pervade humorous interactions on these apps and on similar ones such as Line or Telegram. As Hsieh and Tseng (2017, 412) remark in relation to emoticons, these "represent appealing characters and humorous gestures, thus complementing text messaging in mobile instant messaging to foster perceived playfulness and fun in the interactive communication process." It should be noted that sex- and age-specific constraints exist in the choice and frequency of use of emojis for humorous purposes. Regarding the former, sex-related use, Al Rashdi (2018), Pérez-Sabater (2019), Wirza et al. (2020) and Herring and Dainas (2020), among others, found clear gender-based differences in emoji use. For example, the "face blowing a kiss" emoji tends to be much more popular among female users than among their male counterparts. López-Rúa (2021) adds that "females are more skilled at expressing nonverbal behaviour, and they are more prone to the expression of certain attitudes and emotions which are commonly conveyed through emojis (such as love, happiness, sadness, or empathy). In addition, they are more likely to use ornament and visual aesthetics as a complement to text in their communicative exchanges. All these functions are effectively performed by emojis."

Age also influences the choice of emojis, including those for humorous purposes (see Jones et al. 2020 and Koch et al. 2021, among others). In Spain, for instance, younger generations use the "face with tears of joy emoji" far less frequently than older users. Instead, the former exhibit a striking familiarity with others such as the "loudly crying face" emoji (😭), never found in older users' humorous interactions. Evidence also exists about the utilisation of the skull emoji by young users, conveying the "laughing to death" connotation. Indeed, as Ishmael (2021) correctly emphasises, people over 30 mostly use emojis to convey their literal referents, while "digital natives" might ascribe sarcastic meanings to them or turn them into shorthand for an entirely different interpretation. The skull emoji, despite its meaning of death or hazard to many adults, is said to signify laughing extremely hard for young users.

In any case, the one most typically associated with humour is the "face with tears of joy" emoji (especially for older generations), followed by other variations, e.g. the "rolling on the floor laughing" emoji (🤣). The former occurs very frequently both when qualifying the text next to it (*emoji within* function) and when typed as the only content of a message (*emoji without* function). In the first pattern, as already mentioned, it mainly serves to mark the accompanying text as humorous, also inviting the interlocutor's continuation with laugher. By way of example, Juan uses the "face with tears of joy" emoji in (32) to emphasise the humorous nature of his utterance, and Luis's subsequent utilisation of another emoji equally seeks to avoid that his complaint be inferred as such. Without adding the emojis, these utterances might not have been inferred as these were intended.

(32) Luis: No mas disho na pisha.
[*You didn't reply to me, mate*].
Juan: Sí, te dije "vaya!" 😂😂
[*I did, I said to you "Blimey!"* 😂😂].
Luis: Ahhh es verdad.
[*Ahhh it's true*].
Luis: No te rompas la uña tecleando 😂😂😂
[*Don't break a nail while typing* 😂😂😂].
Juan: Jajajajaja.
[*hahahaha*].
Juan: Las tengo delicadas y ayer me hice la manicura 🤭🤭🤭🤭
[*Mine are delicate and yesterday I had a manicure* 🤭🤭🤭🤭].
Luis: Eso está muy bien.
[*That's very good*].
Luis: Yo las llevo postizas de nácar.
[*I wear false mother-of-pearl nails*].

Secondly, when used on its own (*naked emoji*), the "face with tears of joy" emoji more often than not appears repeated several times and fulfils a widespread function: to close short humorous messaging conversations (Sampietro 2021a, 104). As illustrated in (33), the short conversation frequently stops after the production of the emoji, this being a feature which will be corroborated when analysing patterns in messaging interactions later on in this chapter:

(33) Sara: [Sends- a video showing rain pouring down].
Sara: Mira cómo llueve en Valencia!
[*Look how it's raining in Valencia*].
Luis: 😂😂😂😂

Added to the above, other qualities such as the position of an emoji in the overall interaction entail further pragmatic implications (see Sampietro 2021a, 2021b). In general, if laughter opens a message, it usually does so as an answer to previous humorous remarks. By contrast, if a user places laugh particles or a laugh-connoted emoji at the end of a message, they usually signal that the attached message should be inferred as humorous.

Therefore, emojis are not only useful to mark nonverbal meanings, but also help structure the conversation (Sampietro 2021a, 101). Example (34) below shows both roles in the same dialogue. The first laughing emoji emphasises the humorous quality of the accompanying text, whereas Sarah's second stand-alone emoji is a humorous reaction to the preceding message. In (35), the emoji serves to react humorously to Luis's text. Finally, the laughing emoji appearing in (36) clearly marks the accompanying text as humorous.

(34) Luis: [Sends photo of a T-shirt with a striking text on it].
Luis: 🤦‍♂️
Luis: Es real. Se puede comprar 🤣
[*It's real. You can buy it* 🤣].
Sara: 🤣🤣🤣🤦‍♀️

(35) Luis: When you are stressed, you eat icecream, cake, chocolate and sweets. Why? Because "stressed" spelt backwards is "desserts."
Sara: 🤣🤣🤣

(36) Luis: [Tells Juan about a new job he's been offered].
Juan: Te pagan por todo
[*They pay people for everything*].
Juan: Jolín, qué bien!
[*Geez, how good!*].
Luis: Creo que incluye dos concubinas en el hotel 😂😂😂
[*I think it includes two concubines at the hotel* 😂😂😂].
Juan: Te vas a hacer de oro.
[*You're going to get rich*].
Juan: Jajajajajajaja
[*hahahahaha*].
Luis: Ya veremos.
[*We'll see*].

Somehow, as Qiu et al. (2021, 230) contend, these roles resemble the ones performed by laughter and facial expressions in the management and labelling of utterances as humorous in face-to-face scenarios. When it comes to handling messaging interactions, emojis have proved useful in controlling the flow of a conversation and can additionally act as openings and closings, alongside their role as backchannel devices (Sampietro 2021b). Also similar to face-to-face interactions is the use of the "laugh with tears of joy" emoji at the end of a message as an invitation to laugh. Sampietro (ibid.) provides example (37), where the presence of this emoji in the last turn can be seen as a response to the invitation to laugh:

(37) User 1: Hoy tienes huésped otra vez 🤪
[*Today you have a guest again* 🤪].
User 1: A venido Manu a x el.
[*Manu's gone to look for him*].
User 2: 👍
User 2: Lo que ellos no saben es que mañana a las ocho menos cuarto hay repique de campanas hasta morirse 😂
[*What they don't know is that tomorrow at a quarter to eight there will be church bells ringing to the max* 😂].
User 1: 😂😂😂

5 Turn-Taking Patterns during Humorous Messaging Interactions (WhatsApp)

Humorous messaging interactions follow certain patterns. In previous research (Yus 2021c, 2022b), a qualitative analysis of these patterns was carried out, its main objective consisting in identifying the most frequent turn-taking patterns in dyadic humorous interactions between WhatsApp users. As sub-objectives, this research aimed to examine: (a) how humorous and non-humorous turns combine in the development of a humorous WhatsApp interaction; (b) the role of other discourses that reveal humorous intentions (emojis, laugh particles such as *jaja*...); and (c) the role played by images in the generation of humorous responses (or not) by other users.

Next, Yus (2022c) presented a quantitative analysis of these humorous interactions (see next Section for data and methodology) which has now been extended and updated. This quantitative analysis essentially sought to examine a broader corpus of conversations on WhatsApp and accordingly corroborate the suitability of the patterns previously identified in Yus (2022b). This research also has some sub-objectives, among which stand out the following three: (a) to identify quantitatively recurrent discursive combinations in humorous WhatsApp interactions: (b) to analyse the frequency of use of certain discourses that also convey a humorous intention (e.g. laugh particles, emoji(s)...); and (c) to propose a prototypical schema for humorous WhatsApp interactions depending on the frequency of the different patterns.

5.1 *Corpus and Methodology*

For this study, the dyadic conversations in Spanish between several WhatsApp users were exported via email and kindly sent to me. Added to some of my own WhatsApp interactions, the corpus under analysis amounted to 541,769 words. In addition, the research benefited from friends and students who provided around one hundred screenshots showing examples of conversations that exhibited humorous qualities (according to those informants' opinion).

The next step consisted in extracting from this corpus the interactions which had a marked humorous quality and whose effects were managed in several turns. The analysis was carried out by reading through the corpus and isolating examples of clear humorous intentions, which totalled 2269 interactions, mainly from conversations between users within the age range of 40–60, especially between men or mixed interactions between men and women.

After delimiting this sub-corpus, each example was studied for the purpose of isolating recurring humorous patterns that may yield a typology of humorous interactions on WhatsApp. To avoid an excessive multiplicity of turn possibilities, the scrutiny focused on the first four turns of dyadic humorous interactions between WhatsApp users, insofar as four turns suffice to isolate recurrent patterns while simultaneously avoiding an endless recursiveness of pattern developments during those conversations. The reader is reminded that, in this research, all the messages that a user sends without another user sending their own message constitute a single turn and not successive turns, as already stated above. For example, Luis's message (his turn) in (38) is followed by several messages that Juan sends in a row. For the purposes of this study, Juan's messages would be considered one single turn:

(38) Juan: Lunch en el primer y tercer piso
[*Lunch on the first and third floor*].
Luis: Quedamos a 11:45 y decidimos donde ir
[*Let's meet at 11:45 and we'll decide where to go*].
Juan: Sí, eso
[*Yes, fine*].
Juan: Van a abrir ya
[*They are opening now*].
Juan: Están diciendo dónde nos tenemos que poner
[*They are saying where we are supposed to sit*].
Juan: Estás en el panel de [investigador X]?
[*Are you in the panel by [researcher X]?*].

The analysis isolated several patterns according to the quality of the first turn in the four-turn sequences examined: (a) humorous text; (b) humorous text plus emoji; (c) non-humorous text; (d) non-humorous text plus emoji; (e) single image; (f) image plus humorous text[10]; (g) image plus non-humorous text; and (h) video.[11] Most of these patterns will be studied in this Section, with the exception of (g), whose presence in the corpus is negligible.

The humorous interactions were then grouped together depending on the quality of the subsequent turns, creating one Table for each of the patterns (a-h) listed in the previous paragraph. Figure 5.4 reproduces the first part of the Table for humorous interactions beginning with a humorous text. These have been brought together in accordance with the quality of the second turn, this time "humorous text plus emoji." The same applies to the third turn: again, interactions have been grouped on the basis of the similar quality in this third turn: once more, a "humorous text plus emoji." The analysis proceeded in the same way with the fourth turn.

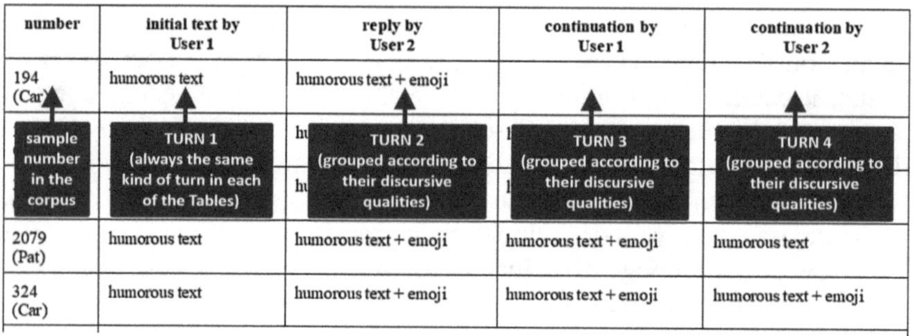

Humorous text

number	initial text by User 1	reply by User 2	continuation by User 1	continuation by User 2
194 (Car)	humorous text	humorous text + emoji		
2079 (Pat)	humorous text	humorous text + emoji	humorous text + emoji	humorous text
324 (Car)	humorous text	humorous text + emoji	humorous text + emoji	humorous text + emoji

Fig. 5.4 Table classifying patterns for interactions beginning with a humorous text

[10] Combinations of different discursive elements -as in "image plus humorous text"- have been identified in this research irrespective of the order in which they appear in the message. For example, AT+E ("approbation text" plus emoji) would fit either of these messages: "Sara: I love it! 😂😂😂 " / Sara: "😂😂😂 I love it!"

[11] There were instances of "humorous text plus sticker" and "non-humorous text plus sticker" too, though the number was negligible. This largely has to do with the age range of the users from which the WhatsApp corpus was obtained: individuals between 40 and 60 years of age. Stickers appear much more frequently in -and even pervade- messaging interactions between young users (adolescents, twenty-somethings, etc.) and cultural constraints exist as well, since stickers are even more common in Asian countries such as China (Yus and Hu, submitted).

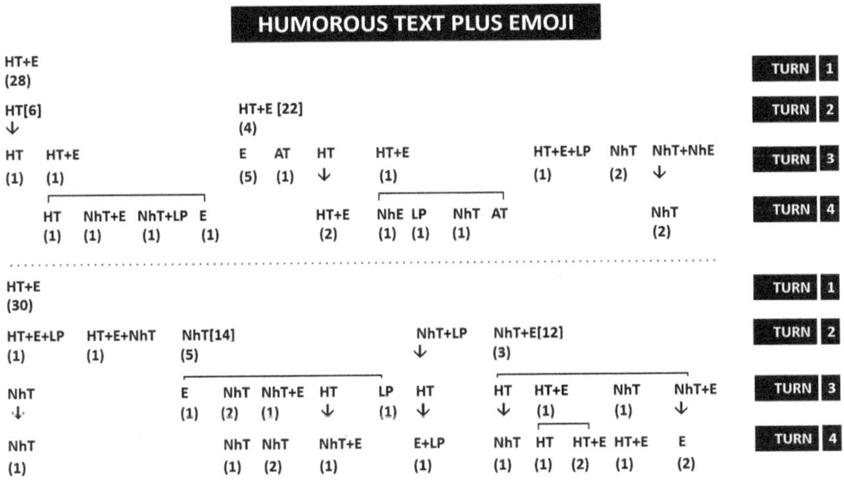

Fig. 5.5 Tree diagrams for the quantitative analysis of humorous WhatsApp interactions. Key: *HT* humorous text, *E* humorous emoji, *AT* approbation text (e.g. I loved this!), *LP* laugh particle (e.g. hahaha), *NhT* non-humorous text, *NhE* non-humorous emoji

Finally, several tree diagrams were set up in order to quantitatively analyse the number of instances that fitted the different patterns (depending on the quality of the first turn) and sub-patterns (according to the quality of the subsequent turns) included in the research corpus. Figure 5.5 shows two of these trees created for some of the WhatsApp interactions which start with a first turn made up of a humorous text plus emoji.

5.2 *Analysis of Turn-Taking Patterns during Messaging Interactions*

Examining the sample of 2269 humorous interactions on WhatsApp provided us with the following numbers and percentages per sample:

(1)	Humorous text	136	(6%)
(2)	Humorous text plus emoji	109	(4.8%)
(3)	Non-humorous text	239	(10.53%)
(4)	Non-humorous text plus emoji	77	(3.41%)
(5)	Single image	1530	(67.4%)
(6)	Image plus humorous text	39	(1.73%)
(7)	Image plus non-humorous text/emoji	35	(1.53%)
(8)	Video	104	(4.6%)

A few preliminary conclusions can be drawn from this initial quantitative delimitation:

1. Against the initial predictions, only about 11% of interactions begin with an explicitly humorous text on its own (6%) or paired with emoji(s) (4.8%). This comes as a surprise, since a humorous text appears to be a clear, explicit way to start a humorous interaction.
2. In fact, it is more common for a user, during an ongoing non-humorous interaction, to suddenly shift it into a *play frame* by sending a message with a humorous intention (about 14% of interactions). This attempt at turning the interaction from a non-humorous frame to a humorous one may be reacted upon with an alignment to the just-initiated play frame or an insistence on sticking to the initially established non-humorous frame, or combinations of both. An example appears in (39), where Olga suddenly transforms a serious conversation about Ramón's mishap into a humorous one. Notice how Ramón's initial reaction is not humorous at all, as shown by the "red with anger" emoji (😡), but he finally aligns himself with it, further developing the conversation within this new "now-mutually-agreed-upon" humorous frame:

(39) Ramón: Sabes?
[*You know what?*].
Hoy me he caido en MediaMarkt
[*Today I fell down at MediaMarkt*].
Olga: Comorrr????
[*Whatttttt?*].
Olga: 😳
Olga: Con tu hijo delante?
[*With your son beside you?*].
Ramón: He tropezado con un borde de ladrillo y he caido[12] de cara sobre la carretera.
[*I tripped over a brick curb and fell face first onto the road*].
Ramón: Pero no me he hecho nada.
[*But I wasn't hurt*].
Olga: Dios mio de mi vida.
[*Oh my God*].

[12] In this chapter, the orthographic mistakes made in the Spanish WhatsApp conversations have been kept unchanged.

Ramón: Y mi hijo venga a reírse.
[*And my son couldn't stop laughing*].
Olga: Habra temblado la tierra...
[*The earth must have trembled*].
Ramón: 😠😠😠
Olga: 😂😂😂😂
Olga: Lo siento.
[*I am sorry*].
Olga: Pero... es muy divertido! Jajaja.
[*But... it's very funny! hahaha*].
Olga: 😂👍😂
Ramón: se ha caido un coche dentro del agujero que he hecho en el suelo
[*A car fell into the hole I made on the ground*].
Ramón: 😀
Olga: Jajaja.
Olga: Me meoooo.
[*I laugh my socks off*].

3. Image is, by far, the most frequently used discourse to start a humorous interaction (67.4%), often as a pretext to generate connectivity and further interactions. However, it will be commented upon below that a high percentage of these single images receives an emoji or laugh particle in reply and the conversation stops at this point, thus invalidating the user's possible attempt to engage in a sustained interaction after having sent the initial image.
4. Videos clearly do not seem to be the most favoured option for initiating a humorous interaction (only 4.6%), possibly because users are aware of their "weight" (in terms of megabytes), which demands high smartphone data connection and data processing levels. Hence users' preference for avoiding them or sending a link to the video, instead.

5.2.1 Pattern 1: First Turn as Humorous Text

This first pattern occurs in 136 humorous interactions (6% of the total sample). These humorous texts are either typed directly in the designated area of the messaging app interface or referred to via link, or copied and pasted from other messaging conversations or even from other online resources.

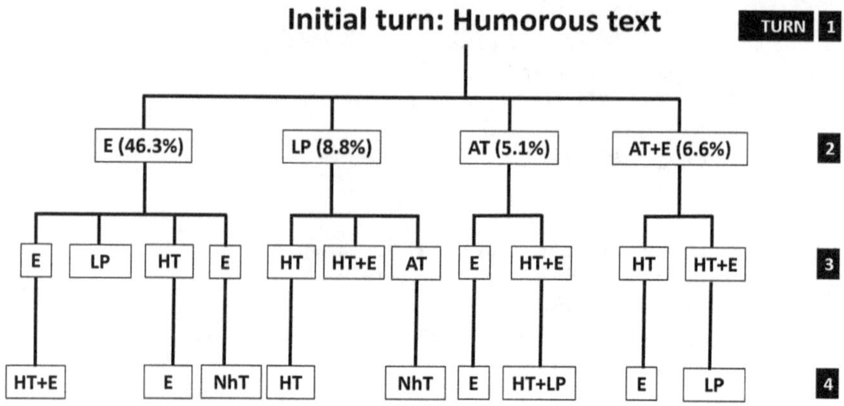

Fig. 5.6 Humorous messaging interactions starting with a humorous text. Key: *E* humorous emoji, *LP* laugh particle, *HT* humorous text, *NhT* non-humorous text, *AT* approbation text

Figure 5.6 shows some of the most prototypical turn sequences beginning with a humorous text. In 46% of the sample, the second turn is an emoji. Of these, the most common pattern contains a reply with a humorous emoji (often repeated several times), the interaction then ending at this point (39% of the sample). This would be a kind of agreed adjacency pair consisting of just a text-based humorous text and an emoji to acknowledge the humorous intention and/or to show appreciation for the sender user's effort to amuse their interlocutor. A few of these frequent two-turn interactions appear in Fig. 5.7, with the first-turn humorous texts translated in (40).

(40) [Top left] -One's got to learn to say NO.
-Fancy a beer?
-I can NOT see why NOT.

[Top right] Waiter, I'll have spaghetti and my wife pizza with mushrooms, eggplant and olives.
-Capricciosa?
-I am pissed off with her.
[This Spanish joke plays with the phonetic similarity of *Capricciosa* (the name of the pizza) and *caprichosa*, an adjective in Spanish denoting someone who is capricious. The sub-sentential utterance

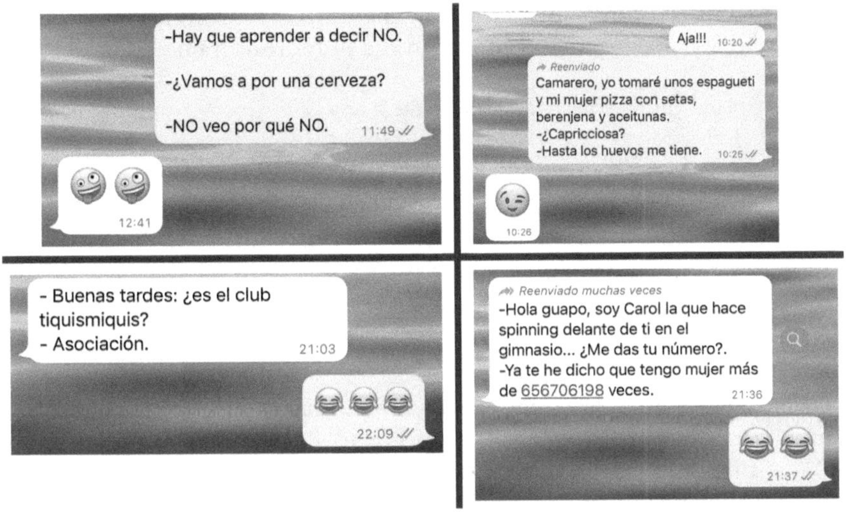

Fig. 5.7 Two-turn interactions with humorous text replied to with emoji

"Capricciosa?" may thus be enriched inferentially into *¿Quiere una pizza Capricciosa?* ("Do you want a Capricciosa pizza?," the most likely candidate interpretation given the previously processed content and bound to be initially selected by the user) and *¿Es su mujer caprichosa?* ("Is your wife capricious?," more unlikely but, as in many other humour instances, eventually imposed as a valid and correct interpretation fitting the next utterance (I am fed up with her), which humorously surprises the addressee user].

[Bottom left] -Good afternoon: Is this the club of picky people?
-Association.

[Bottom right] -Hello, darling. I'm Carol, the one who does spinning in front of you at the gym… Would you give me your number?
-I've told you 656706198 times that I am married.

When the interaction extends to the third and fourth turns, laughter is often reciprocated either with another emoji or with humour-indicating discourses such as laugh particles. This third-turn emoji/particle probably corroborates the humorous effect on the initial user, or at least suggests that the conversation may continue in the humorous frame, as in (41).

(41) Sara: [humorous text as audio file].
Luis: 😂
Sara: 😀😀😀
Luis: Ponte brillo en los labios por lo q pueda pasar luego
[*Apply gloss to your lips, whatever might happen later*].
Luis: 😂
Sara: Uauuuu
Sara: Jajaja
[*hahaha*].

The second most frequent reply to the initial humorous text utilises a laugh particle (e.g. *hahaha*) -amounting to 8.8% of the sample. Again, 60% of these instances exhibit a brief two-turn sequence where the laugh particle brings the short interaction to an end. By way of example, see (42) below, whose humour relies on the polysemy of the noun *sirena* (*siren*, which may mean either "alarm sound" or "mermaid").

(42) Luis: -Guardia: ¿Por qué no se detuvo al escuchar las sirenas?
[*Policeman: Why didn't you stop when you heard the sirens?*].
-Yo: Porque su canto conduce a los hombres a la muerte.
[*Me: Because their singing leads men to their death*].
-Guardia: Sople aqui, por favor.
[*Policeman: Blow here, please*].[13]
Sara: Jajajajajajaja.
[*hahahahaha*].

Third, a habitual continuation of the first humorous turn consists in responding with a single approbation text, sometimes on its own (5.1%) and on other occasions with an emoji attached to it (6.6.%). This way to show appreciation often suffices to assume that the conversation has ended, just like in previous replies (with emoji or laugh particles). 57.2% of approbation texts on their own and 66.7% of approbation texts with

[13] Of course, "blow here" is understood in this joke as the man being ordered to take the breathalysing test by a traffic cop.

emoji(s) serve to acknowledge the humorous effect of the first turn and also to finish the conversation at that point, as in (43–46). Likewise, simplicity tends to characterise third and fourth turn continuations, often made of single emojis[14] or laugh particles, though more elaborate interactions are also possible:

(43) Luis: [*humorous text in audio file*].
Ana: 🤣🤣🤣🤣 buenísimos!
[🤣🤣🤣🤣 *Very good ones!*].

(44) Ana: [*humorous text in audio file*].
Luis: Cierto 😂
[*True* 😂].

(45) Luis: Tengo un duendecillo que me grita.
[*I've got a little elf shouting at me*]
Come on you lazy tiger!!! Get moving!!!
Luis: You've got lots of things to do, so move your feline ass.
Sara: I know.
Luis: 😂
Sara: 😂😂😂

(46) Juan: Doctor doctor, venga corriendo a casa que mi mujer esta dando a luz!!!!!
[*Doctor, doctor, come to my house fast. My wife is giving birth!!!!*].
Es su primer hijo?
[*First son?*].
No hombre joderrrr. Soy su marido!!!
[*No, damn it. I am her husband!!!*].
Sara: 😳😳😳
Sara: 😂😂😂
Sara: Siiii.
[*Yessssss*].
Sara: Malitoooo
[*A bit bad [the joke was]*].
Sara: 😂😂😂
Juan: Malo malo pa matarse
[*Bad to die from*].

[14] This schematic "image replied to with emoji(s)" suits what Georgakopoulou (2017) called *ritual appreciation*: positive assessments of the post and/or the poster, expressed in highly conventionalised language coupled with emoji, which would fit this typical strategy by WhatsApp users of simply replying with an emoji to a humorous text, and also typical as a reply to images used as the first turn (see below).

Finally, it should be noted that this first-turn humorous text occasionally fails to generate the desired humorous effects. In this case, an interesting pattern uses replies with a non-humorous emoji to show disapproval of the text content (second turn); then, the initial user mixes a non-humorous emoji to express agreement with the non-humorous quality (and parallel failed humorous intention) plus a humorous emoji to convey that, at least for them, the text did have a humorous potential. (47) illustrates this.

(47) Juan: Dicen que Antonio Banderas ha cogido el virus porque hace tiempo que no lleva la máscara del zorro.
[*They say that Antonio Banderas caught the virus because it's a long time since he last wore the mask of Zorro*].
Ana: 🤦‍♀️🤦‍♀️🤦‍♀️🤦‍♀️🤦‍♀️
Juan: 🤦‍♂️😂

5.2.2 *Pattern 2: First Turn as Humorous Text plus Emoji(S)*

Even though this pattern resembles the previous one, this time the user emphasises the intended humorous quality of their text by adding emoji(s), a kind of *procedural role* which instructs the interlocutor on how to infer the text properly (stickers and GIFs are mainly used for this purpose in interactions by young generations). A total of 109 interactions in the corpus (4.8%) matches this pattern.

Judging from Fig. 5.8, the most frequent second-turn reply is to reciprocate with a similar "humorous text plus emoji" (20.2%), thus accepting the humorous frame just initiated and resorting to a similar grammatical structure. Subsequent turns commonly maintain the same text-emoji discourse; this is what the two turns of humorous text plus emoji in (48) and the three consecutive "humorous text plus emoji" turns in (49) exemplify.[15]

(48) Ana: Me ha encantado el Hobbit.
[*I loved The Hobbit*].
Luca: Esta bien
[*It's nice*].
Luca: Musha batalla pisha
[*Lotsa battles mate*].

[15] The reader is reminded that for the purposes of this chapter, a turn is conceived of as all the messages that a user sends to another user before the latter sends their own message. As can be seen in (49), Luis and Sara send several messages, but in reality the conversation only contains three turns.

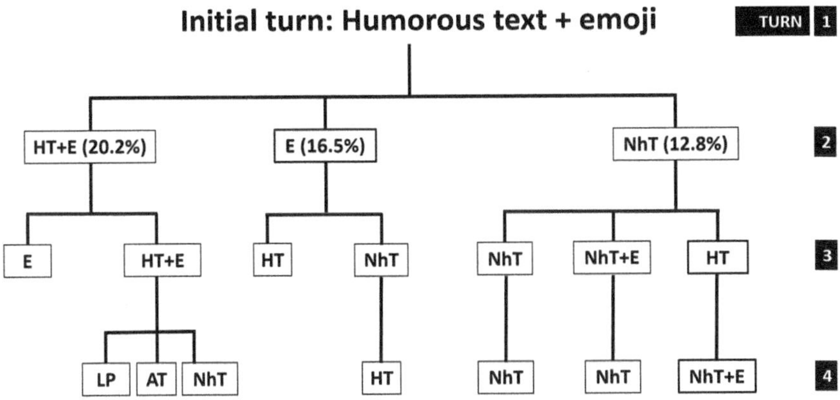

Fig. 5.8 Humorous messaging interactions starting with a humorous text plus emoji. Key: *E* humorous emoji, *LP* laugh particle, *HT* humorous text, *NhT* non-humorous text, *AT* approbation text

Luca: 😂
Ana: Claro. La batalla de los 5 ejercitos.
[*Of course, the battle of the five armies*].
Ana: 😂😂😂
Luca: Po si
[*Yeah*].

(49) Sara: Pero eres beastie boy on the road.
[*But you are a beastie boy on the road*].
Sara: 😂😂😂
Luis: Muevete coño joderrrr piiiii piiiiii joder que mierda de velocidad!!!! 😠😠😠
[*Move on damn it piiiii piiiii damn what a f***ing low speed!!!!*].
Luis: Luis en el coche
[*Luis in his car*].
Luis: 😂
Sara: Siiii.
[*Yesss*].
Sara: El pito es tu mejor aliado.
[*The horn is your best ally*].
Sara: 😂😂😂

This humorous alignment of turns does not always appear in such a crystal-clear fashion. It is often negotiated and, as a result, the interaction ends up moving into and out of the humorous frame. Notice, for example, how Sara in (50) does not initially welcome the humorous frame initiated by Luis. Eventually, though, she agrees to follow the frame by typing a humorous emoji.

(50) Luis: Mas el de Moby que no te voy a devolver 😂
[*Plus [the CD] by Moby that I am not returning to you* 😂].
Sara: Oyesssss 😠
[*Heyyyyy* 😠].
Sara: Q es mi tesoooorooooo.
[*It's my treasureeeee*].
Luis: Tecnicamente es mio, sabessssss o sea
[*Technically it's mine, you know, I mean*].
Luis: Yo puse la pasta.
[*I provided the money*].
Luis: 😂
Sara: Sera posible!😠
[*Can't believe it!* 😠].
Sara: No es cool hablar de pasta...
[*It's not cool to talk about money*].
Sara: 😂😂😂
Luis: En broma si.
[*It is, if one's joking*].
Sara: Ok.

The second most frequent continuation of the first turn consists in replying with an emoji (16.5%). Just like in the first pattern, it commonly happens that the emoji is not only used to acknowledge the successful humorous intention by the first user but also to end the short conversation at this point. The corpus also features a similar structure in which the emoji is accompanied by some kind of approbation text that amplifies the second user's acknowledgement. (51–53) provide us with examples thereof.

(51) Sara: [*humorous text as audio file*].
Sara: 😂😂😂
Luis: Que graciosa
[*How witty*].
Luis: 😊

(52) Juan: [*long humorous text followed by emoji(s)*].
Ana: 😂😂😂😂
Ana: Qué ingenioso!
[*How clever!*].
(53) Luis: [*humorous text as audio file*].
Luis: 😂
Sara: Cariiiiiiii
[*My deaaaar*].
Sara: Mencantaaaa!
[*I loooove it!*].
Sara: me meooooo!!!!
[*I laugh my socks off*].

Finally, a third frequent continuation of the first turn containing a humorous text plus emoji(s) shows a reply with a non-humorous text (on its own or accompanied by emoji). Several cases explain this combination of humorous plus non-humorous text with/without emoji(s). In a first possible situation, the first user is joking but the second infers the text as serious, despite the presence of an emphasising emoji, as in (54). A second option relies on dismissing the humorous intention completely and replying with a non-serious message that prevents a continuation of the play frame, as in (55). A third possibility is for an apparently non-humorous message to become humorous due to some alternative discourse. For instance, *Diosss* (God) in (56) is tinged with a humorous connotation by the attached laugh particle *jaja*:

(54) Luis: Y el domingo me llevas al aeropuerto 😂😂😂
[*And on Sunday you'll take me to the airport* 😂😂😂].
Sara: A q hora?
[*What time?*].
Luis: No no. Es bromita.
[*No no. I am only joking*].
Luis: El vuelo sale a las 15:40.
[*The flight is at 15:40*].
Hora de siesta para Sara.
[*Siesta time for Sara*].
Luis: ♡
(55) Juan: Yo he llevado a mi hijo al cine.
[*I took my son to the cinema*].
Juan: A ver la peli de los Juanes, digo de los simios 😂😂
[*To see the film Planet of the Johns, I mean of the Apes*].

Ana: Me gusta.
[*I like it*].
Ana: Es buena?
[*Is it good?*].
(56) Luis: Me voy a la duchita... Quizas descubra que tengo dedos en los pies cuando se vaya toda la roña.
[*I am going to the shower... Maybe I'll discover that I have toes when all the dirt is gone*].
Luis: 😂
Sara: Diosssss! Jaja
[*God!*].
Sara: Eres palmípedo?
[*Are you web-footed?*].
Luis: Luisipedo.
[*Luis-footed*].
Sara: 😳
Sara: Jaja
Sara: 😂😂😂
Luis: 😃

5.2.3 *Pattern 3: First Turn as Non-humorous Text*

In this case, one of the interlocutors suddenly turns an ongoing non-humorous interaction into a humorous one. 239 interactions (10.53%) fit this pattern. Figure 5.9 shows some of the turn structures that appear more frequently in this pattern.

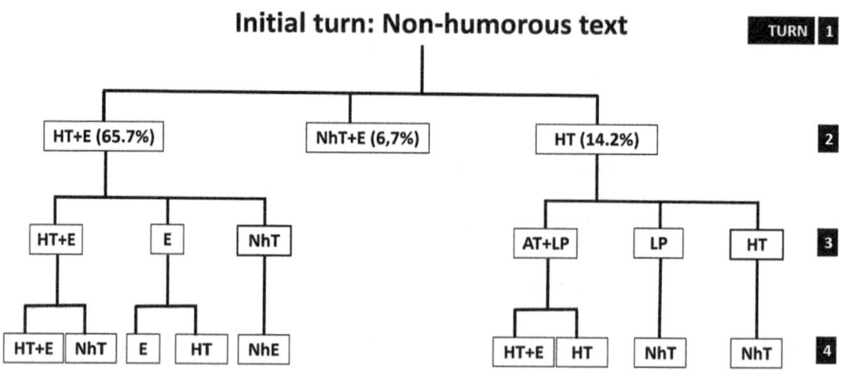

Fig. 5.9 Humorous messaging interactions starting with a non-humorous text. Key: *E* humorous emoji, *LP* laugh particle, *HT* humorous text, *NhT* non-humorous text, *AT* approbation text, *NhE* non-humorous emoji

It has already been mentioned that, in patterns like this, one of the users transforms the interaction into a humorous one. Thus, it should come as no surprise that the most frequent second turn is "humorous text plus emoji(s)," where the emoji plays an emphasising role or that of effectively preventing the attached text from being understood as non-humorous, given that the messages in the interaction have not been humorous so far.

When the "humorous text plus emoji" is introduced, the most frequent third-turn reaction typically produces an alignment with the same kind of message structure: a humorous text plus emoji (20.5%), followed in percentage by third turns with a non-humorous text (15.56%), a naked humorous emoji (12.6%), a non-humorous text plus laugh particle (6.62%) and non-humorous text plus emoji (5.3%). Some examples of the first structure (second turn with a "humorous text plus emoji" replicated in the third turn) can be seen in (57–58).

(57) Sara: Cuidate.
[*Take care*].
Sara: No me ligues mucho.
[*Don't chat up too many girls*].
Luis: Thx.
[*Thx*].
Luis: Con este look "recien levantado con legañas"?
[*With this "just got up from bed and with rheumy eyes" look?*].
Luis: 😂
Sara: Q tu tienes un peligro aun asi...😂😂😂
[*You are dangerous even like that...* 😂😂😂].

(58) Juan: Ahora me echo una crema nueva por las noches
[*Now I apply myself a new cream at night*].
Juan: Se llama...
[*It's called...*].
Ana: Uauuuuu
Ana: Escandalo.
[*Scandal*].
Ana: 😂
Juan: Crema tersa-piel-jurasica
[*Smooth-Jurasic-skin cream*].
😂

Ana: Jaja....
[*haha*].
Ana: Anda yaaaaa
[*Come off it*].
Ana: Q estas to bien.
[*You look really good*].

The second most frequent third turn after a non-humorous text (1st turn) and a humorous text plus emoji (2nd) is to type a non-humorous text (15.56% of the sample). An intention to show that the humorous frame initiated has failed would probably explain the utilisation of this non-humorous text. Alternatively, perhaps the humorous intention has been successful but the addressee user does not feel like continuing the interaction in the new humorous frame. By way of example, the interaction in (59) does not have a humorous status at first. Then, Juan introduces a humorous text plus emoji; however, Ana sticks to the non-humorous quality that the interaction had exhibited until that moment. (60) is also interesting, because Sara uses a humorous emoji to show appreciation of Luis's humorous attempt provided in the shape of a humorous text plus emoji, albeit adding a non-humorous text to insist on sticking to the initial quality of the interaction -subsequently accepted by Luis:

(59) Juan: Ha llegado al hotel un grupo de ancianitos.
[*A group of old people has arrived at the hotel*].
Tipo imserso.[16]
[*Imserso style*].
Juan: Estan cenando tb aquí.
[*They are also having supper here*].
Ana: Españoles?
[*Spanish?*].
Juan: No.
Parecen alemanes o ingleses.
[*They look German or English*].
Yo bajo la media de edad en el restaurante 😂😂😂
[*I lower the average age in the restaurant* 😂😂😂].
Ana: Esta bien el hotel?
[*The hotel is nice?*].

[16] IMSERSO (*Instituto de Mayores y Servicios Sociales* [Institute for the Elderly and Social Services]) arranges low-cost holiday trips or stays in spas -among other services- for Spanish retirees.

Juan: Ufff genial de verdad
[*Ufff, very nice indeed*].
(60) Sara: Ahora te hablo.
[*I'll talk to you in a minute*].
Luis: 👍
Sara: Q dennis me esta enseñando una cosa.
[*Dennis is showing me something*].
Luis: El penis?
[*His penis?*].
Luis: 😂
Sara: En la tele.
[*On TV*].
Sara: 🎉😂😂😂
Luis: Ahhh.
Luis: Ok.

Another possible reason not to acknowledge the user's humorous message plus emoji or not to replicate it with a similar play-frame-based continuation has to do with the situation in which the user produces a text plus humorous emoji in an attempt to be witty but, at the same time, apparently does not seek to divert the conversation towards a humorous frame. In (61), for instance, an intention to show a witty quality seems to underlie Luis's message paired with an emoji, rather than inviting Sara to continue the conversation within the humorous frame (she does not).

(61) Sara: Has estado muy calladitooo.
[*You've been very quieeeet*].
Luis: Ya. Sorry.
[*I know. Sorry*].
Sara: Uauuuuu
Sara: No, q va. No te preocupes.
[*No way. Don't worry*].
Luis: Pero es q cuando quiero concentrarme aparto el móvil.
[*The thing is, when I want to concentrate I put the mobile aside*].
Luis: Mindfulness 😂
Sara: Yo tb he estado haciendo cosas.
[*I've also been doing things*].
Luis: 👍

In a third frequent continuation of the second-turn "humorous text plus emoji(s)," the addressee user reciprocates with a naked emoji (12.6%

of the sample) in the third turn. As it happens with other humorous messaging interaction patterns, this emoji is used both to show appreciation for the humorous attempt and to conclude the interaction at that point. If the interaction continues in subsequent turns, it normally extends the humorous frame with humour-revealing discourses, e.g. another emoji, a laugh particle or a humorous text. This becomes visible in (62–63).

(62) Sara: Saliendo de yoga.
[*Leaving the yoga class*].
Sara: 🙏
Luis: Ommmmmm
Luis: Importante el yoga para aguantar a Luis.
[*Yoga is important to help put up with Luis*].
Luis: 😂
Sara: 😂😂😂😂
Sara: 🆘🆘🆘🆘
Luis: 😃

(63) Luis: Yo acabo de volver de dejarla en la Renfe.
[*I've just returned from taking her to the railway station*].
Sara: Ahhhhh.
Sara: Todo pasa....
[*Everything passes by*].
Luis: Yep.
Sara: Yo oliendo un poco el aguarras a ver si me coloco de una vez por todas😂😂😂
[*I am sniffing a bit of turpentine to check if I get high once and for all*😂😂😂].
Sara: Wildddddd.
Luis: 😃😂😊
Sara: 😊😊

The second most frequent second-turn after a non-humorous turn utilises a humorous text (14.2% of the sample). After this second turn, users normally resort to approbation texts plus laugh particles and/or emojis to express appreciation of the just-initiated humorous frame (26.5% of this pattern). An example appears in (64), where, after a second turn with a humorous text (*se los pondre a la perra*), the third turn contains laugh particles (*jaja*) followed by an approbation text (*me meo*) and a humorous emoji (😂):

(64) Luis: Mañana ire a por tus zapatitos.
[*Tomorrow I'll collect your little shoes*].
Sara: Ay gracias!
[*Oh thanks!*].
Sara: Me hacen mucha ilu.
[*I am very excited about having them*].
Luis: Y se los pondre a la perra.
[*And I'll put them on my dog's paws*].
Sara: Jaja
[*haha*].
Sara: Me meo.
[*I laugh my socks off*].
Sara: 😂😂😂
Luis: 😃
Sara: Le quedaran tope guays o sea.
[*They will look top nice on her, I mean*].
Sara: 😃
Luis: Pos claro o sea no?
[*Of course, I mean you know?*].

5.2.4 Pattern 4: First Turn as Non-humorous Text plus Emoji

This pattern does not abound in the corpus of messaging conversations, matching only 77 interactions (3.41% of the total). In this case, the emoji mainly fulfils a procedural function instructing the addressee user about how the accompanying text, initially non-humorous, should be inferred, or adding a parallel attitude to that attached text. Unsurprisingly, over 90% of the emojis attached to these texts are humorous. Figure 5.10 reproduces some of the recurring patterns.

The most frequent second-turn continuation relies on typing a humorous text plus emoji (37.7%). Other continuations include non-humorous text plus emoji (13%) and non-humorous text (7.8%). In the first case, as remarked earlier, the emoji helps to invalidate a potentially non-humorous interpretation of the text typed next to it. This occurs in the first turns by Juan in (65) and Luis in (66), both of which subsequently develop into a whole interaction within the humorous frame. (67) seems interesting too because, despite the use of the humorous emoji, Sara infers Luis's message explicitly (notice the "sad face" emoji), which in turn compels him to insist that he was joking.

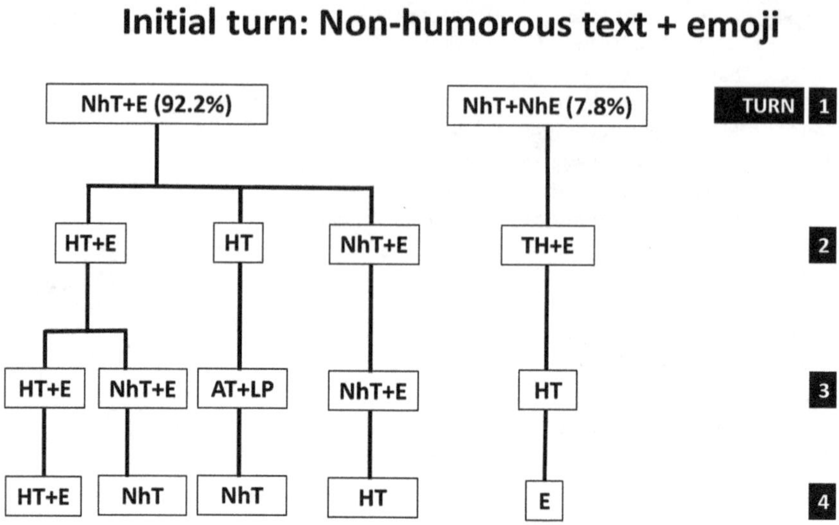

Fig. 5.10 Humorous messaging interactions starting with a non-humorous text plus emoji. Key: *E* humorous emoji, *NhE* non-humorous emoji, *HT* humorous text, *AT* approbation text, *LP* laugh particle, *NhT* non-humorous text

(65) Ana: Respecto a lo otro: solo tienes 5 años + q yo.
[*Regarding the other thing: you're only 5 years older than me*].
Ana: 😃
Juan: An eternity.
Juan: 😂
Ana: Sure.
Ana: 😄
Juan: Pasame el andador, que hoy hace sol.
[*Pass me the walking aid. It's sunny today*].
Ana: Pero si estas to weno y macizo.
[*But you are so hot and muscular*].
Ana: 😂😂😂
Juan: Tu que me miras con wenos 👀
[*Because you are looking at me with kind* 👀].

(66) Sara: Te voy a hacer el ingreso 💰💰💰
[*I am going to transfer the money to you*].
Luis: Thx.

[*Thanks*].
Luis: 115€ con los intereses de demora. Lo siento pero los negocios son los negocios 😃
[*It's 115€ with late payment interest. Sorry but business is business* 😃].
Sara: Diosssss.
[*God*].
Sara: Ya me avisaron q no mezclara dinero con amistad 😂😂😂
[*I was actually warned not to mix money and friendship* 😂😂😂].

(67) Sara: Muy contenta con mi móvil.
[*Very happy with my mobile*].
Sara: 😊😊😊😊
Luis: Querras decir MI móvil 😂
[*You mean MY mobile* 😂].
Sara: Ohhhh. Siiii
[*Ohhh. Yes*].
Luis: Nooooo
Sara: 😔
Luis: Bromita.
[*Little joke*].
Sara: Reality bites.[17]
Sara: 😊😊😂😉😌
Luis: Es todo tuyo.
[*It's all yours*].

As the second most frequent continuation, we find a non-humorous text plus non-humorous emoji. However, this (initial) non-humorous quality of both text and emoji seldom prevents the interaction from expanding towards a humorous frame. Ana's interpretation of the first turn by Juan in (68) illustrates it:

(68) Ana: Cómo estás?
[*How are you?*].

[17] A reference to the film *Reality Bites*. In English in the original WhatsApp conversation.

Ana: Any changes at all?[18]
Ana: 😳
Juan: Rigor mortis. De cuerpo presente 😲
[Rigor mortis. The deceased body 😲].
Ana: Jaja
[*haha*].
Ana: Me meo.
[*I laugh my socks off*].
Ana: En serio.
[*Honest*].
Ana: Dime.
[*Tell me*].
Juan: Estoy algo mejor.
[*I am feeling a bit better*].

5.2.5 *Pattern 5: First Turn as Single Image*

Unlike the previous pattern, this one pervades humorous messaging interactions, reaching 67.4% of all the interactions collected in the corpus. As already hinted, "an image" in this chapter is what the messaging app treats as an image, or expressed differently, a file uploaded from the smartphone's store of images, forwarded from another messaging interaction or downloaded from the Internet. Hence the possibility for these images to include only text, an image on its own, or multimodal combinations of text and image.

Undoubtedly, the most frequent interaction structure fitting this pattern is to react to the image with an emoji (944 instances, 49.8% of the messaging interactions matching this pattern), either (a) humorous (762 instances, 80.7% of all emoji-based replies) or a non-humorous one (42. 4.45%), or even both types of emoji in sequence (130, 13.77%). Several reasons might account for this schematic pattern: on the one hand, this kind of humorous initiative is very common and users normally get constantly bombarded with humorous images. In this case, it does not seem difficult at all to simply type an emoji to express appreciation for the humorous attempt, and possibly also as a way to show a polite attitude towards the first user and to ensure that the message does not go unanswered. In parallel, there may be non-propositional effects involved

[18] In English in the original WhatsApp conversation. The same applies to other non-translated texts in English.

Fig. 5.11 Images replied to with humorous emojis

beyond the humorous appreciation, including gratitude to the user for thinking about him/her and forwarding the image, a feeling of connection and, when certain contextual assumptions become essential to understand the image, feelings of in-group membership and a sense of bonding which emanates from the vivid awareness of shared assumptions that the user's successful interpretation triggers (see Chap. 8).

Of all the humorous interactions that start with a single image, the most common structure is the one featuring an "image replied to by humorous emoji(s)," in which the conversation comes to an end after only two turns (48.1% of the samples fitting this pattern), as it happened with previous patterns too. Consider the examples provided in Fig. 5.11, which contain three text-based and three multimodal humorous images replied to using "laugh with tears of joy" emoji(s). The interaction stops after the emoji has been sent in all of them. The texts accompanying these images are translated in (69) below.[19]

[19] Notice that some of the images in Fig. 5.11 contain the word *Reenviado* (forwarded) at the top. This is a specificity of the WhatsApp interface. In theory, addressee users' awareness that the image was forwarded to them from another messaging interaction should seem annoying, since they were obviously not the first option when sending the image. In reality, though, all WhatsApp users know that these images will circulate massively and take this forwarding as a natural behaviour within the app.

(69) [Top left] -Hello, is this the course for snake oil salesmen?
-No, here we value the management and implementation of transversal synergies.
-Come on, open the door.
[Top middle] EXCLUSIVE: The Spanish government has decided to toughen up the sanctions on Putin and has included him on the list of self-employed workers.
[Top right] -Paco, I think a Caesar's salad is not like this.
-You have no f***ing idea of history.
[Bottom left] -I will no longer depend on Russia… I will produce my own gas.
[Bottom right] -Conjugate the future perfect of "there is some cocido left."
-Croquettes.[20]

Likewise, within this dual-turn structure of the interaction (image replied to using an emoji) the humorous image-based initiative may not always succeed. Despite this happening only in a small percentage of cases (4.45%), users sometimes show that humour failed by resorting to a clearly non-humorous emoji, as can be seen in the interactions collected in Fig. 5.12.[21] The translation of its texts appears in (70).

(70) [Top left] The new English Covid, Filomena storm, the assault to the Capitol, and it's only the 6th day of the year!!! We'll end up missing 2020, you'll see.[22]
[Top right] -I've just read *The Little Prince*.
-Don't be corny, it is called "Foreword."
[The key to the humour of this Spanish meme lies in the similar pronunciation of *principito* (little prince)

[20] *Cocido* -a Spanish dish typical of Madrid- has boiled chickpeas and meat as its main ingredients. At restaurants, if cooks see that some *cocido* meat is left at the end of the day, they often turn it into croquettes for the next day's menu.

[21] Two of the images in Fig. 5.12 are replied to with the "facepalming female" emoji. For me, it clearly indicates that the humorous image-based attempt has been unsuccessful. However, two colleagues have indicated that, for them, the emoji does not really invalidate the appreciation of humour but, rather, indicates that the information contained in the image was a bit excessive or bordering on bad taste.

[22] Filomena, a huge snowstorm named as such by the Spanish "Agencia Estatal de Meteorología" (AEMET, "State Meteorology Agency"), mainly affected Spain between January 6th and 11th, 2021, covering cities such as Madrid, with many feet of snow.

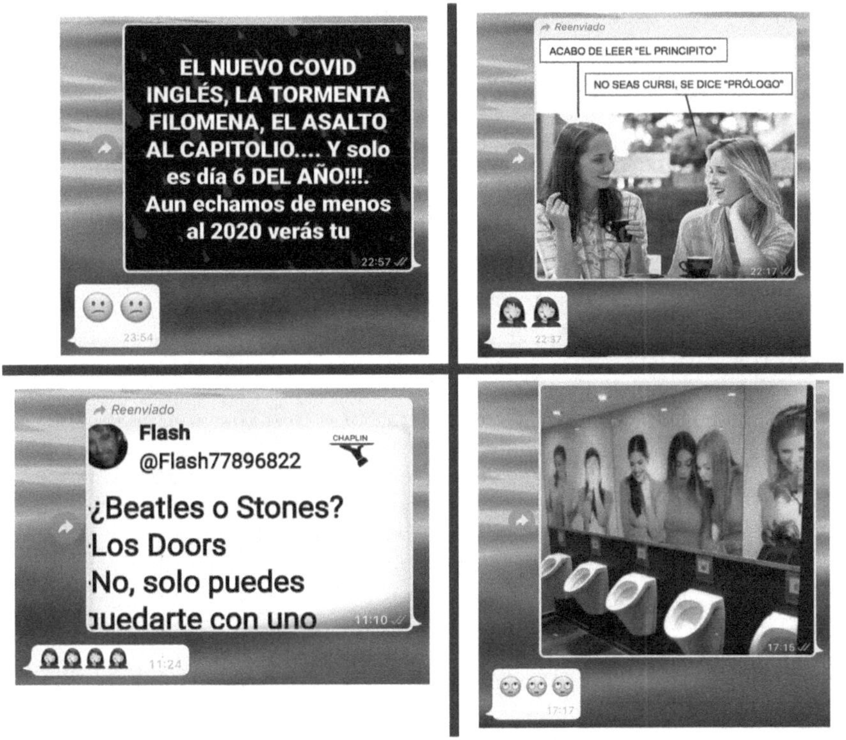

Fig. 5.12 Images replied to with non-humorous emojis

and *principio* (beginning). The second girl thinks that the first girl means "I've read the beginning of the book" upon saying her utterance, and she tries to correct her].

[Bottom left] -Beatles or Stones?
-The Doors.
-No, you can only pick up one.
[Again, the key to the humour of this meme once again lies in the similar pronunciation in Spanish of *Los Doors* (The Doors, the pop group) and *Los dos* (meaning "both of them"). This explains the continuation is "No, you can only pick up one"].

Finally, these dual-turn interactions may contain both humorous and non-humorous emojis (14.2%), thus conveying a mixture of reactions to the image: on the one hand, the humorous intention is acknowledged and appreciated; however, at the same time, some negative quality becomes manifest: either towards the image content or regarding some failed humorous effects involved, or even the user's taste upon sending the image. See a couple of illustrative examples in (71–72) below:

(71) Ana: Text-based image:
-¿Quién es la mujer de Zeus?
[*Who is Zeus' wife?*].
-Hera.
-¡No me digas que se han separado!
[*Don't tell me they have split up!*].
[The potential humour of this image relates to the homophony between *Hera* and the past tense of *ser* (to be) in Spanish (*era* = she was). In this context, although using *Hera* to answer the question "who is Zeus' wife?" clearly refers to the wife's name, a possible but far more unlikely interpretation could likewise be "[she] was" (if the reply is spoken, of course)].
Juan: 🤦‍♂️😂

(72) Sara: Text-based image:
-En una escala del 1 al 10, ¿cómo valoraría su capacidad de comprensión?
[*On a scale of 1 to 10, how would you rate your comprehension skills?*].
-Muy buena.
[*Very good*].
Luis: 🤦‍♂️😂

Continuations of this basic "image-then-emoji" structure do exist; nevertheless, fewer instances appear in our corpus. Predictably, after positive emoji-based feedback from the addressee user, the first user tends to carry on with the interaction by resorting to further humorous messages. One possibility is to type a humorous text with/without humorous meme(s), often reciprocated. In other words, the humorous intention and/or the humorous quality of the image are not only appreciated and acknowledged, but users also agree to continue the interaction within the humorous frame initiated by the image and ensuring thematic coherence across turns. Consider the memes in Fig. 5.13, translated in (73) (left image), (74) (middle image) and (75) (right image) below:

Fig. 5.13 Image-initiated humorous messaging interactions

(73) Juan: Multimodal image. Text: "Ikea launches its first book."
Luis: 😂😂😂😂
Juan: At least, if you go to the Ikea cafè and order a cappuccino, the cream they serve is whipped!!!!😂😂
Luis: 😂😂😂

(74) Juan: Image.
Luis: 😂😂😂
Juan: The iron throne, low-cost style.
Luis: Cardboard throne.
Hahahahaha.

(75) Juan: Text-based image: Hey, Paco, I was told you got married? / Yes, because I didn't like cooking, cleaning or ironing. / Well, and how is it? / Now I am starting to like it.
Luis: 😂😂😂
Juan: Text-based image: I want to get divorced, Paco. / But we're not married yet… / I am rehearsing.
Luis: 😂😂😂

Example (73) plays with two alternative meanings of *montar* in Spanish, namely "to assemble [pieces]" and "to whip [cream]." The humour revolves around the wooden pieces that need assembling (*montar*), just like any Ikea furniture, and the cream, which is whipped (*montada*). The interaction exhibits cunning congruency across the posts supported by emoji use. (74) unfolds from an initial image, with the users alternating in making humorous comments on it. Finally, (75) shows text-based memes used in a row. This time, alongside the inherent humour of the text, effectiveness also lies in the repetition of the same character (*Paco*, a very common affectionate form of the Spanish name Francisco) in both memes.

The second most frequent second turn after an image-based first turn features approbation text plus emoji (147 instances, 9.6%). Pairing these texts with emojis is an effective way to show appreciation for the initial user's intention and/or for the humorous effects generated on the addressee user. Some of the approbation texts are quoted in (76).

(76) a. Bravo! 😂😂😂
b. Qué buenos!!!! 🤣🤣
[*Very good ones!!!* 🤣🤣].
c. Mira que eres gracioso 😉
[*You are so funny* 😉].
d. Right!!! 🤣
e. Genial!! 😝
[*Awesome!!* 😝].
f. Indeed 😂😂
g. Sin duda! 😂😂
[*Undoubtedly!* 😂😂].

A similar function is carried out by the laugh particle, the third most frequent second turn after an initial image-based turn (121 instances, 7.9%). By means of that discourse, either because of a successful humorous intention or just out of politeness, the addressee user expresses acknowledgment and appreciation. As was also the case in previous patterns, most of the interactions involving second-turn laugh particles end at this point, a short dual turn messaging conversation (113 instances, (93.4%).

5.2.6 *Pattern 6: First Turn as a Single Image plus Humorous Text*

This pattern reminds us of the previous one; nonetheless, here the user emphasises or complements the intended humorous effect of the image with some accompanying humorous text. Not many instances in the corpus fit this pattern (39, 1.73%). On this occasion, the most frequent continuation consists in typing a humorous emoji and finishing the conversation at this point, a two-turn interaction which has also pervaded the messaging patterns examined.

The text performs several functions in these short interactions. Sometimes it acts as a humorous remark which does not add any essential information to the one already provided by the image. For instance, in the

Fig. 5.14 Humorous messaging interactions initiated by image plus text

interaction reproduced in Fig. 5.14 (left), we can see Jesus trying to talk to the apostles via a video chat interface (e.g. Zoom, Meet and the like). The image (massively shared among users during the 2020 pandemic in Spain) is humorous by itself, and the accompanying text, *La última cena, versión confinamiento* (The Last Supper, lockdown version) adds no significant information.

Other times, the text has a more *procedural* role, leading the user in the right inferential direction or narrowing the range of possible valid interpretations for the attached image. The image in one of the interactions portrays a Christmas tree with bank notes instead of the typical balls; the adjacent text then complements the image by critically saying who the supposed owner of the tree would be, thus reducing the list of people likely to be the owner of the tree.

Anyhow, a more interesting role for a cyberpragmatics of messaging interactions is the one in which the ultimate intended meaning requires combining partial meanings of text and image to be properly conveyed. Some examples are reproduced in Fig. 5.14 (middle/right). In the interaction shown in the middle, the text next to the image -*En Lepe*[23] *dicen*

[23] In nearly every collectivity (e.g. countries, regions…), another human group can be found that invariably becomes the butt of derogatory jokes in which these target people are unfairly labelled as thick, illiterate, mentally retarded and so on. The English tell jokes about the Irish; the French about the Belgian, etc. In Spain, this kind of joke is directed at people from Lepe, a village in the Southern region of Andalusia.

que han encontrado la efigie de un faraón (In Lepe they say that they have found a pharaoh's effigy)- becomes essential to interpret the image of the plastic bottle correctly. Similarly, in the interaction on the right, hardly anybody could make an adequate inference of the image without the accompanying text: *Cuando tú estás en 2018 pero tu hijo ya va por el 2028* (When you are in 2018 but your son is already in 2028).

5.2.7 Pattern 7: First Turn as Video

As already pointed out above, starting an interaction with a video is not the preferred option on messaging apps when it comes to generating humorous effects on the interlocutor (only 104 instances, 4.6%). One possible reason has been suggested: videos are high in megabytes, demand high processing power in the smartphone and take up a lot of space in the device's hard drive.

Other patterns analysed in this chapter reveal that the most frequent reply choice consists in typing emoji(s) to express appreciation for the video and to acknowledge the user's humorous intention (41.3%) and on most occasions, mirroring previous humorous patterns too, the interaction ends at this point, after only two turns. The same applies to the second most frequent reply: approbation text plus emoji (13.3%), which rarely exhibits a continuation after the second-turn reply.

5.3 The Prototypical Pattern of Humorous Interactions on WhatsApp

The quantitative analysis carried out in the previous Section allows us to draw some conclusions about which the prototypical humorous interaction on WhatsApp might be. Figure 5.15 shows, in bold, prototypical sequences of messaging interactions on WhatsApp by Spanish users.

As can be seen in the items highlighted in bold, when a non-humorous interaction is already in progress, the typical strategy resorts to shifting into a humorous mode by supplying a humorous text plus emoji (HT+E in Fig. 5.15) which is typically reciprocated (and the play frame further sustained) in subsequent turns using a similar pattern. When the humorous interaction starts from scratch, images (IMA), humorous texts (HT) and humorous texts plus emoji (HT+E) frequently serve humorous purposes. Very often, the image is replied to with a humorous emoji (E), and the interaction stops at this point (Ø). The same holds true for humorous texts (HT) as first turn, often continued with an emoji, where the

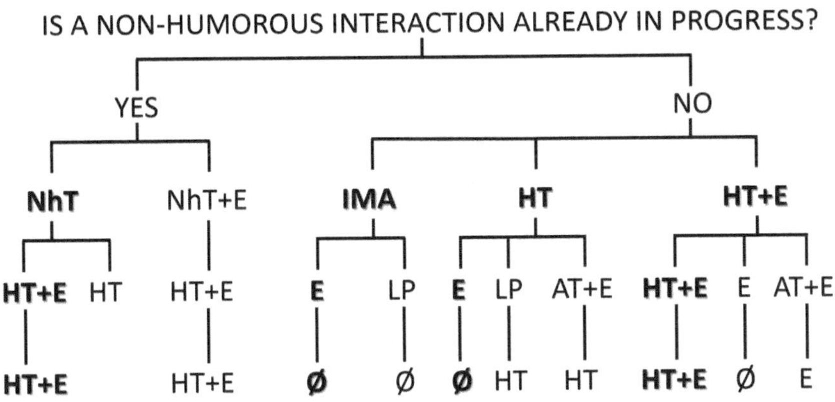

Fig. 5.15 Prototypical humorous messaging interactions on WhatsApp. Key: *NhT* non-humorous text, *E* humorous emoji, *IMA* image, *HT* humorous text, *LP* laugh particle, *Ø* no continuation of the interaction, *AT* approbation text

interaction concludes. However, in the case of humorous text plus emoji (HT+E), the interaction tends to unfold over several turns, usually by exploiting the same discursive structure.

6 East Versus West: Messaging across Cultures

In this chapter, several patterns of humorous messaging interactions have been analysed and exemplified from a corpus of WhatsApp interactions between Spanish users. A final question arises: Are these patterns valid across cultures? Seeking to answer this question, Yus and Hu (submitted) have compared the patterns identified in Spanish WhatsApp interactions to those followed by Chinese users on the app WeChat. Although lack of space unfortunately prevents a thorough pattern-by-pattern comparison and explanation of the outcome(s) of such research, a summary of some relevant findings can be found below.

The contrastive analysis must necessarily begin with an account of what in this book has been labelled ***interface-centred contextual constraints***, also called ***interface affordances*** in the literature. The two aforesaid apps share some basic attributes (for instance, despite being mainly managed through typed text, contextualisation is aided with emoji(s), stickers, GIFs, etc.) as well as limitations (e.g. the system imposes a strict order for the display of messages, often leading to ***disrupted turn adjacency***, which means that, instead of being posted in direct adjacency to the first turn, the second turn ends up in a slot further down on the screen, separated from its actual point of reference by earlier postings). Table 5.4 provides a comparison of other interface affordances.

The examination of both corpora yielded similarities in many humorous patterns, thus confirming our initial hypotheses. For example, we predicted that a humorous attempt by a user would be reacted upon similarly on both apps: mainly by showing appreciation via text, laugh particles or text plus emoji/sticker, among other possibilities. However, we additionally foresaw that cultural constraints would somehow *leak* to the manner in which these humorous interactions are initiated, managed, replied to

Table 5.4 Differences between WhatsApp and WeChat interface affordances

WhatsApp	*WeChat*
It is basically an app for text-, image- and video-based communication and file sharing	It also offers an all-in-one platform for communication, social media, search engine, mobile wallet and e-commerce
Different letter types (bold, italics...)	Not available
Only emojis from the smartphone galleries. Stickers and GIFs are taken from the app or from other sources	Users may choose between the galleries of emojis provided by the smartphone and the unique ones provided by the app itself, also applied to GIFs and stickers. Users may also create images, stickers and memes with their own photos or pictures stored on the smartphone
Regarding users' location, they may send their exact location to other users as a message	Regarding users' location, the app incorporates several location-centred features, namely: *Shake*, *Look Around* and *People Nearby* (see Yus 2021b)
Users' names do not appear on the dialogue screen of dyadic conversations, but they do in messaging groups	Users are identified by their profile images on the dialogue screen
It has a notification feature, which allows users to tell whether the message has been delivered and read (blue double tick)	Not available, but users may "give someone a buzz", a sort of notification that also appears on the smartphone screen
Texts can be deleted any time after being sent, provided that the addressee user still has not read them	Texts can only be deleted a short period of time after being sent, and regardless of whether the addressee user has read them or not

and developed. Actually, one of our specific predictions was that the well-known distinction between individualist and collectivist cultures (and in parallel, that opposing low-context cultures to high-context ones) would also apply, to a greater or lesser extent, to the humorous interactions staged on these apps.

Some substantial research on individualist (e.g. U.S.A.) vs. collectivist (e.g. China) cultures already exists, for instance, concerning the expression and management of emotions. Needless to say, this is not a clear-cut dichotomy of mutually exclusive attributes, since cultures often exhibit mixed qualities (for instance, Spain would roughly stand in between both ends of the individualist-collectivist continuum, see Cheng 2017, 211). A collectivist, high-context culture such as the Chinese one emphasises indirectness and largely relies on paralanguage and other nonverbal cues to convey meaning, sending information more indirectly as well, though, by means of subtler cues (Park et al. 2014, 334). By contrast, communication in low-context environments tends to be more direct and dependent on language, which carries most of the meaning conveyed to other people (Togans et al. 2021, 278).

Likewise, we made the assumption that the way in which humorous interactions are managed on WhatsApp/WeChat might relate to certain cultural communicative patterns, while other interactions will follow a similar humorous structure. The analysis revealed a number of distinctive features specifically when sending a single image for humorous purposes and replying to it. It has been shown earlier in this chapter that a very high percentage of WhatsApp users simply send the humour-connoted image with no accompanying discourse and, on most occasions, the addressee user simply reacts to it with an emoji or a laugh particle and finishes the interaction at this point. This kind of interaction hardly ever takes place on WeChat. Rather, this pattern mainly happens in group conversations, and much more so than in dyadic ones. In these one-to-one WeChat dialogues, the user rarely sends a single image/video to the addressee; they prefer to add supplementary explanatory text or their own comments, both to increase the potential humorous effects and to provoke the addressee user's desire to reply to the message (what in Yus 2014b was referred to as *interactivity trigger*). Very often, if the user simply sends a single image or video, the recipient is likely not to reply. By contrast, an image with additional discourses can attract more attention and trigger more reactions from other users.

This emphasis on complementing images with supplementary discourses clearly has to do with politeness too. For Chinese users, sending an image or video with explanations or other supportive discourses expresses a higher level of respect towards their addressee than doing so with an image or video on its own, insofar as these messages threaten the addressee's *face* and force them to open the app and look at the sender's discourse. The same can be said about discourses such as emojis and stickers. Since cultures vary in their concern with face management and politeness, people from predominantly collectivist cultures like the Chinese will tend to use more stickers and emoji(s) in text messages, particularly in negative, face-threatening situations (Togans et al. 2021, 285).

By the same token, when receiving a picture/video on WeChat, the addressee user will normally reply with an approving verbal-visual-multimodal discourse both to acknowledge the humorous effect and to strengthen ties and ultimately convey solidarity. A mere response with an emoji, so pervasive in the WhatsApp corpus, would be interpreted as impolite or as exhibiting a certain lack of interest in continuing the conversation. From a cultural point of view, the Chinese are more prone to trying to maintain good social relationships with others by displaying a collaborative attitude during conversations, a quality that can be identified in the image-based pattern of humorous messaging interactions as well. Zhang et al. (2021, 264) contend that "playfulness is encoded through emojis in order to discursively resolve the tension between the openness and freedom afforded by the emerging social media culture and the inherited real-life social norms of conservativeness and restraint. That is, emojis support Chinese social media users' pursuit of preserving face and maintaining social harmony."

7 Concluding Remarks

Humour is very frequent in messaging interactions and often the only reason for users to connect with one another. In this chapter, the quantitative analysis of some recurring patterns in these interactions has made it possible to draw several conclusions both from the prevalence of some patterns over others and from the higher or lesser occurrence of certain discourses in the management of humorous interactions as well as in accomplishing the users' humorous intentions.

Just like in the treatment of other kinds of internet humour, this chapter has also examined the role of interface affordances in how humour is planned, inferred or derived from such interactions. Messaging apps may exhibit limitations compared to the contextual richness of other interfaces (e.g. video chat) but users still manage to convey their intentions and obtain the desired (humour-connoted) inferences with the aid of other supportive discourses (stickers, emojis or GIFs, among others) all the same.

References

Adams, Audrey. 2012. Humor Markers in Computer-Mediated Communication. MA Thesis. Texas A&M University-Commerce.

Al Rashdi, Fathiya. 2018. Functions of Emojis in WhatsApp Interaction Among Omanis. *Discourse, Context & Media* 26: 117–126. https://doi.org/10.1016/j.dcm.2018.07.001.

Archakis, Argiris, and Villy Tsakona. 2005. Analyzing Conversational Data in GTVH Terms: A New Approach to the Issue of Identity Construction Via Humor. *Humor* 18 (1): 41–68. https://doi.org/10.1515/humr.2005.18.1.41.

Attardo, Salvatore. 2001. Humor and Irony in Interaction: From Mode Adoption to Failure of Detection. In *Say Not to Say: New Perspectives on Miscommunication*, ed. Luigi Anolli, Rita Ciceri, and Giuseppe Riva, 166–186. Amsterdam: IOS Press.

———. 2002. Semiotics and Pragmatics of Humor Communication. Babel A.F.I.A.L., Special Issue on Humour, 25–66.

———. 2011. Humor. In *Discursive Pragmatics*, ed. Jan Zienkowski, Jan-Ola Östman, and Jef Verschueren, 135–155. Amsterdam: John Benjamins. https://doi.org/10.1075/hoph.8.08att.

———. 2015. Humor and Laughter. In *The Handbook of Discourse Analysis*, ed. Deborah Tannen, Heidi E. Hamilton, and Deborah Schiffrin, 2nd ed., 168–188. Chichester: Wiley Blackwell. https://doi.org/10.1002/9781118584194.ch8.

Attardo, Salvatore, Lucy Pickering, and Amanda Baker. 2011. Prosodic and Multimodal Markers of Humor in Conversation. *Pragmatics & Cognition* 19 (2): 224–247. https://doi.org/10.1075/pc.19.2.03att.

Attardo, Salvatore, Lucy Pickering, Fofo Lomotey, and Shigehito Menjo. 2013. Multimodality in Conversational Humor. *Review of Cognitive Linguistics* 11 (2): 402–416. https://doi.org/10.1075/rcl.11.2.12att.

Bateson, Gregory. 1953. The Position of Humor in Human Communication. In *Cybernetics, Ninth Conference*, ed. H. von Foerster, 1–47. New York: Josiah Macey Jr Foundation.

Bell, Nancy D. 2009. Responses to Failed Humor. *Journal of Pragmatics* 41: 1825–1836. https://doi.org/10.1016/j.pragma.2008.10.010.

Brown, Penelope, and Stephen C. Levinson. 1987. *Politeness: Some Universals in Language Use*. Cambridge: Cambridge University Press. https://doi.org/10.1017/CBO9780511813085.

Cheng, Winnie. 2003. Humor in Intercultural Conversations. *Semiotica* 146 (1/4): 287–306. https://doi.org/10.1515/semi.2003.070.

Cheng, Lifen. 2017. Do I Mean What I Say and Say What I Mean? A Cross-Cultural Approach to the Use of Emoticons & Emojis in CMC Messages. *Fonseca, Journal of Communication* 15: 207–226. https://doi.org/10.14201/fjc201715199217.

Chiaro, Delia. 2018. *The Language of Jokes in the Digital Age*. Abingdon: Routledge.

Chiera, Alessandra. 2014. Language in Interaction: The Role of Conscious Processes in Conversation. *Academic Journal of Modern Philology* 3: 7–16.

Chovanec, Jan. 2011. Humour in Quasi-Conversations Constructing Fun in Online Sports Journalism. In *The Pragmatics of Humour across Discourse Domains*, ed. Marta Dynel, 243–264. Amsterdam: John Benjamins. https://doi.org/10.1075/pbns.210.16cho.

Chovanec, Jan, and Villy Tsakona. 2018. Investigating the Dynamics of Humor: Towards a Theory of Interactional Humor. In *The Dynamics of Interactional Humor. Creating and Negotiating Humor in Everyday Encounters*, ed. Villy Tsakona and Jan Chovanec, 1–26. Amsterdam: John Benjamins. https://doi.org/10.1075/thr.7.01cho.

Chui, Sherman. 2020. A Comparative Study of the Interpretations of Emojis in Between U.S. and Chinese Users. *International Journal of Literature and Arts* 8 (3): 108–118. https://doi.org/10.11648/j.ijla.20200803.12.

Coates, Jennifer. 2007. Talk in a Play Frame: More on Laughter and Intimacy. *Journal of Pragmatics* 39: 29–49. https://doi.org/10.1016/j.pragma.2006.05.003.

Coupland, Nikolas, and Adam Jaworski. 1997. Relevance, Accommodation and Conversation: Modeling the Social Dimension of Communication. *Multilingua* 16 (2–3): 233–258. https://doi.org/10.1515/mult.1997.16.2-3.233.

Cruz-Moya, Olga, and Alfonso Sánchez-Moya. 2021. Humour in Multimodal Times. Insights from Online Interactions among Senior Users of a Whatsapp Group. *Internet Pragmatics* 4 (1): 52–86. https://doi.org/10.1075/ip.00061.cru.

Danesi, Marcel. 2016. *The Semiotics of Emoji. The Rise of Visual Language in the Age of the Internet*. London: Bloomsbury.

dos Reis, Julio, Rodrigo Bonacin Casar, Heiko Horst Hornung, M. Cecília, and C. Baranauskas. 2018. Intenticons: Participatory Selection of Emoticons for Communication of Intentions. *Computers in Human Behavior* 85: 146–162. https://doi.org/10.1016/j.chb.2018.03.046.

Dresner, Eli, and Susan C. Herring. 2010. Functions of the Nonverbal in CMC: Emoticons and Illocutionary Force. *Communication Theory* 20: 249–268. https://doi.org/10.1111/j.1468-2885.2010.01362.x.

———. 2012. Emoticons and Illocutionary Force. In *Philosophical Dialogue: Writings in Honor of Marcelo Dascal*, ed. D. Riesenfel and G. Scarafile, 59–70. London: College Publication.

Durante, Carey B. 2016. Adapting Nonverbal Coding Theory to Mobile Mediated Communication: An Analysis of Emoji and Other Digital Nonverbals. MA Thesis. Lynchburg, Virginia: Liberty University.

Dynel, Marta. 2007. Joking Aside: Sociopragmatic Functions of Conversational Humour in Interpersonal Communication. In *Current Trends in Pragmatics*, ed. Piotr Cap and Joanna Nijakowska, 246–268. Newcastle-upon-Tyne: Cambridge Scholars Publishing.

———. 2008. No Aggression, Only Teasing: The Pragmatics of Teasing and Banter. *Lodz Papers in Pragmatics* 4 (2): 241–261. https://doi.org/10.2478/v10016-008-0001-7.

———. 2009. Beyond a Joke: Types of Conversational Humour. *Language and Linguistics Compass* 3 (5): 1284–1299. https://doi.org/10.1111/j.1749-818X.2009.00152.x.

———. 2011. Joker in the Pack. Towards Determining the Status of Humorous Framing in Conversations. In *The Pragmatics of Humour across Discourse Domains*, ed. Marta Dynel, 217–241. Amsterdam: John Benjamins. https://doi.org/10.1075/pbns.210.15dyn.

Feyaerts, Kurt. 2013. Tackling the Complexity of Spontaneous Humorous Interaction: An Integrated Classroom-Modeled Corpus Approach. In *Irony and Humor: From Pragmatics to Discourse*, ed. Leonor Ruiz-Gurillo and B. Alvarado, 243–268. Amsterdam: John Benjamins. https://doi.org/10.1075/pbns.231.14fey.

Ge, Jing, and Susan C. Herring. 2018. Communicative Functions of Emoji Sequences on Sina Weibo. *First Monday* 23 (11). https://doi.org/10.5210/fm.v23i11.9413.

Georgakopoulou, Alexandra. 2017. 'Friendly' Comments Interactional Displays of Alignment on Facebook and YouTube. In *Social Media Discourse, (Dis)identifications and Diversities*, ed. Sirpa Leppänen, Elina Westinen, and Samu Kytölä, 179–207. Abingdon: Routledge.

Glenn, Phillip. 2003. *Laughter in Interaction*. Cambridge: Cambridge University Press. https://doi.org/10.1017/CBO9780511519888.

Gumperz, John J. 1982. *Discourse Strategies*. New York: Cambridge University Press. https://doi.org/10.1017/CBO9780511611834.

Hay, Jennifer. 2000. Functions of Humor in the Conversations of Men and Women. *Journal of Pragmatics* 32: 709–742. https://doi.org/10.1016/S0378-2166(99)00069-7.

———. 2001. The Pragmatics of Humor Support. *Humor* 14 (1): 55–82. https://doi.org/10.1515/humr.14.1.55.

Herring, Susan C. 2018. Emergent Forms of Computer-Mediated Communication and Their Global Implications. *Linguapax Review* 5: 90–129.

Herring, Susan C., and Ashley R. Dainas. 2018. Receiver Interpretations of Emoji Functions: A Gender Perspective. In *Proceedings of the 1st International Workshop on Emoji Understanding and Applications in Social Media (Emoji2018)*, ed. Sanjana Wijeratne, Emre Kiciman, Horacio Saggion, and Amit Sheth. Stanford: CEUR. https://doi.org/10.1145/3375629.

———. 2020. Gender and Age Influences on Interpretation of Emoji Functions. *ACM Transactions on Social Computing* 3 (2): 1–26. https://doi.org/10.1145/3375629.

Holmes, Janet. 2006. Sharing a Laugh: Pragmatic Aspects of Humor and Gender in the Workplace. *Journal of Pragmatics* 38: 26–50. https://doi.org/10.1016/j.pragma.2005.06.007.

Holt, Elizabeth. 2010. The Last Laugh: Shared Laughter and Topic Termination. *Journal of Pragmatics* 42: 1513–1525. https://doi.org/10.1016/j.pragma.2010.01.011.

Hsieh, Sara H., and Timmy H. Tseng. 2017. Playfulness in Mobile Instant Messaging: Examining the Influence of Emoticons and Text Messaging on Social Interaction. *Computers in Human Behavior* 69: 405–414. https://doi.org/10.1016/j.chb.2016.12.052.

Ishmael, Aiyana. 2021, August 9. Sending Smiley Emojis? They Now Mean Different Things to Different People. *The Wall Street Journal.*

Jones, Lara L., Lee H. Wurm, Gregory A. Norville, and Kate L. Mullins. 2020. Sex Differences in Emoji Use, Familiarity, and Valence. *Computers in Human Behavior* 108: 106305. https://doi.org/10.1016/j.chb.2020.106305.

Knop, Kathanina, Julian S. Öncü, Jana Penzel, Theresa S. Abele, Tobias Brunner, Peter Vorderer, and Hartmut Wessler. 2016. Offline Time is Quality Time. Comparing Within-Group Self-Disclosure in Mobile Messaging Applications and Face-to-face Interactions. *Computers in Human Behavior* 55: 1076–1084. https://doi.org/10.1016/j.chb.2015.11.004.

Koch, Timo K., Peter Romero, and Clemens Stachl. 2021. Age and Gender in Language, Emoji, and Emoticon Usage in Instant Messages. *Computers in Human Behavior* 126. https://doi.org/10.1016/j.chb.2021.106990.

König, Katharina. 2019. Stance Taking with 'Laugh' Particles and Emojis -Sequential and Functional Patterns of 'Laughter' in a Corpus of German WhatsApp Chats. *Journal of Pragmatics* 142: 156–170. https://doi.org/10.1016/j.pragma.2019.01.008.

Lampert, Martin Daniel, and Susan M. Ervin-Tripp. 2006. Risky Laughter: Teasing and Self-Directed Joking Among Male and Female Friends. *Journal of Pragmatics* 38: 51–72. https://doi.org/10.1016/j.pragma.2005.06.004.

Liedtke, Frank. 2001. The Negotiation of Relevance. In *Negotiation and Power in Dialogic Interaction*, ed. Edda Weigand and Marcelo Dascal, 239–252. Amsterdam: John Benjamins. https://doi.org/10.1075/cilt.214.

Long, Debra, and Arthur Graesser. 1988. Wit and Humour in Discourse Processing. *Discourse Processes* 11: 35–60. https://doi.org/10.1080/01638538809544690.

López-Rúa, Paula. 2021. Men ["face with tears of joy" emoji] and Women ["heart" emoji] on Twitter: A Preliminary Account of British Emoji Usage in Terms of Preferred Topics and Gender-Related Habits. *Language@Internet* 19.

Lynch, Owen H. 2002. Humorous Communication: Finding a Place for Humor In Communication Research. *Communication Theory* 12 (4): 423–445. https://doi.org/10.1111/j.1468-2885.2002.tb00277.x.

Maíz-Arévalo, Carmen. 2014. A Pragmatic and Multimodal Analysis of Emoticons and Gender in Social Networks. In *New Insights into Gendered Discursive Practices: Language, Gender and Identity Construction*, ed. Antonia Sánchez Macarro and Ana Belén Cabrejas Peñuelas, 175–197. Valencia: University of Valencia.

Manokaran, Komalata, and Ong Shyi Nian. 2020. The Functions of e-Laughter in Whatsapp Conversations among Students. *Platform* 3 (2): 55–80.

McKay, Isabel. 2015. Laughing with Letters: A Corpus Investigation of the Use of Written Laughter on Twitter. Senior Thesis. University of Michigan.

McKeown, Gary. 2016. Laughter and Humour as Conversational Mind-Reading Displays. In *Distributed, Ambient and Pervasive Interactions*, ed. Norbert Streitz and Panos Markopoulos, 317–328. Cham: Springer. https://doi.org/10.1007/978-3-319-39862-429.

Moalla, Asma, and Wafa Ben Amor. 2020. The Co-construction of Humor in Computer-Mediated Teacher-Student Communication. *Discourse & Society* 32 (1): 81–97. https://doi.org/10.1177/0957926520961631.

Moeschler, Jacques. 1993. Relevance and Conversation. *Lingua* 90: 149–171. https://doi.org/10.1016/0024-3841(93)90065-5.

Nardi, Bonnie A., Steve Whittaker, and Erin Bradner. 2000. Interaction and Outeraction: Instant Messaging in Action. In *Proceedings of the 2000 ACM Conference on Computer Supported Cooperative Work*, Philadelphia, 79-88. https://doi.org/10.1145/358916.358975

Norrick, Neil R. 1993. *Conversational Joking: Humor in Everyday Talk*. Bloomington: Indiana University Press.

Padilla Cruz, Manuel. 2020. Verbal Humor and Age in Cafés and Bars in Seville, Spain. In *Pragmatic Variation in Service Encounter Interactions across the Spanish-Speaking World*, ed. J. César Félix-Brasdefer and María Elena Placencia, 169–188. Abingdon: Routledge.

Panckhurst, Rachel, and Francesca Frontini. 2020. Beyond the Binary: Emoji as a Challenge to the Image-Word Distinction. In *Visualizing Digital Discourse*.

Interactional, Institutional and Ideological Perspectives, ed. Crispin Thurlow, Christa Dürscheid, and Federica Diémoz, 81–103. Berlin: De Gruyter Mouton. https://doi.org/10.1515/9781501510113-004.

Park, Eun Kyung, and S. Shyam Sundar. 2015. Can Synchronicity and Visual Modality Enhance Social Presence in Mobile Messaging? *Computers in Human Behavior* 45: 121–128. https://doi.org/10.1016/j.chb.2014.12.001.

Park, Jaram, Young Min Baek, and Meeyoung Cha. 2014. Cross-Cultural Comparison of Nonverbal Cues in Emoticons on Twitter: Evidence from Big Data Analysis. *Journal of Communication* 64: 333–354. https://doi.org/10.1111/jcom.12086.

Pérez-Sabater, Carmen. 2019. Emoticons in Relational Writing Practices on WhatsApp: Some Reflections on Gender. In *Analyzing Digital Discourse. New Insights and Future Directions*, ed. Patricia Bou-Franch and Pilar Garcés-Conejos Blitvich, 163–189. Cham: Palgrave Macmillan. https://doi.org/10.1007/978-3-319-92663-6_6.

Petitjean, Cécil, and Etienne Morel. 2017. "Hahaha": Laughter as a Resource to Manage *Whatsapp* Conversations. *Journal of Pragmatics* 110: 1–19. https://doi.org/10.1016/j.pragma.2017.01.001.

Poyatos, Fernando. 1975. Cross-Cultural Analysis of Paralinguistic 'Alternants' in Face-to-Face Interaction. In *Organization of Behavior in Face-to-Face Interaction*, ed. Adam Kendon, Richard Harris, and Mary Ritchie Key, 285–314. The Hague: Mouton. https://doi.org/10.1515/9783110907643.285.

———. 2002. *Nonverbal Communication Across Disciplines. Volumen II: Paralanguage, Kinesics, Silence, Personal and Environmental Interaction*. Amsterdam: John Benjamins. https://doi.org/10.1075/z.ncad2.

Priego-Valverde, Béatrice. 2006. How Funny it is When Everybody Gets Going! A Case of Co-construction of Humor in Conversation. *Círculo de Lingüística Aplicada a la Comunicación* 27: 72–100.

Priego-Valverde, Béatrice, Brigitte Bigi, Salvatore Attardo, Lucy Pickering, and Elisa Gironzetti. 2018. Is Smiling During Humor so Obvious? A Cross-cultural Comparison of Smiling Behavior in Humorous Sequences in American English and French Interactions. *Intercultural Pragmatics* 15 (4): 563–591. https://doi.org/10.1515/ip-2018-0020.

Qiu, Jia, Xinren Chen, and Michael Haugh. 2021. Jocular Flattery in Chinese Multi-Party Instant Messaging Interactions. *Journal of Pragmatics* 178: 225–241. https://doi.org/10.1016/j.pragma.2021.03.020.

Ritchie, L. David. 2011. You're Lying to Jesus!' Humor and Play in a Discussion about Homelessness. *Humor* 24 (4): 481–511. https://doi.org/10.1515/humr.2011.027.

Ruiz-Gurillo, Leonor. 2021. Disrupted vs. Sustained Humor in Colloquial Conversations in Peninsular Spanish. *Journal of Pragmatics* 178: 162–174. https://doi.org/10.1016/j.pragma.2021.03.011.

Sampietro, Agnese. 2016. Exploring the Punctuating Effect of Emoji in Spanish WhatsApp Chats. *Lenguas Modernas* 47: 91–113.

———. 2017. Emoticonos y cortesía en los mensajes de WhatsApp en España [Emoticons and Politeness in WhatsApp Messages in Spain]. In *El Español en la Red*, ed. Mabel Giammatteo, Patricia Claudia Gubitosi, and Alejandro Parini, 279–302. Buenos Aires: Iberoamericana Vervuert.

———. 2018. Emoji and Politeness: A Multimodal Account. Paper Delivered at *Sympol11*. Valencia (Spain).

———. 2019. Emoji and Rapport Management in Spanish Whatsapp Chats. *Journal of Pragmatics* 143: 109–120. https://doi.org/10.1016/j.pragma.2019.02.009.

———. 2021a. Emojis and the Performance of Humour in Everyday Electronically-Mediated Conversation. A Corpus Study of Whatsapp Chats. *Internet Pragmatics* 4 (1): 87–110. https://doi.org/10.1075/ip.00062.samp.

———. 2021b. The Use of the 'Face with Tears of Joy' Emoji on Whatsapp: A Conversation-Analytical Approach. In *Proceedings of the15th International AAAI Conference on Web and Social Media (ICWSM)*. Palo Alto, California: AAAI. https://doi.org/10.36190/2021.03.

Schnurr, Stephanie. 2010. Humour. In *Interpersonal Pragmatics*, ed. Miriam A. Locher and Sage L. Graham, 307–326. Berlin: De Gruyter Mouton. https://doi.org/10.1515/9783110214338.2.307.

Siever, Christina Margrit. 2020. 'Iconographetic Communication' in Digital Media. Emoji in WhatsApp, Twitter, Instagram, Facebook -From a Linguistic Perspective. In *Emoticons, Kaomoji, and Emoji. The Transformation of Communication in the Digital Age*, ed. Elena Giannoulis and Lukas R.A. Wilde, 127–147. Abingdon: Routledge.

Siever, Christina Margrit, and Torsten Siever. 2020. Emoji-Text Relations on Instagram: Empirical Corpus Studies on Multimodal Uses of the Iconographetic Mode. In *Shifts towards Image-Centricity in Contemporary Multimodal Practices*, ed. Hartmut Stoeckl, Helen Caple, and Jana Pflaeging, 177–203. Abingdon: Routledge.

Sun, Juhyung, Sarah Lasser, and Sun Kyong Lee. in press. Understanding Emojis: Cultural Influences in Interpretation and Choice of Emojis. *Journal of International and Intercultural Communication*. https://doi.org/10.1080/17513057.2022.2036790.

Tagg, Caroline, and Agnieszka Lyons. 2022. *Mobile Messaging and Resourcefulness. A Post-Digital Ethnography*. Abingdon: Routledge.

Thielemann, Nadine. 2020. *Understanding Conversational Joking. A Cognitive-Pragmatic Study Based on Russian Interactions.* Amsterdam: John Benjamins. https://doi.org/10.1075/pbns.310.

Togans, LaCount J., Thomas Holtgraves, Gyeongnam Kwon, Tania E. Morales, and Zelaya. 2021. Digitally Saving Face: An Experimental Investigation of Cross-Cultural Differences in the Use of Emoticons and Emoji. *Journal of Pragmatics* 186: 277–288. https://doi.org/10.1016/j.pragma.2021.09.016.

Vandergriff, Ilona. 2014. A Pragmatic Investigation of Emoticon Use in Nonnative/Native Speaker Text Chat. *Language@Internet* 11: 4.

Viana, Amadeu. 2013. Humor and Argumentation in Everyday Talk. In *Irony and Humor: From Pragmatics to Discourse*, ed. Leonor Ruiz Gurillo and Belén Alvarado, 219–242. Amsterdam: John Benjamins. https://doi.org/10.1075/pbns.231.13via.

Völkel, Sarah Theres, Daniel Buschek, Jelena Pranjic, and Heinrich Hussmann. 2019 Understanding Emoji Interpretation through User Personality and Message Context. In *Proceedings of MobileHCI '19.* Taipei (Taiwan). https://doi.org/10.1145/3338286.3340114

Wang, Victoria, John V. Tucker, and Kevin Haines. 2012. Phatic Technologies in Modern Society. *Technology in Society* 34: 84–93. https://doi.org/10.1016/j.techsoc.2012.01.001.

Wirza, Yanty, Della Hanifah Nurbaeti, Hana Hanifah, and Hasri Hanifah. 2020. *The Difference in Emoji Usage Between Genders*, 430. Education and Humanities Research: Advances in Social Science.

Yus, Francisco. 2003. El Chat como Doble Filtro Comunicativo [Chat as a Double Communicative Filter]. *Revista de Investigación Lingüística* 2 (5): 141–169.

———. 2005. Attitudes and Emotions Through Written Text: The Case of Textual Deformation in Internet Chat Rooms. *Pragmalingüística* 13: 147–174.

———. 2010. *Ciberpragmática 2.0. Nuevos Usos del Lenguaje en Internet [Cyberpragmatics 2.0. New Uses of Language on the Internet].* Barcelona: Ariel.

———. 2011a. *Cyberpragmatics. Internet-Mediated Communication in Context.* Amsterdam and Philadelphia: John Benjamins. https://doi.org/10.1075/pbns.213.

———. 2011b. En Qué Difieren los Géneros Electrónicos de los Analógicos [In Which Way Are Electronic and Analogic Genres Different?]. Paper Delivered at *Leer y Escribir en Español en la Red. Aprendizaje, Renovación y Propuestas.* University of Comillas (Spain).

———. 2014a. Not All Emoticons Are Created Equal. *Linguagem em (Dis)curso* 14 (3): 511–529. https://doi.org/10.1590/1982-4017-140304-0414.

———. 2014b. El Discurso de las Identidades en Línea: El Caso de Facebook [The Discourse of Online Identities. The Case of Facebook]. *Discurso & Sociedad* 8 (3): 398–426.

———. 2015. The Role of Cognition and Relevance in New Digital Narratives. In *Prospettive Multilingue e Interdisciplinari nel Discorso Specialistico*, ed. Elena Carpi, 81–107. Pisa (Italy): Pisa University Press.

———. 2016a. *Humour and Relevance*. Amsterdam: John Benjamins. https://doi.org/10.1075/thr.4.

———. 2016b. Towards a Cyberpragmatics of Mobile Instant Messaging. In *Yearbook of Corpus Linguistics and Pragmatics 2016: Global Implications for Culture and Society in the Networked Age*, ed. Jesús Romero-Trillo, 7–26. Berlin: Springer. https://doi.org/10.1007/978-3-319-41733-2_2.

———. 2017. Contextual Constraints and Non-Propositional Effects in WhatsApp Communication. *Journal of Pragmatics* 114: 66–86. https://doi.org/10.1016/j.pragma.2017.04.003.

———. 2019. Emoji: A Full Cyberpragmatic Approach. Paper Delivered at the *16th China Pragmatics Conference*. Nanchang (China).

———. 2021a. *Smartphone Communication. Interactions in the App Ecosystem*. Abingdon: Routledge. https://doi.org/10.4324/9781003200574.

———. 2021b. Pragmatics of Humour in Memes in Spanish. *Spanish in Context* 18 (1): 113–135, Special Issue on Humour. https://doi.org/10.1075/sic.00070.yus.

———. 2021c. The Specificity of Interactive Humor on Messaging Applications. The Case of WhatsApp Conversations. Paper Delivered at the *II International Workshop on Advanced Studies of Humor and Gender*. University of Alicante, Spain.

———. 2022a. Layers of Predicted Inferences in Humorous Communication. Lecture Delivered at *ArgLab Research Colloquium*, Lisbon.

———. 2022b. WhatsApp. Interacciones y Humor en la Mensajería Instantánea [WhatsApp. Interactions and Humour on Instant Messaging]. In *Interactividad en Modo Humorístico: Géneros Orales, Escritos y Tecnológicos*, ed. Leonor Ruiz Gurillo, 161–192. Madrid: Iberoamericana Vervuert.

———. 2022c. Diseccionar el Humor en la Mensajería Instantánea. El Caso de WhatsApp [Dissecting Humour in Instant Messaging. The Case of WhatsApp]. Paper delivered at *AESLA 39*. Las Palmas, Spain.

Yus, Francisco, and Xiaolin Hu. submitted. Interactive Patterns in Humorous Messaging Interactions. A Contrastive Analysis of Western (Whatsapp) and Eastern (Wechat) Users. *Contrastive Pragmatics*.

Zhang, Yiqiong, Min Wang, and Ying Li. 2021. More Than Playfulness. Emojis in the Comments of a Wechat Official Account. *Internet Pragmatics* 4 (2): 247–271. https://doi.org/10.1075/ip.00048.zha.

CHAPTER 6

Humour on Social Networking Sites

1 Introduction: Social Networking Sites as "Humour Repositories"

This chapter will address humour on social networking sites (henceforth SNSs), which many equate to the label of ***social media***, despite the latter being a higher-order term. As specified in Yus (2017), the label applies to socially-connoted uses of internet communication, typically comprising SNSs such as Facebook or Instagram, for instance, but it also encompasses other socially-oriented websites or apps, among them those focused on messaging (WhatsApp, WeChat, Telegram or Line, to quote but a few; see Chap. 5); microblogging sites such as Twitter,[1] blogs and video-centred sites (notably YouTube) or apps such as TikTok too. Herring (2013) defined social media as web-based platforms that incorporate user-generated content and social interaction, often alongside or in response to structures and/or (multimedia) content provided by the sites themselves. The generation of content by users, the availability of areas for its publication and sharing, as well as the options to comment

[1] Twitter, initially designed for short 140-character microblogging messages about what the user was doing while posting them, has doubled its character limit (now 280) and has gradually acquired all the features typical of a social networking site (user's profile, area for comments, different types of uploaded content…). In other words, it has somehow *facebooked*, thus becoming just another SNS in the eyes of quite a few users.

F. Yus, *Pragmatics of Internet Humour*,
https://doi.org/10.1007/978-3-031-31902-0_6

on information uploaded by other users crosscuts numerous popular social media sites, among them Facebook, WhatsApp, Twitter, TikTok or YouTube.

Despite their apparent similarity, users utilise social media platforms differently. By way of example, in a study by Rhee et al. (2021) social interaction stood out as an important feature of all four platforms analysed, particularly of Facebook. Nonetheless, the results of this study likewise provided evidence that Twitter, Instagram or Snapchat users did not assign a central role to social interaction. More precisely, according to these authors, while Twitter functioned as a news or entertainment platform, Instagram and Snapchat focused on photo/video and entertainment, above and beyond social interaction platforms.

Furthermore, Yus (2011) already remarked that, in the years when SNSs started becoming popular, these sites were often defined by equating them to an even more general term, namely: Web 2.0. Possible definitions of SNSs include the following:

> Web-based services that allow individuals to (1) construct a public or semi-public profile within a bounded system, (2) articulate a list of other users with whom they share a connection, and (3) view and traverse their list of connections and those made by others within the system. (boyd and Ellison 2007)

> On-line environments in which people create a self-descriptive profile and then make links to other people they know on the site, creating a network of personal connections. Participants in social network sites are usually identified by their real names and often include photographs; their network of connections is displayed as an integral piece of their self-presentation. (Donath and boyd 2004, 72)

> Internet-based, persistent and disentrained channels of masspersonal communication facilitating perceptions of interactions among users, deriving value primarily from user-generated content. (Carr and Hayes 2015, 49)

Research equally provides us with interesting attempts to delimit the main features or attributes of these SNSs, always highlighting the key role played by the profile as the basic centre or *locus* of social networking, where users engage in self-presentations, interact with other users and upload potentially relevant information. The challenge, as pointed out in Yus (2011), lies in how to acquire relevance on SNSs by capturing other users' attention within an environment where everyone can focus on multiple potential sources of satisfaction. Indeed, a profile typically contains a photo, a short description and general information about the user, a list of friends, a number of applications and a wide area for entries and comments (both by the owner of the profile owner and by other users), together with an area for (a)synchronous messaging interactions, plus additional spaces for the publication of short videos (e.g. reels). SNS users hence become *produsers*, a term coined by Bruns (1998, 2006) as a blend of (active) *producer* and (passive) *user* which describes this kind of user who, far from being the classic passive consumer of content, currently plays an active role both in the production of information and in its consumption. An analogous term, *prosumer*, coined back in the 70s by McLuhan and Nevitt (1972), anticipated the emergence of a new kind of media consumer with the ability to assume the roles of *producer* and *consumer* of content.

In addition to the above, a number of authors have suggested elements or qualities of SNSs:

> (a) persistence (communication between users can be stored indefinitely); (b) searchability (with a "search form" we can find information inside these sites); (c) replicability (we can copy and paste content from one area to another); and (d) invisible audiences (many strangers can access the content of the profile, although the software can filter out information intended only for preselected friends) (boyd 2007).

> (a) users are the key element in the whole system; (b) they exhibit a great capacity to generate connections; (c) they offer the possibility of uploading content in multiple formats; and (d) they make it possible to integrate other technologies and applications into the system (Cormode and Krishnamurthy 2008).

> (a) they are accessible from the Net without the need of a special software; (b) inside them, users express the links that bind them with other users clearly; (c) the software has to foster the creation, maintenance and development of interactive connections among users; and (d) these connections need to be visible (Golbeck 2007).

Regarding humour, as the title of this Section suggests, SNSs may be conceptualised as repositories of different humorous discourses and interactions. Thanks to their capacity to host verbal exchanges plus images and multimodal combinations, all kinds of humorous discourses and humorous acts of communication may appear therein, including, among others, messaging interactions (studied in Chap. 5), or memes (Chap. 7), to which must be added the possibility for SNSs to serve as joke repositories (collected instances of humour addressed under relevance theory in Chap. 2).

An important feature of SNSs when it comes to humour is that they typically contain users' comments on SNS photos, videos and status updates often meant to be humorous as well. Although these mainly exhibit an asynchronous quality, on certain occasions users may feel that a synchronous interaction is taking place among those commenting. In any case, users frequently co-construct humour by acting on one another's comments, as will be explained later on in this chapter. Such humorous discourses may be tagged via hashtags, which become essential on sites such as Twitter or Instagram, among others (Weitz 2017, 515), and often play a *procedural role*, instructing users about how the accompanying discourses should be inferred (e.g. as humorous or otherwise). Zappavigna (2021, 298) contends in this respect that hashtags "have a wide variety of functions from coordinating social media discussion, facilitating meta-commentary, linking and referencing ideas, and cracking jokes." Figure 6.1 is proposed in Parini and Yus (2023), as an example of tagging meant to instruct the audience about the proper way to interpret the tagged images. Albeit referring to specific physical places, two layers of digital information

Fig. 6.1 Tagged images (with hashtags) by an Instagram user

are attached to the images: an initial one shaped by the description that the user makes of the visual referent depicted in the image, and a second layer of hashtagged labels that tell the reader how these images in question should be interpreted. The translation of these discursive layers is provided below.

Left image

Description:	Alicante, my hometown. Its coast and maritime façade. Mediterranean and palm trees in April
Tags:	#alicante #alacant #spain #mediterranean #mediterraneaning #coastalliving #coast #sea #blue #rocks #sunset #dusk #sky #april #spring #breathing #feeling #sensations #colours #smells #way #dontstop #goahead #horizon #more #freedom

Middle image

Description:	Sunset in the English Channel. Feel the warmth of it. Orange power
Tags:	#orange #power #warmth #strength #heat #fire #interiorisation #axis #endoftheday #sunset #sunshine #dusk #englishchannel #uk #england #feelthefireinyou

Right image

Description:	Moorish house, Crevillente. Exuberant and exotic. Remote airs to relax and watch life go by
Tags:	#moorishhouse #crevillente #carmenofcampillo #oasis #shelter #morocco #moorishpeople #alhambra #granada #plants #fountains #water #paradise #senses #candles #light #air #ways #feel #smell #tea #greentea #moorishtea #thesouthalsoexists

The important role played by tagging in these images has to do with the fact that the digital information spread on them determines the way in which the visual referent is to be interpreted, additionally providing clues to the feelings and emotions stirred by these images in the user. The latter emphasises the impact caused by the scene on one's senses, alongside a feeling of freedom which pushes the user to go ahead instead of giving up (left image); objective information regarding the referent and associated feelings (middle image), and broader attributes of Moorish culture and the impact on our senses while staying at this Tea House (right image). Needless to say, feelings also stem from the wider availability of tagged discourse when searched on social media. As Yus (2021a, 156–157) remarks, the tagged photo is not only available for viewing by the "tagger users," but also becomes accessible to these users' entire network of friends on the networking site. The same holds true for images or multimodal combinations whose tagging seeks to ensure that they are properly inferred as humorous.

Furthermore, default iconic reactions to users' posts may also indicate the presence of humour. These reactions, generically labelled as *paralinguistic digital affordances* (Yus 2021a, 250), only applied to the famous Facebook Like (thumbs-up icon) at first. However, they later became widespread, a humorous reaction arising as one of the possible default paralinguistic affordances. According to Yus (ibid.), these iconic reactions (like, dislike, amuses me, angers me…) are easily clicked on and therefore users value the humorous iconic reaction (an image of a laughing face) to a lesser extent than humorous typed comments and the subsequent associated interactions as a means towards self-gratification. Overall, the relevance of these affordances seems to lie in quantity rather than quality. Reich et al. (2018) concluded that a user who gives Likes or other iconic reactions matters far less than the sheer number of such reactions received, thus proving the aforesaid preference for quantitative reward. In other words, users who publish a brand-new profile photo of themselves will generally be disheartened to see that it triggers few Likes, even engaging in social comparison with other users, probably. The same is likely to happen when making a humorous attempt with a new post. These non-propositional effects resulting from users' reactions and responses may fall within an initial user's full awareness (this occurs, for example, when individuals consciously deem their self-presentation successful based on the number of affordances received), or they may produce an array of (dis)satisfying effects on the user beyond full conscious assessment.

2 Humorous Discourses on SNSs

The communicative environment of SNSs provides users with different means to fulfil their humorous intentions. These sites allow for the publication of discourses by using different modes (text, image, multimodal combinations), with text also becoming enriched by means of other qualifying discourses (such as emojis, GIFs, stickers, Likes and hashtags, to quote but a few), and enabling in-post threaded interactions or user-to-user interactions in parallel messaging areas inside the same site (Chiaro and Lobanov 2021, 115; Ge 2019, 11; Ge and Gretzel 2018, 66;

Lewin-Jones 2015, 74; McKay 2020). All of these features are deployed across intra- and inter-cultural flavours across the Net. As Nissenbaum and Freud (2021, 5210) correctly argued, the flow of global humour has been found to undergo a user-generated localisation process which "imports some features (such as stereotypes about nonlocal ethnicities), but does so within frames reflecting local affinities."

SNSs are no doubt frequently used with an entertainment or amusement intent. By way of example, Elayan et al. (2022) cited a report concluding that generating humorous effects (or some form of amusement) stands out as the main reason for posting in over 60% of social media users. After all, SNSs offer users a good opportunity to use humour for other purposes such as counter-cultural movements, feminist campaigns and political positioning, among others (Sundén and Paasonen 2021, 234). Nontheless, it is likewise worth underlining that *interface-related constraints* (also called *interface affordances* in the bibliography) largely determine how these humorous discourses are devised, coded, inferred, subsequently commented upon, and ultimately shared on SNSs. Dynel and Chovanec (2021, 152) point in the same direction by highlighting aspects of these media that, one way or another, influence the production of humour, namely: (a) audiences are made up of countless ordinary users who can interact with the poster in myriad ways; (b) social media have introduced technological developments which allow users to construct humorous items and are characterised by creativity and, more often than not, multimodality; (c) the high volume of humorous interactions and items circulated via the internet on a daily basis; and (d) the creativity that these environments let users show to their followers. Regarding the last aspect, Kräussl (2022) claims that discourse spread and recontextualisation are favoured by the design of social media sites, where people create and repost pictures, pieces of news and other users' posts. Instagram and Twitter would be clear examples of fully participatory sites that encourage everyone to create and share humorous content.

Among the potential humorous strategies, incongruity-resolution (IR) is one of the most frequently chosen, both in its *frame-* and *discourse-*based varieties (see Chap. 2 and, more precisely, its application to meme communication in Chap. 7; see also Yus 1997, 2016, 2021b, forthcoming). As already explained in this book, the former (frame-based) relies on inferential clashes while building up an appropriate mental scenario for the comprehension of a humorous discourse. Instead, the latter (discourse-based IR) revolves around the actual interpretation of a discourse, which usually involves playing with the likelihood of referents for pronouns, senses of ambiguous words, various possible adjusted concepts, and so on. Examples of both incongruity-related strategies will be provided in subsequent sections of this chapter (as well as other chapters).[2]

SNS users often take advantage of multiple discursive combinations inside a multimodal discourse to deploy their IR-based humorous intentions (Vásquez 2019; Yus 2019, 2021b). A good example is the soccer-related posts analysed by Messerli and Yu (2018), which contain several categories of discourses filled with text and/or image incongruities (see Table 6.1) but, at the same time,

> both the verbal and visual elements of the individual humorous posts activate particular aspects of the soccer frame and work in relation to expectations based on knowledge of soccer, the domain of professional soccer and the conventions of televisually broadcast soccer. (…) all of these knowledge structures are assumed by original posters to be part of the communal common ground of their recipients, which in turn renders them affordances for humor construction. (p. 231)

Besides incongruity-resolution, a special mention must be made of two other pervasive humorous strategies used on SNSs, more precisely *self-deprecation* (or *self-denigration*) and *jocular mockery*. The former relies on apparently negative comments and reactions that nevertheless end up being interpreted as humorous and with the user ending up unaltered. This is a typical strategy in the so-called *RoastMe humour*, where users exhibit their self-denigrating or self-deprecating sense of humour by willingly laying themselves open to jocular abuse, and "especially when roastees make manifest their shortcomings, which can be humorous stimuli in their own right" (Dynel and Poppi 2020a, 539–540; more on this below). Weitz (2017, 514) also quotes a post that clearly illustrates a self-deprecating humorous strategy:

(1) Think I just got confused for a Tinder match in a coffee shop. The look of relief on her face when I wasn't "Peter" was a tad unnecessary *sulks*. Hope it works out for them. Maybe they'll invite me to the wedding… #meandpeterareliketwins

[2] Examples of frame-based humour on SNSs have been studied in the bibliography. One example is the political tweets analysed in Vásquez (2019). Moalla (2015, 47–50) also found this strategy in the tweets criticising the Tunisian ex-president during the Arab Spring.

Table 6.1 Incongruity types in soccer-centred SNS posts, as proposed by Messerli and Yu (2018)

IR Strategy	*Description*	*Example*
Incongruities in pictures	One or several pictures or videos that contain incongruities are presented either without text or with a caption or post highlighting the incongruity that the target audience is meant to look for in the post	Best kisses in football history: It includes three pictures of soccer players kissing other players or male or female fans, with the poster asking their followers to choose their favourite of the three. Kisses between male players clash with users' background expectations in the football context
Captions recontextualising incongruities in pictures	The posted picture already contains a humorous incongruity and thus can be said to be humorous in itself. However, on this occasion incongruity does not reside at all or at least not entirely within the domain of soccer, which is why work has to be done by the poster to make it become relevant in the football context	Multimodal discourse with incongruity: a depicted picture from the frame of soccer (a goal) clashes with a snowman (pictured in front of it), that bears some human resemblance (it clearly replaces a goalkeeper). This contrast only activates itself when a metaphorical connection is made with an actual player being criticised: "Still more effective on penalties than Oblak"
Reinforcing incongruities in pictures by juxtaposing them with other pictures	To find a humorous soccer-related picture or video and then to combine them with new pictorial content (it can be described as a combination of the first two strategies, since it makes use of a pre-existing incongruity from the soccer domain on the one hand, and on the other hand, it harnesses additional content from a different domain for humorous effect)	A video consisting of two parts, each of them around two seconds long. The first part is a moment taken from the live broadcast of a recent soccer game, in which the referee keeps sticking his tongue out. The second part simply adds video footage of a goat doing similar movements with its tongue

(*continued*)

Table 6.1 (continued)

IR Strategy	*Description*	*Example*
Incongruous collages	Yet another example of the establishment of a metaphorical link between different events. However, rather than achieving this effect in a linear fashion, by juxtaposing different elements, the images themselves are manipulated in order to map the two metaphorical domains	A post in which one picture shows an Atlético de Madrid player running to the sideline to embrace a female supporter, while a man in a white shirt holds on to the player's arm. This image has been altered by the poster in a very simple fashion, by inserting a logo of the club Real Madrid to cover the Atlético player's head, a picture of the UEFA champions league cup to cover the female fan's face, and an Atlético logo to cover the face of the man wearing the white shirt
Juxtaposition of incongruous pictures	The focus is placed on the relationship established between the juxtaposed pictures as well. An incongruity arises from combining two pictures that contrast with each other	A post with player Marcus Rashford scoring for England's national team and two very different reactions of his teammates: A smiling Wayne Rooney (on the right) faces a less than pleased Daniel Sturridge (on the left). Context is needed for proper understanding: Sturridge and Rashford were then competing for a place in the England squad at the Euro 2016
Humorous captions and post texts	To construct humorous incongruities linguistically and use imagery for purely illustrative purposes	A post pokes fun at Manchester City for spending too much money on a single player and contrasts this with another successful club, Italy's Juventus, who have managed to sign a number of top players for free. Instead of listing the names of these players, the creator of the post simply provides all their pictures

(*continued*)

Table 6.1 (continued)

IR Strategy	*Description*	*Example*
Humorous recontextualisations	To present one or several non-humorous pictures and recontextualise them with a specific text	A post brings together two pictures of real Madrid player Gareth Bale, his hair appearing to show a bald spot, and another where he celebrates the champions league victory by putting the cup on top of his head. The caption ("how to cover up your bald spot") recontextualises the second picture and mockingly suggests that Bale is using the cup to cover up the bald spot revealed in the other picture
Juxtaposition of pictures and captions	Non-humorous pictures and captions. Humour emerges, however, when the post creator combines them	A post shows three pictures related to changes of team members at Manchester United on the left as well as icons and text on the right. These pictures establish a chronology of the former coach leaving the club, Mourinho arriving as his replacement, and the rumoured transfer of their Swedish footballer Ibrahimović. The first two icons on the right, which resemble the Nike logo, also serve as check marks identifying the changes as completed. The labels below these marks specify the respective changes. Instead, the third icon, placed next to Ibrahimović, signifies that a program is loading, which parallels the player's situation of unpredictability

(*continued*)

Table 6.1 (continued)

IR Strategy	*Description*	*Example*
Establishing and breaking a pattern	Posts create a sequence of pictures and captions, with two or more of them establishing a pattern, and the final one running against the expectations evoked by this pattern, a case of a mental frame being easy to construct and subsequently invalidated	A post where the first two pictures and captions establish that the two champions league finalists, Real Madrid (left) and Atlético de Madrid (right) are ready for the game, and the final, larger picture of the Barcelona squad expresses in a colloquial register that they, too, are ready for the game, even though they had already been eliminated from the competition at that point

A similar self-deprecating strategy becomes visible in the tweets by Stormy Daniels reacting to critical or insulting comments, as analysed by Dynel and Poppi (2020b). These authors conclude that her strategy does not consist in taking offence or counter-attacking these abusers; she prefers to deploy what most receivers identify as creative humour, which helps to attest her composure and sharp wit. Within this default strategy, "Stormy Daniels boldly admits to, or tacitly concedes to, what is traditionally considered vices, taking the insults on the chin. Such retorts then qualify as self-denigrating or self-deprecating (or self-deprecatory) humour" (ibid., 77). This form of humour allows her to show her ability to laugh at herself, building a positive self-image and tacitly communicating a message along these lines: "I am weak, I admit it. To admit means to be strong" (ibid.).

Jocular mockery, in turn, appears as a common interactional practice whereby the ability of not taking oneself too seriously is valued because of its capacity to reinforce solidarity (Haugh 2010; Mullan 2020, 142). Maíz-Arévalo (2015, 297) proposes the following definition of jocular mockery in the context of SNS interaction: "[it] involves a Facebook user explicitly diminishing something of relevance -e.g., a photograph, comment, etc.- to self or some other Facebook user within a non-serious or jocular frame." Her analysis shows that mockery can be framed via certain discursive devices in face-to-face environments (lexical exaggeration, prosody, gestures…) which are then mirrored online mainly through typographic manipulation or deformation.[3] As possible triggers of jocular mockery, Maíz-Arévalo mentions new locations, new belongings and personal achievements, all of which may be misinterpreted as bragging by the user's audience.

Regardless of the humorous strategy used, those who create humorous discourses on SNSs hold an expectation that their audience will be able not only to turn the humorous discourse into relevant explicit and/or implicated interpretations but also to retrieve from context the information that will allow them to derive the desired humorous effects. The essential role played by context accessibility has been underlined as essential throughout this book and, as relevance theory proposes, it takes place in a *mutual parallel adjustment* with other inferences performed by audiences for the purpose of obtaining explicit and implicated interpretations from these coded discourses on SNS. Crucially, mutual awareness in the audience and (un)successful context accessibility and interpretation, often through the (in)ability to identify intertextual links, generates an offset of feelings across a positive-negative continuum (Locher and Bolander 2015, 144), ranging between in-group *bonding* and out-group *bounding*: on the one hand, mutual awareness of context accessibility causes an offset of affiliation and in-group bonding effects, or expressed differently, an awareness of in-group belonging and communal affiliation; on the other hand, though, lack of accessibility to the necessary quantity and quality of contextual information can evidence the user's lack of group membership (see also Chap. 8). Some research in the bibliography also corroborates this importance of context accessibility for a proper understanding of humour on SNSs:

Vásquez (2019, 75) analyses tweets such as (2) below, which exhibit a blend of colloquial expressions and academic language and can be interpreted as playful criticism of the unnecessary complexity of academic discourse (particularly regarding specialised jargon), as well as of the absurdity associated with other academic phenomena:

(2) Friends don't let friends believe in impact factors.
It's not you. It's your unsubstantiated a priori epistemological assumptions.
I don't always get emotional. But when I do, I call it affect.

[3] Also called *text deformation* in (Yus 2005a), *oralised written text* in Yus (2010, 2011) and *text alteration* in Yus (2021a). Crystal (2001) uses the term *hybrid language*.

Most importantly, optimal understanding of tweets such as those quoted in (2) demands accessibility to certain contextual information, more specifically insider knowledge of and membership in the community of academics. Similarly, Vásquez (ibid.) analyses Tumblr chats based on the capacity to recognise feelings and emotions in the posts which rely on a capacity to share experiences and references for their interpretation:

> Intertextual references are a significant mechanism for community building on the platform (…) shared references and intertextual practices are what enable Tumblr users to discover others on Tumblr with shared interests, leading to the formation of loosely formed communities. (…) only those readers who share similar backgrounds and/or interests as the creator of the Chat -and are thus able to make the necessary cultural associations to interpret the message- would fully understand the humorous dimensions of these digital texts (p. 94).

Tsakona (2020) also analyses instances of SNS humour supported on intertextuality and, consequently, on the audience's ability to retrieve from context the necessary information that allows for these intertextual connections and for the derivation of the expected humorous effects. For instance, she quotes several internet jokes that humorously and ironically criticise a very specific event: a Ryanair flight that landed in Timisoara (Romania) instead of Thessaloniki (Greece), as initially scheduled. These jokes will no doubt make no sense to the users who lack access to this piece of contextual information. Examples of these intertextuality-centred posts include the ones in (3–5).

(3) -Mum, I am going to Thessaloniki.
-Take a Greek-Romanian dictionary [with you].

(4) -Honey, while I was on my way home, I ended up in Romania.
-You scamp, did you go [there] for women?
-It's not what you think…

(5) At the end, Ryanair is really a bargain. With a ticket of, say, €20 you see half Europe. Cool. #Timisoara #Romania #ryanair

The same applies to the *RoastMe* community on Reddit (see below), in which users are only apparently insulted by other users in the community, willingly committing themselves to being the butt of aggressive acts that may well be misunderstood by outsiders who are unaware of the rules[4] of this roasting activity: "Sharing benevolent humor is the primary reason for the functioning of this online community. Its members engage in the humorous activity, cognizant of its overarching purpose and mechanics. Those can be misunderstood by outsiders, not only academics but also media commentators and Internet users who do not participate in the activity" (Dynel and Poppi 2020a, 538).

Finally, it should be noted that two qualities of SNS (and of the internet in general) determine the effectiveness of this inferential strategy of contextualisation aimed at humorous effects. First, the heterogeneous nature of users' audiences, made up of relatives, close friends, acquaintances, students and so on, what Marwick and boyd (2011) labelled as *context collapse*. Upon attempting a humorous communicative strategy, only a portion of the user's audience will be able to access the necessary contextual information while processing the humorous discourse as intended by the initial user. Second, a typical activity on the internet consists in utilising humorous instances posted on one SNS and re-posting it somewhere else (another SNS, a messaging conversation…). This strategy of forwarding and sharing the initial humorous discourse entails re-contextualisation across sites and audiences, thus producing variations across the whole act of communication. After all, upon being published elsewhere, the discourse lands on a different context and is interpreted by a different audience who, once again, may prove unable to retrieve the information that the initial user had predicted for the initial audience.

What community practices such as RoastMe (together with sites revolving around political orientation, gender or ethnic origin, etc.) show us is that, apart from the value of the humorous effects themselves, one major source of relevance stemming from the interactions that take place therein lies in the non-propositional effects generated (see Chap. 8 for a more detailed explanation). Needless to say, among these effects, audience-generated feelings of group membership, of being valued and acknowledged by the community stand out as key to these community members,

[4] "While publicising their faces, roastees must remain anonymous and share no self-identifying details that could help other users to trace their identity or location. Roasters, on the other hand, cannot do 'hating' or 'bullying'; instead, they should aim to make 'an audience laugh' by means of creative jocular comments (cf. the 'unfunny abuse' and 'don't be evil' rules). What is pertinent in the context of the present study is the 'inappropriate flattery rule,' according to which fishing for compliments is not allowed; nor is flirting with a view to prospective dating" (Poppi and Dynel 2021, 436).

who feel the support and connection through weak ties with myriad users (Weitz 2017, 516). A close relationship hence exists between this group-centred offset of effects and other feelings of connection such as *ambient affiliation* (Zappavigna 2011, 2012, 2014, 2022) or *affective publics* (Papacharissi 2015, 2016). Humour on collective SNSs has the capacity to foster and trigger these non-propositional effects that become crucial to understand these sites' current appeal among contemporary users (Yus 2021a).

3 SNS Humour: Single User

Humorous communication on SNSs may be generated by a single user. Very often, users simply collect potentially humorous discourses (memes, photos, screenshots of news items…) and share them with their audiences. Therefore, these individual users act as mere humour repositories. Of more interest for the purposes of this book is to analyse the creative production of humour by a single user without the aid of previously published material. In this section, the tweets of a Spanish female user will be analysed. She explicitly labels her page as humorous and reminds her audience of this quality when criticised for treating apparently serious facts and events humorously. With this aim, a sample of 50 of her tweets was collected between 4th April 2022 and 9th September 2022. Although most of them have a textual nature, some exhibit a multimodal quality. Several humorous strategies were isolated from these tweets, as commented and exemplified below.

1. *Humour based on make-sense frames.* The label *make-sense frame* was introduced in Chap. 2, a label that comprises other frequently used terms in the literature, among them *frame*, *schema* and *script*. In a nutshell, make-sense frames are inferential constructions of suitable (i.e. prototypical) mental situations generated by default (and often sub-attentively) while a discourse is inferred. Several examples of the exploitation of these make-sense frames for the sake of humour can be found in Chap. 2 (see also Yus 2013a, 2013b, 2016). This Twitter user likewise resorts to these mental situations to generate humour (14 instances). Manipulations of make-sense frames include (a) to explicitly contrast or confront information from two dissimilar make-sense frames constructed during the comprehension of the tweet; (b) to add an element in the tweet that seems non-coherent

regarding the overall frame just constructed (typically invalidating the frame generated for the initial part of the tweet); and (c) to depict absurd situations that cannot possibly be framed correctly due to some inadequacy. Consider the tweets in (6–10):

(6) Que haya sido capaz de parir yo solita una criatura de más de cuatro kilos y que no pueda abrir un bote de pepinillos del Mercadona...
[*I was able to give birth to a creature who weighed over four kilos all by myself but now I can't open a can of pickles from Mercadona...*].[5]

(7) Si se os declara alguien y os gusta mucho, decidle que sí... que no os pase como a mí, que por hacerme la interesante y hacerle esperar, a las dos semanas me lo encontré en un bar y ya estaba casado y con un niño de tres años.
[*If someone proposes to you and you like him/her a lot, say yes... Don't let what I went through happen to you. I played hard to get and two weeks later I met him in a bar and he was already married and with a three-year-old son*].

(8) A mí estos días de tanto calor me gusta madrugar para pasar calor ya desde prontito por la mañana.
[*On these days of so much heat, I like to wake up early and suffer the heat already from very early in the morning*].

(9) Los animales más temibles y peligrosos del mundo son: El león africano, el tiburón blanco, y ese flipado que hay en todos los barrios que conduce un Seat León amarillo piolín.
[*The most fearsome and dangerous animals in the world are: the African lion, the white shark, and that freak who can be found in all neighbourhoods driving a tweety-yellow Seat León*].

(10) Cuando parece que estamos saliendo de una pandemia, estalla un volcán, cuando se apaga el volcán, comienza una guerra, terminará la guerra y vendrá a pasar mi suegra unos días a casa, ya lo verás...
[*When it looks like the end of the pandemic is near, a volcano erupts, when the volcano becomes extinguished, a war starts, the war will finish and my mother-in-law will come to spend some days with us, you'll see*].

These examples exhibit manipulations of make-sense frame constructions aimed at generating humour. (6) brings together information from two dissimilar frames that need to be constructed while interpreting the tweet: to give birth and to open a can. (7) presents the reader with a situation whose “framing” is impossible. However, the exaggeration allows

[5] Mercadona is a popular Spanish supermarket chain.

for implications concerning the need to act quick on a prospective relationship. In (8), the frame-based processing of the initial part of the tweet leads the reader to carry out frame-congruent anticipatory inferences about its continuation, which are disconfirmed. (9–10) illustrate the humorous strategy of inserting a discordant element after several previously processed (and mutually coherent) elements have favoured the construction of a specific frame.

2. *Humour based on discourse interpretation*. Some of this user's tweets rely on manipulation of discourse comprehension, 4 of them exploiting ambiguities and/or multiple possible referents (i.e. for indexicals), while another 5 resort to the strategy to exploit the inferential strategy of concept adjustment. The former (ambiguity/referents) appears in tweets such as (11–13):

(11) Lo que puede cambiar la palabra "cómetelo" cuando no tienes hijos a cuando los tienes.
[*The phrase "eat it" can change a lot depending on whether you have kids or not*].

(12) Me estaba acordando del día que le desvalijaron la casa de la sierra a mi tía Carmen y le dijo la policía que se trataba de una banda organizada. "Organizada dice, y me han dejado la casa hecha una mierda."
[*I was remembering the day my aunt Carmen's house in the mountain was stripped bare and the police told her that it was an organised gang. "Organised, they say, and they left my house a mess"*].

(13) Me acuerdo una vez que ligué con un chico, y mientras tomábamos una copa me dijo "menudo trancazo tengo" Luego fuimos a su casa y resulta que estaba constipado.
[*I remember once when I hit it off with a guy, and while we were having a drink he told me "What a cold I've got." Then we went to his house and it turns out he did have a cold*].

The tweet in (11) plays with different possible referents for the indexical *lo* (it) in *cómetelo* (eat it). The one in (12), by contrast, takes advantage of the ambiguity and hierarchical accessibility associated with two possible meanings of *organizada* (organised), one of them being more accessible and likely (i.e. *relevant*) while the other, not initially identified for being much less predictable, becomes foregrounded at the end of the tweet, also triggering the erasure of the initial meaning and subsequent replacement with the new one. Finally, (13) features a tweet that "toys" with two meanings of the idiomatic word *trancazo* in Spanish, namely: "a serious cold" (an illness) or "a big penis" (used in very informal settings). Despite the former being far more likely to be selected as the intended meaning, at the end of the tweet the reader is reminded of the second, less probable interpretation and the audience has to backtrack inferentially and re-interpret the word given the new evidence.

In turn, concept adjustment underlies the humour generated in a number of tweets. As explained in Chap. 2, concept adjustment is applied to coded concepts whose context-free literal meaning tends to be irrelevant (or not relevant enough) and must go through as adjustment process so as to remain communicatively valid. In this way, the eventually inferred concept (called *ad hoc concept* in relevance-theoretic terminology) resembles in meaning but is not exactly the same as the literal meaning of the coded concept. Adjustments may either entail *narrowing* (when the meaning of the coded concept has an excessively general meaning and has to be made more specific -narrower- so that it can become relevant), as it happens with *drink* in (14) below, or *broadening* (when the meaning of the coded concept is too specific and must be rendered more general -broader- to ensure its relevance), as illustrated with *empty* in (15) below:

(14) I am worried about John. He *drinks* too much.
[The literal meaning of "drink" is too general and is narrowed into "drink alcohol"].

(15) Let's go somewhere else. This pub is *empty*.
[The pub is not literally empty (there is a waiter, etc.), so the meaning of the coded concept has to be broadened into a more relevant "with few people"].

This strategy also appears in several of this user's tweets. Let's consider (16–17) below:

(16) Están diciendo que este fin de semana habrá más de 1 millón de desplazamientos en España. Eso porque no cuentan los que hace una madre del salón a la cocina y de la cocina al salón antes de sentarse a ver una serie.
[*They are saying that this weekend there will be more than 1 million journeys in Spain. That's because they don't count the ones a mother makes from the living room to the kitchen and from the kitchen to the living room before sitting down to watch a series*].

(17) Gritamos y gemimos poco para lo bien que nos están follando las petroleras. Esta es mi reflexión de hoy.
[*We scream and moan little for how well the oil companies are fucking us. This is my reflection for today*].

In (16), the coded concept *desplazamientos* (journeys) comprises any movement by people, an excessively broad meaning that has to be narrowed, so that one can regard it as relevant. Initially, the reader is led to infer a very accessible interpretation via narrowing (i.e. "journeys by car across the country") as the *adjusted concept* being meant. However, the second part of the tweet forces the construction of an alternative narrowed concept, that of a person moving around the house. In turn, (17) depicts a metaphor of *follar* (fuck), which requires a certain degree of conceptual adjustment for the verb to be applicable to these companies' actions over its customers.

3. *Humour based on implicated premises and conclusions.* 4 instances in the collected sample from this user base their humorous effects on the audience's ability to infer implicated premises (which work as contextual information) and implicated conclusions (that is, *implicatures*) from the text of the tweet. These implicatures are frequently of a critical kind. For example, part of the humour in tweet (18) lies in the (implicated) critical connotations regarding taxi drivers' continuous reluctance to use their car indicators. Similarly, the negative qualities associated with the TV coverage of the Spanish Cycling Tour (*Vuelta Ciclista a España*), e.g. for being so boring, are implicated, rather than explicitly expressed in (19). Finally, (20) equally implicates the information about the lack of sexual activity when one grows older instead of communicating it via an explicature:

(18) Cuando veo a un taxista dar el intermitente correctamente, siempre pienso que el pasajero que lleva detrás le está apuntando con una pistola y él nos está intentando enviar una señal.
[*When I see a taxi driver use the indicator correctly, I always think that the passenger behind him is pointing a gun at him/her and he/she is trying to send us a signal*].

(19) Y para la operación, ¿qué prefiere que le pongamos, anestesia general, local o la Vuelta ciclista a España?

[*And for the operation, what would you prefer us to give you, general anaesthesia, the local one or La Vuelta?*].

(20) Admites que te has hecho mayor cuando te jode más que se te haya terminado el pan rallado para las croquetas, que los condones.
[*You admit that you've grown older when it bothers you more that you've run out of breadcrumbs for the croquettes, than of condoms*].

4. *Humour based on mutual awareness of context accessibility*. Finally, one major humorous strategy implemented by this user in up to 22 instances (of the sample out of 50 tweets), relies on supposedly shared assumptions and context accessibility by the user and her audience. Most of them rely on what was labelled as *joy of mutual manifestness* in previous research on stand-up comedy monologues (Yus 2002, 2004, 2005b). In these monologues, the derivation of humorous effects very often lies in the comedian's ability to remind the audience about the collective status of certain information and, alternatively, to surprise some audience members with a reminder that some information previously considered private and personal actually holds a collective quality. Tweets such as (21–25) exploit this awareness about the collective nature of certain background contextual information (or private information turned collective):

(21) A mí lo que de verdad se me da bien en la vida, es aparcar a la sombra por la mañana y que a los 5 minutos ya le esté dando el sol al coche para todo el día.
[*What I am really good at in life is parking in the shade in the morning in such a way that, after 5 minutes the sun is already shining on the car and during the whole day*].

(22) Yo no me decepciono más a mí misma intentando memorizar el número de surtidor cuando voy a echar gasolina. Ya directamente digo "el coche blanco." Y si hay dos blancos digo, "el más sucio."
[*I no longer let myself down trying to memorise the pump number when I go to fill up. I directly say "the white car." And if there are two white cars I say, "the dirtier one"*].

(23) Si os gustan las emociones fuertes a medianoche, pegad algo con ventosas en el baño.
[*If you like strong emotions at midnight, stick something with suction cups in the bathroom*].

(24) ¿Vosotros también ensayáis brillantes conversaciones en vuestra mente, pero cuando llega la hora de exponerlas, se os planta un mono con dos platillos en la cabeza que hace que parezcáis gilipollas?
[*You too rehearse brilliant conversations in your head but, when the time comes to expose them, a monkey with two cymbals gets into your head and makes you look like mentally retarded*?].

(25) Hay gente que piensa que independizarse consiste en tener su propia flota de tuppers para que los siga llenando su madre.
[*There are people who think that becoming independent consists in having their own fleet of tupperwares so that their mother continues to fill them*].

The five tweets above resonate with similar experiences by the audience in situations that probably resemble the ones that they have gone through, thus generating an offset of effects through this *joy of mutual manifestness* and the audience's awareness about the collective status of the information conveyed. Tweet (24), in particular, stands out for being shaped as a direct question to the audience, seeking to confirm that the information in the tweet does indeed possess a collective status.

4 SNS Humour: Compiled

Several SNS sites are archives and repositories of humorous discourses, mainly storing textual, visual and multimodal memes or tweets that are likely to cause humorous effects in the audience (and perhaps lead to a viral spread of these discourses). One of these sites will be analysed in this chapter, more precisely the Twitter page *Memes top Best*. Exactly like in the previous Section, 50 posts were collected between 22nd January and 22nd September 2022. The analysis yielded similar humorous strategies underlying these collected discourses that will be exemplified in detail below.

1. *Humour based on make-sense frames*. As in the personal tweets analysed in the previous section, 13 instances of the sample fit a humorous strategy based on manipulating of the audience's mental construction of a suitable make-sense frame for the comprehension of the humorous discourse. Three main sub-strategies were isolated. Firstly, some humorous discourses from this site feature an inferential clash being triggered between the make-sense frame constructed

for the initial part of the discourse and the frame constructed for the subsequent and/or final part. Examples include (26) below, which links two opposed frames in the same tweet by means of similar pronunciations in Spanish (also applicable to English); (27), where the initial part leads the audience to predict a continuation in the profession-related frame, which then becomes invalidated; and (28), in which an initial love-related frame clashes with the need to activate a different frame in the second part of the tweet. Secondly, some tweets defy "commonsense" frame construction by portraying impossible (or very unlikely) situations, which actually play a basic role in their eventual humorous effects. (29) illustrates this mechanism. Finally, some tweets support their humour on totally contradicting the initial part of a constructed frame, even though the frame remains roughly maintained (instead of being abandoned and replaced with an alternative frame, as in other instances). Two examples would be (30) and (31). In the former, the reader expects a commonsense development of the tweet as a dismissal of the information initially provided, aided by the procedural connective *pero* (but), which instructs the reader to infer a contrast with what has already been processed; nevertheless, the end of the tweet surprises the reader by further emphasising the initial part with no contrast whatsoever. As for (31), the list includes an incoherent item that contradicts what the reader has inferred so far in the tweet.

(26) Gym y tonificar se parecen mucho a gin y tónica y eso puede prestar a la confusión.
[*Gym and toning up sound a lot like gin and tonic and that can lead to confusion*].

(27) Quería ser psicóloga pero tengo más potencial como paciente.
[*I wanted to be a psychologist but I have more potential as a patient*].

(28) Es muy duro el silencio de la persona deseada tras preguntarle si te ama, pero el silencio del mecánico tras salir de debajo del coche, no hay angustia que lo supere.
[*The silence of the desired person after being asked if he/she loves you is very hard, but the silence of the mechanic after coming out from under your car, there is no anguish that overcomes it*].

(29) He salido del supermercado con un carrito que se desviaba ligeramente hacia un lado. He llegado a Burgos. Estoy bien. Hace fresquito.

[*I have come out of the supermarket with a trolley that veered slightly to one side. I have arrived in Burgos. I'm fine. It's cool*].

(30) Siempre había pensado que la gente era gilipollas, pero estos últimos años me he dedicado a escuchar a todo el mundo sin prejuzgar, con empatía, tratando de entender sus circunstancias, sus puntos de vista, dispuesto a acercar posturas. Y, efectivamente, la gente es gilipollas.
[*I had always thought that people were assholes, but in recent years I have striven to listen to everyone without prejudging, with empathy, trying to understand their circumstances, their points of view, willing to bring positions closer. And indeed, people are assholes*].

(31) Soy responsable y siempre controlo lo que gasto:
Comida 50€
Internet 20€
Ni puta idea 482€
[*I am responsible and always monitor the money I spend: Food €50/ Internet €20/No fucking idea €482*].

2. *Humour based on discourse interpretation.* Similarly to what was explained in the preceding Section, humorous effects may also derive from manipulations regarding how tweet content is to be inferred (i.e. to turn the coded discourse into an explicit interpretation or explicature). The two major inferential strategies exploited are once more disambiguation and concept adjustment. Concerning the former (6 instances in the sample), the author of the tweet again plays with alternative meanings of a word or phrase, one of which is highly likely and relevant, and hence prone to be selected as the one intended, whereas the second meaning, not initially taken into consideration, is finally proposed as the correct one, the author of the tweet being aware that it was not the reader's initial choice. Le tus look at the tweets in (32–33):

(32) Tengo amigas que van a la discoteca con la misma actitud que cuando van a Ikea: echan un vistazo y si les gusta algo se lo llevan a casa para montarlo.
[*I have female friends who go to the disco with the same attitude as when they go to Ikea: they take a look and if they like something they take it home to assemble it*].

(33) -¡Me estás llevando a la ruina!
-Claro, somos arqueólogos.
-Ah, sí, calla.

[*-You're driving me to ruin!*
-Of course, we are archaeologists.
-Ah, yes, shut up].

The humorous effects achieved in (32) rely on the latent ambiguity of *montarlo* at the end of the tweet. In Spanish it can mean either "to assemble parts" or "to have sex with," and both are possible meanings because the tweet explicitly compares these two senses and includes what in Yus (2020) was called *preparatory discourse.* In short, the term refers to a part of an utterance or dialogue deliberately placed in the joke with the aim of influencing the kind of inference applied to (an)other subsequent piece(s) of discourse inside the pun-based joke. As such, the preparatory discourse has as its main purpose to keep certain information vivid in the hearer's working memory (i.e. the short-term memory store), whose associated encyclopaedic information becomes enacted as part of the overall construction of an appropriate situation for the comprehension of the joke (i.e. the *make-sense frame*). This information is activated in parallel to (and also influencing) the normal relevance-seeking cumulative procedure through which any utterance is interpreted. In the case of (32), these preparatory discourses would be *ir a la discoteca* (go to the disco) and *Ikea*, both of which render the two senses of *montarlo* (assemble it/have sex with him) equally likely. Regarding (33) above, the tweet once again plays with two meanings of a word, this time *ruina* (ruin), both of which are humorously exploited.

Apart from exploiting ambiguities, 4 tweets implement the inferential strategy of concept adjustment, as it also happened in the samples analysed in the previous Section. One possible strategy consists in playing with literal vs. metaphoric uses of the same word. Figure 6.2 shows an example of this adjustment-based strategy. The multimodal discourse attached to the user's tweet depicts several *trampas mortales* (deadly traps) associated with the corresponding animal (fly, mouse, bear). In the first three cases, *trampa* is used literally, and although some inferential conceptual narrowing becomes necessary to turn the general coded referent into more animal-specific inferred concepts, this does not prove inferentially costly due to the accompanying images. By contrast, in the fourth *trampa*, the one applied to a human being, the word is used metaphorically and shaped as a woman's remark: *No hace falta que me regales nada en San Valentín* (You needn't buy me anything on Valentine's Day), which is said by a woman and entails some kind of trap for the man involved, who cannot react properly.

Fig. 6.2 Concept adjustment of *trampa* (trap) in a humorous tweet

3. *Humour based on implicated premises and conclusions.* The Twitter page *Memes Top Best* likewise includes cases where the main humorous potential of the tweet lies in the audiences' ability to retrieve implicated premises (i.e. contextual information) and derive implicated conclusions (implicatures) from its content. This inferential strategy often relates to some attitude towards some state of affairs (often a critical one) that the community managers of a page want to share with the audience (albeit not explicitly but rather as an implicatures). The utilisation of this strategy becomes obvious in 10 tweets of the sample, some of which are reproduced in (34–38) below:

(34) Hay gente a la que no le gusta el vino ni la cerveza y van andando por encima de la acera a nuestro lado, como si fueran personas normales.
[*There are people who don't like wine or beer and walk over the sidewalk next to us, as if they were normal people*].
Implicated: it is impossible not to like wine or beer.

(35) Mi más profunda admiración a toda esa gente que es capaz de pasar unas vacaciones enteras sin colgar ni una sola foto en ninguna red social.
[*My deepest admiration to all those people who are able to spend an entire holiday without posting a single photo on any social networking site*].
Implicated: Posting information on SNSs is addictive and/or difficult to avoid.

(36) Los videojuegos son una pasada. En serio, te dejan vivir las fantasías más salvajes. En los Sims, por ejemplo, puedes tener casa y trabajo.
[*Video games are really cool. Seriously, they let you live out the wildest fantasies. In the Sims, for example, you can have a house and a job*].
Implicated: Nowadays, the prospect of having a house and a job is a fantasy in Spain.

(37) Iba a llenar el depósito al coche para ir a ver a un amigo este finde, pero al final nos vamos al Caribe una semana, que hay que ahorrar.
[*I was going to fill the tank in the car to go and see a friend this weekend, but in the end we are going to stay in the Caribbean for a week, because we have got to save*].
Implicated: The current price of petrol is exorbitant.

(38) He ido a echar gasolina y me ha atendido directamente un señor del banco para pedirme las tres últimas nóminas y la renta.
[*I went to get petrol and I was directly attended by a man from the bank who asked me for the last three pay slips and my income statement*].
Implicated: The current price of petrol is exorbitant.

4. *Humour based on mutual awareness of context accessibility.* Finally, harnessing the mutual manifestness of information, either by reminding the audience about the collective nature of this information or by forcing a reinterpretation of some thought-to-be privately held information as collective, is a humorous strategy used in no less than 18 tweets of the collected sample of tweets from the *Memes Top Best* repository. The information supplied in these tweets will emphasise some users' background assumptions about collectively assumed actions or activities, whereas for other users, the relevance will stem from contradicting and reshaping the private-collective status of certain assumptions. Some examples thereof appear in (39–42).

These tweets connect with some audience members' background knowledge about the situations depicted. Some female users probably agree with how they are dressed to go to the beach (39); other users have probably felt the same upon reluctantly deciding to go to the gym, for instance (40); a number of female users probably felt just as puzzled when trying to buy clothes for the gym (41); and finally, many users have (privately) decided to push the lift button so as to go up on their own, the tweet reminding them that this is in fact a collective habit.

(39) Hay dos tipos de mujeres: las que vamos a la playa con la ropa de ir a comprar droga. Y las que van listas para protagonizar un anuncio.
[*There are two types of women: those who go to the beach with the clothes that we wear when we go to buy drugs. And those who are ready to star in a commercial*].

(40) El argumento de ir a hacer deporte porque luego te sentirás bien aunque te dé pereza empezar, hace aguas cuando ya te sientes bien en tu sofá con tu cerveza.
[*The argument of going to play sports because later you will feel good even if you are too lazy to start, is invalidated when you already feel good on your sofa with your beer*].

(41) Hoy fui a comprarme ropa para el gimnasio y me quedo loca con que la mayoría de ropa de deporte para mujeres sea: compresiva, push up, reductora, realzante, moldeadora... Por dios que quiero unos pantalones no envasarme al vacío.
[*Today I went to buy clothes for the gym and I'm shocked that most sportswear for women is: compression, push up, reducing, enhancing, shaping... For Chrissake, I want some tracksuit bottoms, not getting vacuum packed*].

(42) Ese momento cuando entras al ascensor y oyes que alguien entra al portal y le das rápidamente al botón como si viniese un zombi a comerte.
[*That moment when you enter the lift and you hear someone enter the portal and you quickly press the button as if a zombie was coming to eat you*].

5 SNS Humour: Collective

SNS pages and groups also host users making up cohesive areas delimited by certain attributes too. As already stated, a non-propositional offset from these collective sites may be labelled *bonding* and *bounding* effect, mainly through a mastery of how to design the posts and especially via mutual manifestness of being able to access or retrieve essential information from context that marks these users as legitimate members of the group in question. To put it in another way, the members of these groups not only feel connected to one another through both this mastery of discursive constructions and context accessibility on the site/group (*bonding*), but also know who belongs to this SNS or not thanks to this mutual awareness (*bounding*).

An example of these delimited SNS spaces can be found in the SNS areas where users gather according to their sexual orientation, including feminist sites in which humour targets men and patriarchal society. Similarly, this collective gathering is typical of users who bond via their political orientation (again using humour to criticise other political positions) and race (mainly resorting to humour as a tool to refute racist discourses on these SNSs, see Taylor 2022). As such, SNSs provide users with a perfect venue to create and disseminate humour, especially the one that serves the purpose of challenging hegemonic discourses (Rodriguez 2020, 271).

Regarding political humour on SNSs (but also in relation to other thematically oriented sites), Juzefovics and Vihalemm (2020) contended that "political humour" is an umbrella term for "various artifacts dealing with political issues, people, events, processes, or institutions, designed to elicit laughter and offer various degrees of critical judgement about them," to which they added the significance of engagement and participation through humour on these political sites. They also proposed a distinction regarding how to approach this connection: either from a *functionalist angle* or from a *cognitive theoretical one*. In the former, political humour is seen as an expression of superiority or a "safety valve" for society, or expressed differently, as a release of aggressive feelings. In the latter, we lay the emphasis instead upon the socio-culturally shared patterns of "incongruence" that trigger the laughter.

These authors also mentioned the important contribution by Papacharissi (2016) and especially her coinage of the term *affective publics*, also applicable to these thematic humorous sites (an essential offset of non-propositional effects, see Chap. 8). This scholar proposes the concept of *affective news stream*, where elements of cognition and affect become intertwined and which she, together with Oliveira (Papacharissi and Oliveira 2012) also applied to Twitter news feeds during the 2011 Egyptian uprisings, which exhibited a mix of humour, news sharing, expression of opinions, and emotion (p. 278). Basically, what Papacharissi had in mind when she coined the phrase *affective publics* was the users' involvement in shared storytelling, defined as "networked publics that are mobilized and connected, identified, and potentially disconnected through expressions of sentiment" (Papacharissi 2016, 311). As a consequence of this massive posting, commenting and sharing, these affective publics "produce disruptions, interruptions of dominant political narratives" (ibid., 318).

Another interesting humour-centred community is *RoastMe* on the SNS Reddit (see Kasunic and Kaufman 2018; Dynel 2019; Dynel and Poppi 2019, 2020a 2020b; Poppi and Dynel 2021; Ryen 2022), a specific communal environment where expectations of mutuality of assumptions related to the norms associated with this site become vital, since nonmembers might qualify it as an environment riddled with insults and harassment. Within RoastMe a *roast* is defined as follows:

> a humorous interaction (private or mass-media) in which one or more individuals is/are subjected to jibes, i.e. disparaging remarks, produced by roasters with a view to amusing themselves and others, including the target (the roastee). Although these jibes can be regarded as seemingly aggressive and even potentially offensive, they are free from spite and genuine aggression. Thus, the target, who has willingly agreed to be roasted, can - and perhaps even should (according to the presupposed design) - react positively to these comments and deem them amusing, together with other participants. (Dynel 2019, 3)

As seen in Fig. 6.3, the procedure for RoastMe is: the participant firstly posts an anonymised photo of themselves explicitly offering to get roasted by holding a RoastMe notice, and they subsequently receive comments by the RoastMe community. Thus, RoastMe basically operates with (apparent) insults generated by the members of that Reddit community, the resulting humour being also experienced collectively through a "competition of wits" in parallel to upvotes and metapragmatic user evaluations (Poppi and Dynel 2019). Just like in any other tightly knit community, RoastMe members "show *mutual engagement*, and have a *joint enterprise* and a *shared repertoire* of negotiable resources accumulated over time" (Dynel 2019, 7, italics added).

Crucially, an essential part of this supposedly shared mutuality of assumptions refers to the tacit agreement that these (ritual) insulting practices are performed within a "this is play" humorous frame, i.e. the audience's aggressiveness is not overt but pretended. There is a goal for a

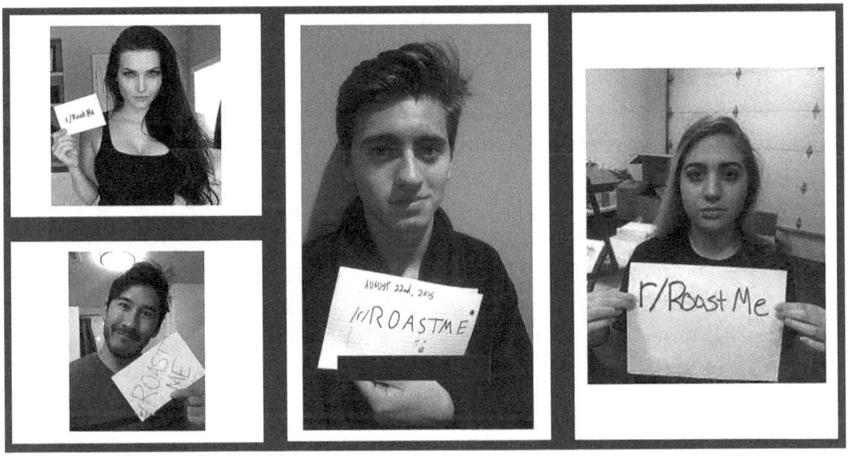

Fig. 6.3 Participants in the RoastMe community on Reddit

collective humour experience, which includes the roastee's, and therefore does not seek to cause offence. This may be misinterpreted, though, by users alien to the community who are unaware of the collective background assumptions holding the preference for humour despite the apparent abusive behaviour. These assumptions are expected to be mutual even though the RoastMe phenomenon has a global scope, cutting across nations and/or different age and ethnic groups, to name but a few.

6 SNS Humour: From Commented Posts and in-Comment Interactions

Humour does not simply lie in users' posts; is also pervades their comments to posts and in further interactions arising between the initial user and their audience. These comments are threaded and visually organised by the SNS system, in an attempt to relieve the effort side of the relevance equation (a positive *interface-related contextual constraint*). However, in-thread interactions turn out to be messy, with sub-interactions taking place too, and mixes of serious and humorous comments abound, which makes it difficult to follow the threads thematically and in sequence. Anyhow, humour in these comments should be conceptualised only as part of the non-propositional effects generated after receiving feedback from others. For example, Sun et al. (2023) emphasise that comments elicit lower loneliness, an effect explained by a higher sense of social connectedness.

Given the structure of SNS comments and in-comment interactions, instead of the prototypical one-to-many or one-to-one dialogues that characterise other media, interactions within comments rather exhibit the qualities of *polylogues*, as suggested in the bibliography (see Marcoccia 2004; Lorenzo-Dus et al. 2011; Bou-Franch and Garcés-Conejos Blitvich 2014; Bou-Franch et al. 2012). The term indicates that comments and user interactions therein cannot be explained from a traditional, conversation-analytic point of view, in which interactions become structured in more or less predictable patterns such as the famous adjacency pair (e.g. question-answer, request-reply, etc.), arranged in organised ways and where interlocutors hold the conversational floor. Instead, interactions within these comments have a complex, flexible, unstable and unpredictable nature, usually showing "a combination of, on the one hand, the orderly, turn-by-turn patterns typical of dyadic conversations and, on the other, 'networked sequences' consisting of adjacent and nonadjacent turns typical of asynchronous interaction" (Bou-Franch et al. 2012, 503).

Such structural properties are likely to have a direct impact on how coherence works within text-based comments on social media, for instance on YouTube (Bou-Franch et al. 2012). Most importantly, although the initial post and the audience's comments appear in clearly delimited areas, it has been demonstrated that users tend to conceptualise posts as a unified entity made up of the initial post plus the comments that it triggers. Ballantine et al. (2015) commented on the way in which the perceptions of a profile owner are influenced by the peer comments and postings that others leave on their profiles (see also Walther et al. 2010). These authors draw from *warranting theory* (Walther and Parks 2002), which signals the importance of the perceived validity of the information about another user that others observe online. The theory mainly argues that individuals rely on the information available online which offers greater warranting value regarding the true qualities of the user offline (what Yus (2021a) referred to as *online-offline congruence*). Since users tend to rely on SNS profiles for this task, and given the users' proneness towards so-called *enhanced selves* (i.e. to post only the most special activities performed by the user), a high likelihood exists that the information gathered from any user's profile will be based on distorted self-presentations and deception when compared to their offline identity and personality. This is where comments and reactions acquire their value: they lie beyond the user's control and allow for a more thorough insight into that user's real qualities: "readers may not believe the self-presentations individuals make in such virtual environments. Online information is more likely to be seen as truthful, depending on the extent to which the observer perceives it to be immune to any manipulation by the person to whom it refers" (Ballantine et al. 2015, 52).

This idea of "user-audience unicity" acquires relevance in certain areas, for example in the comments to prominent politicians' posts often prone to both aligning and discordant or critical reactions (see Chovanec 2018; Hirsch 2020; Rodriguez 2020). Likewise, the degree to which a post is regarded as humorous depends on the (equally humorous) quality of the audience's reactions to it, as well as on the presence of further posts complementing or co-constructing humour. In other words, their ability to co-construct, develop or extend the initial user's humorous intention will impact on the eventual humorous appreciation of the broader audience, including lurkers who do not directly participate but merely browse through posts. A drawback in this regard has to do with the fact that comments to (supposedly) humorous posts exhibit a mixture of humorous and non-humorous remarks, direct replies to the initial post intertwined with more addressee-specific remarks across in-comments interactions (which the SNS normally tries to thread visually, as mentioned above). In short, interactions within the comment section of SNSs such as Twitter exhibit fragmentations that fit the two types proposed by Marcoccia (2004, 120) for newsgroup threads, namely: (a) *bifurcation and the emergence of multiple conversations*, which happens when the various conversations occurring simultaneously involve subgroups of users who participate in only one of the multiple conversations; and (b) *multiple involvement* of some users engaged in several conversations, which can be seen as a marker of a group leadership role or as a way for any given participant to play the "host" role. These attributes allow us to differentiate these interactions from normal everyday face-to-face dyadic or group interactions. By contrast, other authors such as Mullan (2020, 144) suggest similarities in specifically humorous interactions found in both realms. Concerning this, Georgakopoulou (2017, 180) referred to the existence of a clear systematicity in sequential patterns of social media communication, comparable to face-to-face interaction, illustrated by how comments on Facebook exhibit "conversational" features, respondents creating coherence and "tying" their comment with previous ones and with the original post.

When humorous posts are explicitly replied to in a similar vein, several possibilities emerge across platforms. Messerli and Yu (2018, 247–251) list a number of possible reply types:

a. *Humour appreciation.* The audience signals appreciation for the poster's humorous intention, typically expressed with the range of discourses analysed in Chap. 5, including emojis, GIFs, stickers, laugh particles (e.g. hahaha) and appreciation texts (e.g. "I loved it" or "That was funny!").
b. *Humour construction in comments.* Rather than simply reacting appreciatively to humour, like in the first case, comments may also serve to create humorous incongruities. Some of these incongruities simply mirror the one used in the initial post, or new incongruities could be created which typically relate to that initial post in a significant way.
c. *Humour comment or question.* This usually happens when, faced with failed or incomprehensible humour, users decide to resort to the "comment option" to let the initial user know about this unintended effect. In the case of Twitter and Instagram comments, however, Messerli and Yu (ibid.) expected less pressure on followers to acknowledge lack of comprehension, the absence of a comment being most likely to prevail over an explicit acknowledgement of lack of proper comprehension.
d. *Stranded conversations.* It was previously highlighted that these in-thread conversations within the main comment area are very common. Here, commenters break into smaller conversations on their own where the initial user may or not participate.
e. *Multimodal comments.* A unique use found on SNSs such as Facebook or Twitter is the option of multimodal comments such as pictures and memes. Some of these comments include in-comment sub-interactions that are visually marked (threaded comments aligned visually, see Frobenius and Harper 2015).

Mullan (2020) proposed an interesting account of how this interaction involving a humorous post by the user plus its comments unfolds in terms of phases. The initial humorous post in her corpus comprises a picture of dry leaves grouped together using a broom and the text "Does anyone want this pile of dead leaves? I found them in the garden, free to good home" (*phase 1*). The text clearly clashes with the audience's background "commonsense" assumptions about the usefulness of these leaves, and the humorous point of the post is hence easily identified. The audience then acknowledge the scenario (*phase 2*), with one user showing appreciation by accepting the offer and adding to the comical hypothetical (i.e. fictional) scenario. Two participants then engage in co-constructed humour which humorously maintains the mock seriousness of the initial offer. This becomes enhanced by the initial user's contributions, delivered in a seemingly serious manner, unaccompanied by emojis. Other users simply express their appreciation for the user's humorous tweet by means of emojis and Likes. Next, other participants display their positive orientation to this fictional (and humorously absurd) scenario and quickly begin to help with the creation of an imaginary setting (*phase 3*) and escalate the ongoing fictionalisation of the interactions, often with strategies such as jocular mockery and self-deprecation. Overall, several of the exchanges additionally reveal the assumed shared knowledge of this online community by following the traditional format of a post offering something for free, and the subsequent negotiations that can take place, even within a fictional humorous frame like this one that defies background commonsense assumptions, as already remarked.

Another typical humorous situation regarding comments to a humorous post is the one where the initial user either posts a discourse with a clear ironic intention, mostly referring to (or *echoing*, in relevance-theoretic terms) some norm or expectation or commonsense assumption that has not taken place as expected, or produces a text that humorously contradicts the information provided by the image. The former, a humorous use of irony, happens in the multimodal tweet quoted below: User 1 depicts a photo of a man with a critical condition in the emergency room of a hospital and attaches an ironic comment minimising the severity of his condition. The post triggers comments that build upon this contradiction and co-construct the fictionalised "ironic-turned-literal scenario" in which commonsense assumptions about what constitutes a serious health problem become humorously dismissed. Other users even trivialise the seriousness of the man's condition by producing utterly irrelevant tweets (e.g. User 6):

> User 1: [She posts a photo of a man in the emergency room, sitting on a hospital bed. He has been pierced by a large iron bar, entering through his chest and exiting through his back].

"Pues con una tirita ya estaría. ¡SIGUIENTEEE!".

[*Well, a band-aid and sorted out. NEEEXT!*]

User 2: Y por esto ha venido usted a urgencias? Por gente como usted está el sistema colapsado. Se toma un Paracetamol y pida cita con su médico de cabecera.

[*And this is why you came to the emergency room? It is because of people like you that the system has collapsed. Take a Paracetamol and make an appointment with your GP*].

User 1: 🎯 [6]

User 3: Muy bestia el Cupido este que se quedó sin flechas…

[*Such a brute this Cupid, who ran out of arrows*].

User 1: 🎯

User 4: Tal y como está la Seguridad Social, lo mismo se muere. 🙄🙄🙄

[*The way Social Security is at the moment, he'll probably die.* 🙄🙄🙄].

User 5: -No sé, noto como un pinchazo en el pecho.

-Eso van a ser gases. Una de Aerored cada 8 horas y listo.

[*-I don't know, I feel like a puncture in my chest.*

-That's going to be flatulence. Take one Aerored every 8 hours and that'll do].

User 1: 🤣🤣

User 6: Las sabanas de atras van a juego con su camisa o me lo parece a mi?

[*Do the sheets in the back match his shirt or is it just my impression?*].

User 7: No me extraña que con éstas chorradas estén colapsadas Urgencias 😆

[It doesn't surprise me that with this nonsense the Emergency Room is collapsed 😆]

User 8: ¿Le parece a usted que esto es una urgencia?

Ande, ande, ande. Siéntese ahí y espere a ver si hay un hueco y le echamos una mirada.

[*Do you think this is an emergency?*

Come off it. Sit there and wait to see if there's a gap and we'll take a look at it].

User 9: Un vasito de agua y pa casa.

[*A glass of water and off home*].

User 1: 🤣

User 10: Así al pronto, falto de hierro no le veo 👨⚕🤔

[*At first sight, I don't think you have an iron deficiency* 👨⚕🤔].

[6] This emoji seems to convey the metaphorical idea that the previous user's comment has hit the nail on its head, so to speak.

User 11: Qué hartura los que vienen a colapsar urgencias con barras atravesadas que te puede arreglar tranquilamente el médico de cabecera.

[*So fed up with those who come to collapse the emergency room with crossed iron bars that a family doctor can easily fix for you*].

7 SNS Humour: Corporate

7.1 Introduction

An area of SNS communication where humour frequently appears is corporate pages or sites whose community manager produces amusing content, often of a multimodal kind, aimed at overtaking the obviousness of a brand' desire for subsequent audience actions (e.g. purchases of certain products). To implement this "avoidance of an explicit commercial aim" strategy, such brands' community managers seek affiliation and engagement via humour and resort to familiar SNS discourses that blend into the audience's general SNS practices. Grinberg (2022) further underlined the extent to which humour can foster the creation of in-group membership feelings, basically through the audience's capacity to access and retrieve supposedly shared contextual information, as mentioned earlier in this chapter. Grinberg (ibid) exemplifies this *bonding* (in-group) and *bounding* (out-group) non-propositional outcomes of corporate humour by means of the KFC page on Twitter and Facebook, which exhibits active participation in boundary-making by resorting to common identifiers that help to define these in-group/out-group boundaries.

Ge (2019, 18) illustrates this humour-based corporate strategy with the use of animals (e.g. those typically featured in memes such as cats or dogs) and certain people (celebrities, for instance). These may clearly release the potential tension in the consumer-dominated social media space. Yang (2022, 947) equally listed a number of beneficial effects triggered by humour in advertising (see Romell and Segedi 2022), including its capacity to draw the audience's attention (Putri and Ariastuti 2019, 13), thus leading to higher brand recall. A study cited in Yang (ibid.) proved that participants interpreting a humorous ad were more likely not only to recall the commercial they had just viewed over a message conveyed via the traditional, more serious ad format, but also to remember the name of the advertised brand.[7] Similarly, the presence of humour in advertising leads to greater positive ad attitudes. Specifically on social media, humour effectively increases customer engagement leading to more Likes, comments and shares.

Attention should likewise be paid, within the context of corporate humour on SNSs, to how these discourses are both adapted to the specificity of the particular SNS interface and reshaped when the content is interpreted through the small smartphone screens. As stressed in Yus (2023), advertisements on smartphone screens stage a fierce competition for users' attention because they often get in the way of those users' main task upon accessing certain content through a specific app. Similarly, users are not ready to expend as much effort upon attending to these intrusive ads as in website-based advertising, precisely due to this reduced size of the screen and the number of apps for entertainment that the device contains.

7.2 *Humorous Corporate Strategy*

The humorous strategies present in corporate SNS pages mirror the ones already commented upon in this and other chapters of this book (Ge and Gretzel 2018, 65–66). The humorous effect of numerous posts relies on the well-known incongruity-resolution pattern, often by bringing together elements whose processing triggers clashing effects inside the same multimodal discourse (or visual discourse plus firm-initiated comments). Sometimes, typed text may serve this purpose: Pano Alamán and Mancera Rueda (2016, 40–41) offer a good example in the tweet (43), a comment

[7] In this sense, Simpson's (2001) distinction between *reason advertisements* and *tickle advertisements* deserves a special mention. In a nutshell, the former base their effectiveness on the product's inherent quality, and therefore no need exists to adorn the advertisement with witty, funny or surprising effects. The latter, by contrast, employ different techniques to obtain the addressee's attention irrespective of the objective qualities of the product advertised. Simpson (ibid. 594) described reason advertisements as being characterised by the following two attributes: (a) conspicuous product placement with brand name and (if available) company logo visually prominent; and (b) a clear and unambiguous statement of the principal reason to buy the product. Tickle advertisements instead resort to various attention-arousing techniques. Normally, the advertised product and the brand logos (if available) are visually inconspicuous, to which must be added the frequent absence of clearly explicated product claims. As a consequence, the most significant quality of a tickle advertisement is the need for a higher investment of processing effort (ibid. 601–602) that needs to be compensated for with cognitive reward.

directed at *Telepizza* on 3rd April, 2015 by the user *@Sr_Dios* (Mr. God), who "juxtaposes two contexts, two meanings, which are incompatible with each other, therefore, inviting and challenging the community manager of the company to recognise this contrast and activate a process of inference, which must lead to the recognition of the non-serious attitude of the speaker and the interpretation of the (implied) humoristic sense of the message" (p. 41). However, the replies by Telepizza's community manager (44–45), together with the comments made by the initial user (46) and by other users (48, 49) manage to maintain the absurd fictional scenario and generate humour across posts:

(43) @telepizza_es/Servís pizzas a cementerios?
[*Do you serve pizzas to cemeteries*].

(44) si, siempre que este dentro de nuestro zona de reparto. Pero si al tercer día resucitas pide menú de grupo desde 6.50€ cada uno 😄
[*Yes, as long as it is within our delivery area. But if you come back to life on the third day, ask for a group menu from €6.50 each* 😄].

(45) Nuestro repartidor está en el cementerio que nos dijiste @Sr_Dios, pero no hay nadie 😕
[*Our delivery person is in the cemetery that you told us @Sr_Dios, but there is no one* 😕].

(46) Al final he resucitado, si me las podéis mandar a casa como siempre me haríais un favor 😅
[*In the end I rose from the dead, if you can send them home to me as always, you would do me a favour* 😅].

(47) hombre ¡que alegría! Esta Telepizza corre de nuestra cuenta 😄
[*man what a joy! This Telepizza is on us* 😄].

(48) pero sin carne que es viernes santo!!!
[*but without meat, it's Good Friday!!!*].

(49) Ahora, en la web no se si se puede poner la dirección de la tumba...
[*Now, on the web I don't know if you can put the address of the tomb...*].

Humour based on make-sense frames can also appear in corporate SNS humour, the user being led to clashing mental situations constructed to interpret both the tweet and the discourse therein, as in several of the KFC posts that Grinberg (2022) analysed. The tweet by *Cola Cao* (a Spanish company selling cocoa powder) reproduced in (50) below (Pano Alamán and Mancera Rueda 2016, 45) forces the reader to construct and entertain simultaneously two initially unrelated frames in the same tweet: one referred to children's food and another that has to do with technology (smartphones):

(50) Tarda menos en disolverse, que tu hijo en pedir un #smartphone nuevo. #colacao #turbo
[*It takes less time to dissolve, than your child to ask for a new #smartphone*].

Finally, another strategy implemented by community managers is to engage in self-deprecation (i.e. positioning the brand as the butt of the joke), as shown in one example provided in Yus (2023): The insurance company *Progressive*'s ad compares itself to other competitors, capturing the user's attention (or expressed differently, raising their expectations of relevance) by positioning the company as an honest brand, happy to tell users that their competitors are cheaper ("Sometimes our rate isn't the lowest. That's okay. We're happy for you"), which clearly contradicts and erases previous background assumptions associated with typical advertising practices. Besides, the ad appeals to users with a creative graphic and human faces showing lots of emotion, all of which creates intimacy and attachment or empathy. Finally, the ad matches the "culture" of Twitter by not taking itself too seriously as a brand, and using humour and honesty as a means to concoct a perfect mix for a successful Twitter campaign.

7.3 Humorous Corporate Discourse

Humorous discourses on corporate SNS pages range from purely textual discourses, to visual and multimodal ones, with a preference for the latter due to their capacity to attract users' attention. Ge and Gretzel (2018) emphasise this power of images to arouse interest and generate consumer interactions, alongside the skill that some users exhibit in manipulating these images for the sake of humour. This attention-drawing potential of images becomes enhanced by the community manager's tagging and commenting of the photo when posting it. An example is an image posted in the *MediaMarkt* Spain Twitter's page (27th March, 2015), which emphasises the advantages of flat TVs through humour. Two images depict a cat, firstly sleeping on the big top surface of an old TV, and another image featuring the same cat but this time it is struggling to stand on top of a flat TV. The caption, *A los únicos que no les gustan las pantallas planas* (The only ones who don't like flat TVs) frames the image and generates the desired humorous effects while, at the same time, covertly highlighting the advantages of purchasing these products. A clear implicated conclusion from that phrase is: "purchasing this kind of TV represents a good option for everybody (except cats)."

Memes, especially of the multimodal kind, are also pervasive on SNS corporate pages (see Chap. 7). Besides the typical meme discourse created and distributed on the internet (the widespread *image macro*, made up of an image and one or two lines of text at the top and/or the bottom of the meme), corporate memes often show variations of this prototypical discursive schema, as corroborated in Manero Richard's (2022) research. For example, it is frequent for the meme text not to form part of the meme itself and to appear inside the tweet text instead. Secondly, despite memes' tendency to be anonymous, this does not happen in corporate memes. Thirdly, corporate meme creators capitalise on non-viral images such as news or recent widely-known events when creating memes, rather than drawing from traditional meme topics, although community managers do resort to popular existing memes if that proves useful to achieve a successful corporate outcome. For instance, Yang (2022) proposes two types of memes being disseminated via online marketing: *existing memes* and *original memes* (McCrae, 2017). The former include those which, after being around for a while, have gone viral. The latter are developed with the exclusive aim of promoting a certain brand. Needless to say, as Manero Richard (2022) contends, these variations do not prevent the users of these accounts from recognising such occurrences as memes. Furthermore, they sometimes act on these memes by following the humorous behaviour that this genre is prone to trigger, basically through creative modification of the text and/or the image of the received meme.

7.4 *Responses and Reactions to Humorous Corporate Posts*

Beyond the type of humorous discourse used on corporate SNS pages, what matters most is (a) the effects that these discourses generate among the audience (in addition to humorous ones, see Chap. 8); and (b) how these effects impact on the audience's attitude towards the brand, as well as their future activity regarding that brand (purchases, viralisation of key attributes and so on).

First and foremost, corporate humour is a collaborative venture that seeks certain desired effects. As Manero Richard (2022) explains, humorous recontextualisations of the corporate meme abound, including the modification of the text, or the image or of both, most commonly for the purpose of adapting them to their particular context, not only multiplying and modulating the supposedly "unique" meaning that can be attributed to the initial humorous discourse by the community manager, but also eventually revealing the way in which users have interpreted the brand's intended humour. This re-signification procedure evidences the connection of users' comments with the meme proposed by the company, as well as their dependence on it, additionally proving the existence of an intimate link to the genre itself, which, due to its intertextual nature, encourages manipulation on the part of the audience.

Besides, as already mentioned, the capacity that a corporate post has to generate humour also depends on the attributes of the audience's behaviour towards it. Apart from the importance of co-constructing or complementing the humorous post with further humour, the SNS audience's typical reactions (Likes, laugh particles, emojis, GIFs…) likewise play a part in the eventual success of the community manager's humorous attempt. Yang (2022) calls these reactions ***bandwagon cues***, a term that also includes comments and shared content. This author concluded that "the post with a funny meme was perceived as most humorous when it obtained a large number of replies, retweets, and likes, which ultimately led to positive attitudes toward the post and greater intent to share the post online" (p. 955).

Secondly, corporate humour causes a direct impact as far as feelings of group membership and parallel awareness of non-membership are concerned, depending on whether certain contextual information or background knowledge is accessible or not (see Chap. 8). This becomes visible in the case of KFC analysed by Grinberg (2022). This brand uses strategic humorous discourses that determine the audience's in-group/out-group status -referred to as ***boundary work***, which in turn indicates the existence of a pattern in humour utilisation to affect in-group/out-group perceptions on social media between the brand and its online users so that the group's boundaries can be clearly communicated by the organisation, and constantly negotiated too (p. 79).

Thirdly, community managers seek affiliation and engagement with the audience through humour, two non-propositional effects that may clearly compensate for the initial reluctance to process corporate information. As Mondal and Chakrabarti (2019, 153) contended, rather than attempting to boost short-term sales, many brands focus on increasing user engagement, bonding and connection (affective effects), especially by means of branded apps: "the conceptualization of consumer-brand engagement is a set of in-app experiences that influences consumers to become interested, involved, and occupied in doing something and acts as an antecedent to consumer responses such as consumer attention, liking, usage, and word of mouth." As remarked in Yus (2023), engagement with brands proves particularly effective on social media (users' most familiar virtual environment). Brands take advantage of the fact that people keep accessing their social networking sites to avoid the unsatisfactory "pushing" of content on to users and to engage them, instead, by creating relevant content and building up meaningful relationships with users, particularly via humorous posts. Engagement is fostered through interactions with users, their feedback and their involvement with the brand's content. The combination of social media marketing and content on brands' pages creates an optimal ecosystem for user engagement (Ashley and Tuten 2015, 15).

However, attempts to engage the audience humorously sometimes fail. Several instances can be found on SNSs showing several users' negative reactions to attempted humorous effects. Manero Richard (2022) mentions two of these examples from corporate Twitter accounts. The first one portrays one customer with a horrified look on her face upon seeing the balance of her account, accompanied by the text *Cuando tienes que entrar a tu App y queda poco para acabar el mes* (When you have to check your App and the end of the month is near) plus several emojis. A second text reads *¡Veeenga, que el mes acaba ya!* (Come on, the month will soon be over!). Despite being meant to be humorous, the tweet received several negative comments by several users who find it hard to make ends meet, as illustrated in (51). The second tweet is from a streaming company showing the choice of audio in Spanish and subtitles in Spanish as well, with an attached text: *Todos conocemos a esta persona* (We all know this person). Once again, several users posted negative comments such as the ones in (52–54). Others found it amusing, though, and even criticised the users who initially complained.

(51) A vosotros os hará mucha gracia. A nosotros ninguna
[*You probably find it very funny. We don't*].

(52) Los que tienen alguna discapacidad auditiva.
Los que están aprendiendo el idioma.
Los que tienen dislexia.
¿Os estáis riendo de ellos, en serio?
[*Those who have a hearing disability.*

Those who are learning the language.
Those diagnosed with dyslexia.
Are you laughing at them, seriously?]

(53) No tiene ni puta gracia. Hay una comunidad sorda, ¿sabes?
[*It's not fucking funny. There's a deaf community, you know?*].

(54) Aquí el CM ha estado muy muy mal.
[*Here the community manager has got it very very wrong*].

7.5 An Example: Burger King

In an attempt to identify the most typical kinds of humorous posts on SNS corporate pages, 50 tweets from *Burger King España*'s page (henceforth BK) were randomly selected between 3rd March 2022 and 24th September 2022 and subsequently studied and grouped together according to the main humorous strategies devised. Four major categories emerged from this analysis.

1. *Mashups with other media.* 10 instances show a combination of BK-related information and stills from audiovisual discourses such as films or TV series. Their co-presence raises the user's expectations of relevance, thereby compelling them to find the key that links both discourses. These tweets frequently exhibit BK's manipulations of existing stills from other media or sites online, normally by over imposing of juxtaposing BK-related images and adding explicative texts. In one of these tweets, there is a still of the character Marge from the animated TV series *The Simpsons* taking off her coat, and several photos of BK products have been placed on all the inside pockets. The text of the tweet says: *Yo yendo al cine* (Me going to the cinema). In another tweet, two stills from a film features a woman in a car looking at someone who is not framed in the image, and also a man in another car performing a similar action (the audience is further expected to infer that the woman and the man are looking at each other). The accompanying texts are meant to trigger a humorous re-interpretation of these film stills in the new context of BK advertising: The text next to the woman is quoted in (55) below, and the one next to the man appears in (56).

(55) Yo saliendo del autoking con mis patatas gratis.
[*Me leaving the autoking with my free fries*].

(56) Mi colega al que le había dicho que no podía quedar a comer.
[*My friend, the one to whom I had said that I couldn't meet for a meal*].

This strategy of humorous re-interpretation or mash-up of films and TV episodes was labelled *second-order incongruity* in Yus (2021b). Despite these images-captions exhibiting certain congruence, incongruity does occur, though not within the tweet but in relation to the initial film or TV series episode from which these images were taken (e.g. where the actors' gestures initially originated), triggered by other episode plot stimuli and meant to be interpreted differently by the initial audience.

2. *Clashing frames*. This humorous strategy underlies 22 tweets in the sample, with two sub-categories. Frame manipulation generally entails some kind of alteration of the normal (and often sub-attentive) mental construction of a situation to understand a discourse, as already mentioned several times in this book. The first sub-type exploits the co-occurrence of two visual discourses that are somehow incompatible or at least not usually depicted side by side. At times a caption is added providing the link to these apparently dissimilar visual discourses and directing the audience towards the right humorous interpretation. A few examples are quoted in (57–60) below.

(57) Image: A dog leaning on its hind legs and with its front legs resting on the window where BK menus are typically ordered (from a car).
Text: Buenas tardes, no quería dejar la oportunidad de pedirle que me entregue unas patatas gratis. Gracias.
[*Good afternoon, I didn't want to miss out on the opportunity to ask you to hand me some free chips. Thank you*].

(58) Image: A hamburger and a bag of fries filled with ice (instead of the burger and fries respectively).
Text: El menú que necesito para esta ola de calor.
[*The menu that I need for this heatwave*].

(59) Image: Two images of necklaces. The one on the left is a normal necklace with a jewel as a pendant; the one on the right has a piece of pickle instead of the pendant.
Text: Encajar en la sociedad (left image)/Ser feliz (right image).
[*To blend into society/To be happy*].

(60) Image: A BK menu bag in a car surrounded by a seat belt.
Text: La seguridad ante todo.
[*Safety first*].

The second sub-type applies to tweets designed for the purpose of leading the audience into the mental construction of a certain make-sense frame, which is later invalidated. Three BK examples are illustrative. In the first one, a frame is constructed by the audience regarding several pictures of supposedly important events in anybody's life that are visually depicted in the tweet with attached captions, starting with *Nos casamos* (We get married) and followed by *Vivimos felices* (We live happily). Then, the third image abruptly contradicts the initiated frame by proposing a continuation with *Y comemos patatas fritas juntos* (And we eat fries together), which lies very far from the importance of the previous life commitments. The second example portrays Albert Einstein and, supposedly, a quote by him. The audience expects some remark about larger-than-life issues, and this is actually what they obtain from the quote at first: *Nacimos muy tarde para descubrir el fuego, muy temprano para descubrir el espacio* (We were born too late to discover fire, too early to discover space). However, the continuation invalidates that recently constructed frame by equating the mundane action of getting a BK menu to that previous information: *pero justo a tiempo para pillarnos un menu desde 2.99€* (but just in time to grab a menu from 2.99€). Finally, in the third example two panels at the top of the tweet favour the construction of a frame about education and maths teaching: a student is standing by the blackboard to solve a math problem. The student, unable to find the answer to 2×8 on the blackboard, looks at his classmates in search of help, and one of them raises a notice with a 2×8 BK offer that invalidates the initially constructed frame. The initial student finally writes *2×8 = menudo ofertón* (2×8 = what an offer) on the blackboard.

3. *Connecting with the audience's collective background assumptions and desires.* Relevance theory identifies three types of inputs for processing that result in relevant outcomes: (a) to strengthen existing assumptions; (b) to contradict and erase previous assumptions; and (c) to combine with previous assumptions for yielding new fine-grained information. Emphasis has been laid in this chapter on the fact that two key humorous strategies consist in reminding the audience of certain collective habits or reinforcing collective assumptions; and in making the audience remember that certain supposedly

personal habits or beliefs are in fact collective. Six instances from our BK sample play with the status of certain assumptions in the audience. The first one is interesting because it equates the user to a cat facing a dilemma while watching a BK menu: *seguir la dieta o ser feliz* (follow the diet or be happy). The community manager adds the text *La elección está clara* (The choice is clear). Curiously, the tweet communicates, as an implicated premise, that eating BK food is bad to stay fit, which in turn becomes paralleled with another premise: that eating BK food makes one happy, the main reason why the choice should be clear according to BK. Most importantly, this tweet resonates with similar dilemmas that the audience has faced in the past, providing an immediate offset of collectivisation in relation to the feelings involved. Some users may achieve extra effects through the re-conceptualisation of thought-to-be private assumptions that now acquire a collective status. The second example portrays a queue of people labelled with a notice in front of it: *Te critican* (They criticise you), another one with *Te juzgan* (They judge you) and no queue behind a third notice that reads *Te invitan a comer patatas* (They invite you to eat fries). Again, those audience members who have experienced the feeling of not being invited will end up strengthening the collective status of these background assumptions to a significant extent. Finally, the third example compares two images with associated captions: a few chicken nuggets with the caption *En la primera cita* (On the first date) and a huge pile of hamburgers with the caption *Cuando ya sois novios* (When you are already going out). An implicated premise in the tweet is that people tend to take care of their shape during the process of meeting a prospective partner/couple. The tweet likewise communicates (via implicated conclusion) that once the objective of having a partner has been more or less "accomplished," they no longer need to care so much about their health (i.e. they do not mind getting fat), an idea clearly mirrored in the kind of BK food portrayed.

4. *Playing with discourse interpretation.* 10 tweets suit this humorous strategy. Four of them exploit the potential ambiguity of some word or phrase in the tweet. This is the humorous strategy at work in tweets (61–63) below. In (61), the processing of the left image and its text *Cómo me veo* (How I see myself) makes one interpretation of the text *Cómo me siento* (How I feel) on the right very relevant. In accordance with the relevance-theoretic comprehension procedure,

this is the most accessible and hence the only interpretation that should be picked up or considered by the audience. Nevertheless, the image of the famous BK character sitting down makes another interpretation possible and plausible as well: "How I sit down," due to the polysemy of the phrase *me siento* (I feel/I sit down) in Spanish, hence also compatible with the utterance in the panel and, due to the image, equally likely, all of which inferentially puzzles the audience. Ambiguity becomes visible in the tweet (62) through the word *julio*, which has two radically different meanings in Spanish: the name of the famous Spanish singer (*Julio Iglesias*, portrayed) and the month of July (*julio*), both compatible in the context of this tweet, and accentuated by its date of publication (July 2022) and by the community manager's text: *Julio ya llegó* (Julio/July has already arrived). Finally, the tweet (63) portrays a famous panel from the Batman and Robin superhero comic series in which Batman is slapping Robin's face. Batman's utterance contains the word *galleta*, which is polysemous in Spanish, meaning either "a cookie" or "a slap on someone's face." Cunningly, the community manager has managed to make both interpretations equally likely and relevant, thus confusing the audience once more. The "slap meaning" makes sense as a correlate of Batman slapping Robin's face, and the "cookie meaning" is possible because of the audience's previously processed discourse in the panel, more precisely, Robin's utterance mentioning ice cream and Batman speaking about a popular BK menu.

(61) Image: Two images: the famous BK character looking at himself in the mirror (left) and sitting down (right).
Text: Two texts: Como me veo (left)/Como me siento (right).
[*How I see myself/How I feel (vs. How I sit down)*].

(62) Image: Picture of famous Spanish singer Julio Iglesias at a BK restaurant.
Text: Julio ya llegó.
[*Julio/July has already arrived*].

(63) Image: A panel showing superhero Batman slapping superhero Robin's face.
Text: Los helados son para el verano (Robin)/Pues para mí un King Fusión y para ti una galleta (Batman).
[*Ice creams are for the summer (Robin)/Well for me a King Fusion menu and for you a slap/cookie (Batman)*].

The sample of tweets also contains instances of manipulations that affect the processing of the visual discourse, very often through metaphorisation or forced connections of resemblance to the prototypical (i.e. coded) visual referent depicted in a picture within the tweet. Three examples are illustrative. In the first one, we can see a human-like figure falling into an abyss. The accompanying text says *Muerdo la burger. Los ingredientes del otro lado de la Burger* (I bite the burger. The ingredients on the other side of the burger). The creator of the tweet encourages the audience to make metaphoric connections between the human figure falling and the burger's ingredients likewise falling from it. The second tweet features a coded image, a huge cone of fries, which resembles a bouquet of flowers. The text at the top confirms this resemblance: *Que nunca muera el romanticismo* (May romance never die). The audience is thus expected to take the coded image and simultaneously infer a variation of this portrayed image into a more romantically connoted one. Finally, in the third tweet a left-hand-side picture reminds us of a condom wrapper sticking out of a pocket. The interpretation of this visual referent becomes easier thanks to the initial part of the text at the top of the tweet: *Siempre hay que estar ready* [sic] (You always gotta be ready). The image on the right, then, shows the audience a packet of ketchup as an alternative referent of the image, which is possible too, and again aided by the top text in its continuation: *Nunca sabes cuando se te cruzarán unas patatas* (You never know when you're going to come across some fries).

8 Concluding Remarks

Humour appears frequently on SNSs. This chapter has addressed some of the ways in which humour is used on these sites: by a single user, in repositories, on collective sites, within comments and interactions therein, and on corporate sites. A special mention has also been made of SNS interface-related constraints (interface affordances), which allow for the publication of certain discourses ranging from cues-filtered texts to contextually rich images and videos, together with all kinds of supportive discourses, in the fulfilment of a humorous strategy (emojis, laugh particles, Likes and so on). Moreover, some space was devoted to the non-propositional effects (feelings, emotions) resulting from humorous SNS interactions, which go from in-group membership feelings to those associated with attachment and engagement.

References

Ashley, Christy, and Tracy Tuten. 2015. Creative Strategies in Social Media Marketing: An Exploratory Study of Branded Social Content and Consumer Engagement. *Psychology and Marketing* 32 (1): 15–27. https://doi.org/10.1002/mar.20761.

Ballantine, Paul W., Yongjia Lin, and Ekant Veer. 2015. The Influence of User Comments on Perceptions of Facebook Relationship Status Updates. *Computers in Human Behavior* 49: 50–55. https://doi.org/10.1016/j.chb.2015.02.055.

Bou-Franch, Patricia, and Pilar Garcés-Conejos Blitvich. 2014. Conflict Management in Massive Polylogues: A Case Study from YouTube. *Journal of Pragmatics* 73: 19–36. https://doi.org/10.1016/j.pragma.2014.05.001.

Bou-Franch, Patricia, Nuria Lorenzo-Dus, and Pilar Garcés-Conejos Blitvich. 2012. Social Interaction in YouTube Text-Based Polylogues: A Study of Coherence. *Journal of Computer-Mediated Communication* 17: 501–521. https://doi.org/10.1111/j.1083-6101.2012.01579.x.

boyd, danah. 2007, May 13. Social Network Sites: Public, Private, or What? The Knowledge Tree.

boyd, danah, and Nicole Ellison. 2007. Social Network Sites: Definition, History, and Scholarship. *Journal of Computer-Mediated Communication* 13 (1): 210–230. https://doi.org/10.1111/j.1083-6101.2007.00393.x.

Bruns, Axel. 1998. The Future is User-Led: The Path Towards Widespread Produsage. *Fibreculture* 11.

———. 2006. Towards Produsage: Futures for User-Led Content Production. In *Cultural Attitudes towards Communication and Technology*, ed. Fray Sudweeks, Herbert Hrachovec, and Charles Ess, 275–284. Perth: Murdoch University.

Carr, Caleb T., and Rebecca A. Hayes. 2015. Social Media: Defining, Developing, and Divining. *Atlantic Journal of Communication* 23 (1): 46–65. https://doi.org/10.1080/15456870.2015.972282.

Chiaro, Delia, and Nikita Lobanov. 2021. Fandom Versus Citizenship: The "Weirdisation" of Politics. *European Journal of Humour Research* 9 (3): 113–134. https://doi.org/10.7592/EJHR2021X.9.3.527.

Chovanec, Jan. 2018. Irony as Counter Positioning: Reader Comments on the Eu Migrant Crisis. In *The Pragmatics of Irony and Banter*, ed. Manuel Jobert and Sandrine Sorlin, 165–193. Amsterdam: John Benjamins. https://doi.org/10.1075/lal.30.09cho.

Cormode, Graham, and Balachander Krishnamurthy. 2008. Key Differences between Web 1.0 and Web 2.0. *First Monday* 13 (6). https://doi.org/10.5210/fm.v13i6.2125.

Crystal, David. 2001. *Language and the Internet*. Cambridge: Cambridge University Press. https://doi.org/10.1017/CBO9781139164771.

Donath, Judith, and danah boyd. 2004. Public Displays of Connection. *BT Technology Journal* 22 (4): 71–82. https://doi.org/10.1023/B:BTTJ.0000047585.06264.cc.

Dynel, Marta. 2019. Risum Teneatis, Amici?: The Socio-Pragmatics of RoastMe Humour. *Journal of Pragmatics* 139: 1–21. https://doi.org/10.1016/j.pragma.2018.10.010.

Dynel, Marta, and Jan Chovanec. 2021. Creating and Sharing Public Humour across Traditional and New Media. *Journal of Pragmatics* 177: 151–156. https://doi.org/10.1016/j.pragma.2021.02.020.

Dynel, Marta, and Fabio I.M. Poppi. 2019. Risum Teneatis, Amici? The Socio-pragmatics of Roastme Humour. *Journal of Pragmatics* 139: 1–21. https://doi.org/10.1016/j.pragma.2018.10.010.

———. 2020a. Quid Rides?: Targets and Referents of Roastme Insults. *Humor* 33 (4): 535–562. https://doi.org/10.1515/humor-2019-0070.

———. 2020b. Arcana Imperii. The Power of Humorous Retorts to Insults on Twitter. *Journal of Language Aggression and Conflict* 8 (1): 57–87. https://doi.org/10.1075/jlac.00031.dyn.

Elayan, Suzanne, Martin Sykora, Thomas W. Jackson, and Ejovwoke Onojeharho. 2022. 'Are You Having a Laugh?': Detecting Humorous Expressions on Social Media: An Exploration of Theory, Current Approaches and Future Work. *International Journal of Information Technology and Management* 21 (1): 115–137. https://doi.org/10.1504/IJITM.2022.121332.

Frobenius, Maximiliane, and Richard Harper. 2015. Tying in Comment Sections: The Production of Meaning and Sense on Facebook the Self-explicative Organization of Communication Acts on and Through Facebook. *Semiotica* 204: 212–143. https://doi.org/10.1515/sem-2014-0081.

Ge, Jing. 2019. Social Media-Based Visual Humour Use in Tourism Marketing: A Semiotic Perspective. *European Journal of Humour Research* 7 (3): 6–25. https://doi.org/10.7592/EJHR2019.7.3.ge.

Ge, Jing, and Ulrike Gretzel. 2018. Impact of Humour on Firm-Initiated Social Media Conversations. *Information Technology and Tourism* 18: 61–83. https://doi.org/10.1007/s40558-017-0097-0.

Georgakopoulou, Alexandra. 2017. 'Friendly' Comments Interactional Displays of Alignment on Facebook and YouTube. In *Social Media Discourse, (Dis)identifications and Diversities*, ed. Sirpa Leppänen, Elina Westinen, and Samu Kytölä, 179–207. Abingdon: Routledge.

Golbeck, Jennifer. 2007. The Dynamics of Web-Based Social Networks: Membership, Relationships, and Change. *First Monday* 12 (11). https://doi.org/10.5210/fm.v12i11.2023.

Grinberg, Hannah. 2022. "Don't Call Me a Crouton": A Case Study on the Use of Humor in Organizational Relationships on Twitter and Facebook. MA Thesis. Montclair State University.

Haugh, Michael. 2010. Jocular Mockery, (Dis)affiliation, and Face. *Journal of Pragmatics* 42: 2106–2119. https://doi.org/10.1016/j.pragma.2009.12.018.

Herring, S. 2013. Discourse in Web 2.0: Familiar, Reconfigured, and Emergent. In *Discourse 2.0: Language and New Media*, ed. D. Tannen and A.M. Tester, 1–25. Washington: Georgetown University Press.

Hirsch, Galia. 2020. Humorous and Ironic Readers' Comments to a Politician's Post on Facebook: The Case of Miri Regev. *Journal of Pragmatics* 164: 40–53. https://doi.org/10.1016/j.pragma.2020.04.012.

Juzefovics, Jänis, and Triin Vihalemm. 2020. Digital Humor Against Essentialization: Strategies of Baltic Russian-speaking Social Media Users. *Political Geography* 81. https://doi.org/10.1016/j.polgeo.2020.102204.

Kasunic, Anna, and Geoff Kaufman. 2018. "At Least the Pizzas You Make Are Hot": Norms, Values, and Abrasive Humor on the Subreddit r/RoastMe. In *Proceedings of the Twelfth International AAAI Conference on Web and Social Media (ICWSM 2018)*, 161–170. Palo Alto, CA: The AAAI Press. https://doi.org/10.1609/icwsm.v12i1.15020.

Kräussl, Martin. 2022. Analysis of Millennial Humour in Select Instagram Reels. MA Thesis. Brno: Masaryk University.

Lewin-Jones, Jenny. 2015. Humour with a Purpose: Creativity with Language In Facebook Status Updates. *Linguistik Online* 72: 69–87. https://doi.org/10.13092/lo.72.1973.

Locher, Miriam A., and Brook Bolander. 2015. Humour in Microblogging: Exploiting Linguistic Humour Strategies for Identity Construction in Two Facebook Focus Groups. In *Participation in Public and Social Media Interactions*, ed. Marta Dynel and Jan Chovanec, 135–155. Amsterdam: John Benjamins. https://doi.org/10.1075/pbns.256.06loc.

Lorenzo-Dus, Nuria, Pilar Garcés-Conejos Blitvich, and Patricia Bou-Franch. 2011. On-Line Polylogues and Impoliteness: The Case of Postings Sent in Response to the Obama Reggaeton Youtube Video. *Journal of Pragmatics* 43: 2578–2593. https://doi.org/10.1016/j.pragma.2011.03.005.

Maíz-Arévalo, Carmen. 2015. Jocular Mockery in Computer-Mediated Communication: A Contrastive Study of a Spanish and English Facebook Community. *Journal of Politeness Research* 11 (2): 289–327. https://doi.org/10.1515/pr-2015-0012.

Manero Richard, Elvira. 2022. Los Memes. (Re)contextualizaciones y Reacciones en el Discurso Corporativo en Twitter [Memes. (Re)contextualisations and Reactions in Corporate Discourse on Twitter]. In *Interactividad en Modo Humorístico: Géneros Orales, Escritos y Tecnológicos*, ed. Leonor Ruiz Gurillo, 37–82. Madrid: Iberoamericana Vervuert.

Marcoccia, Michel. 2004. On-Line Polylogues: Conversation Structure and Participation Framework in Internet Newsgroups. *Journal of Pragmatics* 36: 115–145. https://doi.org/10.1016/S0378-2166(03)00038-9.

Marwick, Alice, and danah boyd. 2011. I Tweet Honestly, I Tweet Passionately: Twitter Users, Context Collapse, and the Imagined Audience. *New Media and Society* 13 (1): 114–133. https://doi.org/10.1177/1461444810365313.

McCrae, James. 2017, May 8. Meme Marketing: How Brands are Speaking a New Consumer Language. *Forbes*.

McKay, Isabel. 2020. Some Distributional Patterns in the Use of Typed Laughter-Derived Expressions on Twitter. *Journal of Pragmatics* 166: 97–113. https://doi.org/10.1016/j.pragma.2020.05.009.

McLuhan, Marshall, and Barrington Nevitt. 1972. *Take Today: The Executive as Dropout*. New York: Harcourt Brace Jovanovish.

Messerli, Thomas, and Yu Di. 2018. Multimodal Construction of Soccer-Related Humor on Twitter and Instagram. In *The Aesthetics, Poetics, and Rhetoric of Soccer*, ed. Ridvan Askin, Catherine Diederich, and Aline Bieri, 227–255. Abingdon: Routledge.

Moalla, Asma. 2015. Incongruity in the Generation and Perception of Humor on Facebook in the Aftermath of the Tunisian Revolution. *Journal of Pragmatics* 75: 44–52. https://doi.org/10.1016/j.pragma.2014.10.008.

Mondal, Jalaluddin, and Somnath Chakrabarti. 2019. Emerging Phenomena of the Branded App: A Systematic Literature Review, Strategies, and Future Research Directions. *Journal of Interactive Advertising* 19 (2): 148–167. https://doi.org/10.1080/15252019.2019.1647580.

Mullan, Kerry. 2020. Pile of Dead Leaves Free to a Good Home: Humour and Belonging in a Facebook Community. In *Studies in Ethnopragmatics, Cultural Semantics, and Intercultural Communication. Ethnopragmatics and Semantic Analysis*, ed. Kerry Mullan, Bert Peeters, and Lauren Sadow, 135–159. Cham: Springer. https://doi.org/10.1007/978-981-32-9983-2_8.

Nissenbaum, Asaf, and David Freud. 2021. Which Person Walks into a Bar? A Typology of Globally Spread Humor on Twitter. *International Journal of Communication* 15: 5208–5228.

Pano Alamán, Ana, and Ana Mancera Rueda. 2016. Humor and advertising in Twitter: An approach from the General Theory of Verbal Humor and Metapragmatics. In *Metapragmatics of Humor. Current Research Trends*, ed. Leonor Ruiz-Gurillo, 35–56. Amsterdam: John Benjamins. https://doi.org/10.1075/ivitra.14.03ala.

Papacharissi, Zizi. 2015. *Affective Publics. Sentiment, Technology, and Politics*. Oxford: Oxford University Press. https://doi.org/10.1093/acprof:oso/9780199999736.001.0001.

———. 2016. Affective Publics and Structures of Storytelling: Sentiment, Events and Mediality. *Information, Communication and Society* 19 (3): 307–324. https://doi.org/10.1080/1369118X.2015.1109697.

Papacharissi, Zizi, and Maria de Fatima Oliveira. 2012. Affective News and Networked Publics: The Rhythms of News Storytelling on #Egypt. *Journal of Communication* 62 (2): 266–282. https://doi.org/10.1111/j.1460-2466.2012.01630.x.

Parini, Alejandro, and Francisco Yus. 2023. The Discursive Construction of Place Through the Online-Offline Interface. From Physical Locations to Wikispaces. In *The Discursive Construction of Place in the Digital Age*, ed. Alejandro Parini and Francisco Yus, 9–32. Abingdon: Routledge.

Poppi, Fabio I.M., and Marta Dynel. 2021. Ad Libidinem: Forms of Female Sexualisation in Roastme Humour. *Sexualities* 24 (3): 431–455. https://doi.org/10.1177/1363460720931338.

Putri, Amadhea Naidriya, and Marti Fauziah Ariastuti. 2019. Beyond Tweets: Pragmatic Analysis of Humor as a Brand Image in Burger King's Tweets. *Journal of Urban Society's Art* 6 (1): 12–23.

Reich, Sabine, Frank M. Schneider, and Leonie Heling. 2018. Zero Likes – Symbolic Interactions and Need Satisfaction Online. *Computers in Human Behavior* 80: 97–102. https://doi.org/10.1016/j.chb.2017.10.043.

Rhee, Lisa, Joseph B. Bayer, David S. Lee, and Ozan Kuru. 2021. Social by Definition: How Users Define Social Platforms and Why it Matters. *Telematics and Informatics* 59. https://doi.org/10.1016/j.tele.2020.101538.

Rodriguez, Nathan J. 2020. #FamilyTravelHacks: Humor and Political Commentary in Hashtag Hijacking. In *Twitter, the Public Sphere, and the Chaos of Online Deliberation*, ed. Gwen Bouvier and Judith E. Rosenbaum, 267–290. Cham: Palgrave Macmillan. https://doi.org/10.1007/978-3-030-41421-4_11.

Romell, Annika, and Rebecca Segedi. 2022. Humor as a Social Media Strategy. A Mixed-Methods Research on Humor, its Types, Contingencies, and Favorability. MA Thesis. Jönköping University.

Ryen, Marte. 2022. "You've Aged Like Milk on a Radiator": An Investigation of Verbal Humour on R/Roastme. MA Thesis. University of Stavanger.

Simpson, Paul. 2001. 'Reason' and 'Tickle' as Pragmatic Constructs in the Discourse of Advertising. *Journal of Pragmatics* 33 (4): 589–607. https://doi.org/10.1016/S0378-2166(00)00004-7.

Sun, Peng, Xing Lu, Junhui Wu, and Kou Yu. 2023. Receiving Feedback after Posting Status Updates on Social Networking Sites Predicts Lower Loneliness: A Mediated Moderation Model. *Applied Psychology: Health and Well-Being* 15 (1): 97–114. https://doi.org/10.1111/aphw.12378.

Sundén, Jenny, and Susanna Paasonen. 2021. "We Have Tiny Purses in Our Vaginas!!! #Thanksforthat": Absurdity as a Feminist Method of Intervention. *Qualitative Research Journal* 21 (3): 233–243. https://doi.org/10.1108/QRJ-09-2020-0108.

Taylor, Zari. 2022, April–June. "(It) Shouldn't Be Funny But You Can't Help But Laugh": Black Twitter, #TweetLikeThe1600s, and Black Humor Online. *Social Media + Society*. https://doi.org/10.1177/20563051221107631

Tsakona, Villy. 2020. Tracing the Trajectories of Contemporary Online Joking. *Media Linguistics* 7 (2): 169–183. https://doi.org/10.21638/spbu22.2020.202.

Vásquez, Camilla. 2019. *Language, Creativity and Humour Online*. Abingdon: Routledge.

Walther, Joseph B., and Malcolm R. Parks. 2002. Cues Filtered Out, Cues Filtered. In *Computer-Mediated Communication and Relationships. Handbook of Interpersonal Communication*, ed. Mark L. Knapp and John A. Daly, 529–563. Thousand Oaks, CA: Sage.

Walther, Joseph B., David DeAndrea, Jinsuk Kim, and James C. Anthony. 2010. The Influence of Online Comments on Perceptions of Antimarijuana Public Service Announcements on YouTube. *Human Communication Research* 36 (4): 469–492. https://doi.org/10.1111/j.1468-2958.2010.01384.x.

Weitz, Eric. 2017. Online and Internet Humor. In *The Routledge Handbook of Language and Humor*, ed. Salvatore Attardo, 504–518. Abingdon: Routledge.

Yang, Guolan. 2022. Using Funny Memes for Social Media Marketing: The Moderating Role of Bandwagon Cues. *Journal of Promotion Management* 28 (7): 944–960. https://doi.org/10.1080/10496491.2022.2054904.

Yus, Francisco. 1997. La Teoría de la Relevancia y la Estrategia Humorística de la Incongruencia-Resolución. *Pragmalingüística* 3-4: 497–508.

———. 2002. Stand-up Comedy and Cultural Spread: The Case of Sex Roles. Babel A.F.I.A.L., Special Issue on Humour Studies, 245–292.

———. 2004. Pragmatics of Humorous Strategies in *El Club de la Comedia*. In *Current Trends in the Pragmatics of Spanish*, ed. Rosina Márquez-Reiter and María Elena Placencia, 320–344. Amsterdam: John Benjamins. https://doi.org/10.1075/pbns.123.25yus.

———. 2005a. Attitudes and Emotions Through Written Text: The Case of Textual Deformation in Internet Chat Rooms. *Pragmalingüística* 13: 147–174.

———. 2005b. Dave Allen's Stand-Up Monologues: An Epidemiological Approach. In *Thistles. A Homage to Brian Hughes. Volume 2: Essays in Memoriam*, ed. José Mateo and Francisco Yus, 317–344. Alicante: University of Alicante, Department of English Studies.

———. 2010. *Ciberpragmática 2.0. Nuevos Usos del Lenguaje en Internet [Cyberpragmatics 2.0. New Uses of Language on the Internet]*. Barcelona: Ariel.

———. 2011. *Cyberpragmatics. Internet-Mediated Communication in Context*. Amsterdam and Philadelphia: John Benjamins. https://doi.org/10.1075/pbns.213.

———. 2013a. An Inference-Centered Analysis of Jokes: The Intersecting Circles Model of Humorous Communication. In *Irony and Humor: From Pragmatics to Discourse*, ed. Leonor Ruiz Gurillo and Belén Alvarado, 59–82. Amsterdam: John Benjamins. https://doi.org/10.1075/pbns.231.05yus.

———. 2013b. Analyzing Jokes with the Intersecting Circles Model of Humorous Communication. *Lodz Papers in Pragmatics* 9 (1): 3–24. https://doi.org/10.1515/lpp-2013-0002.
———. 2016. *Humour and Relevance*. Amsterdam: John Benjamins. https://doi.org/10.1075/thr.4.
———. 2017. Social Media. In *The Routledge Handbook of Pragmatics*, ed. A. Barron, G. Steen, and G. Yueguo, 550–562. Abingdon: Routledge.
———. 2019. Multimodality in Memes: A Cyberpragmatic Approach. In *Analyzing Digital Discourse. New Insights and Future Directions*, ed. Patricia Bou-Franch and Pilar Garcés-Conejos Blitvich, 105–131. Cham: Palgrave Macmillan. https://doi.org/10.1007/978-3-319-92663-6_4.
———. 2020. Disambiguation Should Not Exist (But it Does in Humour). Paper delivered at the *9th International Symposium on Intercultural, Cognitive and Social Pragmatics* ("Communication in the 21st Century: Intercultural, Cognitive and Social Pragmatics"). Seville, Spain.
———. 2021a. *Smartphone Communication. Interactions in the App Ecosystem*. Abingdon: Routledge. https://doi.org/10.4324/9781003200574.
———. 2021b. Incongruity-Resolution Humorous Strategies in Image Macro Memes. *Internet Pragmatics* 4 (1): 131–149. https://doi.org/10.1075/ip.00058.yus.
———. forthcoming. Memes. In *Introducción al Estudio del Discurso Digital en Español*, ed. Maria Elena Placencia and Alejandro Parini. Abingdon: Routledge.
———. 2023. Finding Relevance in Smartphone Advertising. *Internet Pragmatics* 6 (1): 1–41. https://doi.org/10.1075/ip.00084.yu.
Zappavigna, Michele. 2011. Ambient Affiliation: A Linguistic Perspective on Twitter. *New Media and Society* 13 (5): 788–806. https://doi.org/10.1177/1461444810385097.
———. 2012. *Discourse of Twitter and Social Media: How We Use Language to Create Affiliation on the Web*. London: Bloomsbury.
———. 2014. Enacting Identity in Microblogging through Ambient Affiliation. *Discourse and Communication* 8 (2): 209–228. https://doi.org/10.1177/1750481313510816.
———. 2021. Discourse and Social Media. In *The Bloomsbury Handbook of Discourse Analysis*, ed. Ken Hyland, Brian Paltridge, and Lillian Wong, 295–309. London: Bloomsbury.
———. 2022. Social Media Quotation Practices and Ambient Affiliation: Weaponising Ironic Quotation for Humorous Ridicule in Political Discourse. *Journal of Pragmatics* 191: 98–112. https://doi.org/10.1016/j.pragma.2021.12.003.

CHAPTER 7

Meme-Mediated Humorous Communication

1 Introduction: Meme Discourse

Memes stand out for being one of the most pervasive multimodal discourses on the Net nowadays.[1] Despite having been initially created on websites, now specific smartphone apps for meme generation exist[2] and social networking apps, together with mobile messaging apps, are typical channels through which these memes spread across mass populations. Castaño Díaz (2013, 97) proposes a broad summary of definitions and elements typically associated with internet memes:

> An *internet meme* is a *unit of information* (idea, concept or belief), which *replicates* by passing on via Internet (e-mail, chat, forum, social networks, etc.) in the *shape* of a hyper-link, video, image, or phrase. It can be passed on *as an exact copy or can change and evolve*. The *mutation* on the replication can be by meaning, keeping the structure of the meme or vice versa. The mutation occurs by *chance, addition or parody*, and its *form* is not relevant.

[1] This chapter is an extension and update of previous research on memes carried out in Yus (2018, 2019a, 2019b, 2021b, 2021c, 2021d, 2022, forthcoming-a) and Yus and Maíz-Arévalo (2021, 2023; Maíz-Arévalo and Yus 2021).

[2] At the moment of writing this chapter, a wide range of smartphone *apps* to create memes are available on the *App Store*, namely: *MemesMaker Pro*, *Meme Generator*, *Creador de Memes Lite*, *Imgur*, *Meme Creator*, *Memedroid*, *Simple Meme Creator*, *Dopameme*, *Meme Maker*, *SMS Rage Faces*, and *InstaMeme!*

F. Yus, *Pragmatics of Internet Humour*,
https://doi.org/10.1007/978-3-031-31902-0_7

> An internet meme *depends* both *on a carrier* and on a *social context* where the transporter acts as a filter and decides what can be passed on. It *spreads horizontally* as a virus at a *fast and accelerating* speed. It *can be interactive* (as a game), and some people relate them to creativity. Its *mobility, storage, and reach* are web-based (Hard disks, cell phones, servers, cloud, etc.). They *can be manufactured* (as in the case of viral marketing) or *emerge* (as an offline event taken online). Its *goal* is to be known well enough to replicate within a group.

One specific type of meme that proliferates to a large extent nowadays is the *image macro meme*, a text-image discourse made up of one or two lines of text at the top and/or the bottom of the meme and an image in the middle which lends itself to several possible interpretive combinations (see Sect. 2 below).[3] According to Tay (2015, 49), image macros tend to be simpler to produce, since some computer applications can make it easy to create and alter memes. The widely accepted expression *image macro* refers to an image with a superimposed caption, usually for humorous purposes (see Sect. 4). From this perspective, a macro can be portrayed as the automated processes that users go through in order to add captions to images following the style accepted by the community. As Diedrichsen (2020, 238) contends, "the individual is a cognitive agent who is making individual contributions within a large community, whose dimension and individual participants are however not known to him/her and cannot be known. At the same time, the individual's thoughts and choices may be determined by the cultural cognition that characterises the cultural group he/she is taking part in."

As listed in Arizzi (2019, 55), other types of "text-image memes" include (a) written discourse replacing initial speech in comic bubbles; (b) written discourse organised in surreal conversations, usually placed at the top or bottom of the meme (the words being separated physically, but not functionally, from the image, as they are needed to interpret what the image itself shows), and (c) written discourse replacing the one previously existing in the image, as exemplified by placards working like thought bubbles (where the inner thoughts and beliefs of the person represented

[3] Scott (2022) specified other types, such as *hashtag memes* (where "the inclusion of the hashtag not only connects the different tokens together but functions as a signal that they are part of a family"); and *phrasal templates* ("text-based memes which follow a recognisable template with editable slots. Users customise the template by filling in the slots, and each example describes a different situation or scenario").

are portrayed from inside the image, often with an ironic and irreverent intent). And of course, memes may also draw upon other discursive modes beyond the text-image format. Börzsei (2013), for instance, writes that a meme can consist of a still image, an image with a phrase, a GIF or a video[4]; it may contain a punchline or make a statement with no added text. Certainly, text-only, image or text-image memes are not the only possible discursive modes making up memes. Nowadays, especially among teenagers, many memes are shaped as videos, most frequently on TikTok (see for instance Han and Kuipers 2021).

Milner (2012) also provides an exhaustive taxonomy of meme types. Starting with a differentiation between *remixed images* and *stable images*, he sub-divides the former into *single images* and *stacked images*. Single images are then divided into memes such as annotated stills, macros and quotes; stacked images in turn being divided into rage comics and stacked stills. Finally, stable images may contain drawings, graphs, photos and screenshots, among other types of memes. Milner (ibid., 89) argues that image macros are "one of the clearest examples of interplay of imitation and transformation in the process that guides the construction of memes." These image macros will also be the main type of meme on which this chapter will focus.

The term *meme* initially refers to the *cultural unit* proposed by Dawkins (1976) as a parallel to *gene*, although it also departs from this term substantially:

> We need a name for the new replicator, a noun that conveys the idea of a unit of cultural transmission, or a unit of imitation. "Mimeme" comes from a suitable Greek root, but I want a monosyllable that sounds a bit like "gene." I hope my classicists friends will forgive me if I abbreviate *mimeme* to meme. If it is any consolation, it could alternatively be thought of as being related to "memory," or to the French word *même*. It should be pronounced to rhyme with "cream" (…) Just as genes propagate themselves in the gene pool by leaping from body to body via sperms or eggs, so memes propagate themselves in the meme pool by leaping from brain to brain via a process which, in the broad sense, can be called imitation. (Dawkins ibid. 192).

[4] See Shifman (2012), Guadagno et al. (2013), Xu et al. (2016), Sánchez-Olmos and Viñuela (2017), and Hirsch (2019), among others.

Memes exhibit an ability to *infect* people's minds, and to spread for that matter.[5] Dawkins (ibid.) suggested three main characteristics: (a) *fidelity* (the meme can be readily copied and transmitted from person to person without significant alteration in shape or format), (b) *fecundity* (a high rate at which the information is copied and spreads), and (c) *longevity* (the meme's capacity for survival within a chained spreading process).

From this initial idea of meme, the information that spreads through the Net has been labelled similarly: *internet memes*. This should come as no surprise, since these memes share some properties initially ascribed to memes in general, a crucial one being their power of replication. Wiggins (2019) pictures this capacity as a process divided into three stages, namely *assimilation* (of some discourse prone to being represented); *expression* (it takes a physical shareable form, e.g. photo and/or video) and *transmission* (through a medium such as messaging apps or social networking sites). However, the internet meme likewise differs from the initial conception suggested by Dawkins (Wiggins ibid., 1–20). For example, in addition to being frequently altered by users during the process of sharing and spreading (*no fidelity*), many memes have an ephemeral nature, tied to some newsworthy event that is itself ephemeral as well (no *longevity*, see Wiggins 2020). Obviously, some memes are more likely to spread more widely across user populations due to a number of qualities that make them more appealing (i.e. relevant), and thus prone to being subsequently forwarded. An attempt to conceptualise this appeal was proposed by Spitzberg (2014), for whom six major nested levels of variables may influence or reflect meme diffusion: (a) the meme itself, (b) the user's competence, (c) the various social network structures through which the meme is disseminated, (d) societal contextual factors, (e) geospatial/technical factors, and (f) the criteria of meme fitness and the conceptual criteria indicating the practical outcomes of meme diffusion, which feed back into the original system levels. These levels are briefly summarised in Table 7.1.

Furthermore, no consensus has yet been reached on a definition of internet memes. Several of them are listed below:

[5] Definitions of memes (in general) include those offered by Naughton (2012): "an infectious idea which replicates itself;" Blackmore (1999): "whatever it is that is passed on by imitation;" Knobel and Lankshear (2007, 201): "popular term for describing 'catchy' and widely propagated ideas or phenomena;" and Taecharungroj and Nueangjamnong (2014, 152); "units of information, ideas or mental representations, cultural instructions that are not only self-replicating but also contagious."

Table 7.1 Factors influencing meme diffusion (Spitzberg 2014)

Meme	The key word here is *fitness*, "the adaptive capability of a meme, where adaptation is the potential of the meme to adjust to the constraints and demands of the networks through which the meme is propagated and replicated. Fitness represents a meme's ability to replicate by adapting successfully to environments" (p. 317).
Individual	*Computer-mediated communication competence*, or expressed differently, the extent to which one views the use of digital media in sending a message as effective and appropriate, is what matters most. Effectiveness refers to the degree to which a message fulfils the preferred goals of the communicators engaged in replication, whereas appropriateness has to do with whether or not the message exchange process is seen as contextually adequate (pp. 319–320). Interestingly, competence becomes associated with *source credibility* of the sender user, to such an extent that expectations of relevance may rise simply by identifying the sender (or "spreader") of the meme.
Network	The eventual success of a meme's diffusion is said to depend on the level of receptiveness shown by the social network towards the meme. The social networks in and through which a meme is propagated may occasionally mediate, and probably moderate, the replication of memes. Successful replication is thus likely to depend on the extent to which a social network system facilitates such replication (p. 321).
Society	A number of context features are bound to mediate or moderate the diffusion trajectory of a meme. For example, social groups may be competing for meme attention through the transmission of their own counter-memes, thus taking up the audience's cognitive resources and affecting eventual relevance. Furthermore, "there are various forms of social networks, and their different types, structures, and functions are likely to have differential effects on meme diffusion" (p. 324).
Geo-technical	Geographical location often represents functional intersections of human activity that can be mapped by meme production. For instance, a disproportionate geospatial tweeting about a music event may accurately geolocate a music venue. In addition, several geotechnical features may affect meme replication. Without a doubt, infrastructure trauma or limitations that impede communication technologies and their hardware networks place real limits on meme replication (p. 325).
Outcome	As for the extent to which memes are successful, their competence can be assessed via a variety of efficacy criteria including popularity, velocity, longevity and fecundity (p. 326).

A piece of culture (...) which gains influence through online transmission (Davison 2012).

Amateur media artifacts, extensively remixed and recirculated by different participants on social media networks (Milner 2012, iii).

> Multimodal artefacts remixed by countless participants, employing popular culture for public commentary (Milner 2013a).
>
> Groups of digital items (such as images or videos) that share common characteristics, are created with awareness of each other, and are distributed online by multiple participants (Shifman 2014).
>
> Texts, (i) belonging to *different expressive substances*, and usually *syncretic*, (ii) deriving from a process of *intervention* upon pre-existing texts, (iii) according to *rules* of pertinence and good formation, (iv) that are characterized by a collectively assigned and recognized *efficacy*, (v) in a *playful* spirit, (vi) by the anonymity of the creator, and (vii) by modalities of diffusion that are repetitive, adaptive, appropriative, and -in general- *participative* (Marino 2015).
>
> Any artifact that appears on the Internet and produces countless derivatives by being imitated, remixed, and rapidly diffused by countless participants in technologically mediated communication (Dynel 2016).
>
> A relatively complex, multi-layered, and intertextual combination of (moving) image and text that is disseminated by the active agency of internet users, becoming popular among them (Laineste and Voolaid 2016).
>
> A remixed, iterated message that can be rapidly diffused by members of participatory digital culture for the purpose of satire, parody, critique, or other discursive activity (Wiggins 2019).

Crucially, internet memes have as one of its distinctive features that they are invariably ascribed to a "family" and part of their effective processing is tied to this initial family ascription (Nissenbaum and Shifman 2017, 484, 2018; Segev et al. 2015, 418; Vandelanotte 2021; Vásquez and Aslan 2021). Eschler and Menking (2018) also claimed that memes can become a type of brand, insofar as specific groups of memes converge on recognisable formats, where images and texts are often re-mixed to express new concepts using a familiar formula (see Dynel 2021, 179; Aslan 2022).[6] Diedrichsen (2022, 255) also emphasises the fact that memes are

[6] In this sense, a taxonomy of internet memes was proposed by Diedrichsen (2020), with five main types: *established advice animals*, *situation memes* (they comment on a circumstance chosen by the user), *memetic silliness* (linguistic, visual, embodied, other), *comment memes* (they refer to contributions by other users), and *reaction memes* (they react to other users' contributions).

tied to families that anchor new, innovative forms of meme creation: "when a picture-text combination is finally recognized as a meme, its convention of usage is its usage history. Successful and trending memes draw more instances of themselves, as they reach many users in diverse variations. This gives users an idea of their form, function, and usage, and at the same time inspires more users to create an instance of the meme. This newly created instance will make a novel point that fits into the general usage schema and apply it to new situations."

In this sense, even though family ascription stands out as a key feature of memes,[7] Brooke (2019) considers that if memes are to be treated as a form of communication, they need to have another four qualities. First, the message, whose interpretation entails some form of shared knowledge (expectations of mutual manifestness in relevance theory -RT- terms). Second, memes must evolve and be subjected to alterations and re-mixing by the community of users (see Jiang and Vásquez 2020). Third, this evolution is aided by their malleability, inasmuch as some characteristics may change but some basic features have to be preserved so that they point to the original message. Finally, memes are defined by their virality and capacity to spread. If a meme fails to achieve popularity and shared understanding, it has not succeeded and therefore does not resonate with a culture or community.

2 Text and Image in Memes

A number of interesting conclusions may be drawn from analysing text-image combinations in memes and the role played by such discourses in the eventual interpretation of the multimodal meme as a whole, as well as its capacity to generate humorous effects. Several publications have addressed text-image interfaces.[8] Two proposals are collected in Table 7.2.

In this chapter, following Yus (2019a), the taxonomy of different categories for multimodal combinations in comics devised by McCloud

[7] By contrast, Attardo (2020, 149) remarks that, in most cases, memes are experienced individually (one by one) and acquire the family/group dynamics only at a different level of engagement (i.e. when the person actively seeks out the meme). He proposes to distinguish two levels: *passive fruition*, in which any user may encounter a given instance of a meme by itself, and an *active level*, where the user seeks out the meme and is fully aware of the existence of other memes within the "family" (called *meme cycle* by Attardo, ibid.).

[8] See, for instance, Trifonas (2015), van Leeuwen (2006), Tsakona (2009) and Sarapik (2009), among others.

Table 7.2 Some proposals for text-image combinations

Authors	*Classification*
Nikolajeva and Scott (2000)	(a) *Symmetry* (both image and text transmit exactly the same message); (b) *enhancement* (the image serves to enhance the text adding, as it were, a nuance of meaning that was not expressed by the purely textual part of the message); (c) *complementing* (the antithesis of the previous kind of interaction, when one of the semiotic components offers different information from the other one; (d) *counterpoint* (the textual and visual components provide different perspectives); and (e) *contradictory* (when the former kind of interaction is taken to extreme points and image and text contradict each other).[a]
Cochrane et al. (2022)	(1) *character* (the image is redefined by the text, thereby attributing its actions/reactions to the textual object; (2) *comic* (consecutive images are combined to create a narrative), (3) *comparison* (two consecutive images featuring a facial expression or body language change), (4) *conversation* (at least two entities converse verbally or nonverbally, followed by an image that represents the response of the second speaker to the first), (5) *description* (text is given alongside or overlaid on an image to contextualise what the image is meant to represent), (6) *sign* (a figure interacts with an object that contains text, where the figure imposes an interpretation of the text, and (7) *subtitle* (a screenshot from another piece of media, for example a film).

[a]In her analysis of emoticons, Maíz-Arévalo (2014, 182) reduces them to three: *symmetry*, *enhancement*, and *contradiction*

(1994) for comics will be applied to a corpus of 100 memes randomly selected from the internet. As a matter of fact, only one of McCloud's categories could not be found in our corpus of memes. Alongside McCloud's taxonomy, other sets of categories for text-image relationships of a semiotic (Barthes 1977) and a social-semiotic quality will likewise be mentioned in this study (Gill 2002; Salway and Martinec 2002; Martinec and Salway 2005; Chan 2011). The interest essentially lies, of course, in the text-image relationships that help to achieve specific interpretive outcomes, rather than in the purely semiotic interrelation of modes. By way of example, Cohn (2013) proposed four ways to connect text and image: (1) *inherent* (text and image are part of each other's structures); (2) *emergent* (text and image are directly interfaced with each other); (3) *adjoined* (text and image are integrated but not directly interfaced); and (4) *independent* (text and image are fully separate). Albeit interesting from a purely semiotic point of view, this taxonomy does not seem useful for a cyberpragmatic analysis of memes, since the latter exhibit a rigid placement and quality of both modes. A more fruitful approach, in my view, consists in working out the inferential implications of text-image interrelations and how their combinations yield relevant (and often unexpected) interpretive outcomes.

The main objective will be to analyse the corpus and determine category ascription, assessing the role that text and image play in the eventual interpretation while, at the same time, looking for specific text-image combinations that may prove interesting for a cyberpragmatic account of their relevance for the user processing the meme. Some conclusions may be reached from this analysis, throughout which it is necessary to focus on ascertaining (a) what contribution each mode (text/image) makes to the meme's overall global meaning; (b) whether cases exist in which the text makes little or no contribution to the interpretation of the meme -mainly provided by the image- or if the relationship is just the opposite: the image making little or no contribution to interpret the meme, that is, examples where the image adds little or no meaning to the meme; (c) in which cases text and image combine to generate implicated meanings that may only be obtained after combining the information from both modes; and (d) whether there is some specificity to memes that does not neatly correspond to any of the categories suggested by McCloud (1994) for comics. Several categories can thus be isolated:

1. *Word specific*, where images illustrate but do not significantly add to a largely complete text.[9] In Yus (2019a), 25 instances out of the general corpus of 100 memes were ascribed to this category. Sometimes, the image helps to narrow down the text meaning scope (images equally prevent a potential incongruous interpretations of the text). Consider these memes:

(1)	Top text:	If tomorrow isn't the due day
	Image:	A university student drinking a beer in a pub.
	Bottom text:	then today isn't the do day.
(2)	Top text:	Why make college the 4 best years of your life.
	Image:	Picture of a university student drinking a beer in a pub.
	Bottom text:	if you can make it 6.

[9] This category resembles Barthes's (1977) concept of *illustration*, in which the text is the primary mode and the image plays no substantial role in altering the verbally conveyed meaning. It also suits Martinec and Salway's (2005) *exemplification*, where the text prevails over the image.

In (1–2), despite being more or less autonomously interpreted, the text is more adequately processed next to the image of someone who might possibly utter these words, i.e. a university student. In the meme, the image is the same and it exemplifies the kind of person that would typically produce the utterance. The image narrows down the potential range of speakers of such an utterance, additionally helping the user to ascertain the exact meaning of, for example, *do* in (1) and *make* in (2). Furthermore, thanks to the image, the user can more easily derive a number of implications on a stereotypical university student's attitude to coursework and commitment to university duties in general.

2. *Image specific*, where the image dominates and the words do not significantly add to its meaning. This reminds us of the previous category (word-specific with images illustrating), the difference lying in the fact that the image is central to the meme here: the words play a supplementary exemplifying role. Expressed differently, the words exemplify situations in which the gestures provided by the image might appear (Wu 2014, 1417). Only 7 instances of the 100-meme corpus fitted into this category, which suggests that images generally serve to exemplify, emphasise or amplify the meaning of the text, or combine with the latter in order to generate interpretations which can only be obtained from this combination. However, instances where the image acts as the main source of information (and eventual relevance) in the meme turned out to be far less frequent.

As attested in Yus (2019a), one of the cases in which the picture does dominate occurs when the meme shows a person who has achieved fame for repeatedly saying something. The picture itself is worth the user's attention and the text merely emphasises the attributes of the person depicted therein. In this case, one expects any user to retrieve the specific information justifying the famous person's appearance in the meme from their background knowledge (e.g. what he/she typically said or did that leads to the creation of the meme). An example can be found in (3):

(3) Top text: Either you're naive or have scruples.
Image: Picture of actor Hugh Laurie in his role as Dr. House with an angry look on his face.
Bottom text: I'm not sure which is worse.

3. *Duo specific*, where words and images send essentially the same message. This category mirrors the social semiotics category of *equivalence* (Gill 2002), since the content is communicated both by the image and by its accompanying text, thus causing some degree of redundancy in meaning (Chan 2011, 149). Predictably, hardly any instance of the meme corpus fitted into this category, since one of the features inherent to this kind of meme is the interfacing meanings between text and image. Only meme (4) below might be close to the attributes of this category. Its text refers to happiness, and this feeling is paired with the picture of happiness on a famous actor's face:

(4)	Top text:	You find it offensive. I find it funny.
	Image:	Picture of actor Leonardo di Caprio smiling and proposing a toast.
	Bottom text:	That's why I'm happier than you.

4. *Additive*, where words amplify or elaborate on an image or vice versa. Unlike the previous one, this category appeared frequently in the corpus under analysis. One way or another, up to 37 instances exhibited this text-image relationship in which amplification or elaboration of one mode occurs regarding the other.[10] A typical text-image relationship in this category is the one where the image amplifies or elaborates on the meaning of the adjacent text, as in (5) and (6). In the former (5), the user's background knowledge about Brando and of his role in the film *The Godfather* makes it easier to adjust the concept encoded by the word *fix*. Moreover, the user is guided by the picture when trying to narrow down and connote the meaning of the phrase *the old-fashioned way*, initially broad and somewhat vague. Regarding (6), the image of a famous actor play-

[10] This category reminds us of Barthes's notion of *anchorage*, in which words help the user to reach a more fine-grained interpretation or the image or the other way round. The category likewise resembles social semiotics notions such as: (1) *extension*, where one mode provides new information on the information from the other mode; (2) *enhancement*, where the text adds an informative element to the image or vice versa; (3) *exposition*, in which the image elaborates on aspects of the text or vice versa; and (4) *augmentation*, which involves an image extending or adding new meanings to the text or the text extending the image by providing an additional element (Chan 2011, 154).

ing a dumb character enhances the absurd idea that the character came up with, as described in the meme text:

(5)	Top text:	I think we have to fix this problem.
	Image:	Actor Marlon Brando in the film The Godfather.
	Bottom text:	the old-fashioned way.
(6)	Top text:	I changed all my passwords to "incorrect."
	Image:	Famous actor playing a dumb character.
	Bottom text:	so, whenever I forget, it says, "your password is incorrect."

Frequent and equally ascribable to this category is the abundant series of memes (i.e. "families") which share the same image but contain different texts (this text-image configuration also corresponds to the meme-specific inferential strategy of ***ad hoc visual referent adjustment***, see Sect. 5 below, as well as to the humorous strategy of ***second-order incongruity***, see Sect. 4 below). In this case, the main interest lies in a specific kind of gesture that users find funny (often one made by an actor/actress and reproduced as a film still). The different versions of the text depict situations in which this gesture might appear. These series are based on the so-called *memetic templates*, which allow for both collective and individual actions on eventual memes. As Nissenbaum and Shifman (2018, 295) remarked, individual input is required to create different instances of a meme and the memetic template provides users with a means to express personal experiences or identities, and the individual often draws upon a collectively created template to deliver a personalised message.

5. *Parallel*, where words and image entail different inferential paths without intersecting. This category refers us back to the social semiotics label *exposition*, in which image and text find themselves at the same level of generality (van Leeuwen 2011, 676). Not surprisingly, this category was absent in the corpus, since the eventual interpretation of memes normally relies on the combination of text and image, and it makes little sense to place both modes together in the meme unless these are bound to be somehow related.
6. *Montage*, where words are treated as integral parts of the image. This category typically appears in comics, since artists often skilfully connote texts with iconic connotations, as a result of which both modes become semiotically integrated. Consequently, it is similar to

the social semiotics term *homospatiality*, where different semiotic modes co-occur inside a single spatially bonded homogenous entity. The absence of this category in the corpus of memes has to do with the fact that text type (font, size...) is fixed and imposed upon the user by the available software, which makes a creative *iconisation* of the text impossible.

7. *Interdependent*, where image or words together convey an idea that neither could convey on their own. Not only was this category frequent in the corpus with up to 30 instances, but it also stands out as the one raising the most interest for a cyberpragmatic analysis concerned with how users derive interpretations from the available information. The fact that interpretations from memes in this category cannot be drawn from the partial meanings of text or image taken separately makes the meme highly context-dependent and very significant for the kind of analysis proposed in this chapter.[11] Such image-text complementariness fits instances previously described as *centrifugal multimodality* (Boxman-Shabtai and Shifman 2014), where the image provides one meaning while the written text conveys another.

The most frequent text-image interaction in this category of memes is that in which the information from the image invalidates, to a greater or lesser extent, the information supplied by the text. In (7), for example, the image of Keanu Reeves with a lunatic look on his face makes access to the intended ironical-critical remark easier:

(7)	Top text:	What if Obama needs all of our personal information
	Image:	Lunatic-looking image of actor Keanu Reeves.
	Bottom text:	because he's setting up a matchmaking service and wants us all to find love?

[11] This category also suits Barthes' (1977) term *relay*: "text and image do not 'say the same thing' but convey different, complementary content" (van Leeuwen 2011, 657). This category exhibits the qualities of the social semiotics term *distribution* (juxtaposed images and text jointly constructing information) and *divergence* (the meanings of text and image contradict each other and convey new information out of this contradiction). Besides, it is related to what Jewitt (2016) calls *multimodal ensemble*, where all the modes combine to convey a message's meaning. The information is distributed across modes, and "any one mode in that ensemble is carrying part of the message only: each mode is therefore partial in relation to the whole of the meaning" (p. 73).

Added to the above, text-image combinations characteristically serve to trigger the inference of implications from text, with the help of a connoted image, as in (8), where the activity depicted in the image contradicts the feelings of honour and pride that the soldier should associate with being a marine:

(8)	Top text:	Join the marines they said.
	Image:	A marine holding an umbrella over president Obama.
	Bottom text:	You'll be a hero they said.

Needless to say, the most radical case of text-image relationships yielding a different meaning for the meme than that obtained from the partial meanings of text and image occurs when the image forces the very opposite of the interpretation drawn from the text -typical of ironic discourses. A good example is the series of memes which share the same image of two girls laughing. The image triggers a radically different interpretive path for the texts, invariably related to sex-role connoted information, to such an extent that their interpretation is reversed. Fig. 7.1 provides some examples.[12]

Furthermore, a frequent type of meme ascribable to this category is the series of memes that contain the same images but different texts labelling them, which often triggers a process of metaphorization of these images.[13] The humorous effect lies in the ability of these texts to be compatible with the information provided by the images. Figure 7.2 reproduces an example of one of such series of memes, more specifically the *distracted boyfriend series* (see Lou 2017; Scott 2021, 2022).

[12] Zappavigna (2020) analyses a broader class of memes invariably containing "*and then he said*..." as the top text. Again, as it happens with the memes in Fig. 7.1, the image -always one or several people laughing- invalidates an explicit interpretation of the bottom text, charging it with an ironic interpretive outcome instead.

[13] As Scott (2021, 291) remarks, the interpretation of these memes "depends on the combination of information in the image and the labels. They work together as a multimodal ensemble and if we change the content in the labels, different features emerge in the ad hoc concepts, leading to different implicatures." The reader is reminded that ad hoc concepts are inferred concepts that depart more or less substantially from the literal meaning coded by these words. The processes involved in ad hoc concept formation involve *narrowing*, as in "I am worried about Antonio… He *drinks* too much" (the inferred ad hoc concept is "drinks too much alcohol," narrower than drinking in general), and *broadening* or *loosening*, as in "I'll be ready *in two minutes*," (the inferred ad hoc concept is "in a while," looser than the exact two minutes).

Fig. 7.1 Irony-triggering image-text combinations

Fig. 7.2 Texts labelling and "metaphorising" the images that accompany bthe meme

3 Exploiting Meme Interpretation for the Sake of Humour

Upon finding a meme (for example spotting it on a Facebook profile, or being sent it as a WhatsApp message), the user will have to engage in several inferential strategies which are not meant to be successive but performed in parallel, according to the user's expectations of, and search for, relevance, much in the same way as interpretations in general become conceptualised in relevance theory (RT): interpretative hypotheses –i.e. likely interpretations– are supposedly formulated during a process of mutual parallel adjustment of the explicit and implicit content of utterances (Padilla Cruz 2017, 44). When inferring memes, the determination of the relationship existing between text and image yielding *explicatures* and *implicatures* (both verbal and visual) is hence context-dependent. In the case of *image macro memes*, an expected default order of interpretation prevails if the meme is to be successfully understood (Dynel 2016, 678). More precisely, the processing of memes goes through various inference stages which, rather than being distributed on a strictly linearly basis as in joke texts, are spatially arranged across the modes of image and text. Thus, the inferential processes may be more easily teased apart operationally (and therefore empirically) into various constellations of stages and their successions (Hempelmann and Samson 2008, 626). Six strategies may be isolated in this respect:

Strategy 1. To decode and inferentially enrich the meme's verbal content (top and/or bottom lines of text) in order to obtain the explicit interpretation of the text or *explicature.*

Strategy 2. To derive *implicatures* from verbal content, if these prove necessary to achieve a relevant interpretation for the text of the meme.

Strategy 3. To decode and inferentially enrich the image so that a *visual explicature* can be yielded.

Strategy 4. To derive *implicatures* or *implications* from the image in the meme (i.e. *visual implicatures*), if these are necessary to reach an adequate interpretation of the meme as a whole.

Strategy 5. To infer possible text-image combinations to yield interpretations (typically implicated ones or *verbal-visual implicatures*) that can only result from combining these sources of information (text and image) and not from either of them taken separately (Tsakona 2009, 1172). Very often, the information from the image will lead to *inferential backtracking* (and *re-interpretation*) once the accompanying text has been processed, in the light of the information provided by visual content. On other occasions, the text will force a new interpretation of the image, resulting in either a new *visual explicature* or a previously unforeseeable *visual implicature.* In my opinion, the effects of such text-image combinations seem more interesting for a cyberpragmatic analysis of why memes turn out to be effective (e.g. humorous), since the eventual interpretation demands the user's active participation in mixing different sources of information as a way to ensure an eventually satisfactory (i.e. relevant) interpretation.

Strategy 6. To access as much contextual information as necessary to obtain relevant interpretations out of strategies 1–5 above. In some memes, the reader's background knowledge of current affairs, newsworthy events, political issues, etc. (their literacy) becomes crucial to understanding the meme properly. After all, the meme very often makes little sense if separated from the specific time frame and pieces of news that justified its publication (Kardaş 2012, 208; El Refaie and Hörschelmann 2010, 197; Wiggins 2020). In fact, the effectiveness of memes more often than not lies in how the audience is aware of being able to access the necessary contextual information without which those memes would make no sense whatsoever. Further meme-based interactions may also generate a vivid mutuality of each interlocutor's accessibility to that information. This is also important to underline group barriers depending on mutual awareness of context accessibility:

> Teasing apart the rebellious, ambivalent, and solidarity-building aspects of humor practices requires knowledge of both the context of the outbreak and the layered symbolic meanings used in memes – images combined with text circulated digitally. Specialized language, images of celebrities, and shared templates for developing jokes can come together in a single meme (often connected to current events) that functions both to share information and foster feelings of belonging among members of a subculture – those who are "in" on the joke. Humor is a key practice for creating and maintaining digital subcultures. (Cottingham and Rose in press).

Strategies (1–6) are ultimately influenced by whether the meme is shared (or forwarded) with or without alterations. Evnine (2018, 305) proposes the term *memographic practice* for those instances in which, despite being shared, the meme undergoes mutation -concerning its textual element- at each forwarding. Although copying is not what mainly lies at the heart of the meme ecosystem (which includes a meta-level of activity where examples of these image macros are discussed, commented on, up-voted, downvoted, criticised, collected, replied to in kind, and so on), users often copy memes without mutation.[14] Jakob Nielsen (in Juza

[14] Marino (2015, 52) differentiates three ways of sharing memes: *spreading* (sharing, copying, posting), *transforming* (sampling, remixing, customising) and *imitating* (remaking, re-creating, re-enacting).

2013) formulated the *principle of participation inequality*, according to which 90% of all users behave as passive recipients of information available on the internet and add nothing of their own; 9% sporadically produce their own messages and post them on the Net; and only 1% of the most active users create original content in a constant and purposeful manner.

In my opinion, though, meme alteration as well as the creation of meme families from these alterations are basic ingredients of today's meme ecosystem, insofar as they impact on the user's self-concept. As Knobel and Lankshear (2007, 208–209) contend, the "look" of the meme not always remains constant, and in many ways, these "mutations" often seem to help the meme's fecundity in terms of encouraging people to contribute their own version thereof. Replicability therefore goes hand in hand with remixing as an important practice associated with numerous successful online memes, including actions such as modifying, bricolaging, splicing, reordering, superimposing, to quote but a few (Shifman 2013, 365). And the same holds true for other memes beyond the image-text visual meme on which the analysis performed in this chapter essentially focuses. For example, Shifman (2012, 191) proposed the term *memetic video*, defined as "a popular clip that lures extensive creative user engagement in the form of parody, pastiche, mash-ups or other derivative work. Such derivatives employ two main mechanisms relating to the 'original' memetic video: imitation (parroting elements from a video) and re-mix (technologically afforded re-editing of the video)." As such, these video-memes undergo processes of imitation and/or alteration as well.

The memes reproduced in Fig. 7.3 exemplify memes intimately tied to certain contextual information. These are translated from Spanish in

Fig. 7.3 Memes that demand accessibility to very specific contextual information

(9a-11a), with the explanation for such essential contextual information being offered in (9b-11b).

(9) a. -We are going to jump to light speed.
-Han, wait till 4 am because it's cheaper.
b. To understand this meme, it is necessary to know about the controversy that arose in Spain regarding the increase in the electricity rate in homes and the creation of time slots during which, in theory, electricity would be cheaper (in Spanish "luz" -literally, *light*- is a colloquial way to refer to "electricity").

(10) a. Fernando Simón: "There will only be 2-3 cases of monkey pox." Spain in 2 weeks.
b. This meme cannot possibly be understood without accessing the information on who Fernando Simón is (director of the Centre for the Coordination of Health Alerts and Emergencies in Spain since 2012), well-known for his blunders when predicting the scope and intensity of the Covid-19 pandemic in that country.

(11) a. He is staying!!!
b. The interpretation of this meme is once again far from easy. It reminds viewers of a similar scene between two FC Barcelona players: Piqué and Neymar. The former, hugging the latter just like in the meme, announced that Neymar was staying at the club (which, incidentally, he did not do in the end). The two players have now been replaced with two Spanish politicians, Rajoy (then president of the government, on the right) and Puigdemont (separatist president of Catalonia) in the face of the imminent escape of the latter to a foreign country to avoid inprisonment.

Several qualities of the multimodal meme will determine which of the strategies (1–5) listed above -and aided by contextualisation, strategy 6- will most likely take place first and in what order the other strategies will be performed. Among others, the *salience* of some discursive element in the meme will lead users to focus their attention there before other parts of the meme are processed. While a vast majority of users will firstly be attracted by the image, as demonstrated empirically by Simarro Vázquez et al. (2021), others may tend to process a top-down text-image-text inferential procedure. A similar view applies to comic panels with text (bubbles, captions) and image. As argued in Yus (2008), when it comes to processing visual information satisfactorily, readers are undoubtedly constrained by their biologically rooted tendency to select the most relevant information from visual stimuli. However, different readers will fix their gaze on different visual elements in the panel, although in theory some default "visual areas of interest" can always be isolated therein. Indeed, ever since the technique to track eye direction was developed, it has become clear that people do not pay the same attention to the same items in the image and/or text, and neither do they follow the same order during their perception, and this happens because all images are collated against very personal encyclopaedic background knowledge as well as expectations that significantly influence perception.[15]

This unpredictability may have implications for the eventual assessment of a meme's relevance; for instance, regarding the way in which the intended interpretations from text-image combinations are derived. In theory, the reading path for a meme should start with the image in the middle (visual processing), then move to the top (text processing), and finally focus on the bottom of the meme (text processing). Indeed, the image normally draws the user's attention before the lines of text are interpreted for relevance and this salience leads to an alteration of the eventual cognitive effects if the processing order does not match the initially foreseen one. As van Leeuwen (2015, 457) reminds us, texts are not really linear in their processing. Despite a top-bottom linear reading of the meme being expected on many occasions, reading paths are mainly created by differences in *salience* and depend on the textual or visual element that attracts the reader's or viewer's attention over and above other elements (Kress and van Leeuwen 2006, 218). In this way, visual compositions can establish particular hierarchies between elements to attract the attention and guide the movement of a hypothetical internet user's eyes within and across the different discursive elements of the meme.

It should also be noted that the typical fonts of an image-macro meme, for example the pervasively used one called *Impact*, were designed to draw the reader's attention (Brideau and Berret 2014), and this visual appeal may influence the processing order for text and image in the meme. Moreover, fonts prove convenient for meme creators. The extreme regularity of typefaces allows for the automated generation of internet memes.

[15] Furió (2002) cites two relevant analyses: One by G.T. Buswell (1935), who showed not only that eye movements are irregular and hence non-smooth but also that areas of interest exist in every picture; however, the order in which the eye focuses on these areas and the time spent perceiving them differ from one person to another. And the other, authored by A.L. Yarbus (1967), which provided similar results and additionally acknowledged the key role that expectations play in the choice of the areas on which the eye focuses. The more supposedly relevant information the object contains, the more attention the reader will pay to it.

And no matter what image is being used, this text will still remain legible over any colour or image (ibid.).

In any case, meme interpretation likewise entails inferential strategies to turn the schematic verbal-visual information coded in the meme into a fully contextualised, relevant interpretation. Such strategies resemble those applied to other discourses, and like in verbal humour, the audience's inferential strategies are very often manipulated for the sake of generating these effects.

As already mentioned several times in this book, according to the *underdeterminacy thesis*, a more or less substantial gap always exists between what is coded in a discourse (i.e. said, written, typed…) and what is intended with -and inferred from- this discourse. Indeed, and as highlighted in Chap. 2, the aforesaid strategies include assigning referents for certain words such as indexicals, as in example (12); delimiting the scope of quantifiers, as illustrated with *nothing* in (13); adjusting (i.e. narrowing) the coded concept into a more specific interpretation -see *temperature* in (14); adjusting the coded concept in the opposite direction (to broaden it into a looser interpretation) in cases such as *empty* in (15), whose literal meaning seems too specific to meet the intended interpretation; and recovering elided content in sub-sentential utterances such as *Typical* in (16). Inferences in (12–16) are meant to turn the words of the utterance into a meaningful explicit interpretation or *explicature*. However, the addressee is also very frequently expected to derive *implicatures* such as (17c) from utterances like (17a) with the aid of essential contextual information (17b):

(12) I saw her there yesterday with him.
[*I saw Mary Smith at the party yesterday with Tom Murray*].

(13) There is nothing on TV.
[*There is nothing interesting on TV worth watching*].

(14) Doctor: "This child has a temperature."
[*This child has a higher temperature than he should*].

(15) Let's go somewhere else. This pub is empty.
[*Let's go somewhere else. There is hardly anybody in this pub*].

(16) A: Mary won't answer my calls.
B: Typical.
[*Not answering calls is typical of Mary*].

(17) a. A: Nice cat! Is it male or female?
B: It's three-coloured.
b. All three-coloured cats are female.
c. The cat is female.

Meme interpretation entails analogous inferential strategies, but these are often manipulated for the sake of humour, that is, the creator intends the audience to be perform these strategies in such a way (and order) that their inferences lead to the desired humorous effects. Firstly, one of the basic preliminary stages during comprehension consists in ascribing a syntactic arrangement to the string of words that shape the utterance, the so-called *logical form*. This initial stage of utterance interpretation often takes place sub-attentively, before other inferential strategies turn the words in question into a contextualised interpretation. Theoretically, even though hearers normally come up with a single possible syntactic arrangement or logical form for the utterance, meme creators may impose a second one over the initially relevant one. This is exactly what happens in meme (18), mentioned in Chap. 2 too, which imposes the two parallel logical forms quoted in (19): one likely (a) and the other very unlikely but still possible (b):

(18) [*A male customer at a restaurant talking to a waitress*].
Man: Can I ask you about the menu please?
Waitress: The men I please is none of your business.
(19) a. [The] [menu] [please].
b. [The] [men] [you] [please].

Secondly, some memes play with the inferential ascription of a referent for words such as pronouns, adverbs or proper names. The memes in (20–22) would be examples.

(20) Amor, ¿me compras un celular?
[*My love, would you buy me a mobile phone?*].
-¿Y el otro?
[*And the other one?*].
-El otro me va a comprar una tablet.
[*The other one is buying me a tablet*].
(21) -Le noto nervioso. ¿Es la primera vez que viaja en avión?
[*You look nervous. Is this the first time you are flying?*].
-Si señorita azafata.
[*Yes miss stewardess*].
-No se preocupe todo irá bien.
[*Don't worry. Everything will be fine*].
-Una pregunta, señorita, en caso de que se incendie el avión ¿Por dónde salimos?

[*One question Miss, if the plane catches fire, where shall we leave through?*].
-Por la tele.
[*On TV*].

(22) Image: A customer about to pay at the supermarket].
Worker: You wanna box for those, Sir?
Customer: Nah, I hate violence. Is it cool if I just pay with my card?

In (20), the most likely (i.e. relevant) referent for *el otro/the other one* is "the other mobile phone." Nevertheless, the audience is surprised to find out that another referent is possible: "the other boyfriend." Similarly, meme (21) plays with the polysemy of *salir* in Spanish, which may mean either "to exit" or "to appear on a medium." Although upon reaching the end of the meme, and considering the previously inferred meme discourse, the only possible interpretation of this word is "to exit," the second one eventually prevails over this likely one. Finally, (22) plays with two meanings of *box* (a recipient/to fight) and possibly also two candidate interpretations of *wanna* when said orally ("want to"/"want a"). In the visual context of the meme, despite being more likely and relevant, the former is again invalidated and replaced with the initially less likely meaning.

A third typical strategy plays with the audience's disambiguation of potentially ambiguous words or phrases. Following the RT inferential route, normally one of the senses should be accessible enough to be picked up as the most relevant, the audience not even noticing that the word/phrase is potentially ambiguous in the first place. However, as part of the humorous strategy, this audience is forced either to become aware of multiple simultaneous meanings or to replace the initially relevant choice of an interpretation with another less likely but in theory also possible. Here are several examples:

(23) -¿Mantiene usted relaciones sexuales de manera regular?
[*Do you have sexual intercourse on a regular basis?*].
-E incluso mal.
[*Even badly*].

(24) -¿Dígame?
[*Hello?*].
-¿Es el veterinario?
[*Is it the vet?*].
-Sí.
[*Yes*].

-¿Me puede decir qué come un canario?
[*Can you tell me what a canary eats?*].
-Lo mismo que tú pero con una hora de retraso.
[*Same as you but one hour later*].

(25) Estos días ando un poco bajo de ánimo, así que decidí ir al psicólogo. Cuando llegué a la consulta había un letrero que ponía: "USE LA SOLUCIÓN ALCOHÓLICA." Me fui agradecido por el consejo y el dinero ahorrado en la consulta Ya estoy mejor.
[*These days I'm a little down, so I decided to visit the psychologist. When I arrived at the practice there was a sign which read: "USE THE ALCOHOLIC SOLUTION." I left grateful for the advice and the money saved on the consultation. I'm better now*].

(26) [*Image of a man and a woman smiling while having a drink*].
She: La verdad que es la primera cita que tengo con un piloto.
[*The truth is that it's my first date with a pilot*].
He: ¿Piloto?
[*Pilot?*].
She: En tu Facebook ponías que habías alcanzado los 30.000 pies.
[*On your Facebook profile you said you'd reached 30.000 feet*].
He: Soy podólogo.
[*I am a chiropodist*].

Meme (23) plays with the multiple meanings of *regular*, one related to frequency (the likeliest one picked up initially by the audience), and the other associated with quality, meaning "in not quite a satisfactory way." This second meaning is only taken into account when the meme creator foregrounds it at the end of the meme. The same applies to (24), where *canario* also has two meanings: "the bird," again the most probable and relevant one given the setup of the meme text, and "a person from the Canary Islands" (whose time slot has a one-hour difference with that of the Spanish peninsula). Thirdly, meme (25), which was created in 2020, at the height of the Covid-19 pandemic in Spain, plays with the twofold meaning of *solución alcohólica* (alcoholic solution): "alcoholic gel" and "alcohol as a remedy." The former is the likeliest interpretation in the context of the pandemic, whereas the latter again becomes imposed on this initial relevant interpretation. Finally, *pies* (feet) is the key word in the polysemy-based meme (26). The word *piloto* (pilot) at the beginning of the meme forces a unique interpretation of feet (unit of measurement); the very end of the meme, however, reminds us that *pies* (feet) is also the part of human anatomy that chiropodists specialise in.

Fig. 7.4 Memes playing with literal vs. idiomatic interpretations of meme texts

Fourthly, a typical humorous meme strategy revolves around playing with the literal vs. metaphoric or idiomatic interpretation of words, phrases or even whole utterances. In theory, the metaphoric/idiomatic meaning is supposedly more accessible in inferential terms due to its default mental storage as a unit. Figure 7.4 shows three examples of the "Matías Prats" meme series. This popular TV News presenter in Spain has become well known in Spain for cleverly using this kind of strategy. The three memes portrayed in Fig. 7.4, show a play on words with three Spanish idioms: *estar que echa humo* (to be fuming with anger)*; no estar para tirar cohetes* (to be short of cash -but literally: "to be incapable of launching rockets"); and *librarse por los pelos* (to be a close shave). Cunningly, all three idioms are also compatible, to a certain extent, with the literal interpretations of these texts, as can be seen in the translations provided in (27–29) below.

(27) An arsonist sets a block of flats on fire.
The residents are fuming.
(28) NASA suffers from a budget reduction.
Apparently, they are short of cash.
(29) A woman's flat explodes while she was at the hairdresser's.
One can say it was a close shave.

It should be noted, though, that it would be a mistake to assume that all the users who infer the same meme will come up with exactly the same interpretation. In fact, the meme is processed against a very personal background of each addressee user (one of the *user-related contextual constraints* mentioned in this book), which not only affects both discourse interpretation and related non-propositional effects, but also influences future actions by the user concerning the spread of the meme as a

Fig. 7.5 Sex role-connoted memes

contribution to the user's audience. This happens, for example, with race- and gender-connoted memes (Williams et al. 2016; Milner 2013b; Nee and de Maio 2019; Paciello et al. 2021).

Figure 7.5, reproduces two examples of sexist memes, emphasising stereotypical attributes of men (meme on the left) and women (meme on the right). Upon receiving them, different interactions with individual users will take place depending on their respective beliefs and ideas about women's role compared to that of men (overlapping, overall matching, utterly different, etc.). This was commented upon in Chap. 4 in terms of *user-related contextual constraints*.

4 Incongruity-Resolution Humorous Strategy in Memes

Despite being usually regarded as humorous discourses, memes may also have a clearly critical purpose, in a similar fashion to cartoons in the press (Yoon 2016, 97; Burroughs 2013; Jiang and Vásquez 2020),[16] and they are often referred to as "jokes" even though they rather fit the "instance of humour" label (Dynel 2016, 668; Zappavigna 2020). Indeed, when users receive or find a meme, one of the default expectations is that it will be humorous in some way (Miltner 2014) and that some of the

[16] As Piata (2020, 4) correctly remarks, humour in memes not only pursues to generate humorous effects, but can be used as "a powerful means for voicing critique vis-à-vis contemporary social and/or political issues" too.

coherence-building strategies between the combined information from text and image are bound to be manipulated seeking humorous effects (Johann and Bülow 2019). For instance, Brown (2013, 189) comments that memes can be sorted broadly into two categories: *absurdist humour* and/or *social commentary*; nevertheless, a study about memes revealed that out of nineteen mainstream memes published until 2007, seventeen had humour as their key component, and this imbalance probably still exists nowadays. Certainly, millions of comedic memes online poke fun at many different aspects of culture, and it must be added that some image macro memes such as the ones analysed in this chapter have a clearly humorous nature, since they exhibit the typical incongruity-resolution pattern of humorous discourses (see Yus 2016, 2017 for an account of this strategy), even though variations become visible which are inherent to this medium.

Certainly, incongruity-resolution (henceforth IR) stands out as one of the most frequently used humour-generating strategies. As analysed in Chap. 2, Suls (1972, 1977, 1983) conceptualised it as arising from inferential conflicts that hearers encounter when processing the verbal content of a joke. An analysis of jokes was carried out in Yus (2016, 2017) with the aim of detecting which incongruity-resolution patterns might be singled out. Two major groups were proposed and also commented upon in Chap. 2: on the one hand, many instances of humorous texts fit a discourse-centred IR helped by a manipulation of inferential strategies such as disambiguation, reference assignment, concept adjustment and so on (*discourse-based incongruity*). The polysemy of "grass" in (30) and its exploitation offers an example. On the other hand, a different group of jokes bases incongruity on the hearer's construction of an appropriate mental situation (frame, schema, script...) to make sense of what is happening in the story depicted within the joke (what in Yus 2013a, 2013b, 2016 was called *make-sense frame*), which turns out to be eventually incorrect (*frame-based incongruity*), as in joke (31):

(30) There was a sign on the lawn at a drug re-hab centre that said "Keep off the grass."

(31) A fellow in a bar noticed a woman, always alone, who came in on a fairly regular basis. After the second week, he made his move. "No thank you," she said politely. "This may sound rather odd in this day and age, but I'm keeping myself pure until I meet the man I love." "That must be rather difficult," the man replied. "Oh, I don't mind too much," she said. "But it has my husband pretty upset."

Table 7.3 Incongruity-resolution patterns in memes (Yus 2021c)

		Type of incongruity	*Role of image*
31.33%	8.66%	Frame-based	The image plays no role
	18.00%	Frame-based	The image aids
	4.67%	Frame-based	The image is essential
38.67%		Discourse-image based	The image is essential
21.34%	8.00%	Discourse-based	The image plays no role
	7.34%	Discourse-based	The image aids
	6.00%	Discourse-based	The image is essential
8.66%		No incongruity	

Although Lugea (2019) claims that this humorous strategy has scarcely been applied to the study of memes, Yus (2021c) analysed 150 randomly selected memes from an IR perspective, and these two major IR patterns suggested for jokes (*discourse-* and *frame-based*) were also found in memes (plus a third pattern arising from clashes between text and image). The role played by the image in the meme was examined as well, with three main cases: (a) the image plays no role in IR, (b) the image aids in IR and (c) the image is essential in IR. The cases resulting from the combination of these parameters yielded the 7 patterns listed in Table 7.3, together with their percentage of occurrence in the corpus.

As seen in Table 7.3, only 8.66% of corpus memes exhibited no IR pattern (and possibly no humorous intention either). The most frequent was the one where incongruity arises from clashes between the text and the image in the meme (near 40%); this makes sense, given the inherently multimodal quality of memes. An example would be those memes which combine visual classical art samples clashing with very colloquial texts that accompany these classical images in the so-called *classical art memes*: "humor in Classical Art Memes differs from other manifestations of meme-based humor in that it arises from incongruity between the *stylistic varieties* evoked in its inputs: the text and the image, the former containing a colloquial linguistic expression and the latter a classical-style artwork. In other words, humor in Classical Art Memes is stylistic, arising from juxtaposing the low variety in the message to the high variety in their image" (Piata 2020, 175).

Notice, also, that this is the only pattern in which no differentiation is made depending on the role of the image. The reason is that if the image plays an important role in contrasting its information to the accompanying text, the role of the image necessarily has to be essential. For the other categories, though, there is a threefold distinction of image roles. The 7 categories listed in the previous table will now be briefly explained.

1. *Frame-based IR, image plays no role.* In this category, the reader builds up a frame for the joke which becomes invalidated, the image playing no role in such IR pattern (especially in text-only memes), a kind of *cumulative inferential contrast.*[17] An example is (32), where the top text leads to construct a joke-like IR pattern and its continuation is invalidated. In addition, the image seems to play no role whatsoever in the derivation of humorous effects. The same applies to the text-based Spanish meme in (33), already mentioned in Chap. 2, in which the audience cannot help but construct a sexual frame for the meme, which once again becomes invalidated at the end.

(32) Top text: A guy walks into a bar...
Image: A rooster.
Bottom text: He has a family of four and a drinking problem.

(33) -Ya no tenemos edad para quedarnos con las ganas.
[*We are too old to be left with the desire*].
-¿Tú crees?
[*You think so?*].
-Claro y los dos queremos ¿no?
[*Of course and both of us want this, don't we?*].
-Sí, tienes razón.
[*Yes, you're right*].
-Camarero, 10 croquetas más por favor.
[*Waiter, 10 more croquettes, please*].

[17] Alba Milà García (pers. comm) argues that these memes with apparently unrelated text-image combinations normally contain thematically homogeneous texts for the same single image, and therefore readers are alerted to the kind of text that they may encounter upon detecting the image. I agree with her, but this seems to be a higher-order processing path that saves mental effort at the initial stages of the inference of those memes and creates more precise expectations of relevance by foregrounding possible kinds of texts associated with the image. A similar claim is made in Lin et al. (2014) concerning a particular kind of meme template, the *Socially Awkward Penguin*, which "describes awkward and uncomfortable life situations. When an experienced reader sees this meme, he knows that the captions are a joke about awkward situations, without even actually reading the text." However, my point is that even if mental effort is saved during the identification phase of meme comprehension, the user still has to solve the incongruity without the aid of the image in the meme.

2. *Frame-based IR, the image aids.* In this category, two varieties may be distinguished. Firstly, there are instances where the image is compatible with the top text but not with the bottom text. This increases the potential effect of the incongruity, insofar as the initial interpretation selected for the top text receives corroboration through the validating interpretation of the image in the meme. Three examples of this appear in Fig. 7.6. The memes on the left and on the right portray the image of an angry-looking woman which is compatible with the top text, but the bottom text turns out incongruous. As for the meme in the middle, the hippy-looking girl in the image may once again be compatible with the top text, but it is definitely not compatible with the bottom text.

Secondly, the opposite may occur, or expressed differently, albeit compatible with the bottom text, the image turns out to be incongruous with the top text. This time, the difficulty to understand the incongruous second text is somehow alleviated by the matching image. Memes (34–35) illustrate this case. In (34), the interpretive impact of the bottom text seems incongruous with the top text, but the image of an actor who is famous for his revenge-related films allows us to understand the real impact of that strong bottom text. The same applies to (35), in which, despite being once more incompatible with the top text, the image of an actor whom everybody knows for the drug-related TV series *Breaking Bad* is perfectly compatible with the bottom text:

Fig. 7.6 Memes in which the image is compatible with the top text but not with the bottom text

(34)	Top text:	Borrowing our tools? If not returned,
	Image:	Photo of actor Liam Neeson.
	Bottom text:	I will find you and kill you.
(35)	Top text:	I just met you and this is crazy.
	Image:	Photo of actor Aaron Paul.
	Bottom text:	But do you want some meth?

3. *Frame-based IR, the image is essential.* A key role corresponds to the image in this category when it comes to properly understanding the IR pattern, often widening the gap between the initial incongruity and the eventual resolution, and sometimes even aiding in the resolution of the initial incongruity. An example of the former case appears in (36) below, where the image of Jesus and his followers sharpens the contrast between the top text and the bottom text, and the text of the meme would make little sense without this image. Meme (37) is different, this time helping with the interpretation, since the photo of Trump becomes essential to understand the textual incongruity correctly:

(36)	Top text:	What is best in life?
	Image:	Jesus surrounded by his devoted followers.
	Bottom text:	Crush your enemies. See them driven before you. Hear the lamentations of other women.
(37)	Top text:	Says he'll create 25 million new jobs.
	Image:	Donald Trump.
	Bottom text:	Went bankrupt 4 times.

4. *Discourse-image based IR.* This category shows an image which clashes with the accompanying text and hence it is invariably essential to arrive at the intended humorous interpretation of the meme. A first group of memes such as those in (38–39) exhibit plain text-image contrast:

(38)	Top text:	I want to go to Taco Bell.
	Image:	Woman weeping intensely.
	Bottom text:	But I'm on an all-carb diet.
(39)	Top text:	I'm hungry.
	Image:	Woman weeping intensely.
	Bottom text:	But I already brushed my teeth.

A second group is made up of memes that trigger ironic interpretations, as it happened in Fig. 7.1 above. And a third group comprises the frequent instances referred to as *second-order incongruity* in Yus (2021c). As already mentioned in this book, this label applies to images that are taken from films or TV programmes (e.g. stills) which are re-used in the different context of a meme. On this occasion, incongruity does not lie so much in the clash between the image and the text *inside* the meme, but rather in that occurring between the text and the image as it was initially produced in the context of the film or the TV programme. A similar strategy comes into play in the so-called *photomanipulated memes* (Tay 2015), also known as *photoshop memes* (Tella 2018), which are approached similarly to the use of green screens in filmmaking, since some portion of an image is cropped out and placed in an alternative setting (the meme). Some of the *LOLitics memes* analysed by Tay (ibid.) adopt this format. Although *photomanipulation* and *photoshopping* demand an extra set of skills (and an increased effort in production, and perhaps in reception as well, demanding intertextual links to the initial visual environment of the cropped image), they are ultimately not difficult to create, especially with free software availability.

5. *Discourse-based IR, the image plays no role.* This time, incongruity arises when inferring the information supplied by the text of the meme (via polysemy, words with similar pronunciation, phrase ambiguity...) without the image helping at all in enhancing incongruity or aiding in its resolution. For instance, "get high" in the top text of (40) is polysemic and the initial interpretation is invalidated by the bottom text, the image playing no role whatsoever in this IR pattern:

(40)	Top text:	Let's all get high
	Image:	Photo of a black man.
	Bottom text:	Grades on our finals.

6. *Discourse-based IR, the image aids.* Here the image proves helpful in directing the user towards one of the senses of a word or a phrase in the top text. Thus, the image of the philosopher Kant in (41) contributes to entertain the ambiguity of meme:

(41)	Top text:	I want to stop philosophizing
	Image:	A portrait of philosopher Kant.
	Bottom text:	But I Kant.

7. *Discourse-based, the image is essential.* This final category portrays the image as key to make sense of the humorous intention of the meme as a whole. Two examples are provided in Fig. 7.7, where the top text contains an ambiguous phrase. In the meme on the left, the ambiguity is conveyed through *covered*. The image of the Muslim man saves mental effort upon selecting an interpretation for the top text, which will inevitably be inferred as "should be covered [with clothes]." Then, the bottom text invalidates this choice and reminds the audience of a latent, less relevant (though still possible) interpretation: "should be covered [by social security]." The same happens with the phrase *beating women* in the meme on the right: paired with the image of a fierce-looking man, it inevitably favours the interpretation of these words as "hurting women."

Yus (2022) explained this kind of text-image combination relating it to what was called *preparatory discourse* in Yus (2020). Summing up, and as already mentioned in this book, the term broadly refers to discourses that the speaker strategically places in a joke for the purpose of leading the hearer in a specific inferential direction, and was defined as follows: "Part of an utterance or dialogue that is intentionally situated in the joke in order to influence the kind of inference applied to (an)other piece(s) of discourse inside the joke." As such, a preparatory discourse has as its main purpose to keep certain information vivid in the hearer's working memory (i.e. the short-term memory store), whose associated encyclopaedic information is enacted as part of the overall construction of an appropriate mental scenario to comprehend the joke (*make-sense frame*, see Yus 2013a, 2016). Such situational labelling occurs in parallel to (and also influencing) the normal relevance-seeking cumulative procedure through which we interpret any utterance. Consider these examples:

(42) Contraceptives should be used on every conceivable occasion.
(43) Two antennas met on a roof, fell in love and got married. The ceremony wasn't much, but the reception was excellent.

In (42), the "pregnancy schema" (*make-sense frame*) is already active in the hearer's mind thanks to the strategic appearance of *contraceptives* as a preparatory discourse at the beginning of the joke. This word makes the initially more accessible or relevant "imaginable" interpretation clash and co-occur with the "prone to pregnancy" interpretation, humorous effects stemming from this co-occurrence of interpretations. The same applies to (43), where two preparatory discourses may be identified. Firstly, the word *antennas* gives the hearer access to associated conceptual material (to provide television signal to single houses or buildings; the quality of this signal may vary depending on its location, and so on and so forth). And, secondly, the phrase *got married* also refers the hearer back to related elements within that make-sense frame (e.g. it involves a formal performance, guests are then invited to meet at a subsequent banquet or party...). The aforesaid information acquires prominence through the inference of these two preparatory discourses, which in turn influence how the word *reception* is eventually inferred (and ambiguously entertained) at the end of the joke.

This proposal may also be valid for the memes in Fig. 7.7, this time conceptualised as *visual preparatory discourses.* Here, the images would work as visual preparatory discourses that lead the viewer to select a specific interpretation of *be covered* (to wear clothes) and *beating women* (hurting women), both of them subsequently becoming invalidated, thus forcing the audience to backtrack and replace them with other meanings.

Fig. 7.7 Images in memes working as *visual preparatory discourses*

5 *Ad hoc* Visual Referent Adjustment in Memes

This is an inferential strategy that is frequently at work in memes due to their typical "meme family ascription" (and also in visual metaphors too, see Yus 2009). This strategy has been labelled as *ad hoc visual referent adjustment*, due to its resemblance with verbal *ad hoc* concept adjustment (Yus 2021a, 2021c). This inferential strategy for meme comprehension places different texts attached to the very same image belonging to a meme family and constrain the interpretations initially inferred from the visual referent of that image, a kind of *modal affordance* (Jewitt 2016, 72), where the ultimate interpretation of the visual mode is constrained by the verbal mode.

Concept adjustment, as proposed by RT, has so far been only applied to verbal communication in the relevance-theoretic literature (but see Yus 2021a, 2021c). In a nutshell, and as commented upon previously in this book, during the interpretation process, the hearer adjusts prototypical concept encoded by a word so that it can meet their expectations of relevance. The outcome of this adjustment is an *ad hoc concept* which resembles, but is not identical to, the stabilised concept coded by the word (Carston 2002, 322).

The innovative inferential concept-related strategy found in memes is that, in addition to the usual concept adjustment required for verbal content (involving *narrowing* or *broadening* or both as it happens in many metaphors), sometimes the user also has to engage in an inferential adjustment, though this time applied to the referent of the image in the meme. This takes place in several series of memes (i.e. *families*) which share the same image and where users change the accompanying text in humorous ways. Such texts trigger slightly different interpretations of the prototypical image referent, which is why the inferential strategy leading to these slightly altered interpretations may be called *ad hoc visual referent adjustment*.

Users are aware that there are many different texts for the same image in meme families and know that sometimes the relationship between image and text in the meme is far from straightforward. A frequent example can be found in memes with an image of a person making a certain gesture. Upon finding an instance of this series of memes, the user will infer the gesture portrayed in the image, albeit not simply as its typical (i.e. default) interpretation of the gesture, but also with added interpretive (i.e. *ad hoc*) inferential variations depending on the text appearing above and below the image, a proper case of adjustment but here applied to the

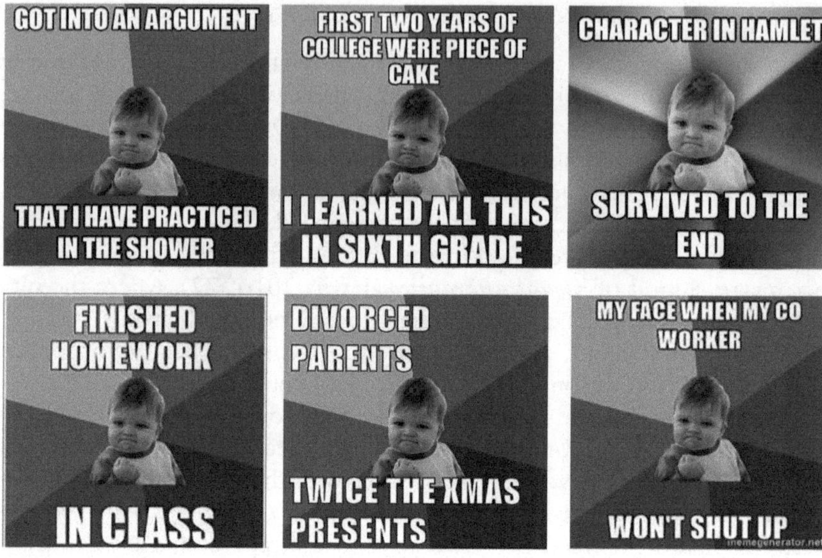

Fig. 7.8 *Ad hoc* visual referents in a series of memes

referent of the gesture depicted in the image. On some occasions, the resulting *ad hoc visual referent* will be *narrower* than the prototypical, default coded referent provided by the image. Other times, the user will infer a *broader* referent than the default one instead. The outcome will be, once again, an *ad hoc visual referent* that meets the user's expectation of relevance upon interpreting the meme, and works specifically for this meme and not for other image-text relationships identified in the remaining memes of the same series (i.e. a repeated image with different texts attached to it).

Take, for instance, the memes depicted in Fig. 7.8. The prototypical nonverbal behaviour depicted in the image (the little child's gesture and hand movement) is generally interpreted as the child being proud of having achieved some goal. However, this default, prototypical interpretation has to be adjusted (either narrowed or broadened) so as to correctly match the kind of feeling enacted by the actions described in the texts placed above and below that same image in those memes. Hence, the *ad hoc visual referent* inferred for the gesture will change when accompanied by the text *Finished homework in class* (more like "sheer pride") or by the text

Divorced parents. Twice the Xmas presents (roughly "intense joy"). In all of these instances, the user needs to adjust the referent of the gesture according to the accompanying text, even though the gesture (and its default coded prototypical meaning) remains identical across this *meme family*.

6 The Specificity of Covid-19 Memes

During the coronavirus pandemic that broke out in 2020 -and, above all, during the lockdown of the whole Spanish population that took place between March and May of that year, as well as in many other countries around the world- memes circulated massively on social networking sites and messaging apps. They played an essential role in relieving the sadness derived from the constant loss of human lives caused by the virus, in adding a note of humour to a painful stage in the lives of millions of people, in emphasising the mutuality of information about day-to-day life during the pandemic, and in alleviating the collective grievance provoked by the deprivation of freedom, the loss of jobs, etc.[18]

The subtleties of communication during the Covid-19 pandemic will be added to the prototypical schema of communication through memes reproduced in Fig. 7.9. The schema starts with a user who wants to share a meme with an audience. This meme-based communicative act depends on a series of *user-related contextual constraints* such as, for example, their personality, age,[19] or current mood and the cultural environment to which they belong (Cancelas-Ouviña 2021; Mifdal 2022), together with other "inherited" features, e.g. the user's sex and ethnic origin (Gbadegesin 2020; Harlow et al. 2020; Dynel and Messerli 2020; Bischetti et al. 2021;

[18] Martínez-Cardama and García-López (2021) trace the five stages of grief across the timeframe during which Covid memes were produced: denial, anger, bargaining, depression and acceptance.

[19] In general, memes are associated with young users. Cabrera Franco (2021) remarks that "the meme is above all a discourse for the youth due to the technological appropriation that it demands, the references to contemporary popular culture into which they are integrated, and their daily use on digital social networks of which they are themselves the largest users" (my translation). Aronson and Jaffal (2022, 526) add that the use of memes by the younger generations equally provides them with a means to criticise older generations, since young people's memes broadly "draw on sarcasm and popular culture references to both reproduce and create shared generational experiences and social space in opposition to older generations."

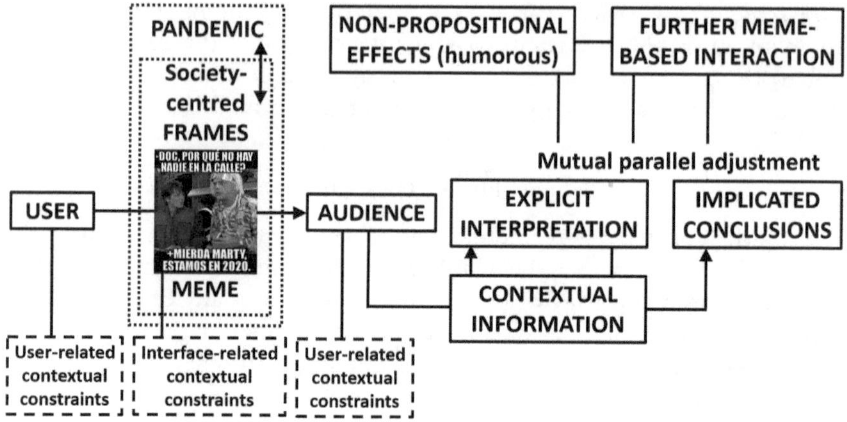

Fig. 7.9 Prototypical schema of meme-mediated communication

Outley et al. 2021).[20] This "sender user" produces a meme focused on the pandemic that more or less noticeably evokes ideas and assumptions supposedly shared by the whole community that was suffering the consequences of both the pandemic and the lockdown at that time. This would fit Kecskes (2014) notion of *core common ground*, general and broad background information supposedly shared by a whole community, as it happens with information regarding the pandemic. A parallel type suggested by Kecskes (ibid.), namely *emergent common ground*, is pervasive on the Net, given the heterogeneous quality of user's audiences (*context collapse*) and the difficulty to predict intersecting areas of mutuality among these users. According to Diedrichsen (2022, 255), both types of common ground are found in meme-related communication:

> For the production of memes and their appreciation by fellow users, the core common ground is the shared interest and expertise in popular culture and social media content. A meme's character as a sign is generally an emergent one, as there is no previous convention for the particular form-meaning

[20] Dynel and Messerli (2020, 213) propose the concept of *nation memes*, "which encompasses not only digital ethnic humour but also digital humour about peoples, sociocultural and historical facts and phenomena, which meme creators consider to be typical of a particular nation. It is evident that cultural scripts will vary according to the meme creators' perspectives."

> constellation. Digital media bear a flood of new contents in every minute, and not every one of them becomes a meme with a usage convention. When a new picture-text combination appears, participants may eventually tune in on a common usage and a recognizable form-meaning correlation. Productions that do not catch on with other users will not reach meme status. Therefore, with the dynamicity and fast pace in which internet contents are created and shared, there is an aspect of emergent common ground to any meme usage, as there is great uncertainty as to whether a given convention is stable enough to be relied upon.

The expectation about the existence and mutuality of such knowledge will largely depend on whether the interpreting audience is a single interlocutor or includes multiple users. Certainly, if it does not take place between two single users, internet communication notoriously exhibits a heterogeneity of audiences that makes predictions of accessibility to this contextual source less fine-grained. Indeed, today's *context collapse* scenario (Marwick and boyd 2011) features users with a highly heterogeneous array of friends, relatives and acquaintances in their messaging apps, as well as on their social networking sites. Such audiences may eventually react to the intended pandemic-related interpretation and expected background information in radically different ways, to which must be added the presence of those lurkers whose comprehension of the meme frequently lacks an appropriate mutuality of contextual information with the user who posted the discourse (included in what Gal et al. 2022, call *contextual knowledge*). Predictably, many users tend to create pandemic-related memes with an expectation of context accessibility and remain "on the safe side" by relying on very general background information on this painful period, or easy-to-access commonsense assumptions about the world that we were then forced to live in, as well as regarding society as a whole.

Interface-related constraints are also at work in meme-based communication. By way of example, memes are not shared in the same way on messaging apps and on social networking sites, especially as regards the options to comment on and further interact from that initial meme-based message.

In any case, the audience will use the information provided by the text, the image or the convergence of both discursive modes in the meme to extract an explicit interpretation and, if necessary, some implicated conclusion (implicature) from the meme. Context accessibility becomes crucial for both, and these inferential strategies (explicature, implicature, access to contextual information) are performed in parallel. Furthermore, the act of sending the meme can trigger subsequent sustained interactions centred upon the pandemic. In Covid-19 memes, though, the non-propositional effects (feelings, emotions, and a collective mutual awareness of Covid-related information) generated by these memes stand out as one of the major sources of relevance for the users involved, adding a humorous note to the users' collective suffering and emphasising more or less novel behaviours due to lockdown, among other things.

Rivas Carmona and Calero Vaquera (2020) propose a classification of Covid-19 memes into four types: (1) memes that portray a critical and vindictive behaviour, e.g. against imposed anti-Covid rules, highlighting the negative impact of lockdown on people's health, against politicians (or authorities, governments…) and their Covid-referred policies…; (2) emotionally laden memes stemming from empathy, gratitude, compassion or sympathy, to quote but a few feelings; (3) playful memes solely aiming at making users have a good time amidst the collective suffering; and (4) memes that underline the truthfulness or falsity of Covid-related information. Regardless of the type, however, many users intuitively feel that the effect of Covid-19 memes goes beyond merely generating humorous effects and that these memes have undoubtedly played a key role in the media ecosystem that brought people together and alleviated their suffering in 2020. This specificity has already been addressed in several studies, two of which will be singled out and analysed in the next Sections of this chapter.

6.1 Covid-19 Memes and the Incongruity-Resolution Pattern

Yus and Maíz-Arévalo (2021, 2023) compared 150 Covid-19 memes in Spanish with the 7-case proposal of Yus (2021c) reproduced in Table 7.3 above, their incongruity-resolution (IR) patterns being contrasted too. The outcome of this analysis appears in Table 7.4, which also includes non-Covid meme percentages between parentheses for the sake of comparison.

The first outstanding feature of the contrasted corpora is that a higher percentage of Covid-19 memes need no incongruity-resolution pattern to convey the message, generate effects and arouse the interest of a potential audience (29.30% as opposed to 8.66% in non-Covid memes). This probably happens because making pandemic-related information mutually manifest to others and reflecting on the new life imposed on Spanish citizens (lockdown) suffice to generate the desired effects, without the need

Table 7.4 Incongruity-resolution patterns in Covid-19 memes (Yus and Maíz-Arévalo 2021, forthcoming)

		Type of incongruity	*Role of image*
38.00% (31.33%)	**21.30%** (8.66%)	Frame-based	The image plays no role
	0.70% (18.00%)	Frame-based	The image aids
	16.00% (4.67%)	Frame-based	The image is essential
24.00% (38.67%)		Discourse-image based	The image is essential
8.70% (21.34%)	**7.30%** (8.00%)	Discourse-based	The image plays no role
	0.70% (7.34%)	Discourse-based	The image aids
	0.70% (6.00%)	Discourse-based	The image is essential
29.30% (8.66%)		No incongruity	

for an explicit IR pattern. These memes propose alternative interpretations of popular media discourses (11.4%), signal collective mutuality of general background assumptions (20.5%) and strengthen the collective status of Covid-related information (66.1%). This last topic is sub-divided into topics such as: criticism of government's actions to tackle the pandemic[21] (6.9%); expected behaviour to prevent a further spread of the virus (16%); people's overall habits during the lockdown (18.2%); and the impact of both the pandemic and the lockdown on people's wellbeing (11.25%).

Regarding frame-based incongruities, a high percentage in the Covid-19 corpus centre their humorous strategy on this strategy, especially those memes in which the image plays no role (21.30% against 8.66% of non-Covid memes). A possible explanation lies in the fact that users do not need any linguistic manipulations to transmit their pandemic-related message and generate the intended effects, which is why they prefer either to emphasise the mutual awareness of collective frames that, until the advent of the pandemic, seemed normal and were taken for granted or to invalidate them in the backdrop of the 2020 lockdown. Almost 90% of the frame-based memes in which there is no image or where it plays no role whatsoever entail an inferential clash with parallelly retrieved

[21] Among the many studies on this overlay of Covid memes and political criticism, see Gibson (2021) for an account of how memes related to the pandemic were used in South Africa to criticise the government; Ndlovu (2021) in the Zimbabwean context; and Nabea (2021), and also Githinji and Omwoha (2021) with regard to Kenya.

Covid-specific background assumptions that become essential to understand the meme. An example can be found in meme (44a), which clashes with the addressee user's background information (44b), and whose resolution demands accessibility to contextual information (44c). Similarly, the text-based meme in (45a) would have been a normal complaint to make in non-Covid times, given the commonsense information in (45b). However, this information clashes with pandemic-related assumption (45c):

(44) a. Última hora: Marruecos intercepta una patera llena de madrileños. [*Breaking news: Morocco intercepts a boat (patera) filled with people from Madrid*].
b. These boats are normally filled with African migrants, not people from Madrid.
c. Nobody is allowed to leave their houses during lockdown, but people from Madrid will do the utmost to reach their second residences on the coast despite lockdown, even if illegally.

(45) a. Dan lluvia para el viernes. Se nos va a joder el finde. [*They forecast rain for Friday. It's going to ruin our weekend*].
b. Weekends are normally the time of the week to enjoy ourselves, go out, have fun.
c. People cannot leave their homes due to the pandemic.

Such pandemic-centred assumptions mix up with other background assumptions that may also prove necessary to understand the meme properly. For example, Aronson and Jaffal (2022) claim that Covid-19 memes also work on a generational basis. Younger generations critically mingle ironically treated Covid-19 information with very specific assumptions drawn from their own store of beliefs and cultural representations (see Yus forthcoming-b). The Facebook group under analysis, *Zoom Memes for Self-Quaranteens*, is filled with critical irony by younger users, and "the combination of references to popular culture during their youth with sarcasm makes many of the memes incomprehensible to older generations" (p. 527).

Furthermore, the image is essential in 16% of frame-based Covid-19 memes (compared to 4.67% of non-Covid ones). Normally, these memes have as their aim to clash with an existing background frame (30.43%), to impose Covid-related information on an existing frame (30.43%), and to trigger a clash with stored information on visual referents or on the "syntax" of combined images (39.1%). The last case seems interesting, because the resolution to the incongruity detected at the visual level can only be

Fig. 7.10 Memes that exploit the user's stored background information on images and their "syntax"

reconciled by retrieving certain pandemic-specific information. A few examples are supplied in Fig. 7.10 (Yus and Maíz-Arévalo 2023: 21).

The first meme in Fig. 7.10 portrays a striking mixture of two people in charge of safety on the beach (Baywatch). Instead of holding lifesavers, as could be expected from the stored visual syntax of such an image, they carry a huge ruler and a protractor, which puzzles the audience. The resolution necessarily demands retrieving the contextual information in (46a) below. The second meme equally gives food for thought: although the text at the top ("Day 856 of lockdown. A6 Madrid-Coruña") is compatible with the image, the user cannot help being struck by its anomalous syntax, which combines a motorway and a jungle in a single, worrying picture. In turn, the third meme resorts to another surprising type of visual syntax bringing together a beach and the number display typically used in markets to show whose turn it is. Once again, the user needs to access pandemic-related contextual information such as (46b) below to be able to resolve the incongruity in this awkward visual syntax. Finally, the fourth meme contains no text and the humorous strategy entirely revolves around the anomaly of its visual image syntax. This time, the juxtaposition of two dogs and the Holy Week procession confuses the user, resolution being only possible by accessing and humorously combining two Covid-centred pieces of information from context, as quoted in (47a-b) below.

(46) a. After a decrease in Covid-19 infections, people were again allowed to go to the beach but strict distancing measures had to be taken. Some workers were hired to ensure that the law was enforced.

b. After a decrease in Covid-19 infections, people were again allowed to go to the beach, and one of the measures to prevent the spread of the virus was to control the number of people who could gather at the beach at specific times of the day.

(47) a. Faithful believers will do the utmost to follow the Holy Week procession outdoors despite lockdown.

b. People can only leave their homes to go to the supermarket or walk their dogs.

Continuing with the seven-case proposal of IR patterns (Yus 2021c) now applied to Covid-19 memes, case four of clashes between text and image (the latter being essential) was deemed very important, and even a distinctive pattern of meme-based communication (38.67%). When it comes to Covid-related memes, fewer of them resort to this pattern (24%) because users prefer to implement frame-based strategies, as already highlighted. The analysis yielded that 52.8% of these memes draw on text-image incompatibility to generate critical implications, to underline collective background assumptions (22.2%) as well as collective fears linked to the pandemic (8.33%), and to impose an alternative interpretation of images (16.6%). Figure 7.11 collects some of these memes. On the left, the meme's text ("I am going to the supermarket -Mercadona- Do you want anything?") should look incompatible with the image; however, the initial clash is resolved via background assumptions about the risks that going to the supermarket during the pandemic entailed. The meme in the middle equally contains a text ("First day of school after lockdown") which does not seem to match with the image. The context of the

Fig. 7.11 Memes where text and image clash to generate pandemic-related implications

pandemic allows for the derivation of implications based on collective fears, though. Finally, both the top text ("Humankind in 2020") and the bottom text ("Teachers teaching online") in the meme on the right impose alternative critical (i.e. metaphorical) interpretations of adjacent images taken from the film *Titanic*. The sinking ship now metaphorically reflects the decline of the human species under the virus, which does not prevent teachers from sticking to teaching despite the inevitable outcome, as connoted by the picture of the band playing on the deck of the ship upon her imminent sinking.

The analysis of our corpus likewise identified text-based memes without an image or in which the image played no role at all in the relevance of the eventual interpretation; the percentage was similar to the one found in non-Covid memes (around 8%). The key to effectiveness in these memes lies in: the ambiguities between the literal and figurative/idiomatic senses of words or phrases (10%); certain inferential strategies performed to understand the text (20%); and especially, the generation of ambiguities where an initial relevant interpretation becomes invalidated and has to be replaced with another supposedly less relevant one (70%). Meme (48) shows an example of play with literal (49a) and metaphorical (49b) interpretations of *lavarse la manos* (wash one's hands). Meme (50) humorously exploits the strategy of disambiguation for *prórroga* (extra time in sport matches vs. extended lockdown during the pandemic). While interpreting this meme, the initial relevant interpretation (51a) biased by the barrage of pandemic-related information arriving at people's smartphones at that time (extended lockdown) is invalidated and has to be replaced with another interpretation (51b) that had hitherto not been taken into account (extra time in sport matches).

(48) El coronavirus no acabará con ningún político de este país, porque si en algo son buenos es en lavarse las manos.
[*Coronavirus will not kill any politician in this country, because if there's something they are good at, is at washing their hands (of things)*].

(49) a. Literal: To clean one's hands to prevent the spread of the virus.
b. Metaphorical: To avoid responsibility on a certain matter, specifically on the control of the pandemic and increasing deaths.

(50) Yo creo que otra prórroga es una barbaridad. Deberíamos ir a penaltis ya.
[*I think another extension is ridiculous. We should go straight to the penalty shootout*].

(51) a. We should not extend lockdown any further.
b. We should not have another extra time in this football match.

6.2 *Covid-19 Memes and "The Joy of Sharing"*

Another account for the impression that Covid-19 memes fulfil supplementary functions beyond the mere generation of humorous effects is proposed by Yus (2021d),[22] basically claiming that the aim of these Covid-19 memes was, one way or another, to emphasise the fact that users share certain Covid-related information and, more specifically, the feelings associated with the mutual awareness of sharing this information. Five distinctive strategies became clear:

1. The first strategy is the use of Covid-19 memes as a therapeutic tool to cope with the collective suffering during the pandemic. Just like it happened with other harmful events such as the 11S attacks to the Twin Towers in New York (see Kuipers 2002), self-deprecating humour and overall laugh at the challenges imposed on a whole population trigger a certain alleviation of collective suffering (Flecha Ortiz et al. 2021; Ponton 2021, 769). Several authors point in the same direction:

> Humor helps individuals alleviate stress, mitigate suffering, and dissipate feelings of anxiety, and grants people a sense of power and control in helpless situations (Blaber et al. 2021).
>
> Humor helps explore cognitive alternatives in response to stressful situations and reduces the negative affective consequences of a real or perceived threat. Hence, turning to humor during a crisis helps manage stress and maintain emotional well-being (Abel 2002).
>
> Telling jokes during trying times, for example, can 'provide for the cathartic release of anxiety or anger while bringing people together and reinforcing the boundaries between in- and out-group' (Hernan 2016, in Agbese and Agbese 2021).
>
> A person displaying humour is able to laugh at their own shortcomings and difficult circumstances despite the emotional intensity of the negative experiences (Aslan 2022).

[22] This reference refers to a lecture available at: https://www.youtube.com/watch?v=wCCkyR663D8

Fig. 7.12 Covid-19 memes shared among users to alleviate collective suffering

> During lockdown, making people laugh was a way to communicate emotions and stay in touch. [It] triggered positive emotions and created a mental state which acted as a "social lubricant" (Amici 2020).

Similarly, Covid-19 memes perform an alleviating role at a time of collective suffering during the pandemic (Ernest-Samuel 2021, 162). For example, the memes in Fig. 7.12, whose texts are translated in (52) below, serve as a humorous way to cope with the stress and suffering due to the impossibility of travelling because of the pandemic (meme on the left), of carrying out normal lives because of the imposed lockdown (middle) and to alleviate the stress caused by the virus to the whole Spanish population (right).

(52) a. Change of plans for Easter.
b. Stay at home but lead normal lives.
c. Here, painting a mandala to relax.

2. The second strategy consists in playing with existing background information (*frames*) supposedly shared by the whole population. This time, unlike what happened with the frame-based incongruities encountered while processing the text of the meme, the incongruities contained in these Covid-19 memes refer us back to broader frames regarding what life used to be like before the pandemic, a life that people took for granted until the pandemic turned it upside

down. The humorous exploitation of specific *make-sense frames* constructed to understand the meme texts is found, as attested in memes (53–54), though much less frequently than those which emphasise broader incongruities with stored frames about pre-Covid lifestyle. Again, achieving a mutuality of this information suffices to obtain the desired effects: to be reminded of what was lost in our way of life due to the virus.

(53) Me estoy volviendo loca sin ir al gym, con esta semana ya van 5 años. [*I am going crazy without going to the gym; this week it's been 5 years already*].

(54) Día 26 del confinamiento. Me he montado un gimnasio en casa… TAMPOCO VOY.
[*Day 26 of lockdown. I have set up a gym at home… I AM NOT GOING EITHER*].

3. A third strategy has to do with revealing areas of mutually of information via successful meme communication. This contextual information becomes necessary to understand the meme properly, its mutuality (mutual manifestness in RT terminology) being additionally *revealed* when the user succeeds in correctly interpreting the meme.[23] The effect is a sort of *joy of mutual manifestness* derived from this mutual awareness of the mutual manifestness of this specific Covid-related information[24]

For example, proper comprehension of meme (55) requires the retrieval of information (56) from context and its successful interpretation (and possibly further meme-based interaction between users) will trigger a vivid perception of the mutual manifestness of this pandemic-related information. The same applies to visual information. Figure 7.13 illustrates how the effectiveness of these mainly visual memes relies on the audience's

[23] See Chłopicki and Brzozowska (2021) for an application of this idea to Covid memes in the Polish context.

[24] As analysed in Chap. 6, the notion of *joy of mutual manifestness* was initially proposed for the outcome of many stand-up comedy monologues (see Yus 2004, 2005, 2016). In these monologues, the comedian very often bases the humorous effects on reminding the audience of the collective status of certain assumptions and, on some occasions, on reminding the audience that previously thought-to-be personal assumptions are actually collective and shared by all the audience in the venue.

Fig. 7.13 Covid-19 memes whose correct interpretation demands access to specific contextual information

ability to retrieve from context information about people's utterly unjustified obsession with collecting toilet paper during the lockdown (see Hermes and Kopitz 2022).

(55) Image: A dog on a sofa. It looks really exhausted.
Text: Pero si ya me has sacado 38 veces hoy.
[*You've taken me out for a walk 38 times already today*].

(56) During lockdown in Spain, people could only leave home to get food or take the dog for a walk, so dog owners took their dogs for a walk very frequently.

Ponton and Mantello (2021, 50) also mention the obsession with toilet paper, specifically regarding a meme in which a supermarket trolley is situated next to the famous screaming person by Munch. Several questions arise upon seeing this striking combination of items:

> 'why is this person screaming'?, 'what could they be looking at'?, 'what relevance could this image have in the current social climate'?, and so on. In a process of explication, possible answers suggest missing information, perhaps a voice only audible to the figure in the image, saying for example that 'supermarkets have run out of toilet paper'. The question of frame/script is also relevant; in this image it is that of classical (post-modern) art. The associations of Munch's painting are generally described in terms of existential

angst, alienation and the like. While this may be entirely appropriate for the condition of man in the time of Covid-19, the social satire concerns the fact that there really is no point stock-piling toilet paper, an irrelevant item in the current context.

4. A fourth strategy seeks to emphasise the phatic quality of Covid-19 memes and its usefulness as a means to trigger further interaction and obtain an offset of feelings of connectedness or co-presence, and eventually a sense of bonding and of being supported among the users involved in the act of meme communication (Bauer and Ngondo 2022, 48; Powell 2020; O'Boyle 2022, 460). In Yus (2021a) a trend is mentioned about today's internet interactions occurring as an attempt to satisfy phatic needs, rather than to provide users with objectively relevant information. In general, as Miller (2008) contended, we are currently witnessing a shift from dialogue and communication meant to facilitate an exchange of substantive content, to a situation where the actual maintenance of a network has become the primary focus. Thus, communication is now subordinated to the role of the simple maintenance of users' networks and to the notion of a connected presence.[25] Such phatic use of Covid-19 memes suits the label *affiliative humour* proposed in Martin et al. (2003), for whom the *raison d'être* of memes is to help people relate to other users and facilitate relationships. In fact, the analysis of Covid-19 memes carried out in Maíz-Arévalo and Yus (2021) revealed that affiliative humour was, by far, the most frequent type of humour in these memes (51%, as opposed to 27% of aggressive humour, 9% of self-enhancing humour, and 13% of self-deprecating humour). This comes as no surprise because during the pandemic users tried to promote unity (the "we-are-all-in-the-same-boat" idea). This was also linguistically reflected in the use of inclusive pronouns and 1st person plural verbs, and the assumption of essential shared knowledge to use intertextuality referents (sociocultural background knowledge, e.g. songs).

[25] The presence is *ambient*, "in the sense that such networks foster not only dialogical communication in explicit interactions but also forms of communion around shared practices such as hashtagging and the production of memes where users do not necessarily engage in direct exchanges" (Zappavigna 2020, 205).

5. Finally, a strategy used in Covid-19 meme communication pursues to emphasise mutuality of information via successful retrieval of the essential information to derive implicatures from the explicit verbal-visual discourse of the meme. In this case, the successful inferential outcome reinforces the mutuality of the contextual information needed to draw these implicatures effectively. For example, in meme (57) the contextual information (58) allows the audience to obtain the implicature (59) and at the same time triggers a mutual awareness regarding this contextual information. The same applies to (60), whose implicature (62) necessarily demands access to the contextual information supplied in (61). The successful inferential outcome once more reveals the mutuality of this information between the sender user and addressee user.

(57) Top text: Esta no es la mascarilla con la que fuiste al cole esta mañana.
[*This is not the mask you went to school with this morning*].
Image: Father talking to his son, who is wearing a face mask.
Bottom text: No, esta es mucho más chula! Me la cambié con Diego y él se la cambió a Lucas.
[*No, this one is much cooler! I exchanged mine with Diego and he exchanged his with Lucas*].

(58) Information from context:
a. People have to wear face masks due to the pandemic.[26]
b. Sharing face masks is a clear source of contagion among people.

(59) Implicature:
This child is putting his classmates' health and his at risk.

(60) Image: Booths of the famous April Fair in Seville, upon which big labels of *Estanco* (Tobacconist's), *Tintorería* (Dry Cleaner's) and *Peluquería* (Hairdresser's) have been placed.

(61) Information from context:
a. During lockdown, Spanish people were only allowed to leave their houses in order to perform essential activities.
b. During lockdown, collective festivities and celebrations were prohibited.

[26] See Dynel (2022a, 2022b) and Nabea (2021) for analyses about the specificity of Covid meme humour based on wearing face masks.

(62) Implicature:
People in Seville will do the utmost to get to celebrate their April Fair.

7 Concluding Remarks

In this chapter, several strategies to generate humour through the use of memes have been thoroughly described and exemplified, with special emphasis on the famous incongruity-resolution pattern. Some attention has also been devoted to the specificity of humour from Covid-19 memes, providing possible explanations to why users find them different from normal memes.

In sum, and without the shadow of a doubt, memes stand out as one of the most pervasive humorous discourses on the Net nowadays, and the variability in the discursive modes that shape them (text-only, image-only, text-image), alongside other formats such as video, makes memes become a very interesting discourse for the objectives of this book.

References

Abel, Millicent H. 2002. Humor, Stress, and Coping Strategies. *Humor* 15 (4): 365–381. https://doi.org/10.1515/humr.15.4.365.

Agbese, Aje-Ori, and Edeanya Agbese. 2021. 'Coromentality': Nigerians' Use of Memetic Humour During the COVID-19 Lockdowns. In *Digital Humour in the Covid-19 Pandemic. Perspectives from the Global South*, ed. Shepherd Mpofu, 75–100. Cham: Palgrave Macmillan. https://doi.org/10.1007/978-3-030-79279-4_4.

Amici, Patrizia. 2020. Humor in the Age of Covid-19 Lockdown: An Explorative Qualitative Study. *Psychiatria Danubina* 32 (Suppl. 1): 15–20.

Arizzi, Cristina. 2019. Digital Memes and US Pop Politics. Dynamism and Pervasiveness of a Digital Genre in the Mobile Web Era. *Lingue e Linguaggi* 30: 45–64. https://doi.org/10.1285/i22390359v30p45.

Aronson, Pamela, and Islam Jaffal. 2022. Zoom Memes for Self-Quaranteens: Generational Humor, Identity, and Conflict During the Pandemic. *Emerging Adulthood* 10 (2): 519–533. https://doi.org/10.1177/21676968211058513.

Aslan, Erhan. 2022. Days of Our 'Quarantined' Lives. Multimodal Humour in COVID-19 Internet Memes. *Internet Pragmatics* 5 (2): 227–256. https://doi.org/10.1075/ip.00075.asl.

Attardo, Salvatore. 2020. Memes, Memeiosis, and Memetic Drift: Cheryl's Chichier She Shed. *Media Linguistics* 7 (2): 146–168. https://doi.org/10.21638/spbu22.2020.201.

Barthes, Roland. 1977. *Image-Music-Text*. London: Fontana.

Bauer, Janell C., and Prisca S. Ngondo. 2022. Moms, Memes, and Mitigating Pandemic Stress: Exploring Themes and Implications in an Academic Mamas' Facebook Group. *Women's Studies in Communication* 45 (1): 45–69. https://doi.org/10.1080/07491409.2022.2030607.

Bischetti, Luca, Paolo Canal, and Valentina Bambini. 2021. Funny but Aversive: A Large-Scale Survey of the Emotional Response to Covid-19 Humor in the Italian Population During the Lockdown. *Lingua* 249. https://doi.org/10.1016/j.lingua.2020.102963.

Blaber, Zlatinka, Guergana Gougoumanova, and Barry Palatnik. 2021. COVID-19 Editorial Cartoons: Theories of Humor Perspectives. *Israeli Journal of Humor Research* 10 (1): 6–42.

Blackmore, Susan. 1999. *The Meme Machine*. Oxford: Oxford University Press.

Börzsei, Linda K. 2013. Makes a Meme Instead: A Concise History of Internet Memes. *New Media Studies Magazine* 7: 152–183.

Boxman-Shabtai, Lillian, and Limor Shifman. 2014. Evasive Targets: Deciphering Polysemy in Mediated Humor. *Journal of Communication* 64 (5): 977–998. https://doi.org/10.1111/jcom.12116.

Brideau, Kate, and Charles Berret. 2014. A Brief Introduction to Impact: 'The Meme Font.'. *Journal of Visual Culture* 13 (3): 307–313. https://doi.org/10.1177/1470412914544515.

Brooke, Siân. 2019. 'There Are No Girls on the Internet': Gender Performances in Advice Animal Memes. *First Monday* 24 (10). https://doi.org/10.5210/fm.v24i10.9593.

Brown, Gavin. 2013. Web Culture: Using Memes to Spread and Manipulate Ideas on a Massive Scale. *Interface* 13: 187–193.

Burroughs, Benjamin. 2013. FCJ-165 Obama Trolling: Memes, Salutes and an Agonistic Politics in the 2012 Presidential Election. *The Fibreculture Journal* 22: 258–277.

Cabrera Franco, Tonatiuh. 2021. Significando desde el Encierro: El Meme como Auto Representación Juvenil de la COVID-19 [Meaning from Lockdown: The Meme as Youth's Self-Representation of Covid-19. *Boletín sobre Covid-19* 2(18).

Cancelas-Ouviña, Lucía-Pilar. 2021. Humor in Times of COVID-19 in Spain: Viewing Coronavirus Through Memes Disseminated via WhatsApp. *Frontiers in Psychology* 12. https://doi.org/10.3389/fpsyg.2021.611788.

Carston, Robyn. 2002. *Thoughts and Utterances*. Oxford: Blackwell. https://doi.org/10.1002/9780470754603.

Castaño Díaz, Carlos Mauricio. 2013. Defining and Characterizing the Concept of Internet Meme. *Revista CES Psicología* 6 (1): 82–104.

Chan, Eveline. 2011. Integrating Visual and Verbal Meaning in Multimodal Text Comprehension: Towards a Model of Intermodal Relations. In *Semiotic Margins. Meaning in Multimodalities*, ed. Shoshana Dreyfus, Susan Hood, and Maree Stenglin, 144–167. London: Continuum.

Chłopicki, Władysław, and Dorota Brzozowska. 2021. Sophisticated Humor against COVID-19: The Polish Case. *Humor* 34 (2): 201–227. https://doi.org/10.1515/humor-2021-0015.

Cochrane, Leslie, Alexandra Johnson, Aubrey Lay, and Ginny Helmandollar. 2022. "One Does not Simply Categorize a Meme": A Dual Classification System for Visual-Textual Internet Memes. *Proceedings of the Linguistic Society of America* 7 (1). https://doi.org/10.3765/plsa.v7i1.5260.

Cohn, Neil. 2013. Beyond Word Balloons and Thought Bubbles: The Integration of Text and Image. *Semiotica* 197: 35–63. https://doi.org/10.1515/sem-2013-0079.

Cottingham, Marci D., and Ariana Rose. in press. Tweeting Jokes, Tweeting Hope: Humor Practices during the 2014 Ebola Outbreak. *Health Communication*. https://doi.org/10.1080/10410236.2022.2045059.

Davison, Patrick. 2012. The Language of Internet Memes. In *The Social Media Reader*, ed. Michael Mandiberg, 120–134. New York: New York University Press.

Dawkins, Richard. 1976. *The Selfish Gene*. Oxford: Oxford University Press.

Diedrichsen, Elke. 2020. On the Interaction of Core and Emergent Common Ground in Internet Memes. *Internet Pragmatics* 3 (2): 223–259. https://doi.org/10.1075/ip.00033.die.

———. 2022. Common Ground in Linguistic Theory and Internet Pragmatics: Forms of Dynamic Multicultural Interaction. In *The Cambridge Handbook of Intercultural Pragmatics*, ed. Istvan Keckses, 245–273. Cambridge: Cambridge University Press. https://doi.org/10.1017/9781108884303.011.

Dynel, Marta. 2016. 'I Has Seen Image Macros!' Advice Animal Memes as Visual-verbal Jokes. *International Journal of Communication* 10: 660–688.

———. 2021. COVID-19 Memes Going Viral: On the Multiple Multimodal Voices Behind Face Masks. *Discourse & Society* 32 (2): 175–195. https://doi.org/10.1177/0957926520970385.

———. 2022a. La vida de los memes de mascarillas del COVID-19: Un estudio diacrónico del panorama memético durante la pandemia [The Life of Covid-19 Face Mask Memes: A Diachronic Study of the Memetic Panorama During the Pandemic]. *Comunicar* 72. https://doi.org/10.3916/C72-2022-06.

———. 2022b. Memefying Deception and Deceptive Memefication: Multimodal Deception on Social Media. In *From Lying to Perjury. Linguistic and Legal Perspectives on Lies and Other Falsehoods*, ed. Laurence R. Horn, 139–161. Berlin: De Gruyter. https://doi.org/10.1515/9783110733730-007.

Dynel, Marta, and Thomas C. Messerli. 2020. On a Cross-Cultural Memescape: Switzerland through Nation Memes from within and from the Outside. *Contrastive Pragmatics* 1: 210–241. https://doi.org/10.1163/26660393-bja10007.

El Refaie, Elisabeth, and Kathrin Hörschelmann. 2010. Young People's Readings of a Political Cartoon and the Concept of Multimodal Literacy. *Discourse:*

Studies in the Cultural Politics of Education 31 (2): 195–207. https://doi.org/10.1080/01596301003679719.

Ernest-Samuel, Gloria Chimeziem. 2021. Social Media Audience's Interpretation of Selected Humor Memes on Coronavirus Pandemic in Nigeria. In *Digital Humour in the Covid-19 Pandemic Perspectives from the Global South*, ed. Shepherd Mpofu, 145–164. Cham: Palgrave Macmillan. https://doi.org/10.1007/978-3-030-79279-4_7.

Eschler, Jornan, and Amanda Menking. 2018, June 4. 'No Prejudice Here': Examining Social Identity Work in Starter Pack Memes. *Social Media + Society*. https://doi.org/10.1177/2056305118768811.

Evnine, Simon J. 2018. The Anonymity of a Murmur: Internet (and Other) Memes. *British Journal of Aesthetics* 58 (3): 303–318. https://doi.org/10.1093/aesthj/ayy021.

Flecha Ortiz, José A., Maria A. Santos, Evelyn Lopez Corrada, and Virgin Dones. 2021. Analysis of the Use of Memes as an Exponent of Collective Coping During Covid-19 in Puerto Rico. *Media International Australia* 178 (1): 168–181. https://doi.org/10.1177/1329878X20966379.

Furió, Vicenç. 2002. *Ideas y Formas en la Representación Pictórica* [Ideas and Forms in Pictorial Representation]. University of Barcelona: Edicions de la Universitat de Barcelona.

Gal, Noam, Zohar Kampf, and Limor Shifman. 2022. SRSLY?? A Typology of Online Ironic Markers. *Information, Communication & Society* 25 (7): 992–1009. https://doi.org/10.1080/1369118X.2020.1814380.

Gbadegesin, Victoria O. 2020. Gender Ideology and Identity in Humorous Social Media Memes. *Digital Scholarship in the Humanities* 35 (3): 529–546. https://doi.org/10.1093/llc/fqz039.

Gibson, Sarah. 2021. 'South Africa Laughs in the Face of Coronavirus': Presidential Addresses, Face Masks, and Memetic Humour in South Africa. In *Communicating COVID-19. Interdisciplinary Perspectives*, ed. Monique Lewis, Eliza Govender, and Kate Holland, 277–298. Cham: Palgrave Macmillan. https://doi.org/10.1007/978-3-030-79735-5_14.

Gill, Talia. 2002. Visual and Verbal Playmates: An Exploration of Visual and Verbal Modalities in Children's Picture Books. Unpublished BA (Hons) Thesis, University of Sydney.

Githinji, Keziah Wangui, and Joyce Omwoha. 2021. The Use of Meme and Hashtags on Twitter Towards Government Response During the COVID-19 Curfew Announcement from 1 June to 14 June 2020. In *Digital Humour in the Covid-19 Pandemic. Perspectives from the Global South*, ed. Shepherd Mpofu, 295–317. Cham: Palgrave Macmillan. https://doi.org/10.1007/978-3-030-79279-4_14.

Guadagno, Rosanna E., Daniel M. Rempala, Shannon Murphy, and Bradley M. Okdie. 2013. What Makes a Video Go Viral? An Analysis of Emotional

Contagion and Internet Memes. *Computers in Human Behavior* 29: 2312–2319. https://doi.org/10.1016/j.chb.2013.04.016.

Han, Xiao, and Giselinde Kuipers. 2021. Humour and TikTok Memes During the 2020 Pandemic Lockdown: Tensions of Gender and Care Faced by Chinese Mothers Working from Home. *China Information* 35 (3): 393–419. https://doi.org/10.1177/0920203X211049634.

Harlow, Summer, Jerrica Ty Rowlett, and Laura-Kate Huse. 2020. 'Kim Davis Be Like…': A Feminist Critique of Gender Humor in Online Political Memes. *Information, Communication & Society* 23 (7): 1057–1073. https://doi.org/10.1080/1369118X.2018.1550524.

Hempelmann, Christian F., and Andrea C. Samson. 2008. Cartoons: Drawn Jokes? In *The Primer of Humor Research*, ed. Victor Raskin, 609–640. Berlin: Mouton de Gruyter. https://doi.org/10.1515/9783110198492.609.

Hernan, Andrew. 2016. Joking through Hardship: Humour and Truth-Telling among Displaced Timbuktians. *African Studies Review* 59 (1): 57–76. https://doi.org/10.1017/asr.2016.4

Hermes, Joke, and Linda Kopitz. 2022. 'We Can Sh*t for Another 10 Years.' Toilet Paper, Pandemic Politics and Cultural Citizenship. *Continuum* 36 (2): 244–259. https://doi.org/10.1080/10304312.2021.1998373.

Hirsch, Galia. 2019. Hitler's Out of Dope: A Cross-Cultural Examination of Humorous Memes. *Journal of Pragmatics* 149: 25–39. https://doi.org/10.1016/j.pragma.2019.06.003.

Jewitt, Carey. 2016. Multimodal Analysis. In *Handbook of Language and Digital Communication*, ed. Alexandra Georgakopoulou and Tereza Spilioti, 69–84. Abingdon: Routledge. https://doi.org/10.4324/9781315694344.ch4.

Jiang, Yaqian Jiang, and Camilla Vásquez. 2020. Exploring Local Meaning-Making Resources. A Case Study of a Popular Chinese Internet Meme (*biaoqingbao*). *Internet Pragmatics* 3 (2): 260–282. https://doi.org/10.1075/ip.00042.jia.

Johann, Michael, and Lars Bülow. 2019. One Does Not Simply Create a Meme: Conditions for the Diffusion of Internet Memes. *International Journal of Communication* 13: 1720–1742.

Juza, Marta. 2013. Internet Memes -Creation, Distribution, Social Meaning. *Media Studies* 55: 1–15.

Kardaş, T. 2012. No Laughing Matter: Visualizing Turkey's Ergenekon in Political Cartoons. *Middle East Critique* 21 (2): 203–223. https://doi.org/10.1080/19436149.2012.6885872012.

Kecskes, Istvan. 2014. *Intercultural Pragmatics*. Oxford: Oxford University Press. https://doi.org/10.1093/acprof:oso/9780199892655.001.0001.

Knobel, Michele, and Colin Lankshear. 2007. Online Memes, Affinities, and Cultural Production. In *A New Literacies Sampler*, ed. Michele Knobel and Colin Lankshear, 199–227. Berlin: Peter Lang.

Kress, Gunther, and Theo van Leeuwen. 2006. *Reading Images: The Grammar of Visual Design*. 2nd ed. London: Routledge.

Kuipers, Giselinde. 2002. Media Culture and Internet Disaster Jokes. Bin Laden and the Attack on the World Trade Center. *European Journal of Cultural Studies* 5 (4): 450–470. https://doi.org/10.1177/1364942002005004296.

Laineste, Liisi, and Piret Voolaid. 2016. Laughing Across Borders: Intertextuality of Internet Memes. *European Journal of Humour Research* 4 (4): 26–49. https://doi.org/10.7592/EJHR2016.4.4.laineste.

Lin, Chi-Chin, Yi-Ching Huang Lin, and Jane Yung-jen Hsu. 2014. Crowdsourced Explanations for Humorous Internet Memes Based on Linguistic Theories. In *Proceedings of the Second AAAI Conference on Human Computation and Crowdsourcing (HCOMP 2014)*. AAAI. https://doi.org/10.1609/hcomp.v2i1.13169.

Lou, Adrian. 2017. Multimodal Simile. The "When" Meme in Social Media Discourse. *English Text Construction* 10 (1): 106–131. https://doi.org/10.1075/etc.10.1.06lou.

Lugea, Jane. 2019. The Pragma-Stylistics of 'Image Macro' Internet Memes. In *Contemporary Media Stylistics*, ed. Helen Ringrow and Stephen Pihlaja. London: Bloomsbury.

Maíz-Arévalo, Carmen. 2014. A Pragmatic and Multimodal Analysis of Emoticons and Gender in Social Networks. In *New Insights into Gendered Discursive Practices: Language, Gender and Identity Construction*, ed. Antonia Sánchez Macarro and Ana Belén Cabrejas Peñuelas, 175–197. Valencia: University of Valencia.

Maíz-Arévalo, Carmen, and Francisco Yus. 2021. 'Laughing together, coping together': The role of humorous memes in the Covid-19 crisis. Paper delivered at the *17th International Pragmatics Conference*. Winterthur.

Marino, Gabriele. 2015. Semiotics of Spreadability: A Systematic Approach to Internet Memes and Virality. *Punctum* 1 (1): 43–66. https://doi.org/10.18680/hss.2015.0004.

Martin, Rod A., Patricia Puhlik-Doris, Gwen Larsen, Jeanette Gray, and Kelly Weir. 2003. Individual Differences in Uses of Humor and Their Relation to Psychological Well-Being: Development of the Humor Styles Questionnaire. *Journal of Research in Personality* 37 (1): 48–75. https://doi.org/10.1016/S0092-6566(02)00534-2.

Martinec, Radan, and Andrew Salway. 2005. A System for Image-Text Relations in New (and Old) Media. *Visual Communication* 4 (3): 337–371. https://doi.org/10.1177/1470357205055928.

Martínez-Cardama, Sara, and Fátima García-López. 2021. Ephemeral Mimetics: Memes, an X-ray of Covid-19. *The European Journal of Humour Research* 9 (4): 35–57. https://doi.org/10.7592/EJHR2021.9.4.558.

Marwick, Alice, and danah boyd. 2011. I Tweet Honestly, I Tweet Passionately: Twitter Users, Context Collapse, and the Imagined Audience. *New Media & Society* 13 (1): 114–133. https://doi.org/10.1177/1461444810365313.

McCloud, Scott. 1994. *Understanding Comics: The Invisible Art.* New York: Harper Collins.

Mifdal, Mohamed. 2022. Covidly Humorous Memes: Coping, Social Cohesion and Power Dynamics of Humour During the Pandemic in Morocco. *European Journal of Humour Research* 10 (3): 189–210. https://doi.org/10.7592/EJHR2022.10.3.688.

Miller, Vincent. 2008. New Media, Networking and Phatic Culture. *Convergence* 14: 387–400. https://doi.org/10.1177/1354856508094659.

Milner, Ryan M. 2012. The World Made Meme: Discourse and Identity in Participatory Media. PhD Thesis. University of Kansas.

———. 2013a. Pop Polyvocality: Internet Memes, Public Participation, and the Occupy Wall Street Movement. *International Journal of Communication* 7: 2357–2390.

———. 2013b. Hacking the Social: Internet Memes, Identity Antagonism, and the Logic of Lulz. *The Fibreculture Journal* 22: 62–92.

Miltner, Kate M. 2014. 'There's No Place for Lulz on Lolcats': The Role of Genre, Gender, and Group Identity in the Interpretation and Enjoyment of an Internet Meme. *First Monday* 19 (8). https://doi.org/10.5210/fm.v19i8.5391.

Nabea, Wendo K. 2021. The Discursive Counter-Power of Internet Memes in Response to the Management of the Covid-19 Pandemic in Kenya. *English Academy Review* 38 (2): 117–134. https://doi.org/10.1080/10131752.2021.1988484.

Naughton, John. 2012. *From Gutenberg to Zuckerberg: What You Really Need to Know about the Internet.* London: Quercus.

Ndlovu, Mphathisi. 2021. Humour in the Time of COVID-19 Pandemic: A Critical Analysis of the Subversive Meanings of WhatsApp Memes in Zimbabwe. In *Digital Humour in the Covid-19 Pandemic. Perspectives from the Global South*, ed. Shepherd Mpofu, 259–277. Cham: Palgrave Macmillan. https://doi.org/10.1007/978-3-030-79279-4_12.

Nee, Rebecca Coates, and Mariana de Maio. 2019. A 'Presidential Look'? An Analysis of Gender Framing in 2016 Persuasive Memes of Hillary Clinton. *Journal of Broadcasting & Electronic Media* 63 (2): 304–321. https://doi.org/10.1080/08838151.2019.1620561.

Nikolajeva, Maria, and Carole Scott. 2000. The Dynamics of Picturebook Communication. *Children's Literature in Education* 31 (4): 225–239.

Nissenbaum, Asaf, and Limor Shifman. 2017. Internet Memes as Contested Cultural Capital: The Case of 4chan's /b/ Board. *New Media & Society* 19 (4): 483–501. https://doi.org/10.1177/1461444815609313.

———. 2018. Meme Templates as Expressive Repertoires in a Globalizing World: A Cross-Linguistic Study. *Journal of Computer-Mediated Communication* 23 (5): 294–310. https://doi.org/10.1093/jcmc/zmy016.

O'Boyle, Neil. 2022. WhatsAppening Donald: The Social Uses of Trump Memes. *European Journal of Cultural Studies* 25 (2): 458–462. https://doi.org/10.1177/13675494211004596.

Outley, Corliss, Shamaya Bowen, and Harrison Pinckney. 2021. Laughing While Black: Resistance, Coping and the Use of Humor as a Pandemic Pastime among Blacks. *Leisure Sciences* 43 (1-2): 305–314. https://doi.org/10.1080/01490400.2020.1774449.

Paciello, Marinella, Francesca D'Errico, Giorgia Saleri, and Ernestina Lamponi. 2021. Online Sexist Meme and its Effects on Moral and Emotional Processes in Social Media. *Computers in Human Behavior* 116. https://doi.org/10.1016/j.chb.2020.106655.

Padilla Cruz, Manuel. 2017. Conceptual Competence Injustice and Relevance Theory, a Reply to Derek Anderson. *Social Epistemology Review and Reply Collective* 6 (12): 39–50.

Piata, Anna. 2020. Stylistic Humor Across Modalities. The case of Classical Art Memes. *Internet Pragmatics* 3 (2): 174–201. https://doi.org/10.1075/ip.00031.pia.

Ponton, Douglas M. 2021. "Never in my Life Have I Heard Such a Load of Absolute Nonsense. Wtf." Political Satire on the Handling of the Covid 19 Crisis. *Russian Journal of Linguistics* 25 (3): 767–788. https://doi.org/10.22363/2687-0088-2021-25-3-767-788.

Ponton, Douglas M., and Peter Mantello. 2021. Virality, Contagion and Public Discourse. The Role of Memes as Prophylaxis and Catharsis in an Age of Crisis. *Rhetoric and Communications* 46: 44–63.

Powell, Julie M. 2020. <3 I Am Tracy: Meme Culture, Coping, and Community During the COVID-19 Pandemic. In *Pandemics and Epidemics in Cultural Representation*, ed. Sathyaraj Venkatesan, A. Antara Chatterjee, David Lewis, and Brian Callender, 193–211. Cham: Springer. https://doi.org/10.1007/978-981-19-1296-2_13.

Rivas Carmona, María del Mar, and María Luisa Calero Vaquera. 2020. Pandemia y Posverdad: El Iimpacto de la Covid-19 en la Comunicación por WhatsApp [Pandemic and Post-Truth: The Impact of Covid-19 on Whatsapp Communication]. *Prisma Social* 31: 110–154.

Salway, Andrew, and Radan Martinec. 2002. Some Ideas for Modelling Image-Text Combinations. University of Surrey, Department of Computing.

Sánchez-Olmos, Cande, and Eduardo Viñuela. 2017. The Musicless Music Video as a Spreadable Meme Video: Format, User Interaction, and Meaning on YouTube. *International Journal of Communication* 11: 3634–3654.

Sarapik, V. 2009. Picture, Text, and Imagetext: Textual Polylogy. *Semiotica* 174 (1/4): 277–308. https://doi.org/10.1515/semi.2009.03.

Scott, Kate. 2021. Memes as Multimodal Metaphors. A Relevance Theory Analysis. *Pragmatics & Cognition* 28 (2): 277–298. https://doi.org/10.1075/pc.21010.sco.

———. 2022. *Pragmatics Online*. Abingdon: Routledge.

Segev, Elad, Asaf Nissenbaum, Nathan Stolero, and Limor Shifman. 2015. Families and Networks of Internet Memes: The Relationship Between Cohesiveness, Uniqueness, and Quiddity Concreteness. *Journal of Computer-Mediated Communication* 20: 417–433. https://doi.org/10.1111/jcc4.12120.

Shifman, Limor. 2012. An Anatomy of a YouTube Meme. *New Media & Society* 14 (2): 187–203. https://doi.org/10.1177/1461444811412160.

———. 2013. Memes in a Digital World: Reconciling with a Conceptual Troublemaker. *Journal of Computer-Mediated Communication* 18: 362–377. https://doi.org/10.1111/jcc4.12013.

———. 2014. *Memes in Digital Culture*. Cambridge, MA: The MIT Press.

Simarro Vázquez, María, Nabiha El Khatib, Phillip Hamrick, and Salvatore Attardo. 2021. On the Order of Processing of Humorous Tweets with Visual and Verbal Elements. *Internet Pragmatics* 4 (1): 150–175. https://doi.org/10.1075/ip.00060.sim.

Spitzberg, Brian H. 2014. Toward a Model of Meme Diffusion (M3D). *Communication Theory* 24: 311–339. https://doi.org/10.1111/comt.12042.

Suls, Jerry M. 1972. A Two-Stage Model for the Appreciation of Jokes and Cartoons: An Information-Processing Analysis. In *The Psychology of Humor: Theoretical Perspectives and Empirical Issues*, ed. J.H. Goldstein and P.E. McGhee, 81–100. New York: Academic Press. https://doi.org/10.1016/B978-0-12-288950-9.50010-9.

———. 1977. Cognitive and Disparagement Theories of Humour: A Theoretical and Empirical Synthesis. In *It's a Funny Thing, Humour*, ed. A.J. Chapman and H.C. Foot, 41–45. Oxford: Pergamon Press. https://doi.org/10.1016/B978-0-08-021376-7.50012-7.

———. 1983. Cognitive Processes in Humor Appreciation. In *Handbook of Humor Research, Vol. 1: Basic Issues*, ed. P.E. McGhee and J.H. Goldstein, 39–57. New York: Springer-Verlag. https://doi.org/10.1007/978-1-4612-5572-7_3.

Taecharungroj, Viriya, and Pitchanut Nueangjamnong. 2014. The Effect of Humour on Virality: The Study of Internet Memes on Social Media. Paper delivered at the *7th International Forum on Public Relations and Advertising Media Impacts on Culture and Social Communication*. Bangkok.

Tay, Geniesa. 2015. Binders Full of LOLitics: Political Humour, Internet Memes, and Play in the 2012 US Presidential Election (and Beyond). *European Journal of Humour Research* 2 (4): 46–73. https://doi.org/10.7592/EJHR2014.2.4.tay.

Tella, Akin. 2018. Humour Generation and Multimodal Framing of Political Actor in the 2015 Nigerian Presidential Election Campaign Memes. *European Journal of Humour Research* 6 (4): 95–117. https://doi.org/10.7592/EJHR2018.6.4.2018.tella.

Trifonas, Peter Pericles. 2015. Text and Images. In *International Handbook of Semiotics*, ed. Peter Pericles Trifonas, 1139–1152. Berlin: Springer. https://doi.org/10.1007/978-94-017-9404-6_53.

Tsakona, Villi. 2009. Language and Image Interaction in Cartoons: Towards a Multimodal Theory of Humor. *Journal of Pragmatics* 41: 1171–1188. https://doi.org/10.1016/j.pragma.2008.12.003.

van Leeuwen, Theo. 2006. Word and Image. In *Encyclopedia of Language and Linguistics*, ed. Keith Brown, 2nd ed. Amsterdam: Elsevier. https://doi.org/10.1016/B0-08-044854-2/00562-9.

———. 2011. Multimodality. In *The Routledge Handbook of Applied Linguistics*, ed. J. Simpson, 668–682. Abingdon: Routledge. https://doi.org/10.4324/9780203835654.ch47.

———. 2015. Multimodality. In *The Handbook of Discourse Analysis*, ed. Deborah Tannen, Heidi E. Hamilton, and Deborah Schiffrin, 2nd ed., 447–465. Oxford: Wiley Blackwell. https://doi.org/10.1002/9781118584194.ch21.

Vandelanotte, Lieven. 2021. Creative Constructs, Constructions, and Frames in Internet Discourse. *Constructions and Frames* 13 (1): 160–191. https://doi.org/10.1075/cf.00050.van.

Vásquez, Camilla, and Erhan Aslan. 2021. "Cats Be Outside, How about Meow": Multimodal Humor and Creativity in an Internet Meme. *Journal of Pragmatics* 171: 101–117. https://doi.org/10.1016/j.pragma.2020.10.006.

Wiggins, Bradley E. 2019. *The Discursive Power of Memes in Digital Culture. Ideology, Semiotics, and Intertextuality*. Abingdon: Routledge. https://doi.org/10.4324/9780429492303.

———. 2020. Memes and the Media Narrative. The Nike-Kaepernick Controversy. *Internet Pragmatics* 3 (2): 202–222. https://doi.org/10.1075/ip.00032.wig.

Williams, Amanda, Clio Oliver, Katherine Aumer, and Chanel Meyers. 2016. Racial Microaggressions and Perceptions of Internet Memes. *Computers in Human Behavior* 63: 424–432. https://doi.org/10.1016/j.chb.2016.05.067.

Wu, Shuxuan. 2014. A Multimodal Analysis of Image-Text Relations in Picture Books. *Theory and Practice in Language Studies* 4 (7): 1415–1420. https://doi.org/10.4304/tpls.4.7.1415-1420.

Xu, Weiai Wayne, Ji Young Park, Ji Young Kim, and Han Woo Park. 2016. Networked Cultural Diffusion and Creation on YouTube: An Analysis of YouTube Memes. *Journal of Broadcasting & Electronic Media* 60 (1): 104–122. https://doi.org/10.1080/08838151.2015.1127241.

Yoon, InJeon. 2016. Why Is it not Just a Joke? Analysis of Internet Memes Associated with Racism and Hidden Ideology of Colorblindness. *Journal of Cultural Research in Art Education* 33: 92–123.

Yus, Francisco. 2004. Pragmatics of Humorous Strategies in *El Club de la Comedia*. In *Current Trends in the Pragmatics of Spanish*, ed. Rosina Márquez-Reiter and María Elena Placencia, 320–344. Amsterdam: John Benjamins. https://doi.org/10.1075/pbns.123.25yus.

———. 2005. Dave Allen's Stand-Up Monologues: An Epidemiological Approach. In *Thistles. A Homage to Brian Hughes. Volume 2: Essays in Memoriam*, ed. José Mateo and Francisco Yus, 317–344. Alicante: University of Alicante, Department of English Studies.

———. 2008. Inferring from Comics: A Multi-Stage Account. In *El Discurs del Còmic (Quaderns de Filologia, Estudis de Comunicació, vol. III)*, ed. Pelegrí Sancho Cremades, Carmen Gregori Signes, and Santiago Renard, 223–249. Valencia: University of Valencia.

———. 2009. Visual Metaphor Versus Verbal Metaphor: A Unified Account. In *Multimodal Metaphor*, ed. Charles Forceville and Eduardo Urios-Aparisi, 145–172. Berlin: Mouton de Gruyter. https://doi.org/10.1515/9783110215366.

———. 2013a. An Inference-Centered Analysis of Jokes: The Intersecting Circles Model of Humorous Communication. In *Irony and Humor: From Pragmatics to Discourse*, ed. Leonor Ruiz Gurillo and Belén Alvarado, 59–82. Amsterdam: John Benjamins. https://doi.org/10.1075/pbns.231.05yus.

———. 2013b. Analyzing Jokes with the Intersecting Circles Model of Humorous Communication. *Lodz Papers in Pragmatics* 9 (1): 3–24. https://doi.org/10.1515/lpp-2013-0002.

———. 2016. *Humour and Relevance*. Amsterdam: John Benjamins. https://doi.org/10.1075/thr.4.

———. 2017. Incongruity-Resolution Cases in Jokes. *Lingua* 197: 103–122. https://doi.org/10.1016/j.lingua.2017.02.002.

———. 2018. Identity-Related Issues in Meme Communication. *Internet Pragmatics* 1 (1): 113–133. https://doi.org/10.1075/ip.00006.yus.

———. 2019a. Multimodality in Memes: A Cyberpragmatic Approach. In *Analyzing Digital Discourse. New Insights and Future Directions*, ed. Patricia Bou-Franch and Pilar Garcés-Conejos Blitvich, 105–131. Cham: Palgrave Macmillan. https://doi.org/10.1007/978-3-319-92663-6_4.

———. 2019b. Incongruity-Resolution Patterns in Meme Communication. Paper delivered at the *International Conference on Verbal Humor*. Alicante (Spain).

———. 2020. Disambiguation Should Not Exist (But it Does in Humour). Paper delivered at the *9th International Symposium on Intercultural, Cognitive and Social Pragmatics* ("Communication in the 21st Century: Intercultural, Cognitive and Social Pragmatics"). Seville, Spain.

———. 2021a. *Smartphone Communication. Interactions in the App Ecosystem.* Abingdon: Routledge. https://doi.org/10.4324/9781003200574.

———. 2021b. Pragmatics of Humour in Memes in Spanish. *Spanish in Context* 18 (1): 113–135, special issue on humour. https://doi.org/10.1075/sic.00070.yus.

———. 2021c. Incongruity-Resolution Humorous Strategies in Image Macro Memes. *Internet Pragmatics* 4 (1): 131–149. https://doi.org/10.1075/ip.00058.yus.

———. 2021d. It's All about Sharing. Covid-19 Memes beyond Meme Discourse Interpretation. Paper delivered at *Humor in the Time of Cholera*. Warsaw, Poland.

———. 2022. Layers of Predicted Inferences in Humorous Communication. Lecture delivered at *ArgLab Research Colloquium*, Lisbon.

———. forthcoming-a. Memes. In *Introducción al Estudio del Discurso Digital en Español*, ed. Maria Elena Placencia and Alejandro Parini. Abingdon: Routledge.

———. forthcoming-b. Irony and the Internet. In *The Cambridge Handbook of Irony and Thought*, ed. Raymond W. Gibbs and Herbert L. Colston. Cambridge: Cambridge University Press.

Yus, Francisco, and Carmen Maíz-Arévalo. 2021. Humorous Effects from Covid-19 Memes. The Role of Multimodal Combinations. Paper delivered at the *17th International Pragmatics Conference*. Winterthur, Switzerland.

———. forthcoming. Interpreting Covid-Related Memes: The Role of Inferential Strategies and Context Accessibility. In *The Pragmatics of Humour in Interactive Contexts*, ed. Esther Linares Bernabéu. Amsterdam: John Benjamins.

Zappavigna, Michele. 2020. "And then He Said... No one Has more Respect for Women than I Do." Intermodal Relations and Intersubjectivity in Image Macros. In *Shifts toward Image-Centricity in Contemporary Multimodal Practices*, ed. Hartmut Stöckl, Helen Caple, and Jana Pflaeging, 204–225. Abingdon: Routledge.

CHAPTER 8

Beyond Humour: Relevant Affective Effects

1 Introduction: Affective Attitude and Affective Effects

Non-propositional effects (feelings, emotions…[1]) are important in any communicative scenario, ranging from face-to-face interactions to internet-mediated communication. In fact, besides the intention to communicate certain information (a set of assumptions) propositionally (i.e. as explicatures and/or implicatures), the speaker (or internet user) normally holds the intention that their current feelings and emotions be communicated as well (*affective attitude*), often because these feelings which become attached to the propositional content may largely determine how the latter is eventually interpreted. Similarly, addressees not only obtain a propositional interpretation from the utterance but also infer the attached affective

[1] In this chapter, feelings and emotions will be roughly treated as similar phenomena under the umbrella terms *affective attitude* (intended) and *affective effect* (derived). Caffi and Janney (1994) did propose a differentiation between *feelings* (broad, complex class of subjective personal sensations or states of inner physiological arousal); and *emotions* (a restricted subset of empirically investigable phenomena within this general class that are relatively transitory, of a certain intensity, and are attached to, or triggered by, particular objects, ideas, or outer incentive events). See also Downes (2000). Wharton (2016, 30), Wharton and Strey (2019, 265) and Wharton and de Saussure (2022) detach emotions from feelings and sensations on the grounds that emotions involve an interaction between three types of elements: cognitive; qualitative; and physiological.

F. Yus, *Pragmatics of Internet Humour*,
https://doi.org/10.1007/978-3-031-31902-0_8

attitude in parallel and, crucially, derive their own feelings and emotions from the interpreted content (*affective effects*) too. Most importantly, these may form part of what the speaker/user intended to convey, or *leak* from the act of communication beyond their intention and, nevertheless, they often result in a relevant outcome for the addressee. In other words, apart from the typical objective of pragmatic research, namely explicit and/or implicated propositional information, another two areas are particularly interesting for the purposes of this chapter: (a) people not only mean to communicate propositions but also the non-propositional information attached to them. In the words of Gibbs et al. (2002, 129) words, likewise at work in communication, non-propositional affective and emotional intentions exist that speakers may, to varying degrees, "wish to make manifest by having listeners draw, again to varying degrees, different inferences about the speaker's emotional state of mind." And (b) non-propositional information about the communicator's affective states may be deliberately conveyed but affective effects are additionally likely to *leak* from the act of communication beyond the communicator's intentions and still result in a relevant outcome for the addressee; see Leggitt and Gibbs (2000) for an application of this idea to irony comprehension.

It can hardly be denied that, as Caffi and Janney (1994, 328) specified, pragmatics should primarily focus on *emotive communication*, i.e. the intentional signalling of "affective information in speech and writing in order to influence partners' interpretations of situations and reach different goals," and not on *emotional communication*, qualified as the spontaneous, unintentional leakage or bursting out of emotion in speech. However, it becomes important, especially due to the topic covered in this book, to highlight that numerous intentional internet-mediated acts of communication also generate a *leakage* of non-propositional effects which may lie within the audience's conscious awareness or not, but often prove relevant to the user's audience. This chapter precisely addresses the way in which humorous communication on the Net, mainly intended to generate an offset of non-propositional effects in the shape of amusement or even laughter, equally generates a number of important and relevant non-propositional outcomes that may add to the relevant content of the discourse produced or even compensate for the lack of relevance that the audience could find therein.

An example of the extent to which the identification of affective effects matters for proper understanding was suggested in Yus (2016) with regard to irony comprehension. According to relevance theory, understanding ironies entails the identification of the speaker's dissociative attitude towards some event, norm, previous utterance or expectation that did not turn out as expected; hence the tendency for ironies to be mainly conveyed with a critical connotation. Nonetheless, ironies may likewise be inferred as humorous or at least embedded in a non-critical attitude, for which purpose the identification of the speaker's affective attitude (or to put it in another way, their feelings/emotions upon producing the irony) becomes crucial. This is illustrated by the conversation quoted in (1), where John ironically criticises Mary's reluctance to call him. However, Mary's identification of the accompanying positive affective attitude makes her react humorously, instead of taking John's utterance as blunt criticism in the shape of an irony (Yus 2016, 232):

(1) [*John calls Mary on the phone*].
Mary: Hi John! How're things?
John: I am fine! I've just thought... Since Mary is always calling me, today for a change I'll make the call.
Mary: Hahaha. Poor thing... You are right, I should call you more often, but you seem soooo happy to call your friend, don't you? hahaha.
John: Hehehe... Of course, Mary... A pleasure.

On the internet, broad categories of feelings and emotions are normally inferred correctly thanks to their (supposed) universality (e.g. anger, happiness, sadness...). It should be noted, though, that a certain degree of cross-cultural variability exists both in the coding of emotions (words used in their verbal communication) and in the nonverbal expression of these feelings/emotions that can influence how they are inferred within an environment such as the internet, where people all over the world can converge on the same webpage or app (see, for instance, Ameka 2002, 30).

2 Relevance Theory and Non-Propositional Information

Although relevance theory (henceforth RT) has usually shown reluctance to address the communication of non-propositional information as part of its scope, recent developments point in the direction of incorporating such non-propositional information as an important part of human communication (including internet-mediated interactions). Quotes such as the ones provided below illustrate this initial "resistance."

> There is a very good reason for anyone concerned with the role of inference in communication to assume that what is communicated is propositional: it is relatively easy to say what propositions are, and how inference might operate over propositions. No one has any clear idea how inference might operate over non-propositional objects: say, over images, impressions or emotions. Propositional contents and attitudes thus seem to provide the only relatively solid ground on which to base a partly or wholly inferential approach to communication. (Sperber and Wilson 1995, 87)

> relevance theory is a theory of communication, and it defines communication rather narrowly in conceptual terms. Communication involves providing evidence for a range of intended effects, and while this leaves room for images and emotions to play a role as causes or consequences of an appropriate interpretation, they cannot be part of that interpretation unless embedded into a conceptual description. (Deirdre Wilson, in de Saussure and Wharton 2020, 193)

However, in their seminal book *Relevance*, Sperber and Wilson (1995) do acknowledge that sometimes what is communicated proves harder to grasp than in normal strongly communicated propositional terms, its interpretation being more open-ended too. An often-cited example is (2).

(2) Mary and Peter are newly arrived at the seaside. She opens the window overlooking the sea and sniffs appreciatively and ostensively. When Peter follows suit, there is no one particular good thing that comes to his attention: the air smells fresh, (…) all sorts of pleasant things come to mind, and while, because her sniff was appreciative, he is reasonably safe in assuming that she must have intended him to notice at least some of them, he is unlikely to be able to pin her intentions down any further. (Sperber and Wilson 1995, 55)

Clearly, Peter cannot grasp which assumption(s) Mary actually feels and intends to communicate to him when she sniffs ostensively. Therefore, according to the RT explanation, Peter would infer an array of weak implicatures about Mary's intentions, a subset of which is probably meant by Mary while Peter derives others on his sole responsibility (see Moeschler 2009, 456–458; Clark 2020, 435; Wharton 2021, 327; Wharton et al. 2021, 262). This entails the paradox of invariably embedding non-propositional information in a *propositional mould* (or expressed differently, weak implicatures are still propositions). My position differs from this one, as asserted in previous research (Yus 2015, 2016, 2018b, 2018c, 2022): non-propositional information may be mentally represented and derived as weak implicatures, but very often this information is inferred non-propositionally as well, which implies some kind of scalability of inferred possibilities between propositional information (weak implicatures) and non-propositional effects (e.g. replicated feelings). By way of example, perhaps in (2) above Mary could not pin down her feelings in the shape of a distinctive proposition to be communicated, and Peter may catch a glimpse of what Mary is feeling by replicating her feelings (consequently not needing to represent them mentally). Wharton and de Saussure (2022, 671) also seem to acknowledge this kind of scale: Someone who is experiencing certain sensations and feelings will perhaps pay a high degree of attention to perceptual inputs that they would probably not even notice in other normal circumstances. Once cognition comes into play, they will be equipped with an newly defined set of goals, and directed to prioritised inferential processes. Also interestingly, these authors opt for a mutual influence of both types of information: "it is not that the recovery of affective effects has nothing to do with the derivation of cognitive effects, but rather that the two dimensions may interact. This happens in particular when the hearer infers that the emotion was deliberately displayed by the speaker. However, this is in no way necessary: an utterance may achieve its communicative affective effects without any further need for relevance" (p. 672).

In this sense, extensive research has been devoted to *mirror neurons*, those responsible for our ability to understand quickly and instinctively what others feel and experience, engaging in what is typically known as *emotional contagion*. In short, mirror neurons single out facial expressions, intonations, etc. to grasp the person's feelings/emotions, which becomes essential for empathy. Therefore, we can in theory feel what others feel without needing to mentally represent (propositionally) their feelings.

Other authors also align with this view. For example, de Saussure and Wharton (2020, 185) remarked that "the communication of propositional or conceptual contents is only one dimension of human communication, which also necessarily involves the direct manifestation of mental states -sensations, emotions, feelings- which are hard to capture in propositional or conceptual terms." Following along the same lines, Wharton (2021, 334) stated that

> feelings need not be conscious at all. Nor are feelings represented propositionally. Having a "feeling" that today is going to be a good day, or that you have performed well in an exam, differs from "believing", or even in one sense "thinking" the same thing. As far as I can see, the closest the standard relevance theory view gets to the notion of "feeling" I propose is the notion of an "impression." But in relevance theory an impression is characterised as an array of weakly manifest propositions (consciously represented or not) and propositions, it is my contention, are not the right currency to exchange for feelings.

Thus, concerning the communication of non-propositional information (feelings, emotions), RT's initial position is that such feelings and emotions must be intended by the communicator propositionally (even if in weak terms) and inferred as such by the addressee. However, plenty of feelings and emotions circulate on the internet that do not fit this RT mould. Yus (2022) listed four possible situations for the communication of non-propositional information, three of which do not neatly fit the default RT analysis, as shown in Fig. 8.1.

Top left situation (Fig. 8.1). This case is addressed by RT: Feelings form part of what is intended in the sender user's act of communication, and the audience recovers them as affective effects that complement other propositional cognitive ones.

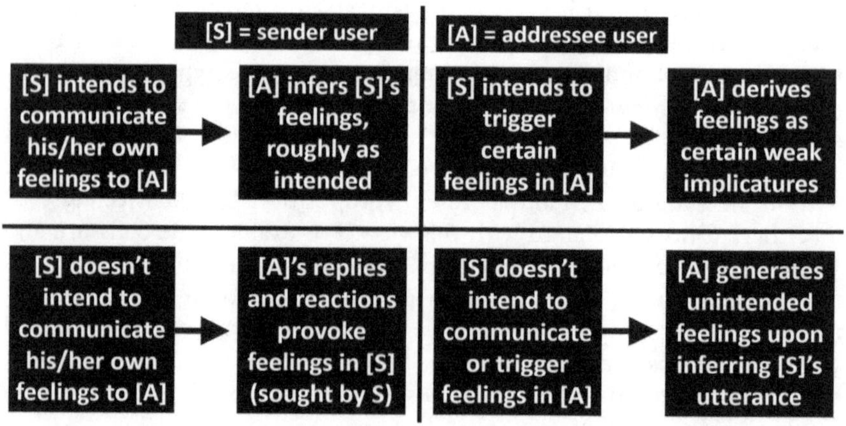

Fig. 8.1 Possible situations in the communication of non-propositional information online

Top right situation (Fig. 8.1). This case is not fully addressed by RT: The feelings are not part of what the sender user intends to communicate to his/her audience, but non-propositional effects that they intend to trigger in the addressee users beyond interpreting the initial user's utterance. Yus (ibid.) illustrates this situation with an advertisement available online in (3) and described in (4):

(3) https://vimeo.com/191630470
(4) Lucía and her parents are in a car driving to a village to spend their holidays. Lucía looks really angry. Her mother explains that she looks frustrated because she thinks that the girls at the village are not going to remember her and she is not going to fit into their group. Then Lucía starts receiving messages from a WhatsApp group made up of those girls. They type that they are waiting for her, inviting her to a party, and so on. Lucía smiles… her face glows with happiness upon feeling acknowledged and wanted by these girls.

How would a cyberpragmatic analysis of (3–4) proceed? A logical approach would consist in interpreting those girls' messages as coded utterances that need inferential enrichment, additionally considering enhancing messaging strategies that might determine the way in which their interpretations are eventually obtained. The messages that Lucía receives on her smartphone, reproduced in (5a-8a), are translated in (5b-8b), their contextualised intended interpretations being added in (5c-8c), with further comments provided in (5d-8d). Notice how the alterations of plain text and additions of other discourses such as emojis have pragmatic value (i.e. they are *relevant*), influencing Lucía's eventual interpretation towards a more "oral" feel and directing her in a certain inferential direction:

(5) a. Cndo llegas??
 b. [*When are you arriving??*].
 c. [We are eager to know] when you are arriving at the village.
 d. (eagerness is conveyed by question mark repetition)
(6) a. T estamos esperando!!! 😍😍😍
 b. [*We're waiting for you!!!* 😍😍😍].
 c. We are [anxiously] waiting for you. [we love your company].
 d. (being anxious is conveyed via exclamation repetition; loving the girl's company is generated through emoji use).
(7) a. Hoy hay plan en casa de Ana!!! 👯👯👯
 b. [*There's a plan at Ana's* 👯👯👯].

c. Today there is [a party] at Ana's [and we're going to have fun].
d. (the coded concept *plan* is narrowed into the more fine-tuned *party*; the "fun" connotation is conveyed via the emoji of a dancing woman).

(8) a. T apuntas? 🙏🙏🙏
b. [*Will you join us?* 🙏🙏🙏].
c. [We would love it] if you joined us.
d. (the eagerness of meeting the girl is conveyed via emoji use).

Despite being correct, such cyberpragmatic analysis is insufficient. What about the intense feelings of happiness that Lucía experiences upon seeing her expectations contradicted (a truly relevant outcome) and realising that she is in fact welcomed by the other girls? A good pragmatic account of this kind of interaction involves attention to the relevant non-propositional effects inferred (like those derived by Lucía). And in general, the claim is that such effects may also become relevant even if the sender user has not overtly sought them. This chapter precisely deals with non-propositional effects that are triggered by humorous internet-mediated communication acts, often leaking from these acts and inferred in parallel to the humour-connoted effects.

Bottom left situation (Fig. 8.1). This case is not neatly addressed by RT: The feelings are not part of what the sender user intends to communicate, nor are they effects that they want to trigger in the addressee, but feelings that the user wants the audience to trigger in themselves by means of Likes, comments, and overall audience validation.

Bottom right situation (Fig. 8.1). RT does not address this case either: Despite not being part of what the sender user intends to communicate, feelings are effects that the addressee generates beyond the user's intention (by their own responsibility), and therefore these affective effects should not be an object of analysis for pragmatics or RT.

More recent RT-based research has more explicitly included non-propositional effects in the picture of communication and understanding that RT provides, albeit still focusing exclusively on the intentional communication of non-propositional information that is inferred as such (therefore, *leaked* relevant affective effects beyond the communicator's intention would lie outside RT's scope of analysis. In short, RT aims "to look for a set of pragmatic principles and mechanisms that can deal with the full range of overtly intentional communicative acts: verbal and non-verbal, showing and telling, determinate and indeterminate, literal and figurative, propositional and non-propositional" (Wilson and Carston 2019, 34).[2]

[2] This Section is an extension and update of the research carried out in Yus (2018a, 2018c).

3 Relevant Non-Propositional Effects from Internet Humour

3.1 Positive Non-Propositional Effects at a Personal Level

Humorous texts produce personal-level non-propositional effects mainly associated with users' identity shaping and self-esteem. For example, being able to master the expected inferential strategies involved in deriving the desired humorous effects will increase the user's self-assurance (Baym 1995). These strategies often entail finding the right intertextual links or background contextual information that serve both to properly infer humorous discourses online and to test users' competence (Laineste 2013, 32). Furthermore, mastering the production and the eventual successful outcome of a humorous attempt typically relates to labels such as extroversion and high self-esteem (Kurtzberg et al. 2009, 390), these being likewise generated through internet humour. On the whole, showing mastery at the production and interpretation of humour makes someone be regarded as socially competent and liked by peers (Pennington and Hall 2014, 2), a kind of validation also pursued in virtual environments.

Identity-related non-propositional effects are often expected in humorous acts of communication, even though they may remain beyond the user's full assessment. Indeed, as du Preez and Lombard (2014, 260) correctly pointed out, the construction of identity mainly takes place through interpersonal interactions, and is influenced by the social and physical environment as well. However, while a user may try to portray an ideal construction of the self while staying online, with full awareness of the underlying identity-related intention, in most instances this performance is not viewed as a conscious act, and it partly remains subconscious, depending on the situation (environment and audience). In other words, although the performance of a specific identity act may be deliberate, it is not entirely (or necessarily) a conscious act. My point in previous research has been that it might have a non-propositional nature too, based on feelings and emotions within or devoid of a propositional format, and placed along an intentional-unintentional continuum.

Identity-related effects may equally stem from the individual user's awareness of having the capacity to interpret the internet discourse adequately with the aid of context, as already stated, and being aware of this interpretive capability may impact on the user's self-awareness. For instance, this becomes particularly noticeable in the case of memes, which often demand specific background knowledge as part of the context needed to see what the user is getting at (see Chap. 7). Users, upon realising that they were able to obtain the intended interpretation, become aware of their status with respect to a collectivity of users. An example is found in Milner (2012, 93) concerning the meme in Fig. 8.2, whose correct interpretation requires the retrieval of background knowledge about information which is, of course, expected and its mutuality (***mutual manifestness*** in RT terms) taken for granted by the meme sender, and also acknowledged by the addressee user, who feels an offset of identity-enhancing effects from a satisfactory interpretation. Among other inferential operations, for the correct interpretation of this particular meme in

Fig. 8.2 A meme demanding a high degree of contextualisation

Fig. 8.2 the addressee user has to (a) infer the referent of "my God" (Steve Jobs) and adjust the coded concept of "God" metaphorically (i.e. broadened to fit an individual into the scope of the coded word *God*); (b) access the background knowledge about the type of meme depicted (Hipster Barista); and (c) use background knowledge related to hipsters loving Apple products, alongside some extra background knowledge on Nietzsche and the circumstances in which that phrase was produced.

3.2 Positive Non-Propositional Effects at an Interactive Level

Internet humour produces a number of effects related to virtual interactions and their management. Among others, the following effects are worth commenting upon.

1. *Value of an environment for interactions.* Humour facilitates the maintenance and desirability of choosing certain environments for online interactions, together with an impact on the eagerness to participate. Users, then, feel compelled to cooperate and preserve the group's interactional activity through sustained humour-centred participation. An example where the importance of humour has been underlined is sports live text commentaries (Chovanec 2011, 244; 2012, 142), where humour proves useful to keep the channel open and the audience interested in staying on the site, even when nothing worth commenting upon is taking place. Similarly, Marone (2015, 76–77) studied internet fora, concluding that humour sometimes functions as a two-way discursive icebreaker: humorous messages are intended to attract comments; but users also create them as gateways to the conversation. Humorous statements are hence followed up by more comments and this chained discursive reaction ensures the continuity of the conversation. Consequently, the effects generated somehow have to do with the on-going construction and the building-up of humorous interactional sequences, as was analysed in Chap. 6 when dealing with comments and replies to social networking site posts. Speakers frequently signal humour appreciation by incorporating or building on the play frame, which in turn can trigger further elaboration in a chain of humour, with humour leading to more humour (Vandergriff 2010, 242).

Furthermore, inference takes different directions depending on where the discourse appears (as a *Facebook* entry, as a *WhatsApp* message to a group…) and on other users' comments, which become "attached" as an indissoluble part of its meaning (see Ballantine et al. 2015; Literat and van den Berg 2019; Dewi 2019). Therefore, the user's identity takes shape in a variety of ways depending on these placements and other users' discursive reactions. Nonetheless, they may lead to unwanted misunderstandings if placed in a de-contextualised scenario (du Preez and Lombard 2014, 259).

2. *Exploitation of shared discursive conventions.* Within cyberpragmatics (Yus 2011), the utilisation of orality features to compensate for the lack of vocal information (through repeated letters, capitalisation, creative use of punctuation marks) and visual information (with the aid of emojis, stickers and GIFs, among others) in typed messages has a clear pragmatic value because they alter the way in which the discourse is eventually interpreted. As already mentioned in this book, the playful or explicitly humorous implementation of these innovative techniques often appears as the sole purpose sought with the production of a discourse; and, even more importantly, they may sustain the development of the whole online conversation, with users humorously building and commenting on these creative conventions, thus producing in-group bonding upon mastering the use of such oralising strategies (Hübler and Bell 2003, 279–280; Shifman 2019, 47–48). This creative play with genre conventions becomes particularly noticeable in the viral humour of *LOLCats* (Miltner 2014; Katz and Shifman 2017), already cited in the previous chapter, where expectations on text style (the so-called *LOLspeak*) play a key role in their ultimate humorous (and viral) effect, complemented with text-image combinations as well as intertextuality. No wonder, "participants explained that using the wrong font or diverging from stylistic expectations essentially ruined it for them" (Miltner ibid.). In other words, this altered language made no sense outside the community of users, which ultimately created a vivid enhancement of in-group solidarity as well as feelings of collective bonding through the successful production and comprehension of that language (Zappavigna 2012, 103). Examples of LOLspeak utterances include the one provided in (9) (Miltner 2014):

(9) Lolspeak: Ohai! I wud like tu b in deh focus groop, if it am alrite wif u
English: Hi! I would like to be in the focus group, if that is alright with you

3. *Encouragement of participation and interaction.* Internet humour may also produce effects on users' willingness to engage in virtual interactions and sustain them. For example, online journalists have been encouraged to harness humour in their interactions with readers because it fosters engagement and participation, and the same applies to corporate social media pages, as highlighted in Chap. 6. Since people often use humour to seek, gain and maintain connections on social networking sites, underestimating the role of humour as a connective device would be a gross mistake: "A little humor may go a long way in helping them better connect with current and potential followers" (Holton and Lewis 2011). Similarly, Hübler and Bell (2003, 280) underlined the role of what they call *threads of constitutive laughter* in mailing list communities, where interactions are boosted by inter-connected participation simply because humour has a capacity to generate more comments and replies than serious topics. These interactions frequently involve employing joint or co-constructed humour, in which users provide instant humorous reactions to each other (Chovanec 2011). As North (2007, 551) would put it, humour

> needs to be choreographed to fit coherently within the unfolding interaction, and when successful, it both builds on what has preceded it and is further elaborated by what follows. As a result, humorous comments are often tied into a network of cohesive relationships, with ambiguities providing links across different lexical chains. The textual cohesion, like the humor, is jointly constructed, and both reflects and helps to constitute the social cohesion of the group.

In a similar fashion, Mak (2014, 266) studied humour in professional and workplace instant-messaging interactions, concluding that these served relational purposes and effects. Even when the content is plainly humorous, the possibility exists for it to cause the effect of improving, maintaining, and enriching interpersonal communication, as well as closeness among colleagues, helping to maintain work-life balance through bonding and companionship. The same holds true for the interactions analysed in Holcomb (1997), where students used joking to accomplish a variety of interactional tasks ranging from building rapport with their peers to saving face, and exploring or negotiating (in a relatively safe way) thresholds between different ways of thinking and behaving.

3.3 Positive Non-Propositional Effects at a Medium-Sized Group Level

Humour is a constitutive marker of specificity in medium-sized internet groups (internet fora, blog communities, social networking site groups, messaging groups, etc.), which often exhibit humour due to their capacity to stress membership, solidarity, social levelling, and areas of mutuality. Several of these aspects, will be addressed below.

1. *Marker of group boundaries and membership*. As mentioned in other sections of this book, the rules governing both humour generation and the capacity for humour appreciation, including the essential retrieval of information from context, cause effects related to group belonging (in-group *bonding*) and an awareness of differentiation from other groups (out-group *bounding*). Norrick (2003) correctly stated that joking not only establishes and enhances group cohesion but also serves to control what sorts of talk and behaviour seem acceptable to participants in the interaction; and the same applies to online environments, where users strengthen delimited group boundaries too (Hübler and Bell 2003, 280–281):

> While jokes aid in social affiliation and group formation, they can similarly be used to target 'others'. The kinds of humour that are shared socially and the participants who find it 'funny' define who the 'others' are. Hence, jokes also function socially and politically to divide groups, particularly in generating and reinforcing social boundaries, social distance and inequalities. Those laughing at an 'out-group' foster greater social affiliation and decreased social distance with their 'in-group', while simultaneously creating and/or increasing social distance against their target. (Nasreen 2021, 149).

For these authors, individuals strategically construct humorous discourses that feel appropriate within a group, and the successful derivation of non-propositional effects from these discourses establishes discursive boundaries for that group (Gal 2019, 733; Locher and Bolander 2015,

143; Simis-Wilkinson et al. 2018, 321–322). Sometimes, these boundaries are made more explicit when users in one group mock and humorously target the other group.

Therefore, humour somehow allows users to fit into the community and simultaneously constitutes or reshapes that community. In the same vein, Marone (2015, 67) claimed that forum-based community users resort to humour for the purpose of avoiding disruptions of the bonding atmosphere, as well as to soothe critiques and foster dialogues. Nevertheless, humour also builds on the information which can be understood exclusively by the members of a community, a sort of insider's code that "needs to be deciphered in order to achieve a knowledgeable and legitimate participation. (…) [U]sers establish unwritten rules of participation based on specialist knowledge that strengthen the cohesiveness of the community and define its identity by separating insiders from outsiders" (ibid., 77).

In a nutshell, humorous interactions entail social desirability and acceptance of group-marking specificity, producing a group-connoted offset of affinity, trust, shared enjoyment and satisfaction, what Bormann (1972) labelled as *in-groupness*. Additionally, as already mentioned and illustrated with *LOLspeak*, the use of certain jargons, styles of text deformation and vocabulary may act as a barrier erected from discursive specificity, since only those who master the type of discourse exchanged within the medium-sized community will both feel part of the group and accepted by its members.

Also fitting this sub-section, a detailed account of identity effects from meme creation and interpretation was proposed in Yus (2018a) (see also Chap. 7). The initial stage, *decoding* of the meme, may generate non-propositional offsets of group membership. Certainly, users' awareness of their command at the initial recognition of the discourse as an instance of a meme together with its intended basic replicability function may influence users and make them aware of belonging to a certain group of those who manage and are fully up to date on the kind of specific information that is currently exchanged on the Net. Tracing the "family" (or genre) to which memes belong likewise enables users to know their level of competence at this meme identification, and signals which further actions may or may not be taken. Furthermore, the identification of the of meme's discursive qualities is indicative of appropriateness and, ultimately, of group membership. As summarised by Shifman (2014b, 342), participants tend to mould their memetic contributions according to a small number of formulations. The apparent rigidity of users who work within a few generic patterns may in fact perform an important social function: following shared pathways for meme production becomes vital to create a sense of community in today's fragmented world.

Likewise, a proper meme interpretation demands shared knowledge within the internet group, and their processing generates cultural capital, insofar as internet memes relate both to their unique creation processes and to the social dynamics surrounding them. "Meme literacy" influences users' status inside online communities and indicates membership (Nissenbaum and Shifman 2017, 486). Similarly, memes have been noted to show participants' discerning use of intertextual media, mixing and matching popular culture references to demonstrate affective affinities with others (Kanai 2016; Rieger and Klimmt 2019; Diedrichsen 2020; Gearhart et al. 2020; Jiang and Vásquez 2020; Zenner and Geeraerts 2018, 169).[3] An example can be found in the Covid-19 memes (10–11) reproduced in Aslan (2021, 52). The first one entails "intertextual winks" about the actor's films and their associated soundtracks that not every user will be able to retrieve from encyclopaedic knowledge. The second one in turn demands access to the personality of the character Sheldon in the TV series *Big Bang Theory*:

(10) Image: A photo of actor John Travolta.
Text: John Travolta was hospitalized for suspected COVID-19, but doctors now confirm that it was only a Saturday Night Fever, and they assure everyone that he is Staying Alive.

(11) Image: A photo of actor Jim Parsons (as Sheldon) spraying disinfectant into the air and covering his mouth.
Text: All of a sudden, everyone has become Sheldon.

[3] An interesting approach in this direction is that of ***networked individualism*** (Wellman 2001, 2002), which stands somewhere in between the joy of being individual and that of feeling the group's approval. Shifman (2014b, 33–34) summarises this idea as follows: we witness an era of accelerated individualisation, and hence people are expected to fashion a unique identity and image and by doing so actively construct their own unique selves. However, at the same time, individuals enthusiastically participate in the shaping of social networks, thus demonstrating an enduring human longing for community bonding. User-generated versions of a meme may serve both purposes: on the one hand, users who exhibit their individuality show their digital literacy, uniqueness, and creativeness. But at the same time, what they upload as individuals frequently relates to common, widely shared rules or formulas. As a result, users simultaneously indicate and construct their individuality and their affiliation to the larger community.

Denisova (2019, 32) also referred to memes being coded with mutuality of expectations and therefore eventually confusing certain audiences because they may have varying abilities and skills to read the community-bonding background information: "Those who are unfamiliar with the rules of digital discussion and styles of the Internet slang, or possess limited awareness of the broader sociopolitical context may consider memes meaningless. In order to be able to read a meme, one has to be digitally savvy or at least have basic familiarity with this format of communication. In some instances, memes can impede the inclusivity of communication."

In this sense, it seems that the identity achieved through group norm fitting, group validation and in-group enhancement (i.e. social identity and social bonding) resulting from humorous acts of communication on the internet becomes more essential for users than identity enhanced by being unique at creating something beyond the norms imposed by the group (Konstantineas and Vlachos 2012; Guadagno et al. 2013; Newton et al. 2022; Gal et al. 2015, 1700; Denisova 2019, 10). Postmes and Baym (2005, 224) agree with this priority of the social when underlining that personal identities "are simultaneously properties of the group itself because they could not exist without some degree of consensus from the group." Similarly, Milner (2012, 42) stated, regarding memes, that these "are often produced on sites where social collectives come together and define themselves at least loosely as a group. (…) Mediated cultural participation means dispersed social collectives can more thoroughly engage with others who share similar social identities." Finally, Tsakona (2018, 234) points in the same direction when highlighting the fact that many online communities often consist of members brought together exclusively by the humorous discourse that they produce and circulate among them online, humour helping to strengthen social cohesion via enhancement of their common attitudes and values, as well as through framing their shared knowledge and views in humorous, agreed-upon acceptable ways (see also Mullan 2020, 149).

This effect likewise happens in the case of so-called *oppositional identity work*, or expressed differently, the explicit acts of identity construction by members of subordinated groups, who attempt to transform a discrediting identity into a crediting one via humorous discourse creation. Users focus on a ridiculed or stigmatised aspect of social identity and turn it into one that could become a mark of pride and belonging (Eschler and Menking 2018).

2. *Awareness of shared knowledge within group.* Humour provides an ideal test to check who has access to the necessary background knowledge and assumptions of mutuality needed to make the most of humorous effects; to which must be added, once again, that it generates positive effects regarding group membership and identification, as remarked elsewhere in this book (e.g. the chapter on humour in social networking sites). Locher and Bolander (2015, 143) rightly point out that when humour relies on shared knowledge it creates closeness and an in-group feeling, additionally maintaining a group identity. Likewise, the same instances of humour can also exclude those lacking access to that basic supposedly shared information. Baym (1995) suggested that humour positions members (of the internet forum under her analysis) as necessarily competent, assumed to have a detailed awareness of intertextual elements mentioned in the postings. Similarly, Holton and Lewis (2011) argued that humorous messages often require at least some prior knowledge of the subject matter being discussed, and are more readily accepted by individuals with shared knowledge and emotional constructs who can collectively decipher their meanings. The same applies to the "cultural intertextual winks" whose tracing is demanded to interpret memes (see, for example, Tay 2012, 62) and which may produce an offset of non-propositional effects upon correct understanding.

A variation of this reliance on mutuality occurs when mutuality is not expected, but rather revealed, or expressed differently, when it occurs as a process of discovery. As already explained (for example in Chap. 6), sometimes humour provokes either a reinforcement of background collective assumptions or unveils this collective quality through the individual user's realisation that previously thought-to-be private information is in fact widely shared and collective. Chen (2014) provided us with an example about a website for user-generated comics, where members "rant about the issues they face in life and seek solace from a sympathetic audience who also grapple with similar problems (…). [They gather online] to laugh at each other's misfortunes, not to feel superior to others, but to revel in the fact that many netizens have experienced similar events" (ibid., 693–694).

3. *Group bonding and solidarity.* This effect closely relates to the requirement or discovery of mutuality areas in humorous communication, since this mutuality enhances or favours bonding and solidarity among the members of a community, both online and offline (see Dynel 2020 for an analysis of the *r/IncelTears community* on Reddit with this solidarity-based connotation). For Zappavigna (2012, 152), developing solidarity serves the most important humour function, as reported in internet research. For example, according to Hancock (2004, 58), humour enhances bonds between individuals by highlighting a shared sense of humour or common ground, which may prove especially appropriate within an online environment. In offline gatherings and casual conversations, these bonds and areas of mutuality among friends are easily emphasised on the fly. However, offline clues tend to be inhibited in text-based interactions, since the scenarios for these interactions become virtualised and are likely to lack the necessary contextual information (see Yus 2007). Therefore, it seems that humour may compensate for offline ways of bonding when interlocutors cannot take advantage of the usual trappings of face-to-face interactions to convey interpersonal information and reinforce mutuality areas.

Jocular mockery or self-deprecating humour have also proved useful to build up bonding and solidarity. As Hübler and Bell (2003, 281) correctly stated, when being the object of laughter, individuals can identify with each other and keep one another's interests in mind. And the goodwill shown in making oneself the butt of a joke de-emphasises hierarchy and at the same time subtly incorporates the other primary components of ethos by conveying an intelligent resourcefulness and a modest character (see also Maíz-Arévalo 2015; Kurtzberg et al. 2009, 380–381).

Solidarity is also present in the action of sharing a meme (Yus 2018a), which involves expecting the addressee to find the meme worth processing, probably through an offset of humorous effects and feelings of group membership or connection that compensate for the mental effort involved in its interpretation. As Aslan (2022) correctly remarks, "when users engage in memetic humour, they signal themselves as individuals playing a game and having fun as well as a sense of belonging to or a membership of a particular group, or more metaphorically speaking 'being in the same boat' as others. In fact, humour in internet memes often emerges in a particular group or community and might represent an inside joke."

Small wonder then that *sharing* and *participatory culture* have arisen as key terms in today's conceptualisation of the *Web 2.0* (Shifman 2014a, 19; Gofton 2017, 28; Wiggins and Bowers 2015, 1891; Rieger and Klimmt 2019). Therefore, meme communication does not merely have to do with passing information along to other users, but rather -and mainly- with sharing a social phenomenon and a jointly constructed discourse tightly linked to solidarity-building comments and reactions to it.[4] Users' work on memes equally entails a significant bearing on identity, "because each semiotic resource employed to create, modify, or comment on a particular meme lends itself to (in)validation by other members and signifies a potentially important choice with regard to community affiliation" (Procházka 2018, 78; see also Lovink 2019, 121). A similar example is the pervasiveness of nonsensical memes. Katz and Shifman (2017, 837) link their proliferation to issues of phaticness and community bonding (see also Varis and Blommaert 2015):

> The circulation of nonsensical memes, in which referential meaning is often completely obscured, serves as a phatic nod; through this gesture, participants not only convey information about themselves (namely, that they are light-hearted and humorous) but also negotiate their affiliation to meme culture, demonstrating that they are attuned to earlier nonsensical forms and to the people generating them. Thus, if what has been depicted in the literature as emotive meaning is formed after one acknowledges (through cognition) referential meanings, affective meaning is a pre-cognitive phatic marker of affiliation.

4. *Feelings of being valuable/valued to/by one's community.* One of the trends in present-day internet is the abundance of user-generated content, from which relevant effects may result in gratification for being productive and useful to the group or community despite the effort involved. When it comes to humour, this becomes particularly noticeable because this user-generated content frequently creates solidar-

[4] As Meikle (2016, 50–51) asserts, communication through social media is an unfinished process of circulation and connection, of relationships and associations. Each new sharing strategy thus opens up different kinds of connectivity and different possibilities for meaning, each one consequently affording various content circulation options to other people. Each connection both establishes new relations between individuals and reveals previously invisible connections. Internet memes are forms of easily remixed texts and images that are intrinsic to this social media environment.

ity through the audience's co-construction and acknowledgment, a clear positive non-propositional effect. Sites such as *Jokes from Russia*, analysed by Gorny (2009), base their success on user-generated information for the community, a significant feature that enables users to become co-producers rather than passive readers of the website and, more importantly, co-responsible for its eventual success.

The internet community may also acknowledge the value of a user's contribution. An example is memes. When posted or forwarded, their *audience validation* of the meme makes the user "stand out" from the crowd, feel unique and valued by the other community members, and even more so if the meme has been altered and generates further humorous effects. Nonetheless, even with unaltered memes, the group becomes identified both by the choice of who the meme is transferred to and by the group's acknowledgment about the acceptability of the transfer (audience validation).[5]

3.4 Positive Non-Propositional Effects at Large-Sized Group Level

Humour generates effects among large-sized groups such as nations, professions or sexes as well. These effects may have a negative nature, when unfair broad stereotypes spread through different online platforms, as happens with sex-role stereotypes (Shifman and Lemish 2010, 2011, 2012; Paciello et al. 2021). However, humour may also produce positive non-propositional effects at a large scale. The following aspects deserve attention.

1. *Cultural specificity of processing information.* Internet humour may stress broad national values. Examples thereof include the politics-centred viral spread of memes, exemplified in the discourses analysed by Baran (2012) on Estonian politics, which can only be understood by those aware of the political events which have taken place in that country.

[5] In this sense, Arizzi (2019) focuses on users' decisions to manipulate an existing image in the meme, with processes such as: (a) a change is made to one part of the image, usually without adding any text to it; (b) a part of the image is copied and pasted into another image, e.g. a well-known painting; (c) the image is changed and other elements, typically captions, are added; and (d) the image is not changed, but other elements, once again mostly captions, are included.

The internet disseminates information globally too, and the aforementioned specificity is likely to be misunderstood across countries, even though jokes often undergo cultural adaptations and the resulting discourses often end up being roughly acceptable if the topic addressed is universal, as illustrated by the jokes that spread worldwide in the aftermath of the 9/11 terrorist attack (Boxman-Shabtai and Shifman 2015, 522). In general, however, humour appreciation offers an insight into the specificity of a culture or society, since it is often tied to the particular context of creation and has a specific audience in mind, in this case a broad group such as one's own nation.

2. *Mutual awareness of broad values.* Humour reveals attributes of our social context and helps to enhance their mutuality. An example is the travel blog *Expatriates' Talk* studied by Cappelli (2008), which builds large-group centred solidarity with Italians by laughing at Americans, and simultaneously maintains group solidarity with co-nationals by also laughing at Italians themselves. Interestingly, the blog also produces a group's initiation effect by increasing commitment to the group of expatriates who are the only ones able to fully understand the richness of the cultural interplay behind these users' words, even behind self-deprecation.

4 Concluding Remarks

Non-propositional effects become crucial for human communication in general, and even more so on the internet. In this chapter, these effects have been reviewed mainly as a parallel (and *leaked*) outcome of humorous acts of communication which take place online. Although they may be sought by the sender user, very often these effects are generated beyond the user's intention; and this quality does not prevent them from proving relevant to the audience. Non-humorous effects such as feelings of self-worth, solidarity, in-group acceptance, collective values, communal acceptance and so on (all of them highly valued by internet users) often appear as a complement to the main humorous effect initially intended in the act of internet-mediated communication.

References

Ameka, Felix K. 2002. Cultural Scripting of Body Parts for Emotions. On 'Jealousy' and Related Emotions in Ewe. *Pragmatics & Cognition* 10 (1/2): 27–55. https://doi.org/10.1075/pc.10.1-2.03ame.

Arizzi, Cristina. 2019. Digital Memes and US Pop Politics. Dynamism and Pervasiveness of a Digital Genre in the Mobile Web Era. *Lingue e Linguaggi* 30: 45–64. https://doi.org/10.1285/i22390359v30p45.

Aslan, Erhan. 2021. When the Internet Gets 'Coronafied': Pandemic Creativity and Humour in Internet Memes. In *Viral Discourse*, ed. Rodney H. Jones, 49–60. Cambridge: Cambridge University Press.

———. 2022. Days of our 'quarantined' lives. Multimodal humour in COVID-19 internet memes. *Internet Pragmatics* 5 (2): 227–256. https://doi.org/10.1075/ip.00075.asl.

Ballantine, Paul W., Yongjia Lin, and Ekant Veer. 2015. The Influence of User Comments on Perceptions of Facebook Relationship Status Updates. *Computers in Human Behavior* 49: 50–55. https://doi.org/10.1016/j.chb.2015.02.055.

Baran, Anneli. 2012. Visual Humor on the Internet. In *Estonia and Poland: Creativity and Change in Cultural Communication. Vol. 1: Jokes and Humor*, ed. Liisi Laineste, Dorota Brzozowska, and Wladyslaw Chłopicki, 144–158. Tartu: EKM Teaduskirjastus.

Baym, Nancy K. 1995. The Performance of Humor in Computer-Mediated Communication. *Journal of Computer-Mediated Communication* 1 (2) JCMC123. https://doi.org/10.1111/j.1083-6101.1995.tb00327.x

Bormann, Ernest G. 1972. Fantasy and Rhetorical Vision: The Rhetorical Criticism of Social Reality. *Quarterly Journal of Speech* 58 (4): 396–407. https://doi.org/10.1080/00335637209383138.

Boxman-Shabtai, Lillian, and Limor Shifman. 2015. When Ethnic Humor Goes Digital. *New Media & Society* 17 (4): 520–539. https://doi.org/10.1177/1461444813506972.

Caffi, Claudia, and Richard W. Janney. 1994. Toward a Pragmatics of Emotive Communication. *Journal of Pragmatics* 22 (3-4): 325–373. https://doi.org/10.1016/0378-2166(94)90115-5.

Cappelli, Gloria. 2008. "Expats' Talk": Humor and Irony in an Expatriate's Travel Blog. *Textus* 21 (1): 1–26.

Chen, Shih-We. 2014. Baozou Manhua (Rage Comics), Internet Humor and Everyday Life. *Continuum* 28 (5): 690–708. https://doi.org/10.1080/10304312.2014.941334.

Chovanec, Jan. 2011. Humour in Quasi-Conversations Constructing Fun in Online Sports Journalism. In *The Pragmatics of Humour across Discourse Domains*, ed. Marta Dynel, 243–264. Amsterdam: John Benjamins. https://doi.org/10.1075/pbns.210.16cho.

———. 2012, January. Conversational Humor and Joint Fantasizing in Online Journalism. In *Language and Humor in the Media*, ed. Jan Chovanec and Isabel Ermida, 139–162. Newcastle upon Tyne: Cambridge Scholars Publishing.

Clark, Billy. 2020. Identity Inferences: Implicatures, Implications and Extended Interpretations. *Language and Literature* 29 (4): 424–445. https://doi.org/10.1177/0963947020969568.

de Saussure, Louis, and Tim Wharton. 2020. Relevance, Effects and Affect. *International Review of Pragmatics* 12: 183–205. https://doi.org/10.1163/18773109-01202001.

Denisova, Anastasia. 2019. *Internet Memes and Society. Social, Cultural, and Political Contexts.* Abingdon: Routledge. https://doi.org/10.4324/9780429469404.

Dewi, Udiana Puspa. 2019. 'How Would You Meme This': Playful Identity Constuction on Instagram Meme Commentaries. Paper Delivered at *Konferensi Linguistik Tahunan (Kolita)* 17. Jakarta.

Diedrichsen, Elke. 2020. On the Interaction of Core and Emergent Common Ground in Internet Memes. *Internet Pragmatics* 3 (2): 223–259. https://doi.org/10.1075/ip.00033.die.

Downes, William. 2000. The language of Felt Experience: Emotional, Evaluative and Intuitive. *Language and Literature* 9 (2): 99–121. https://doi.org/10.1177/096394700000900201.

du Preez, Amanda, and Elanie Lombard. 2014. *The Role of Memes in the Construction of Facebook Personae Communicatio* 40 (3): 253–270. https://doi.org/10.1080/02500167.2014.938671.

Dynel, Marta. 2020. Vigilante Disparaging Humour At R/inceltears: Humour as Critique of Incel Ideology. *Language & Communication* 74: 1–14. https://doi.org/10.1016/j.langcom.2020.05.001.

Eschler, Jornan, and Amanda Menking. 2018, June 4. 'No Prejudice Here': Examining Social Identity Work in Starter Pack Memes. *Social Media + Society*. https://doi.org/10.1177/2056305118768811

Gal, Noam. 2019. Ironic Humor on Social Media as Participatory Boundary Work. *New Media & Society* 21 (3): 729–749. https://doi.org/10.1177/1461444818805719.

Gal, Noam, Limor Shifman, and Zohar Kampf. 2015. 'It Gets Better': Internet Memes and the Construction of Collective Identity. *New Media & Society* 18 (8): 1698–1714. https://doi.org/10.1177/1461444814568784.

Gearhart, Sherice, Bingbing Zhang, David D. Perlmutter, and Gordana Lazić. 2020. Visual Intertextuality Theory. Exploring Political Communication and Visual Intertextuality Through Meme Wars. In *Handbook of Visual Communication. Theory, Methods, and Media*, ed. Sheree Josephson, James D. Kelly, and Ken Smith, 367–379. Abingdon: Routledge.

Gibbs, Raymond W., John S. Leggitt, and Elizabeth A. Turner. 2002. What's Special About Figurative Language in Emotional Communication? In *The Verbal Communication of Emotions*. In *Interdisciplinary Perspectives*, ed. Susan R. Fussell, 125–149. Mahwah: L.E.A.

Gofton, Pete. 2017. Music, Memes and Meaning: A Semiotic Analysis. *Musicology Research* 2: 27–46.

Gorny, Eugene. 2009. More than Humor: Jokes from Russia as a Mirror of Russian Life. In *Internationalizing Internet Studies. Beyond Anglophone Paradigms*, ed. Gerard Goggin and Mark McLelland, 79–95. Abingdon: Routledge.

Guadagno, Rosanna E., Daniel M. Rempala, Shannon Murphy, and Bradley M. Okdie. 2013. What Makes a Video Go Viral? An Analysis of Emotional Contagion and Internet Memes. *Computers in Human Behavior* 29: 2312–2319. https://doi.org/10.1016/j.chb.2013.04.016.

Hancock, Jeffrey T. 2004. LOL: Humor Online. *Interactions* 11 (5): 57–58. https://doi.org/10.1145/1015530.1015557.

Holcomb, Christopher. 1997. A Class of Clowns: Spontaneous Joking in Computer-Assisted Discussions. *Computers and Composition* 14 (1): 3–18. https://doi.org/10.1016/S8755-4615(97)90035-9.

Holton, Avery E., and Seth C. Lewis. 2011. Journalists, Social Media, and the Use of Humor on Twitter. *Electronic. Journal of Communication* 21: 1–2.

Hübler, Mike T., and Diana C. Bell. 2003. Computer-Mediated Humor and Ethos: Exploring Threads of Constitutive Laughter in Online Communities. *Computers and Composition* 20 (3): 277–294. https://doi.org/10.1016/S8755-4615(03)00036-7.

Jiang, Yaqian Jiang, and Camilla Vásquez. 2020. Exploring Local Meaning-Making Resources. A Case Study of a Popular Chinese Internet Meme (*biaoqingbao*). *Internet Pragmatics* 3 (2): 260–282. https://doi.org/10.1075/ip.00042.jia.

Kanai, Akane. 2016, October–December. Sociality and Classification: Reading Gender, Race, and Class in a Humorous Meme. *Social Media + Society*, 1–12. https://doi.org/10.1177/2056305116672884

Katz, James E., and Limor Shifman. 2017. Making Sense? The Structure and Meanings of Digital Memetic Nonsense. *Information, Communication & Society* 20 (6): 825–842. https://doi.org/10.1080/1369118X.2017.1291702.

Konstantineas, Charalambos, and George Vlachos. 2012. *Internet Memes: Humor in Late Modernity and Encroachment Upon the Mainstream*. Oxford: Interdisciplinary.net.

Kurtzberg, Terri R., Charles E. Naquin, and Liuba Y. Belkin. 2009. Humor as a Relationship-Building Tool in Online Negotiations. *International Journal of Conflict Management* 20 (4): 377–397. https://doi.org/10.1108/10444060910991075.

Laineste, Liisi. 2013. Funny or Aggressive? Failed Humor in Internet Comments. *Folklore* 53: 29–46. https://doi.org/10.7592/FEJF2013.53.laineste.

Leggitt, John S., and Raymond W. Gibbs. 2000. Emotional Reactions to Verbal Irony. *Discourse Processes* 29 (1): 1–24. https://doi.org/10.1207/S15326950dp2901_1.

Literat, Ioana, and Sarah van den Berg. 2019. Buy Memes Low, Sell Memes High: Vernacular Criticism and Collective Negotiations of Value on Reddit's MemeEconomy. *Information, Communication & Society* 22 (2): 232–249. https://doi.org/10.1080/1369118X.2017.1366540.

Locher, Miriam A., and Brook Bolander. 2015. Humour in Microblogging: Exploiting Linguistic Humour Strategies for Identity Construction in Two Facebook Focus Groups. In *Participation in Public and Social Media Interactions*, ed. Marta Dynel and Jan Chovanec, 135–155. Amsterdam: John Benjamins. https://doi.org/10.1075/pbns.256.06loc.

Lovink, Geert. 2019. *Sad by Design. On Platform Nihilism*. London: Pluto Press.

Maíz-Arévalo, Carmen. 2015. Jocular Mockery in Computer-Mediated Communication: A Contrastive Study of a Spanish and English Facebook Community. *Journal of Politeness Research* 11 (2): 289–327. https://doi.org/10.1515/pr-2015-0012.

Mak, Chun N. 2014. Humor, Small Talk, and the Construction of Identity and Power in Workplace Instant Messaging. PhD Thesis. Hong Kong: The Chinese University of Hong Kong.

Marone, Vittorio. 2015. Online Humor as a Community-Building Cushioning Glue. *European Journal of Humor Research* 3 (1): 61–83. https://doi.org/10.7592/EJHR2015.3.1.marone.

Meikle, Graham. 2016. *Social Media. Communication, Sharing and Visibility*. Abingdon: Routledge. https://doi.org/10.4324/9781315884172.

Milner, Ryan M. 2012. *The World Made Meme: Discourse and Identity in Participatory Media*. PhD Thesis. University of Kansas.

Miltner, Kate M. 2014. 'There's No Place for Lulz on Lolcats': The Role of Genre, Gender, and Group Identity in the Interpretation and Enjoyment of an Internet Meme. *First Monday* 19 (8). https://doi.org/10.5210/fm.v19i8.5391.

Moeschler, Jacques. 2009. Pragmatics, Propositional and Non-propositional Effects: Can a Theory of Utterance Interpretation Account for Emotions in Verbal Communication? *Social Science Information* 48 (3): 447–464. https://doi.org/10.1177/0539018409106200.

Mullan, Kerry. 2020. Pile of Dead Leaves Free to a Good Home: Humour and Belonging in a Facebook Community. In *Studies in Ethnopragmatics, Cultural Semantics, and Intercultural Communication. Ethnopragmatics and Semantic Analysis*, ed. Kerry Mullan, Bert Peeters, and Lauren Sadow, 135–159. Cham: Springer. https://doi.org/10.1007/978-981-32-9983-2_8.

Nasreen, Zobaida. 2021. 'Have You Not Got a Sense of Humour?': Unpacking Masculinity Through Online Sexist Jokes During the COVID-19 Pandemic. *Society and Culture in South Asia* 7 (1): 148–154. https://doi.org/10.1177/2393861720977632.

Newton, Giselle, Michele Zappavigna, Kerryn Drysdale, and Christy E. Newman. 2022, January–March. More than Humor: Memes as Bonding Icons for Belonging in Donor-Conceived People. *Social Media + Society*. https://doi.org/10.1177/20563051211069055

Nissenbaum, Asaf, and Limor Shifman. 2017. Internet Memes as Contested Cultural Capital: The Case of 4chan's /b/Board. *New Media & Society* 19 (4): 483–501. https://doi.org/10.1177/1461444815609313.

Norrick, Neal R. 2003. Issues in Conversational Joking. *Journal of Pragmatics* 35 (9): 1333–1359. https://doi.org/10.1016/S0378-2166(02)00180-7.

North, Sarah. 2007. 'The Voices, the Voices': Creativity in Online Conversation. *Applied Linguistics* 28 (4): 538–555. https://doi.org/10.1093/applin/amm042.

Paciello, Marinella, Francesca D'Errico, Giorgia Saleri, and Ernestina Lamponi. 2021. Online Sexist Meme and its Effects on Moral and Emotional Processes in Social Media. *Computers in Human Behavior* 116: 106655. https://doi.org/10.1016/j.chb.2020.106655.

Pennington, Natalie, and Jeffrey A. Hall. 2014. An Analysis of Humor Orientation on Facebook: A Lens Model Approach. *Humor* 27 (1): 1–21. https://doi.org/10.1515/humor-2013-0053.

Postmes, Tom, and Nancy Baym. 2005. Intergroup Dimensions of the Internet. In *Intergroup Communication: Multiple Perspectives*, ed. Jake Harwood and Howard Giles, 213–238. New York: Peter Lang.

Procházka, Ondřej. 2018. A Chronotopic Approach to Identity Performance in a Facebook Meme Page. *Discourse, Context & Media* 25: 78–87. https://doi.org/10.1016/j.dcm.2018.03.010.

Rieger, Diana, and Christoph Klimmt. 2019. The Daily Dose of Digital Inspiration 2: Themes and Affective User Responses to Meaningful Memes in Social Media. *New Media & Society* 21 (10): 2201–2221. https://doi.org/10.1177/1461444819842875.

Shifman, Limor. 2014a. Internet Humor. In *Encyclopedia of Humor Studies*, ed. Salvatore Attardo, 389–393. London: Sage.

———. 2014b. *Memes in Digital Culture*. Cambridge, MA: The MIT Press.

———. 2019. Internet Memes and the Twofold Articulation of Values. In *Society and the Internet How Networks of Information and Communication are Changing Our Lives*, ed. Mark Graham and William H. Dutton, 2nd ed., 43–57. Oxford: Oxford University Press. https://doi.org/10.1093/oso/9780198843498.003.0003.

Shifman, Limor, and Dafna Lemish. 2010. Between Feminism and Fun(ny)mism. Analysing Gender in Popular Internet Humour. *Information, Communication & Society* 13 (6): 870–891. https://doi.org/10.1080/13691180903490560.

———. 2011. "Mars and Venus" in Virtual Space: Post-Feminist Humor and the Internet. *Critical Studies in Media Communication* 28 (3): 253–273. https://doi.org/10.1080/15295036.2010.522589.

———. 2012. Virtually Blonde. Blonde Jokes in the Global Age and Postfeminist Discourse. In *The Handbook of Gender, Sex, and Media*, ed. Karen Ross, 88–104. Oxford: Wiley-Blackwell. https://doi.org/10.1002/9781118114254.ch6.

Simis-Wilkinson, Molly, Haley Madden, David Lassen, Su Leona Yi-Fan, Dominique Brossard, Dietram A. Scheufele, and Michael A. Xenos. 2018. Scientists Joking on Social Media: An Empirical Analysis of #overlyhonestmethods. *Science Communication* 40 (3): 314–339. https://doi.org/10.1177/1075547018766557.

Sperber, Dan, and Deirdre Wilson. 1995. *Relevance. Communication and Cognition*. 2nd ed. Oxford: Blackwell.

Tay, Geniesa. 2012. *Embracing LOLitics: Popular Culture, Online Political Humor, and Play*. MA Thesis. Canterbury: University of Canterbury.

Tsakona, Villi. 2018. Online Joint Fictionalization. In *The Dynamics of Interactional Humor. Creating and Negotiating Humor in Everyday Encounters*, ed. Villi Tsakona and Jan Chovanec, 229–255. Amsterdam: John Benjamins. https://doi.org/10.1075/thr.7.10tsa.

Vandergriff, Ilona. 2010. Humor and Play in CMC. In *Handbook of Research on Discourse Behavior and Digital Communication: Language Structures and Social Interaction*, ed. Rotimi Taiwo, 235–251. Hershey: Information Science Reference. https://doi.org/10.4018/978-1-61520-773-2.ch016.

Varis, Piia, and Jan Blommaert. 2015. Conviviality and Collectives on Social Media: Virality, Memes, and New Social Structures. *Multilingual Margins* 2 (1): 31–45. https://doi.org/10.14426/mm.v2i1.55.

Wellman, Barry. 2001. Physical Place and Cyberplace the Rise of Networked Individualism. In *Community Informatics. Shaping Computer-Mediated Social Relations*, ed. Leigh Keeble and Brian D. Loader, 17–42. Abingdon: Routledge.

———. 2002. Little Boxes, Glocalization, and Networked Individualism. In *Digital Cities II: Computational and Sociological Approaches*, ed. Makoto Tanabe, Peter van den Besselaar, and Toru Ishida, 10–25. Berlin: Springer. https://doi.org/10.1007/3-540-45636-8_2.

Wharton, Tim. 2016. That Bloody So-and-so Has Retired: Expressives Revisited. *Lingua* 175–176: 20–35. https://doi.org/10.1016/j.lingua.2015.08.004.

———. 2021. Relevance. Communication and Cognition and…? *Pragmatics & Cognition* 28 (2): 321–346. https://doi.org/10.1075/pc.21013.wha.

Wharton, Tim, and Louis de Saussure. 2022. The Pragmatics of Emotion, Argument and Conflict. In *Language and Emotion. An International Handbook*, ed. Gesine Lenore Schiever, Jeanette Altarriba, and Bee Chin Ng, vol. 1, 664–680. Berlin: De Gruyter Mouton. https://doi.org/10.1515/9783110347524-032.

Wharton, Tim, and Claudia Strey. 2019. Slave of the Passions: Making Emotions Relevant. In *Relevance, Pragmatics and Interpretation*, ed. Kate Scott, Billy Clark, and Robyn Carston, 253–266. Cambridge: Cambridge University Press. https://doi.org/10.1017/9781108290593.022.

Wharton, Tim, Constant Bonard, Daniel Dukes, David Sander, and Steve Oswald. 2021. Relevance and Emotion. *Journal of Pragmatics* 181: 259–269. https://doi.org/10.1016/j.pragma.2021.06.001.

Wiggins, Bradley E., and G. Bret Bowers. 2015. Memes as Genre: A Structurational Analysis of the Memescape. *New Media & Society* 17 (11): 1886–1906. https://doi.org/10.1177/1461444814535194.

Wilson, Deirdre, and Robyn Carton. 2019. Pragmatics and the Challenge of 'Non-propositional' Effects. *Journal of Pragmatics* 145: 31–38. https://doi.org/10.1016/j.pragma.2019.01.005.

Yus, Francisco. 2007. Virtualidades Reales. In *Nuevas Formas de Comunidad en la Era de Internet [Real Virtualities. New Forms of Community at the Internet Age]*. Alicante: University of Alicante, Servicio de Publicaciones.

———. 2011. Cyberpragmatics. In *Internet-mediated communication in context*. Amsterdam and Philadelphia: John Benjamins. https://doi.org/10.1075/pbns.213.

———. 2015, September. Should Relevance Theory Analyse What is Non-propositional, Non-intentional But Yet Affects the Eventual Relevance? Paper delivered at *Relevance Round Table Meeting 4*. Institute of English Studies, Jagiellonian University of Kraków.

———. 2016. *Humour and Relevance*. Amsterdam: John Benjamins. https://doi.org/10.1075/thr.4.

———. 2018a. Identity-Related Issues in Meme Communication. *Internet Pragmatics* 1 (1): 113–133. https://doi.org/10.1075/ip.00006.yus.

———. 2018b. Attaching feelings and emotions to propositions. Some insights on irony and internet communication. *Russian Journal of Linguistics* 22 (1): 94–107. https://doi.org/10.22363/2312-9182-2018-22-1-94-107.

———. 2018c. Positive Non-Humorous Effects of Humor on the Internet. In *The Dynamics of Interactional Humor. Creating and Negotiating Humor in Everyday Encounters*, ed. Villi Tsakona and Jan Chovanec, 283–304. Amsterdam: John Benjamins. https://doi.org/10.1075/thr.7.12yus.

———. 2022. Pushing Cognitive Pragmatics Beyond its Comfort Zone: Smartphone-mediated Communication of Feelings and Emotions. In *Lecture delivered at ESTIDIA Conference*. Alicante: University of Alicante.

Zappavigna, Michele. 2012. *Discourse of Twitter and Social Media: How We Use Language to Create Affiliation on the Web*. London: Bloomsbury.

Zenner, Eline, and Dirk Geeraerts. 2018. One Does not Simply Process Memes: Image Macros as Multimodal Constructions. In *Cultures and Traditions of Wordplay and Wordplay Research*, ed. Esme Winter-Froemel and Verena Thaler, 167–193. Berlin: De Gruyter. https://doi.org/10.1515/9783110586374-008.

Index[1]

[1] Note: Page numbers followed by 'n' refer to notes.

F. Yus, *Pragmatics of Internet Humour*,
https://doi.org/10.1007/978-3-031-31902-0

FSC
www.fsc.org
MIX
Papier | Fördert gute Waldnutzung
FSC® C083411

Kolibri 360 GmbH
Ferdinand-Jühlke-Straße 7
99095 Erfurt, Deutschland
produktsicherheit@kolibri360.de